NEW AFRICAN EXPLOITS
The Diaries of William Stairs
1887-1892
Ed. Roy MacLaren When he died in 1892, aged just 28, William Stairs had already helped Henry Stanley to rescue Emin Pasha, the last of Gordon's Sudan lieutenants, and secured Katanga for the Belgians as part of the Congo Free State. His lively diaries speak of hardships, hazards, encounters with slavers and cannibals, exotic flora and fauna, and clashing cultures. They also open a bloody window on the imperial scramble for Africa. Liverpool UP 1998 £32.95 HB 423pp Illus

[23540]   **£8.99**

African Exploits
The Diaries of William Stairs, 1887–1892

A record of the experiences of a young Canadian caught up in European expansion into Africa in the 1880s, *African Exploits* provides a disturbing record of Willam Stairs's two African expeditions and the devastating clash of cultures that occurred during the imperial scramble for the "dark continent."

Born in Halifax, Nova Scotia, Stairs (1863–1892) attended the Royal Military College Kingston, Ontario, before being commissioned in the British army. Wearying of peacetime soldiering, he volunteered in 1887 to participate in Henry M. Stanley's final trans-African expedition to rescue Emin Pasha, the last survivor of "Chinese" Gordon's lieutenants in the Sudan. The expedition emerged almost three years later in Zanzibar, a reluctant Pasha in tow, having left a trail of havoc and suffering behind it.

Stairs promptly volunteered for a second expedition in Africa to secure Katanga for King Leopold II of the Belgians as part of his controversial Congo Free State. The expedition succeeded, but at the price of suffering, destruction, and Stairs's own life: he died of malaria at the end of the expedition at the age of twenty-eight.

Few diaries of the period convey better than Stairs's the nature and course of imperial expeditions in Africa during the nineteenth century and the psychological and moral corruption caused by absolute power. Stairs's diaries of the Emin Pasha Relief Expedition present a candid, personal account of the long and arduous venture, including an unflattering assessment of Stanley, whom Stairs described as cruel, secretive and selfish. The Katanga diaries, written more as an official than a personal account of the expedition, were intended partly to provide information useful to those intent upon exploiting the African hinterland.

African Exploits is the most complete published collection of Stairs's diaries, with a new translation from French of the Katanga diaries, which no longer exist in the original English. Roy MacLaren's introduction and conclusion set Stairs's adventures in the colonial context of the era and analyse the psychological effects of his experiences.

The Hon. ROY MACLAREN is the High Commissioner for Canada to the United Kingdom of Great Britain and Northern Ireland.

A studio portrait of late 1886 or early 1887 of William Grant Stairs taken in London shortly before his departure for the Congo on the Emin Pasha Relief Expedition. (New Brunswick Museum, Saint John, N.B.)

African Exploits

The Diaries of William Stairs, 1887–1892

ROY MACLAREN

Liverpool University Press

© McGill-Queen's University Press 1998
ISBN 0-85323-722-0

Legal deposit first quarter 1998
Bibliothèque nationale du Québec

Printed in Canada on acid-free paper

This edition published in Europe by Liverpool
University Press

McGill-Queen's University Press acknowledges the
support of the Canada Council for the Arts for its
publishing program.

British Library Cataloguing-in-Publication Data
A British Library CIP record is available.

Typeset in Times 10/12.

Contents

Preface

I wrote this book – or more accurately edited these diaries – when I was the Minister of International Trade of Canada. That role entailed much long-distant travel, prolonged periods on aircraft when, briefing books having been read, understood and inwardly digested, there still remained time to contemplate the trans-African career of a young Victorian from Halifax, Nova Scotia. The progress of William Stairs across Africa took its toll on those living in the path of his two expeditions, an obvious and deplorable toll. Less obvious but also deplorable was the impact on Stairs himself. To understand that dual impact provided a challenge not happy but at least always diverting from the more immediate tasks of understanding the impact of tariff and non-tariff barriers, the external dimensions of national competition regimes or product standards or the rise of regional trade groupings in light of the creation of a new world trade organization. From Ottawa to Marrakech, from Buenos Aires to Kinabalu, others, including frequently my wife, accompanied me, but seldom absent from the table in the arm rest was Stairs. In a sense, the result of those long flights is this book.

I thank Elizabeth Wightman for readying the manuscript for publication. I thank Diane Mew for her sensitive editing, arising both from her inherent skills and from a love for and knowledge of Africa. And finally I thank the Jackman Foundation for its publishing grant which ensured that the high quality standards of McGill-Queen's University Press could be fully met.

The cadet leaders of the class of 1882 at the Royal Military College of Canada in Kingston, Ontario. William Grant Stairs is seated, second from the left. (Massey Library, Royal Military College of Canada)

The Royal Military College football team of 1881. Stairs is standing second from the left. (Massey Library, Royal Military College of Canada)

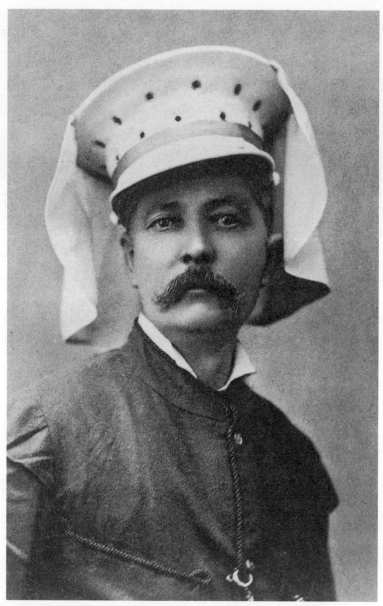

Henry Morton Stanley (1841-1904) in the tropical hat which he made for himself, and which in time became something of a popular symbol of the explorer. (Royal College of Surgeons in Ireland)

William Stairs (1863-1892) in the obligatory studio portrait, photographed in Cairo in 1889 (in freshly laundered caravan kit, complete with spear now in the McCord Museum, Montreal). (Royal College of Surgeons in Ireland)

A photograph of Emin Pasha (1840-1892) when Governor of the Equatorial Province of the Sudan, taken in Khartoum in March 1882, six years before he and Stanley met on the shores of Lake Albert Nyanza on 29 April 1888. (Royal Geographic Society)

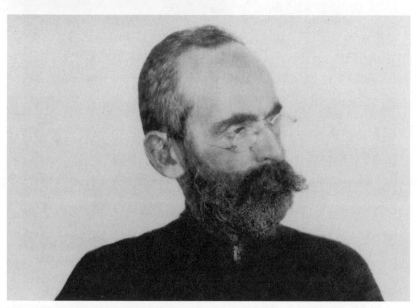

This photograph of Emin Pasha, probably taken in 1889, is one of the few extant from his last years. It may have been taken in Zanzibar, following Emin's reluctant trek to the coast with the stubborn Stanley, who had insisted that he must be rescued. (Royal Commonwealth Society Collection: Cambridge University Library)

Tippu Tib, the slaver whose mother was an African and whose father was a Muscat Arab. With his extensive network of followers, he played a central role in the uneven advance of the Emin Pasha Relief Expedition and in the fate of its Rear Column. (Royal Commonwealth Society Collection, Cambridge University Library)

Major Edmund Musgrave Barttelot (1859-1888) who was killed when in command of the dormant Rear Column. (Royal College of Surgeons in Ireland)

James Jameson (1856-1888), an amateur botanist, a traveller and sensitive amateur artist and the only married officer on the Expedition, who abetted in the murder and eating by cannibals of a young African girl. (Royal College of Surgeons in Ireland)

Arthur Jeremy Mountenay Jephson (1859-1908) who accompanied Emin Pasha on his long and perilous journey through the southern Sudan to ascertain whether his rebellious garrisons there wished to withdraw. Emin and Jephson were fortunate to escape execution at the hands of the rebels. (Royal College of Surgeons in Ireland)

Thomas Heazle Parke (1857-1893), the Anglo-Irish army surgeon who was the medical officer of the Expedition and for whom Stairs had the greatest admiration: "he is a ripping chap ..." (Royal College of Surgeons in Ireland)

Captain Robert Nelson (1853-1892), an Indian Army cavalry officer and a veteran of wars in southern Africa, pursued his comforts with all the single-minded purpose of an old soldier, but when he was left behind for a prolonged period with many of the caravan's sick, he almost succumbed himself. (Royal College of Surgeons in Ireland)

Herbert Ward (1863-1919) who subsequently became a noted sculptor, remained with the Rear Column and sketched the encounter with Tippu Tib (q.v.) which contributed to the fateful decision of Major Edmund Bartellot to keep the Rear Column at its river base rather than to attempt the hazardous overland trek to rejoin Stanley. (Royal College of Surgeons in Ireland)

Introduction

This is a book that can be read on two levels. The first level is that of an adventure story. The diaries of William Grant Stairs of Halifax, Nova Scotia, provide a day-to-day account of two expeditions prominent in the scramble for Africa that seized the imagination of many Europeans – and even some Americans – during the last decades of the nineteenth century. Few diaries of survivors of the "scramble" convey better the nature and course of such expeditions than those of Stairs. Here it is all in abundance: the hazards from hostile terrain and the encounters with slavers and cannibals; the exotic fauna and flora; the threats of isolation and starvation; the hardships and the formidable logistics of driving a caravan across a continent; the confusions of clashing cultures; the sordid and violent whites who regarded blacks as savages. For a total of almost four years Stairs experienced it all, finally succumbing to recurrent malaria, one of the many diseases that plagued expeditions as they pushed through strange lands where few – and frequently no – Europeans had penetrated.

Stairs's diaries are compelling by their immediacy, for he was a trained, perceptive, and lively observer of all that he met in the new world of Africa. At this level, his diaries offer the type of raw material from which the ripping yarns of Rider Haggard, G.A. Henty, and the *Boys' Own Paper* were fashioned.

But Stairs's diaries can be read on a second and more disturbing level. Beyond the adventure story is reflected a more indirect but no less realized – if unintentional – account of the psychological transformation of a young man. Stairs was an army officer, a skilled surveyor and engineer, but he was inexperienced in dealing for sustained periods with people of wholly different backgrounds, values, and understandings. His prolonged encounters with central Africans, even if they had been at arm's length, would necessarily have had an impact upon him. However, the gradual transformation of Stairs from an open, light-hearted, easy-going subaltern into someone who would condone or even himself join in acts of great brutality reflects the corruption wrought by the absolute power that had been given to him. By the end of our story, Stairs has been transformed by his experiences. And the result was neither edifying nor pretty.

◆   ◆   ◆

Stairs's decision to go to Africa in 1887 flows directly from the fact that two years before, Major General Charles Gordon, the governor general of the Sudan, had been killed in Khartoum. It is thought that he died shortly before dawn on 25 January 1885, speared by a follower of the Moslem leader, the Mahdi.

The claims of the Mahdi to both spiritual and temporal supremacy over the Sudan had initially aroused only derision amongst its Egyptian governors. Here was yet another fanatic of the type the desert was wont to produce. But the Mahdi's victories over Egyptian garrisons in the Sudan convinced increasing numbers of Sudanese – if not Egyptians – that this was in fact the long-awaited messiah. Around the sacred green banner of the Mahdi concentrated the forces of both religious fervour and popular unrest. From the deserts in the south, the Mahdists had gradually extended their control over most of the Sudan, which culminated after a long siege in their capture of Khartoum and the death of Gordon. Three days after his death, the small vanguard of a much larger and long-awaited British relief expedition finally approached Khartoum – and then turned back, having learned that the Mahdists had triumphed and that Gordon was dead.

The British public had followed with anxiety the long siege and the laborious ascent of the Nile by the cumbersome force sent too late to relieve Khartoum. The shock and anger was profound when the news reached London of the death of one of the most popular heroes of Victoria's long reign. Demands for revenge were immediately heard throughout Britain, but eventually there grew the recognition, however reluctant, that nothing was to be gained from further expenditure of British lives and Egyptian money in attempting to recover for Egypt the great desert wastes of the Sudan.

Gladstone, the prime minister at the time of Gordon's death, had never been enthusiastic about Britain's involvement in either Egypt or the Sudan. His successor, Lord Salisbury, was content to leave the Mahdists to their own preoccupations in the Sudan on two conditions: that they did not attempt to advance down the Nile on Egypt itself and that no European power sought to exploit the Sudanese uncertainties by moving to establish itself across the headwaters of the Nile. Until the British had reason to re-enter the Sudan, they would simply seal it off. The Mahdists, in one of Salisbury's memorable observations, could be left "to keep the bed warm."

With this decision, London regarded Egypt's always uncertain hold on the Sudan as having ended – or at least having been suspended indefinitely. "The whole Expeditionary Force" Winston Churchill later wrote,

– Guards, Highlanders, sailors, Hussars, Indian soldiers, Canadian voyageurs, mules, camels, and artillery – trooped back forlornly over the desert sands, and behind them the rising tide of barbarism followed swiftly, until the whole vast region was submerged. For several months the garrison at Kassala under a gallant Egyptian maintained a desperate resistance, but at last famine forced them to surrender, and they shared the fate of the garrisons of El Obeid, Darfur, Sobat, Tokar, Sinkat, Sennar and Khartoum.[1]

One by one the Sudanese provinces had fallen to the Mahdists, including one governed by an Austrian officer and another by a former British merchant seaman. By April 1884 only a single province of the Sudan remained unconquered: the southernmost province, Equatoria, near where the Nile emerges from Lake Albert Nyanza. The governor of Equatoria Province was a German physician, one Emin Pasha.

◆   ◆   ◆

Emin remains a complex, enigmatic figure. About his early life – until his arrival in the Sudan at the age of thirty-five – little is known. What little there is comes largely from a two-volume biography written shortly after his death by his cousin, George Schweitzer, who was at some pains to present Emin in the best light.[2] In the absence of much corroborative evidence, it can only be left to the individual reader to judge the dependability of the Schweitzer biography.

The following, however, seems accurate. Eduard Karl Oskar Theodor Schnitzer, the man who was to become Emin Pasha, was born on 28 March 1840 at Oppeln in Prussia. His family, which was Jewish, moved when Schnitzer was two years old to Neisse where his father, a wool merchant, died three years later. Shortly thereafter, Schnitzer was baptized in the Lutheran Church and, later, went to a Roman Catholic school. From the age of eighteen to twenty-four, he attended successively the universities of Breslau, Königsberg, and Berlin, ultimately graduating as a medical doctor in 1864. However, for some unstated reason, he did not qualify to practise medicine in Prussia and was considered unfit for service in the army. As his homeland was asserting its hegemony over the other German states, Schnitzer began to look abroad, first attempting to enlist in the French expeditionary force which was to place Maximilian of Austria on the throne of Mexico. Having been rejected, Schnitzer departed abruptly for Constantinople, where it seems that he hoped to find employment (as many Europeans had done before him) as a physician in the service of Turkey. By December 1864 he was in the minute Albanian port of

Ativari, practising medicine and becoming at some point during the next six years the port quarantine and district medical officer. A remarkable linguist, Schnitzer had become fluent in English, French, Italian, Turkish, Greek, Arabic, Persian, Albanian, and several Slavonic languages, as well as, of course, German. Later he was to add African languages to his extensive repertoire. Equally, Schnitzer had used his inquiring, methodical, and eclectic mind to add an increasingly impressive knowledge of botany and ornithology to his knowledge of medicine.

Schnitzer was to spend a total of almost ten years in Albania, the final period on the personal staff of the Turkish governor of northern Albania, possibly as a tutor to his children. During his decade in Albania, Schnitzer travelled extensively through much of the ramshackle Ottoman Empire (he later appeared knowledgeable about corners even more obscure than Albania). His cousin-biographer says that Schnitzer became involved in a variety of political intrigues. Schnitzer himself confirmed this years later to a British army officer, but what exactly he did during that decade of wandering amongst the Turks and their satrapies remains uncertain. The British officer recorded that Emin had to flee Constantinople for having helped to write anti-government newspaper articles, but that he "had been specially promoted to a Majority for distinguished conduct on the battle-field."[3]

However all that may be, two facts emerge clearly enough. At some point the Lutheran Schnitzer converted to Islam, worshipping regularly in mosques. Slight and deeply tanned by the Mediterranean sun and publicly acknowledging himself a true follower of Mohammed, Schnitzer was able to pass readily amongst Turks and Arabs. Life in the lands of the Sublime Porte evidently appealed to him. With the exception of one brief interlude, he spent the twenty-eight years from 1864 to his death in 1892 within or on the marches of the Ottoman Empire.

The one brief interlude during which Schnitzer absented himself from the Ottoman Empire followed the death of the aged governor of northern Albania in 1875. With the governor's young widow (who was a Transylvanian Christian), her three children and several servants, Schnitzer visited his remarried mother and relatives in the small – and no doubt astonished – town of Neisse. Apparently wearying of the charms of his supposed wife and of his homeland, he returned to the Ottoman Empire, abandoning the Transylvanian and her children to fend for themselves in Bismarck's Germany. His family did not hear from him for the next fourteen years. Schnitzer became a Turkish citizen and never returned to Europe.

It seems clear that everywhere Schnitzer went he was liked. He was a learned, gentle, kindly and observant, if procrastinating, eccentric. He was a scholar, a naturalist who, wherever he was, took unceasing delight in the world around him, recording in his meticulous notebooks the details of the fauna and flora with which he lived in such evident harmony. Even the African explorer Henry

Morton Stanley, who had a monumental ego, later joined briefly in the unanimous praise of Emin's generous and unassuming character and of his scholarship.

Perhaps that constitutes all that one can know with much certainty about the early life of Schnitzer. Why he decided to go to Egypt and the Sudan in 1875 can only be a matter of conjecture. He paused briefly in Alexandria and Cairo, long enough to practise medicine to avoid complete destitution there. He reached Khartoum, penniless, in December 1875. In that small, overcrowded, and foetid capital of the Sudan, he was still nominally within the bounds of the Ottoman Empire. The Sudan was administered as a province of Egypt, but since Egypt continued to recognize the suzerainty of Constantinople (however slight that hegemony might be in day-to-day terms), Schnizter in the Sudan remained within the realm of the Porte.

When Schnitzer arrived, "Chinese" Gordon, famed in Britain for the exploits of his "Ever-Victorious Army" in distant China, was also in Khartoum. It was the first of Gordon's two long sojourns in the Sudan, initially as governor of Equatoria and later as governor general of the whole of the Sudan. When Gordon was governor of Equatoria, the writ of the Porte – or of Egypt – ran only occasionally and haphazardly. The British had not yet intervened directly in Egypt (that was not to be until 1882), the Suez Canal had been open only six years earlier and the notoriously extravagant Khedive of Egypt was still striving, in a desultory sort of way, to ward off complete bankruptcy.

Gordon was much on his own in Equatoria, 1,800 kilometres south of Khartoum. The only physician in the province, an Egyptian, had returned to Cairo. In his place, Gordon recruited Schnitzer who arrived in Equatoria in May 1876. Schnitzer visited Khartoum only once more, in March 1882. He was never to see Gordon again.*

Before his departure for Equatoria, Schnitzer had spent less than six months in Khartoum, but that was time enough to change his name. Perhaps intent upon appearing in every respect a Moslem, he had adopted the name of Mohammed Emin Effendi and was known for the remainder of his life as Emin

---

*In addition to Gordon, Henry Morton Stanley was the second Englishman with whom Schnitzer was eventually and much less happily to be associated. Gordon, having employed Schnitzer as the medical officer of Equatoria, promptly dispatched him on a peace-making mission southward to Buganda, the neighbouring black kingdom which was understandably wary of the intentions of the "Turks" to the north. In 1876, during the first of several quasi-diplomatic sojourns in Buganda, Emin must have heard much about the unexpected visit of Stanley to Buganda the year before, during his harrowing, three-year overland expedition from Zanzibar to the mouth of the Congo.

("the faithful one"): Dr Emin until 1878 when he was promoted by the Khedive of Egypt to bey and in 1886 to pasha (the title by which he was thereafter known).

Following Gordon's resignation of his gubernatorial appointment in Equatoria in late 1876 and his departure for Britain, two Americans and an Egyptian were successively appointed governor of Equatoria. Finally, in 1878, Emin was made governor, a post he was to fill for the next eleven years.

Gordon had done much to establish garrisons across the province, but neither he nor Emin had promising material with which to work in their efforts to suppress the ubiquitous slave trade. At British instigation, the slave trade in west Africa had been suppressed many decades before, but Arab slavers of east Africa continued to evade the Royal Navy patrols in the Indian Ocean. Emin could do little or nothing about cutting off the source of the slaves south of Equatoria when a significant number of the Egyptian and northern Sudanese soldiers in the stations were "convicts, criminals, and men who were deported to Equatoria from Egypt ... As Emin observed, the Equatorial Province has always been considered a sort of Egyptian Siberia by the authorities at Cairo".[4]

Cairo was not much interested in this most distant of its Sudanese provinces. Always near bankruptcy itself, Egypt had no money to invest in a territory so distant from its more immediate concerns. In the face of the continuing expansion of the Mahdists both southward toward Equatoria as well as northward toward Khartoum, the most that Cairo could do was to call upon Emin to withdraw from Equatoria with his garrisons. Cairo could not, however, be certain that Emin would even receive the order or, if he did, that he would carry it out. In February 1886, more than one year after Khartoum had fallen to the Mahdi, Emin finally received the order from the Egyptian prime minister to make his way, with his garrison, to Zanzibar.

Emin's response was to do nothing. As was his wont, he procrastinated, offering a variety of reasons why it was best for him to stay at Wadelai, his minute provisional capital sixty kilometres north of Lake Albert Nyanza. From there he contended that he might somehow withstand the Mahdists and establish a viable entity which could be turned over preferably to the British or, if necessary, to the Congo Free State (the personal fiefdom of Leopold, the King of the Belgians for which Emin had a healthy dislike). The only word in more than two years of his whereabouts reached Europe in early 1887. News had arrived in Zanzibar that Emin was still alive, but that he was isolated at Wadelai with the Mahdists presumably advancing on him from the north and with hostile blacks hemming him in on the south.

◆   ◆   ◆

The man eventually chosen to find Emin, either to provide him with the arms and other supplies which it was assumed that he must desperately need or to encourage him to come away with his garrisons, was Henry Morton Stanley. George Bernard Shaw once described Stanley as "the wild-beast man, with his elephant rifle, and his atmosphere of dread and murder, breaking his way by mad selfish assassination out of the difficulties created by his own cowardice." It is a dramatic but not, all in all, an inaccurate description.

Stanley was not a lovable man. He was as unlike Emin Pasha as anyone could be. Whereas from all accounts Emin was patient, generous, kindly, and charitable, Stanley is frequently portrayed as the opposite : impatient, miserly, cruel, difficult and intolerant. Freudians readily find the reasons for his mean, sulphurous, and complex ego in his extraordinarily difficult childhood. Certainly the character of anyone who had the misfortune to pass his or her illegitimate childhood amidst Victorian poverty – and the illegitimate Stanley had endured destitution, brutality, and opprobrium aplenty – could hardly emerge unscathed.

Illegitimacy in itself was not so rare an occurrence in Victorian England as later generations were to assume, but in Denbigh, Wales, it was, as everywhere, a pronounced stigma. There John Rowlands – like Schnitzer, Rowlands was later to assume another name, that of Henry Morton Stanley – was born on 28 January 1841, eleven years after Schnitzer's birth. Rowland's illegitimacy and his rejection by his mother soon resulted in his relegation to the workhouse in nearby St Asaph. What little instruction he received there was from an apparently loutish schoolmaster. Eventually Rowlands departed for the slums of Liverpool and from there sailed later to the more promising shores of the new world.

Following his arrival in New Orleans in 1859, Rowlands, aged eighteen, was employed by a prosperous British cotton merchant, one Henry Stanley, whose name Rowlands soon assumed, despite a subsequent falling out with his kindly mentor. It was as Henry Stanley that Rowlands enrolled in the Confederate army in the Civil War.

Upon being taken prisoner at the Battle of Shiloh in 1862, Stanley switched sides, joining an Illinois artillery battery and later, after a brief and unhappy interlude in Britain, enlisting in the United States navy, from which he promptly deserted.

There is obscurity about Stanley's service on both sides in the American Civil War, but that is true of much of Stanley's life. Throughout, his memory remained both selective and inventive – perhaps not surprising in one who had been made to feel an outcast even by his mother and who had always to live by his wits. In any event, it is certain that in 1866, Stanley travelled from the United States to Turkey, his first encounter with the Moslem world. The following year he was back in the United States, observing the extermination of the Indians across the western plains. Somewhere along the way he seems to have been employed or retained by the raffish – what Livingstone had flatly

called the disreputable – *New York Herald* as a sort of roving reporter.*
Certainly by 1868, when Stanley was in Abyssinia accompanying a British
expeditionary force, he had become its formally accredited correspondent.

The short, dark, hardy, mistrustful, and aggressive correspondent of the *New
York Herald*, travelling in Europe and the Levant, was, however, not much noted
until 1871 when his enterprising publisher set him the complex challenge that
was to make him famous. Bennett charged Stanley with finding the famous
missionary, David Livingstone, who was assumed to be in danger somewhere
in central Africa. After almost a year on an arduous trek inland from Zanzibar,
Stanley finally encountered the great missionary on the shores of Lake
Tanganyika and asked him his immortal question – and so assured his own
fame. After travelling more than four thousand kilometres in a little more than
a year, Stanley returned to a London which, although never having heard of him
before, promptly lionized him. An audience with Queen Victoria, controversial
lecture tours in Britain and the United States (where Livingstone's brother
John, a farmer in Ontario, joined Stanley on public platforms) and his hurriedly
published bestseller, *How I Found Livingstone*, all confirmed Stanley's sudden
fame. There soon arose, however, awkward questions about who Stanley really
was, including his illegitimate birth. Dark stories began to circulate about his
floggings and manaclings of his more recalcitrant porters and his indifference,
if not hostility, toward his two European companions, both of whom had died
on the expedition. "The contrast with Livingstone's unfailing gentleness and
forebearance (not to mention the obvious similarities between Stanley's
methods and those of the Arab slavers) was too pointed to be lost on those of
Stanley's audience, who thought the whipping and shooting of Africans no fit
occupation for an Englishman and a gentleman, and who concluded, quite
correctly, that Stanley was neither."[5] Stanley was never quite able to free himself
of his origins or to dispel the conviction among the upper classes of Victorian
society that basically he was a bounder. One British officer on the Abyssinia
campaign had described him as "a howling cad" and another who later observed
him at close quarters for three years concluded succinctly that Stanley was
"off his chump" and an "utter brute and cad."

Stanley, now regarding himself as a permanent employee of the *New York
Herald*, accompanied a British force sent in 1874 to the Gold Coast. The

---

*When Stanley was first employed by the *New York Herald*, its founder, James Gordon
Bennett Sr. was already transferring its management to his son, James Gordon Bennett
Jr. The father, who had emigrated to Nova Scotia from Scotland, had begun his profes-
sional life in 1820 as a school teacher in Dartmouth, before moving on to Boston (as so
many Nova Scotians did). For more details of Stanley's relations with Bennett Jr. see C.
Don Seitz, *The James Gordon Bennetts, Father and Son* (Indianapolis, 1928).

following year, this time on behalf of both the *Daily Telegraph* of London and the *Herald* of New York, Stanley led an expedition to explore much of then unknown central Africa to help open those vast areas to trade and the suppression of Arab slavers. Stanley began at Zanzibar, as he had done on his Livingstone expedition. Almost three years later, he had crossed Africa, emerging at the mouth of the Congo. Of the 359 people who had set out with him from Zanzibar, only eighty-two returned. Along the way, the expedition had killed Africans by the hundreds. A high price had been paid in terms of human suffering, but as a result of the expedition much more was known in Europe about the Congo, lakes Victoria Nyanza and Tanganyika, and the plains and mountains of central Africa.

That Stanley managed to cross the continent at all was in part due to the support of an Arab slaver, Tippu Tib, with whom Livingstone had travelled in 1867. Almost as courageous and determined as Stanley himself, Tippu Tib had put aside his search for slaves and ivory long enough to accept $5,000 from Stanley to provide porters and a few fellow Arabs – with himself at their head – to help Stanley's expedition over one of the most difficult stretches of what was throughout a hazardous journey. And Stanley himself had demonstrated that persistent determination which, of all his varied traits, was the one which saw him through ordeals few other men could have sustained.

Upon his return to Europe, Stanley was for a second time enthusiastically acclaimed, although questions were again asked about his brutal treatment of Africans and why it was that no European had survived either of his two expeditions. For his part, Stanley soon recognized that his knowledge of the Congo was prized by those who hoped to exploit the riches of that great river's watershed. Few were more interested in Stanley's findings than King Leopold II of the Belgians.

♦   ♦   ♦

"A more unlikely candidate as standard-bearer of civilisation in the Dark Continent than ... Leopold II of the Belgians would be difficult to imagine. Overweight and bearded like an Old Testament patriarch, Leopold was a liar, swindler, lecher, and master of machiavellianism. This was the man who was to be the architect of Stanley's fortunes during the last half of his life, yet he as clearly called forth the dark side of Stanley's nature as Livingstone had elicited the good."[6] Leopold II (1835–1909) had ascended the Belgian throne in 1865, upon the death of his father, Leopold I, Queen Victoria's "dearest uncle." As a young man, he had travelled extensively in the Middle and Far East and by the 1880s he was eager to obtain – somehow – colonies. Most other European nations already had colonies. Leopold, but not the Belgians themselves, eagerly joined Germany and Italy, the other two latecomers to the colonial scene, in the general scramble for the remnants of the earlier overseas ventures of Britain,

France, Spain, and Portugal. Initially, Leopold's vain ambitions extended to the purchase of Sarawak, the Philippines, Angola, or even a province of Argentina. However, when the people of Belgium continued to exhibit no enthusiasm for the expenses and international complications involved in colonies, the rapacious Leopold turned instead to the idea of a commercial company which could serve as his personal vehicle for colonial exploitation. After canvassing possibilities in China, Leopold finally struck on the Congo, partly as a result of what Stanley had written about it, but mainly as a route to the headwaters of the Nile, which held endless fascination for him.

In his search for like-minded entrepreneurs for his proposed venture in central Africa, Leopold soon began discussions with such noted British explorers as James Grant and Samuel Baker and the steamship owner, William Mackinnon. No one was attempting to do more to open central Africa to trade – other than, in a different way, Stanley himself – than that dynamic, self-made Scottish millionaire.[7] A devout member of the Free Church of Scotland who had flourished in the steamship business in India, Mackinnon shared the growing conviction, endorsed by Livingstone, that the opening of Africa to commerce would prove to be the only effective way of suppressing the hated slave trade, which despite the valiant efforts of Royal Navy squadrons based on Zanzibar, was still flourishing across the Indian Ocean.

In their intermittent and faltering forays to exploit the hinterland of Africa, British entrepreneurs had occasionally some indirect support from their government, but efforts to proclaim either the Congo or Uganda British colonies met with continued rebuffs from Whitehall. As late as 1883, a popular book about colonialism stated, "the policy of England discourages any increase of territory in tropical countries already occupied by native races ... and there is much truth in the dictum of an eminent living statesman, that England had already black subjects enough."[8] Lord Derby, the British foreign secretary when Leopold was embarking upon his colonial enterprises, wrote to his colleague, Lord Granville, "there is something absurd in the scramble for colonies."[9] That laconic and reluctant imperialist, Lord Salisbury, the prime minister from 1885 to 1886 and 1886 to 1892, was no less puzzled. "When I left the Foreign Office in 1880, nobody thought about Africa. When I returned to it [as prime minister and foreign secretary] in 1885, the nations of Europe were almost quarrelling with each other as to various portions of Africa which they could obtain. I do not know the cause of this sudden revolution [in seeking African colonies]. But there it is."[10]

Mackinnon's first collaboration with Leopold had been in 1876, five years after he had received a British government contract to operate a mail steamer service from Aden to Durban via Zanzibar, the island which had become the base for central African exploration. In 1876 Mackinnon, along with several other members of Britain's Royal Geographic Society and delegations from across Europe, had participated in Leopold's Brussels Geographic Conference.

The conference had been convened by the king in the certain knowledge that among his subjects there would be no enthusiasm for the colonial ventures he envisaged. But Leopold also knew that, given the nature of those whom he had invited, the conference would enthusiastically support his idea of opening up central Africa by an association of national committees reporting to an international commission presided over by, not surprisingly, King Leopold II. If his own subjects would not endorse his ambitions, then the *Association Internationale Africaine* would be Leopold's principal instrument to establish bases at both the mouth of the Congo and on the opposite side of Africa at Zanzibar for the exploitation of the interior. Although Britain's Royal Geographic Society soon decided against participation, Mackinnon, J.F. Hutton of the Manchester Chamber of Commerce, and several other British entrepreneurs of the "Mackinnon clan" remained steadfastly committed, convinced that vast new markets for manufactured goods were waiting to be claimed in the Congo.

While Leopold was pursuing his colonial ambitions through a loose network of committees in countries where individuals were eager, for their own ends, to support his schemes, Stanley had completed his epic three-year crossing of Africa from east to west, descending the Congo to its mouth in 1877. It was now evident to Leopold and those eager to support his schemes that the best way to penetrate the upper Congo would be to establish a string of stations reaching inland from Zanzibar. For this task, Leopold asked General Gordon, an arch opponent of the slave trade, to establish the stations, but it was not until 1883 that Gordon finally agreed to enter the Congo service, only to accept instead at the last minute the British government's somewhat reluctant request to him to go to Khartoum to attempt to bring away the Egyptian garrison besieged there by the Mahdists.

Meanwhile, in the Congo itself, Stanley had accepted an offer from Leopold to be its administrator. In his book, *The Congo and the Founding of its Free State*, Stanley described his work from 1879 to 1884 in enthusiastic terms. He was never one to understate his own contributions to any project, but there is no question that Leopold owed more to Stanley than to anyone else in opening the Congo. One student of the period has stated flatly, "To him Leopold owed everything."[11]

The viability of Leopold's faltering but highly personal *Association Internationale Africaine* (and its no less infirm successor, the *Association Internationale du Congo*) was always in question, given the continuing absence of international recognition, clear national backing, and even such symbols as a flag. Leopold responded with a campaign to gain international recognition for a Congo Free State (or states). At the persistent urging of Henry Sanford, the U.S. minister to Belgium, the United State Senate was prompt to oblige in April 1884. Encouraged by the Senate's support, Mackinnon and Hutton worked to promote British recognition, inducing such trade-minded groups as the Manchester Chamber of Commerce to adopt suitable resolutions:

The Chamber ... hereby expresses its warm sympathy in the earnest efforts of His Majesty the King of the Belgians to establish civilization and free trade on the Upper Congo; it also trusts that the independent state or states proposed to be founded there may be recognized by all nations, and that the beneficient work now inaugurated may be ultimately extended throughout the whole of that river from its sources to its mouth.

Leopold's idea of a tariff-free state in the Congo accorded with the emphasis on the benefits of free trade in Stanley's frequent articles, letters, and lectures. If the British government declined to take the Congo for itself, then at least the Congo should be preserved for the free trade of all nations. Certainly France should not have it. Thus there was widespread recognition among British commercial interests that no other option existed but to recognize Leopold's *Association Internationale Africaine* as an anomaly in a world where either nation states or colonies were the standard if not exclusive concept of how people should be governed. The Foreign Office was far from sharing this sanguine view of such an unusual arrangement. Nevertheless, in December 1884 it reluctantly agreed to recognize the *Association* as having all the attributes – or their equivalent – of a nation state, including a flag. Despite misgivings about some of the practices of the *Association*, both Britain and Germany realized that the only alternative would be to cede the lower Congo to Portugal and to recognize a much larger role inland for France. Neither alternative was acceptable. The result was that a West Africa Conference in Berlin in 1884–85 gave general recognition to the Congo Free State. Leopold, with the notable assistance of Bismarck, had achieved his political goal. Now the way was open for the economic exploitation of the Congo. For its part, Germany would content itself with a large slice of east Africa, a nibble of west Africa and much of southwest Africa.

By the summer of 1885 Mackinnon, Hutton, and Stanley had joined together to propose a railway around the great cataracts at Stanley Pool on the Congo River which had so endangered Stanley's crossing of Africa. Stanley himself was restless about his own role – or lack of a role – in the exploitation of the Congo. He was being paid a retainer of £1,000 annually by Leopold, but the king had left him unemployed in London. He eagerly joined in the elaborate proposal which would have given a largely British company the right to exploit a considerable area of the Congo basin as well as to build the railway.

Leopold's response to this ambitious British project was to play for time, hoping that he might himself be able to put together another consortium, largely French and German, to do the same things that the British group had proposed. In the light of Leopold's silence, Stanley was increasingly uneasy as the months passed, seeking reassurance that he retained the king's confidence. On 18

September 1886 Stanley wrote despondently to Mackinnon, "every day the King is closing the Congo against the English and seems resolved to make it more and more Belgian."[12]

Stanley's misgivings about Leopold's real intentions proved to be well-founded. The proposal of the British consortium, which would have made the Congo basin a new sphere of British commercial dominance, was not surprisingly rejected by Leopold, ostensibly because the British activities would be incompatible with the sovereignty bestowed upon the Congo Free State by the Berlin Conference. Leopold knew full well that the British commercial interests would relegate him to a lesser role in the Free State. "In short, if the [British] syndicate's proposals had been accepted, the proposed company would have enjoyed such powers and immunities that the Congo Free State would certainly have become a British sphere of influence, and might well have become a British possession in everything but name."[13]

The British consortium's proposals were rejected in September 1886, at the very time when Stanley was becoming increasingly uneasy about his future employment by Leopold. Coincidentally, however, a pressing reason arose for Stanley to return to Africa. He welcomed a tentative query whether he would lead an expedition to relieve the last survivor of Gordon's lieutenants in the Sudan, Emin Pasha. Almost twenty years had passed since Stanley had "rescued" Livingstone. Here was something to do, some action to end the maddening inactivity in London that had begun more than two years before when he had returned from his five years as Leopold's administrator of the Congo.

♦   ♦   ♦

During the month following the rejection by Leopold of the proposals of the British syndicate, there had arrived in London news that the plight of Emin Pasha, isolated in the southern Sudan, was in some way or other becoming serious. Dr Wilhelm Junker, the Russo-German explorer, had managed to make his way south from Emin's base at Wadelai to the station near Lake Victoria Nyanza of a Scottish missionary, Alexander Mackay. The Kabaka of Uganda was systematically killing Mackay's Christian converts and threatening him and his two fellow missionaries but, against all odds, Junker succeeded in reaching Zanzibar in September 1886. The British consul general there cabled the Foreign Office an urgent appeal for the relief of both Emin and Mackay. A noted Scottish missionary and explorer, Robert Felkin, who knew Equatoria, added his voice to the growing interest in the plight of Emin Pasha.

The Foreign Office, however, did little. A vain appeal to protect the missionaries was sent to the Kabaka – by the unpromising but only route of Arab slavers. Emin, it appeared, needed supplies but it was not at all clear that he wanted to leave Africa. By October letters from Emin, having reached Zanzibar, had been forwarded to London and published there. The result was a yet greater interest in succouring the last of Gordon's lieutenants. In the popular mind, the national disgrace of Gordon's death would be repeated if Emin were to suffer a similar fate. The British government indicated, however, that it would not fund an expedition and would not regard itself responsible for its fate if disaster were to overtake it. Salisbury, for his part, was quite clear that any attempt to relieve Emin Pasha should be left to Germany. "It is really their business, if Emin is a German."[14]

Salisbury's reference to Emin's German origins was a reflection both of his continuing indifference to the "scramble for Africa" (he was gradually to change his mind) and of the growing German presence there. At the end of October 1886, Britain and Germany effectively divided east Africa between them. North of Zanzibar a line was drawn inland to Lake Victoria. Everything to the south of the line was German; everything to the north was British. The Sultan of Zanzibar had been stripped of most of his mainland possessions which had gone to Germany.

Nothing in the Anglo-German agreement, however, needed to be seen as a deterrent to Mackinnon's promotion of an Emin relief expedition. Mackinnon, partly at the prompting of Sir John Kirk, the British consul general in Zanzibar, agreed to chair a committee. The Congo railway project having been pre-empted by Leopold, a relief expedition might be an opportunity, in Hutton's words, "to further the objects of the syndicate as far as possible."[15] The expedition would be led by Mackinnon's collaborator, Stanley.

◆   ◆   ◆

It remained unclear, however, whether Emin wanted to be rescued or, indeed, what he wanted. With the advance of Mahdist forces both north and southward in the Sudan, and especially following the news of the fall of Khartoum and the death of Gordon in January 1885, Emin had begun to plan a withdrawal of all his garrisons farther southward to Wadelai. However, some of the Egyptian garrisons declined to withdraw, convinced as they were that Khartoum had not fallen and that somehow reinforcements from Egypt would come to them from the north and certainly not from the south. In Wadelai, Emin began to think of attempting to hold on to Equatoria, or at least to the southern portion of it, until he could hand it over intact to the British as "a service to mankind and lending an advance to civilisation ..."[16] Several years before, Emin had written to the Anti-Slavery Society in London, offering the vision of the two southernmost provinces of the Sudan united under European rule, which would banish slavery and slaving. In addition, the region could generate the revenue, largely through the export of ivory, to be self-sufficient. Further, even as the Mahdists advanced southward, the few letters received from Emin made it clear that he did not want to leave his province. As late as April 1887, when Stanley was already making his way up the Congo ostensibly to rescue him, Emin was quite certain that he wanted to remain in Africa, preferably where he was. "For twelve long years I have striven and toiled, and sown the seeds for future harvest ... Shall I now give up the work because a way may soon open to the coast? Never!"[17]

Here were seeds enough for any amount of later misunderstanding and mutual antagonism. Stanley, having failed to induce Livingstone to leave Africa with him, was unlikely to leave Emin where he was, merely seeing his role as delivering ammunition and other stores to him. Emin must either resettle where Mackinnon wanted him or leave central Africa.

During the autumn of 1886 there was little question in the minds of those who were aware of Emin's plight that his situation was deteriorating. Few were more interested in organizing a relief expedition than the British syndicate. For its part, the British government began to look with more favour upon a private initiative as reducing public pressure to take any action itself. In light of Leopold's opposition to the British syndicate, Mackinnon had gradually lost interest in central Africa and had not responded to Hutton's urgings to consider opening a direct route to the Nile from the east coast. Now, however, a relief expedition promised to open up much new territory as it passed from Zanzibar to Emin's supposed whereabouts on the shores of Lake Victoria or on the banks of the upper Nile. Although there can be no doubt about the authenticity of the desire of Mackinnon and Hutton to find and help Emin, there is equally no doubt that they also saw in the expedition a welcome opportunity to prepare the way for greater British commercial exploitation in east and central Africa. As early as 29 September 1886, Mackinnon had written that if Stanley were to lead an expedition to relieve Emin, "the opportunity which his going there offers of extending British influence from the coast up to Wadelai is one which if ... not taken advantage of now, will be lost for ever."[18] Emin himself was evidently ready to cooperate. In November 1886 letters arrived in London from him, offering to remain as governor of Equatoria if Britain would assume responsibility for it.

Having declined the offer of the remarkable young explorer, Joseph Thomson, to lead a relief expedition, and having secured Stanley's prompt agreement to do so, Mackinnon gave further expression to his commercial ambitions by commissioning Stanley to negotiate with the Sultan of Zanzibar for trading posts on the mainland coast. They would form the necessary base for a trade route inland to Emin's Equatoria province. At the same time, Mackinnon was seeking in London a royal charter for a new company, the Imperial British East Africa Company, since Leopold had rejected his earlier proposal for a British company to exploit the Congo basin.*

---

*The Imperial British East Africa Company received its royal charter in September 1888.

Mackinnon's recent ventures into Africa had met with a singular lack of success and Leopold's were going nowhere. Now, with the "push" of Stanley again unleashed in central Africa, a new start might be made to open the upper Congo to commercial interests. Mackinnon regarded the Emin Relief Expedition and his Imperial British Africa Company as happily combining two distinct but compatible interests. The expedition would not only be an expression of Christian principles but would also establish a route to the great lakes of east Africa and to the upper Nile. With the supplies delivered to him by Stanley, Emin would be enabled to hold on in Equatoria or elsewhere in east Africa, thereby providing a base for the exploitation of the region by the British syndicate (which had been initially described in a memorandum with the dual and revealing title of "Syndicate for Establishing British Commerce and Influence in East Africa and for Relieving Emin Bey").

By January 1887 Leopold understood what was afoot. Although wanting to remain friendly with British entrepreneurs eager to join in the exploitation of the upper Congo, he sought also to preserve a major role for himself by forcing the proposed expedition to follow the Congo route. The Germans would soon push inland from the Indian Ocean. Now was the moment for Leopold to secure for himself the upper Congo. Accordingly, the king intervened in the plans to organize a relief expedition by reminding both Mackinnon and Stanley that he still had first call upon Stanley's services. If the committee persisted in its plan to use an eastern route from Zanzibar, the king would find it impossible to release Stanley. But if instead the committee saw the wisdom of Stanley beginning at the mouth of the Congo, a flotilla of Free State riverboats would be made available to carry the expedition up the river (the river boats were vital; it was, after all, steam that enabled Europeans to penetrate Africa). Instead of beginning and ending in Zanzibar, the expedition would begin at the mouth of the Congo and end at Zanzibar. Stanley would cross the African continent a second time, but this time from west to east.

Mackinnon did not object to Leopold's demand, although it meant that Mackay and his fellow missionaries in Uganda could expect no help from the expedition. On the other hand, the employment of the expedition to forge a permanent link between the Nile and the Congo rivers might actually assist Mackinnon's fledgling Imperial British East Africa Company to establish itself in the area. In any event, Mackinnon had little choice but to acquiesce in the Congo route if Stanley were to lead the expedition, given the king's prior claim on him.

In early January 1887 Stanley met twice with the king in Brussels to agree on the broad details of the expedition – additional to the relief of Emin. The proposed route from the upper Congo to the upper Nile would help realize the king's long-standing ambition to establish a link between the two great rivers, as well as reinforcing his claim to the eastern Congo. And, best of all, these goals might be achieved at no cost to himself.

Once the Congo route had been agreed upon, the king raised the possibility of using the expedition as a means of consolidating the hold of the Free State on the vast, unsecured region centred on Stanley Falls. Leopold had concluded that there was only one way in which he could run his writ throughout the upper Congo: Stanley must recruit Tippu Tib. The Arab trader and slaver and erstwhile travelling companion of both Livingstone and Stanley now effectively controlled a vast area under the nebulous authority of the Sultan of Zanzibar. He must become instead the Congo Free State's governor at Stanley Falls. The poacher must become the gamekeeper.

◆   ◆   ◆

Tippu Tib, or Hamed ben Muhammed el Murjebi to give him his real name, was about forty-seven years old when Leopold first began to envisage him as governor of Stanley Falls. Born in Zanzibar about 1830 of a Muscat Arab merchant and an African mother, Tippu Tib was typical of the "Arabs" along the east coast of Africa who had made their way inland in the mid-nineteenth century in search of ivory and slaves. Generally such people were in fact of mixed Arab and African parentage and in some cases the "Arab" was simply a black who had adopted Arab ways, including conversion to Islam.

Tippu Tib, while still a young man, had travelled on his father's behalf from Zanzibar to the upper Congo where his guns had gradually subdued the spears of the warlike Manyuema people. Tippu Tib's organizational acumen was such that he eventually came to control the whole vast area through an elaborate structure of middlemen and slaves. It was said that in his exploits on the upper Congo, the frequent tap of the hammers of his muskets had given Hamed ben Muhammed his onomatopoeic sobriquet of "Tippu Tib".

Having once established himself astride the upper Congo, Tippu Tib had strengthened his hold to the point where he and his cohorts not only controlled the ivory and slaves who were despatched mainly to Zanzibar, but were also a barrier to the growing pretentions of Leopold to the area. In his assertion of authority over the Manyuema region of the upper Congo, Tippu Tib regarded himself as acting under the suzerainty of the Sultan of Zanzibar, whose shadowy claims over an indefinite extent of the hinterland Tippu Tib had always recognized. (It was under the Sultan that Tippu Tib had assisted, successively, Livingstone, the British explorer Verney Cameron, and Stanley in their African travels). Eventually, when the claims of the Congo Free State and those of the Sultan of Zanzibar collided on the upper Congo, Tippu Tib remained loyal to the sultan (a fellow Muscat Arab).

However, by the time of the Emin Relief Expedition, the sultan's authority along the upper Congo had been seriously eroded by the claims of the Germans from the east coast and of Leopold from the west. When Stanley arrived in Zanzibar with his expedition, he knew that his chances of success would be enhanced if Tippu Tib could reconcile the Arabs to its presence on the upper Congo. For his part, Leopold had decided that he would need to come to terms with Tippu Tib if the Congo Free State were to succeed in asserting its claim over the Manyuema region. Tippu Tib, in turn, had reluctantly concluded that the authority of the Sultan of Zanzibar could not withstand the growing claims of European powers to various pieces of his domains, whether it was the Germans to coastal areas or Leopold to the upper Congo. With Stanley in Zanzibar, a deal was finally agreed. Tippu Tib would become the governor of Stanley Falls for the Congo Free State and fly its blue flag. However, he would retain full freedom to kill elephants for their tusks – and his underlings could still pursue their slaving. In Zanzibar Tippu Tib also agreed with Stanley that, in return for ammunition and powder, he would provide the expedition with six hundred carriers to help it move from the upper Congo to Lake Albert. Tippu Tib, however, regarded this deal with reservation. With good reason, he believed Stanley to be a cheat and a liar who never kept a bargain unless it was to his own advantage.

◆   ◆   ◆

Stanley's second mandate from King Leopold was to tell Emin Pasha that if he chose not to follow the advice of the Egyptian government to evacuate his province, he would be welcomed into the service of the Free State to keep open the route between the Nile and the Congo. Evidently unknown to Leopold, however, Stanley personally favoured Mackinnon's offer to Emin of settlement near the shores of Lake Victoria Nyanza. There Emin's garrisons would provide the base for the expansion of the Imperial British East Africa Company into Uganda and the upper Congo. Mackinnon presumably was convinced that Stanley regarded himself primarily as his agent and not Leopold's, even if Stanley remained formally in the employ of the king. (Mackinnon's confidence was not misplaced. Upon his return from Africa, Stanley stated explicitly if disingenuously to Mackinnon, "I considered myself only as your agent" and requested Mackinnon, in the flowery dedication to him of *In Darkest Africa*, to "accept much of the professions of [my heart] which has been pledged long ago to you wholly and entirely.")

There is ambiguity if not duplicity in all this. Stanley, although beginning at the mouth of the Congo instead of at Zanzibar, would nevertheless eventually reach Mackinnon's continuing field of interest, central and east Africa. There Stanley could attempt to realize Mackinnon's goal of establishing a trade route between the east coast and Emin's province of Equatoria. In short, Leopold would get something of what he wanted if Stanley could help consolidate the hold of the Free State along the upper Congo. Mackinnon would get something of what he wanted in east Africa if Stanley could establish a string of trading posts from Equatoria to the Indian Ocean. There was, it could be argued, something for everyone. Both Leopold and Mackinnon would realize at least some of their ambitions, even if Stanley was in effect working for both at the same time.

As one biographer of Stanley has written perceptively,

> There was a conflict between Mackinnon's aims and Leopold's ... and not just in the sense that a Congo itinerary for the relief expedition seemed to tip the balance in favour of Congo interests over East African ones. Which side was Stanley on? Almost certainly the answer is, his own. He did not confide the scope of Mackinnon's ambitions to Leopold, nor Leopold's offer to Emin to Mackinnon ... Stanley was playing both ends against the middle, manoeuvring for personal advantage. Ever the opportunist, Stanley's main aim was the enhancement of his own reputation and glory ...[19]

On this ambiguous and even contradictory basis, Stanley set about organizing his third and final expedition to central Africa.

♦   ♦   ♦

When Stanley received from Mackinnon confirmation that the Emin Relief Expedition would go forward, he was in Vermont on one of his highly profitable lecture tours. Following his arrival back in London on Christmas Eve, he found the War Office, the Admiralty, the Colonial Office, and the Foreign Office all collaborating informally in helping to equip the expedition. For his part, Mackinnon had agreed that his own British India Steamship Company would transport the expedition from Zanzibar around the Cape of Good Hope to the Congo (with coal partly provided by the Admiralty). The Egyptian government readied Remington rifles and ammunition and cloth for trading purposes. In Cairo, sixty-one Sudanese soldiers (many of them veterans of the Gordon relief expedition of two years before) were recruited. In Zanzibar, the British consul general was instructed to seek the cooperation of a decidedly unenthusiastic sultan in recruiting four to six hundred porters to await the arrival of the expedition. On the other side of Africa, on the lower Congo, no such porters were available, but Free State steamers were to stand by to carry the expedition up the navigable portions of the river. In Britain, a nine-metre open steel boat, divided into twelve portable sections weighing thirty-five kilograms each, was packed for shipment. Stanley arranged to introduce into Africa the latest Winchester repeating rifles, using smokeless powder, when most of the arms available to the Arabs and others were inferior breech-loaders. Even more menacingly, Stanley also took with him a machine gun, patented by Hiram Maxim only three years before (and not to be adopted by the British army for another two years). Unlike earlier machine guns, the Maxim was operated not by a hand crank but by water-cooled propellant gases which fired smokeless bullets at the rate of eleven per second.* Burroughs and Welcome, the pharmaceutical firm, donated nine specially equipped medicine chests. Fortnum and Mason, that indispensable provisioner of African expeditions, packed forty loads of its choicest supplies for Stanley, including champagne to celebrate the relief of Emin.

The food from Britain , however, was far from adequate for even the brief duration which Stanley had grossly underestimated that the expedition would take. Food, it was hoped, would be available from tribes along the proposed route. Stanley had already crossed Africa once, from east to west, and should have known better. The porters simply could not carry all the food the expedition would need. It must either forage along the route or starve. The expedition would be well beyond the reach of a cash economy, so the traditional barter goods were dispatched to Zanzibar to be loaded for the Congo: almost 27,000 metres (more than fifteen miles) of cloth, almost two tons of beads, and one ton of wire (which for Africans had both decorative and utilitarian value). Added to this already formidable load were two tons of gunpowder, 350,000 percussion caps, 100,000 rounds of Remington ammunition, and large amounts of cartridges for the fifty Winchesters and the Maxim gun. Not all of the ammunition was intended for the use of the expedition itself. A major portion was to be handed over to Emin Pasha who, it was thought, desperately needed it.

When Stanley left London on 21 January 1887 to embark for Zanzibar, his expectations of how quickly he could reach his goal were, as usual, wildly optimistic. He forecast that his expedition would disembark at the mouth of the Congo within two months (that is, by the end of March 1887). The Free State steamers would promptly carry the expedition far up the great river, beyond its confluence with its tributary, the Aruwimi. A rapid march would then take the expedition to its destination, Lake Albert Nyanza, where it was assumed that Emin was eagerly awaiting it. Thereabouts Stanley and Emin would meet by the middle or end of July 1887. The women and children of Emin's Egyptian garrisons would be sent westward to a base camp for despatch back down the Congo on steamers. Stanley would then march the main body of his expedition and Emin and his Egyptian soldiers eastward to Zanzibar. By the end of 1887, the expedition would embark in Zanzibar on its return journey to Britain, the crossing of Africa having taken about eleven months.

◆   ◆   ◆

---

*Maxim's donation of a machine gun to the expedition gave rise to Hilaire Belloc's succinct definition of the difference between the European and the African: "Whatever happens we have got / The Maxim gun and they have not". The Maxim gun of the Emin Relief Expedition was to linger on in Africa; Frederick Lugard used it, battered and unreliable although it had then become, in Uganda in 1892.

In the event, the expedition took almost three years. The terrain it passed through, its reception by both the natives en route and by Emin, and its eventual results were wholly unlike anything Stanley had envisaged as he sat in his rooms on Bond Street in London in early January 1887, hastily organizing the expedition and reviewing the flood of applications from volunteers.*

Stanley for the first time in his African travels included army officers in his arrangements. Many were eager to join in an adventure with which the tedium of peacetime soldiering in Britain could not possibly compete. Although it was not an official expedition, as was the vast armada of 1884 despatched to save Gordon in the Sudan, the presence of army officers and the provision of supplies suggested the indirect support of the War Office, and indeed the officers who volunteered had no difficulty in obtaining leave from the adjutant general. They gave the Emin Relief Expedition rather more of a military character than had been the case with Stanley's two earlier expeditions (for example, the porters and other African recruits were organized into companies, each headed by a white officer). From among the hundreds of applications Stanley received during the four weeks that he was in London (and briefly Brussels), he hurriedly selected nine. Of the nine, one student of the Emin Relief Expedition has written, perhaps a little ungenerously, "none of them [were] exceptional."[20] They were certainly a mixed bag, but several displayed a fortitude and resourcefulness that were by any measure exceptional.

The senior in rank among the nine volunteers, *Major Edmund Musgrave Barttelot* (1859–88), aged twenty-seven, was introduced to Stanley by a mutual friend in the India Office. Barttelot was a veteran of campaigns in Afghanistan, the Northwest Frontier of India, and the Sudan (on the Gordon relief expedition). He had risen rapidly in the army, although he had initially failed to win entry to Sandhurst (a Russian war scare of 1878 had opened the way). From Cyprus in late 1886, Barttelot had returned home on sick leave. After several months of recuperative fox hunting, Barttelot was told by his friend in the India Office of the proposed expedition. Barttelot saw both Mackinnon and Stanley briefly,

---

*Stanley cannot have been surprised at the deluge of applications (which, according to *The Times*, eventually numbered four thousand). Earlier in May 1874, when news of his second expedition to Africa spread through Europe, he said that he had received more that twelve hundred applications (including from three generals and five colonels): seven hundred from Britain, three hundred from the United States, one hundred each from France and Germany. Stanley had greeted many of these offers with incredulity and derision. Some would "take me up in balloons or by flying carriages, make us all invisible by their magic arts, or by the science of magnetism would cause all savages to fall asleep while we might pass anywhere without trouble. Indeed I feel sure that, had enough money been at my disposal at the time I might have five thousand Englishmen, two thousand Frenchmen, two thousand Europeans." *(Through the Dark Continent,* vol. I, p.5).

but no record remains of why Stanley, who was no great admirer of regular officers (generally feeling at a social disadvantage in their presence) promptly appointed Barttelot as his second in command.

Barttelot was soon to prove to be incompatible with Stanley and ill-equipped for the unorthodox tasks assigned to him. From their first interview Stanley must have wondered about Barttelot's suitability, but perhaps he allowed himself to overrule his own misgivings by an eagerness to accommodate indications from the War Office that Barttelot's inclusion would be welcome. Certainly Barttelot's family was well placed to assert influence on his behalf – he was the second son of Colonel Sir Walter Barttelot, MP – and both Lord Wolseley and Sir Redvers Buller endorsed his application to Stanley (Barttelot had known both in Egypt and the Sudan).

On the other hand, Major-General Henry Brackenbury, who had also been on the Gordon relief expedition, evidently warned Stanley against Barttelot. Brackenbury may have recalled that in the Sudan Barttelot had killed a recalcitrant – and presumably thirsty – porter from Aden who had, against orders, tapped a water container. Herbert Ward, one of the officers of the Emin Relief Expedition who had the opportunity to observe Barttelot at close quarters for many months, concluded that the major viewed things "through the strict, stern, rigid spectacles of discipline and with the autocratic manner of the British officer .... He was a stranger to African manners and speech, with the ever-present suspicion of everyone and everything which this disadvantage must always excite."[21] Another officer of the expedition, John Rose Troup, added more succinctly Barttelot "had an intense hatred of anything in the shape of a black man."[22]

James P. Jameson (1856–88), aged thirty-one, had shot game in the Canadian Rockies, travelled in Borneo, and spent four years in southern Africa largely pursuing his botanical interests. He was the only married officer of the expedition, but a small daughter and a pregnant wife (his second child was born when he was on the expedition) did not deter him from eagerly volunteering. His awareness of the expedition came, however, by chance. He later recalled: "Curious how one's fate turns upon a hair sometimes. Had I not gone to _____'s rooms that Sunday morning, and read that paper whilst he was dressing, I should probably never have been here now, for most likely I should not have heard of the Expedition until it was just starting."[23] To ensure his inclusion, Jameson, a rich man, responded to the hint that a contribution of £1,000 to the expedition's funds would secure him a place.

Jameson knew Barttelot and his family. He had also known Herbert Ward (see below) when they were both employed by the Congo Free State. For Ward, Jameson was the "perfect antithesis" of Barttelot: "one of the finest and bravest men it has ever been my lot to meet."[24] In any case, Jameson and Barttelot soon became close friends, Barttelot later praising Jameson as being "sweet-tempered as a woman, courageous, honest, and a friend of all." [25]

The Anglo-Irish *Arthur Jeremy Mounteney Jephson* (1858–1908), aged twenty-eight, was the son of a Church of England rector. Jephson was rather at loose ends, having spent a few years as a cadet in the merchant navy and as a companion to his rich aunt, the Countess de Noailles. He was well travelled in India, but "On some members of the Committee Mr. Jephson made the impression that he was unfitted for an expedition of this kind, being in their opinion of too 'high class'. But the Countess ... made a subscription in his favour to the Relief Fund of £1,000, an argument that the Committee could not resist ..."[26]

Captain Robert Henry Nelson (1853–1892), aged thirty-four, the son of a Leeds solicitor and an old Harrovian, was on extended leave from the noted Indian Army cavalry regiment, Methuen's Horse. Nelson had served for extended periods in several corners of Africa (as had Ward, Jameson, Troup, and Bonny). Stanley damned him with the faint praise of having been "fairly distinguished in Zulu campaigns." In fact, Nelson had soldiered with distinction in Bechuanaland and with Baker's Horse in the South African War of 1879–1880.

John Rose Troup (1855–1912) aged thirty-one, the son of General Sir Colin Troup of the Indian Army, knew something of what awaited him. Along with Jameson and Ward, he had served in the Congo Free State and spoke fluent Swahili. In 1884 Stanley had reported to Brussels that Rose Troup was "a thoroughly good officer. No doubt in a short time, as opportunities offer, his services will be more fully recognized, and a position fitting his superior qualities may be found for him."[27]

Stanley had intended to take as physician Rolph Leslie, a graduate of the University of Toronto, who had been with both him and his successor, Sir Francis de Winton, in the Congo Free State. Leslie, however, declined to sign Stanley's contractual obligation not to publish anything for six months after the conclusion of the expedition without the addition of the proviso, "except in the case of my reputation being attacked." As this was unacceptable to Stanley, the application of *William Bonny* (1842–1899), aged forty-five, was accepted. Bonny had recently bought himself out of the Army Medical Department where he had been a sergeant. Only a year younger than Stanley himself, he had served in southern Africa and travelled in South America. Barttelot was later to describe him as "a mixture of conceit, bravery and ignorance ... his continual cry is that he is every bit as good as we are, and must be treated the same" (Bonny's bravery had received recognition in the award of the Distinguished Service Order).

In Alexandria, however, the Anglo-Irish *Thomas Heazle Parke* (1857–1893), aged twenty-nine, of the Army Medical Department had been urged by Barttelot, a friend from their service together three years before on the Gordon relief expedition, to leave behind him the boredom of the British garrison and to volunteer for adventure up the Congo. Having qualified as a surgeon in Dublin in 1879, Parke had entered the army two years later. He promptly obtained from the War Office the necessary unpaid leave of absence.

Herbert Ward (1863–1919), aged twenty-four, had wandered about the world from the age of fifteen. He had lived in Borneo and New Zealand. The three years preceding the Emin Relief Expedition he had spent first in the employment of the Congo Free State (when he had met Stanley and Troup). In deciding in the Congo to volunteer for the expedition, he wrote confidently, "I know Stanley and would not come to him as an entire stranger."[28] Stanley was fortunate to recruit Ward. It was to the detriment of the whole expedition that he was to be left with the Rear Column instead of being assigned to the advance column where his undoubted courage, resourcefulness, perseverance and stamina would have counted for much.

Stanley's personal servant, *William* (or, more properly, *Wilhelm) Hoffman* (1867–c.1940) was a young German living in London whom Stanley had first employed in November 1884 to accompany him to the Berlin Conference where Stanley had served briefly as a technical adviser to the United States delegation. In Stanley's writings – as in those of the officers – Hoffman remains a shadowy figure, without definition and little more than an unscrupulous buffoon of Cockney upbringing. Emin, in his diaries, does not even mention meeting his fellow German. Bonny, who had reason to recognize a thief and a liar when he saw one, being himself adept in such matters, regarded Hoffman as both.

The final European on the expedition, *William Grant Stairs* (1863–92) of Halifax, Nova Scotia, was in fact the first accepted by Stanley on the grounds that his application was "so sensible."

◆   ◆   ◆

Named after his grandfather, William Grant Stairs was born in Halifax on 28 February 1863, the sixth child and second son of John Stairs and his second wife Mary Morrow.* The Stairs were a Belfast family which had flourished as shippers and merchants, first in Grenada, then Philadelphia, and eventually Halifax. Stairs's grandfather, William, who had founded the prominent Halifax firm of William Stairs and Son and Morrow, was a member of the Legislative Assembly and the eighth mayor of Halifax. A cousin was president of the Nova Scotia Steel and Coal Company, Royal Securities, and the Eastern Trust Company. Proudly independent, the Stairs family was ardent in its opposition to Confederation, convinced that Nova Scotia could flourish alone.

---

*John Stairs was forty years old when his second son was born. He was to predecease him by four years, dying of cancer in France in 1888. The family was amongst the more prosperous in Halifax. For a portrait of a less affluent community than that of the Stairses, see Judith Fingard, *The Dark Side of Life in Halifax* (Halifax, 1989).

In 1871, Stairs's mother, having borne eleven children, died. The following year, when Stairs was nine years old, his father married his children's governess, Isabella Holbrook of Saint John, New Brunswick. At "Fairfield," the large family house on the affluent North West Arm in Halifax, Stairs had received his first training before being sent for his primary education at Fort Massey Academy, a boys' school recently begun by a local teacher.

John Stairs, however, had decided upon British schooling for his son, who sailed for Liverpool in 1875. Following three years at Merchiston Castle School in Edinburgh, where one of his contemporaries remembered Stairs as "shy and reserved in the presence of the master, but active and playful among the students," he returned to Canada to begin four years at the Royal Military College in Kingston, Ontario. Stairs's uncle, Alfred Jones, was minister of militia at the time of his application.

When in early September 1878 Stairs, then just fifteen, alighted from the Montreal train at Kingston's squat limestone station, the Royal Military College of Canada was only two years old. The original class of RMC cadets was just beginning the second half of its four-year course. The college was still small, the initial class numbering only eighteen (the revered "Old Eighteen" whose names every succeeding class was expected to memorize). Stairs was cadet no. 52.

In establishing the Royal Military College, the Liberal government of Alexander Mackenzie had two goals in mind: it sought officers for the Canadian militia, and, at least as important, it wanted an additional source of trained engineers to help encompass the vast territories of the new Dominion and to identify and exploit its resources. Given provincial claims to education, what better source than a national military college – the only federal school in Canada – to train mainly engineers for both military and civil employ? Scarlet tunics bestowed a prestige on the soldiers of the Queen Empress, but there was never any doubt in the minds of either the staff or the students that the basic vocation of the new college was to provide a level of training broadly comparable to that of the universities in Montreal or Toronto. It was, after all, a civil and not a military career that awaited most RMC graduates.

Throughout Stairs's four years at the college, it was experiencing growing pains, including the disruptions of additional construction, but it was nevertheless soon widely acknowledged a success. Seven British officers, a Canadian serving in the British army, and five Canadian civilians formed the instructional staff which, when Stairs arrived, was still finding its feet and adapting where necessary British military traditions to the Canadian environment. The curriculum was designed to produce the type of graduate that the Mackenzie government had originally envisaged. Joined with courses in fortification and military engineering, artillery, military law and administration, and surveying were geometry, physics, chemistry, and geology. A professor from Queen's University eagerly augmented his meagre salary by offering instruction in English, French, and German. The daily routine was strict but not harsh. Team sports were much encouraged as likely to enhance the leadership skills of the gentlemen cadets. Stairs was on the football team.

The War Office had agreed that, upon completion of the four-year course, a RMC cadet was to be regarded as being as well prepared for a commission in the British army as a graduate of Sandhurst. Stairs spent the statutory four years at RMC, graduating on 5 June 1882 at the age of nineteen with a first-class certificate. His competence in his small class had been recognized by his appointment as one of the cadet sergeants. Although Stairs did well, being diligent and industrious, he was nevertheless not among the top four cadets who were offered British army commissions in 1882.* On 13 May 1881, as his final term at the college was ending, Stairs wrote to a cousin in Halifax, "I have not yet exactly decided what I shall do after leaving. Probably as I can't get a commission, I will take up [civil] engineering, though it depends on what the old man says."

Stairs spent most of the three years after his graduation employed by the New Zealand Trigonometrical Survey. Presumably the family business in his native Halifax did not appeal and the challenge of the Canadian west was, in a sense, being realized as the Canadian Pacific Railway neared completion. New Zealand needed civil engineers and surveyors. In the rough country around Hawkes Bay on the east coast of the north island, Stairs and the survey team were frequently on the move, living in their small camps for only a few weeks at most. On visits to the town of Napier, race meetings provided diversion. In the bush, boar hunts and shooting birds (including black swans) for the camp pot offered some recreation, but for the most part Stairs's life was uneventful, consisting largely of laying out roads and mapping by trigonometry. In July 1883, at age twenty, Stairs wrote from Napier to his cousin in Halifax, "By Jove, strange how the profession of surveying is overdone in the colonies! Still I think I will keep on learning it and go up some time for my exam when I know enough practical work. I am going right clean through the mill now, doing a regular labourer's work in addition to book and calculus work."

Stairs never did sit his surveyor's examinations. Unexpectedly, he was offered a commission in the Royal Engineers. The sudden threat of another war between Russia and Britain, thirty years after the Crimean War, brought Stairs in 1885 the commission that had eluded him in Kingston three years earlier. When in

---

*Writing on 19 March 1881 to a cousin, also a former RMC cadet, Stairs noted how several cadets of the classes preceding his had been awarded commissions in the British army: "Straubenzee [later Colonel Arthur Hope van Straubenzee, 1861–1946] is stationed to the 101st Regiment at Halifax ... he will make a good officer and knows a darned sight more than most of those raw boned Jimmys that play polo and do something else that you know."

March 1885 a Russian army annihilated an Afghan force in Transcaspia, it seemed for a brief period that an expansionist-minded Russia might clash with a Britain determined as always to exclude any major power from the borders of its Indian empire. The Sudan was still in turmoil and British troops were spread thinly throughout the Empire, garrisoning distant outposts as well as Egypt. The War Office realized that in any war with Russia there would be a shortage of junior officers. Accordingly, on 15 April 1885, the Colonial Office informed Ottawa that a total of twenty-six commissions were to be offered to suitable RMC graduates, additional to the four commissions awarded annually. Ten were to be in the Royal Engineers.

From distant New Zealand, Stairs learned of the unexpected opportunity. After two years and nine months in the New Zealand bush, he hurriedly and successfully applied for a commission in the Royal Engineers. On 30 June 1885, aged twenty-two, he was gazetted a lieutenant. He was soon in Britain at "the Shop," the Royal Engineers' depot at Chatham, where he joined his new corps for further training. In the event, the threat of war with Russia came to nothing and peacetime soldiering in southern England soon seemed dull. After little more than a year of such a routine life and following a brief visit to Halifax, Stairs decided to volunteer for the Emin Relief Expedition.

In his diary account of the expedition, Stairs nowhere says why he sought to join it or whether he, like Jameson, had learned of it from newspaper accounts. However, in the diary of his second African journey Stairs wrote:

Here I am again in the midst of a caravan, camping amidst the grasses and trees, far from the great world and all its bustle. How good it feels! Despite all the worries, difficulties, bad food, and the certainty of fevers, I find this life, for a variety of reasons, vastly superior to that which one lives within the four walls of a barracks.

Three months ago I was at Aldershot, in the company of the best fellows in the world, enjoying their agreeable society, an exquisite special friend and the town nearby. I was not, however, happy in the true sense of the word. I felt my life was passing while I was doing nothing worthwhile. Now, I travel across the coastal plain with more than 300 men under my orders. My least word is law. I am truly the chief.

In seeking adventure overseas, Stairs was doing what several of his RMC contemporaries did, especially in India. The appeal of empire was strong; the more exotic the imperial destination the better. During the later years of Victoria's long reign, her great empire increasingly offered young Canadians both challenge and adventure in its self-appointed mission to spread Christianity, commerce and civilization. No longer did the frontiers of Canada contain their ambitions: the completion of the transcontinental railway had seen to that. Instead, young Canadians such as Stairs increasingly regarded their homeland as one part of a growing empire where they could join – as their several inclinations dictated – in the now global search for "gold, God or glory." Stairs and many of his classmates would have known instinctively what Stephen Leacock meant when he proclaimed, "I ... am an imperialist because I will not be a colonial." The whole wide empire was for Stairs and his fellows part of their natural birthright, just as much as Canada itself was. As his diaries testify, Stairs happily regarded himself as a champion of empire. By the end of his short life, however, he had become its victim.

◆   ◆   ◆

Whatever his immediate reasons for choosing Africa over India, Stairs simply addressed a terse note to Stanley at his lodgings at 160 New Bond Street. Stanley later recalled, "As I was then receiving applications by the hundred from all ranks, his letter would doubtless have escaped attention had it not been for the clear, direct, concise form of the application. It read very different [*sic*] and was so sensible compared to the others that it arrested the attention, and consequently I became anxious to secure him."[29] Lord Wolseley, the adjutant general, knew well and admired that type of young officer – he had been one himself in the Canadian northwest in 1861–70. He promptly approved the applications of both Barttelot and Stairs for extended leave.*Stanley's method of selection and enlistment was dangerously cursory. One of the few formalities that the volunteers performed was to sign an undertaking:

I _____ agree to accompany the Emin Pasha Relief Expedition, and to place myself under the command of Mr. H.M. Stanley, the leader of the Expedition, and to accept any post or position in that Expedition to which he may appoint me. I further agree to serve him loyally and devotedly, to obey all his orders and to follow him by whatsoever route he may choose, and to use my utmost endeavours to bring the Expedition to a successful issue. Should I leave the Expedition without his orders, I agree to forfeit passage money, and to become liable to refund all moneys advanced to me for passage to Zanzibar and outfit.

Mr. H.M. Stanley also agrees to give £40 for outfit, and to pay my passage to Zanzibar, and return passage to England, provided I continue during the whole period of the Expedition. I undertake not to publish anything connected with the Expedition, or to send any account to the newspapers for six months after the issue of the official publication of the Expedition by the leader or his representative.

In addition to the outfit, Mr. Stanley will supply the following: tent, bed, Winchester rifle, one revolver, ammunition for the same, canteen, a due share of the European provisions taken for the party – besides such provisions as the country can supply.

---

*Wolseley approved leave without pay for Barttelot and Stairs as requested in Stanley's letter of 5 January 1887, despite the fact that Stanley had misspelled the names of Barttelot and even of Wolseley himself.

Stanley's contractual prohibition on the volunteers publishing anything about the expedition for six months after his own account appeared may seem characteristically churlish, but it was in fact well considered, if one accepts the premise that Stanley, as leader, was entitled to a head start. Certainly most of the ten volunteers were fully capable of writing books (unlike the few Europeans on Stanley's two earlier expeditions). They kept diaries which, in several cases, formed the bases of books about the expedition.* Margery Perham, in writing about Stairs's contemporary in Africa, Frederick Lugard, has noted,

> ... the trek itself, apart from the success of its ultimate objective, was a comprehensive test of a man's powers, physical, administrative, and moral, especially where routes had to be found through unmapped and unknown country. Lugard's generation fully realized this, for they were reading eagerly, one by one, the detailed, dramatically illustrated records of the explorers and pioneers as they came out hard upon the conclusion of each exciting and competitive journey in Darkest Africa.

Stairs was no exception to the long line of travellers who intended to offer to an eager public a profitable account of their adventures. Stairs's diary of the Emin Relief Expedition gives, at first reading, the impression of a candid, lively account that he set down daily and it thereafter remained unchanged. In fact, Stairs did not write his diary in the form available to us today. Rather he jotted down in pencil his thoughts and impressions in rough notebooks (one of which survives in the Public Archives of Nova Scotia) and later drew upon his jottings to write his diary. Even if one of the rough notebooks were not extant, the internal evidence in the final journals would point to the same conclusion. In his entry for 16 February 1888, Stairs writes, "though it is now nearly three months after this date that I write this, still in my rough notes I remember putting down that I told Stanley ..." Elsewhere (for example, in the entries for 4 February and 13 December 1888) Stairs describes events which in fact occurred several days after the date given for the diary entry.

The tone of Stairs's diary is, moreover, highly uneven. Those passages of the greatest spontaneity and vigour may represent the transcriptions of a few days' vintage. Other passages, such as his rather studied recollections of life in Nova Scotia, leave the impression of a later and conscious insertion to meet a perceived need. Yet other passages, less certain in their handling, may have been reconstructed entirely from memory.

---

*Details of the books about the expedition by Stanley, Parke, Jameson, Barttelot, Troup, Ward, Jephson, and Hoffman are included in the bibliography.

Stairs's final diary is in five journals, totalling approximately 145,000 words, neatly written in ink and almost entirely free of corrections or emendations. What did Stairs intend to do with his three years of writing and rewriting? That he was editing with an eye to eventual publication can scarcely be doubted. He knew, as Stanley had so abundantly demonstrated, that there was a widespread demand on both sides of the Atlantic for accounts of the "dark continent." Thomas Parke, the army surgeon on the expedition, in pressing a ghost writer to rewrite his diaries, noted, "there is so much money to be made." Further, Stairs appears to have been ambitious for advancement in the army – or elsewhere – and the fame of a successful expedition would obviously reflect well on him.

Again, internal evidence alone would suggest that Stairs intended either to publish his diaries or to base a book upon them (as did Parke, utilizing his own journals). Occasionally in his entries Stairs employs the rhetorical salutations of "dear reader" or "gentle stranger." Additionally, he speaks at several points of being unable to say all that he might, hardly a reservation one would feel in writing an entirely private journal.

What eventually Stairs would have done with his journals can perhaps be inferred from two major articles he prepared for the widely read periodical, *The Nineteenth Century.** In his two articles, Stairs rewrites his diary accounts (which he had already, in the sense noted above, edited and re-edited) of the many months he spent at Fort Bodo and of the return trek to Zanzibar and offers them as his original diary entries. His degree of rewriting in *The Nineteenth Century* articles can be gauged from the examples included here, following his diary entry for 28 April 1888.

If any additional evidence is needed that Stairs intended sooner or later to publish his own account of the Emin Relief Expedition it is contained in a flat statement by one of his brothers. In his will, Stairs had left his diaries to his stepmother but specified that they were not to be published in Stanley's lifetime. In 1908, sixteen years after Stairs's death and four years after Stanley's, Henry Stairs, a younger brother, canvassed the family for opinions about publication, urging only that the derogatory passages about Stanley and certain unspecified "personal references" be deleted. Henry was in no doubt about his brother's desire to see the diaries published: "Will fully intended that the information contained in the diaries should be made available."[30] Nevertheless, Stairs's diaries of the Emin Relief Expedition were never published.

◆   ◆   ◆

---

*These articles, "Shut up in the African Forest" and "From the Albert Nyanza to the Indian Ocean," were published in *The Nineteenth Century*, in January and June 1891, one year after Stanley's highly successful *In Darkest Africa*.

In 1950 Stairs's diaries of the Emin Relief Expedition were deposited by a sister in the Public Archives of Nova Scotia. The fate of Stairs's diaries of his later Katanga expedition – which he commanded – was very different. They were less personal diaries than a running account prepared for *Compagnie du Katanga* in Brussels, in whose employ Stairs returned to Africa in 1892. Stairs's contract stipulated that he should keep a daily account of the Katanga expedition. As a result, his diaries lack the spontaneity of his Emin expedition diaries, being more carefully considered and more concerned with providing information useful to those intent upon exploiting the African hinterland than describing personal vexations or satisfactions.

A second major liability which reduces the vivacity of Stairs's Katanga diaries is that they are available only in French translation. Following Stairs's death from malaria on the east coast of Africa in mid-1892, a summary account of his expedition was published in *Le Mouvement Géographique* in late 1892. His Katanga diary, somewhat edited, was translated into French and published in nine instalments by Leopold's journal, *Le Congo illustré*, in 1893 (a total of approximately 58,000 words, less than half his Emin Relief Expedition diaries). For the present publication, I have translated the edited diaries back into English. The result is not entirely successful, having lost along the way the lively Victorian idiom which Stairs habitually employed. Almost no writing, however vivid, can readily withstand translation from English into French and back into English.

Chapter One

On 20 January 1887 Stairs sailed for Aden on the Navarino *of Mackinnon's British India Steam Navigation Company. The week before, Barttelot had sailed for Alexandria. Stanley, after interviews with Leopold in Brussels, would cross the Mediterranean for Cairo to discuss the expedition with Sir Evelyn Baring, the omnipotent British agent, and with the decidedly less omnipotent Egyptian Government.*

20th January [1887] Thursday
... Left London by the 12.08 p.m. train for Gravesend, saying "Good-bye" to Twining, Nanton and Duff* ... Went down with Col. J. Grant, an old African explorer. Got on the S.S. *Navarino* about 2 p.m. and said farewell to Col. Grant.**

---

*Twining, Nanton, and Duff, were, like Stairs, all graduates of the Royal Military College of Canada and all engineers. They were en route to India where they were to spend many years of notable service.

Twining, later Major-General Sir Philip Geoffrey Twining, KCMG, CB, MVO (1862–1920), was born in Halifax six months before Stairs. He was commissioned in 1886 in the Royal Engineers as a result of the threat of war with Russia that had also brought Stairs his commission. Twining served in India from 1887 to 1891 when he was sent to Mombasa with three other officers to survey with another ex-RMC cadet, Huntly Mackay (see note on p.60), a railway route to Lake Victoria Nyanza. The survey having been completed a year later, Twining returned to the Royal Military College of Canada as an instructor and later professor of engineering. He was again in India on engineering, railway, and survey work from 1899 to 1914 (aside from service in the Boxer Rebellion). He was Adjutant of the British First Army in the First World War and later Director of Fortifications and Works at the War Office.

The *Navarino* is a steel steamer of 3,400 tons, very old and uncomfortable. No smoking room and poor accommodation; belongs to the British India Steam Navigation Company.

We have about 70 passengers in the saloon, mostly all bound for India and Ceylon. On board are Jephson and Nelson of the Expedition. The usual amount of smoking and talking goes on; most of the passengers are young fellows on their way to India – 3 or 4 being in the army and some in the Civil (Indian) Service.

21st Friday

... The *Navarino* is a very poor sailer; we make on an average a little over 9 knots, our fastest to-day being slightly over 10.

Commenced reading Stanley's *How I Found Livingstone*[1] had forgotten most of it, as I read it about six years ago [presumably at the Royal Military College, Kingston]. Started a novel called *Violet Jermyn* [or *Tender and True*] by [James] Grant, finished it to-day.

Set my aneroid to "sea level" this morning, to test its qualities to-morrow and next day.

◆   ◆   ◆

Nanton, later Brigadier-General Herbert Colborne Nanton, CB, CIE (1863–1935), served in the Riel Rebellion of 1885 and thereafter on the Northwest Frontier of India for several years. He was in the South African War and was chief engineer of the Indian Expeditionary Force in France during the First World War.

Duff, later Colonel George Mowat Duff, CIE (1862–1926), the son of Colonel John Duff of Kingston, was Cadet no. 51 at RMC. Following two years with the Canadian Pacific Railway in Ontario, he was commissioned in the Royal Engineers a year after Stairs. Duff embarked for India shortly after saying farewell to Stairs in London and spent most of the next twenty years on military and civil engineering assignments in the Punjab and on the Northwest Frontier. He served in Burma with Stairs's brother-in-law, George Bourke (see note on p.60). Duff retired from the army in 1919, following service in the First World War.

**Lieutenant-Colonel James Augustus Grant (1827–1892) was a member of the Emin Relief committee and donor to its funds. When a captain in the Indian Army, Grant had won fame as the companion of his friend John Speke in their epic effort to identify the headwaters of the Nile (1861–1863). Grant wrote of his relations with Speke, "not a shade of jealousy or distrust or even ill temper ever [came] between them on their wanderings" (*A Walk Across Africa*, p. ix). Stairs does not record what he learned from Grant during the two hours which they spent together on the train to Gravesend, but later Grant was to describe the fate of Stanley's Rear Column as "a disgusting affair."

24th Monday
...Took Barttelot's dog [Satan] for a run on the steerage deck. Stanley's donkey [Ned] is a first-rate traveller and stands well up to his feed.

Saw the Spanish coast early this morning ...

◆   ◆   ◆

29th Saturday
Kept close to the Algerian coast all day. A range of mountains is visible, shown on the chart to be 5,000 to 6,000 feet at its highest point. The Mediterranean to-day was perfect, water seeming to be getting much bluer and the sun shines as on Lake Ontario in midsummer.

Passed the town of Algiers at 8.30 – seems to be a very large place, judging from the number of lights visible. Read a good deal to-day and finished the second volume of Stanley's *Congo* ...[2]

"Ned", Stanley's donkey, had a field day of it. We gave him a walk round the ship, all the youngsters having rides on him. He was in great form, but a little stiff after his confinement in the horse box.

◆   ◆   ◆

31st Monday
Passed Gozo at daybreak and sailed into Malta about 7.30 a.m. Got up, had my bath and dressed and went ashore with Jephson and Ritherdon of the Madras Staff Corps (4th Pioneers). We walked up to the Imperial Hotel and had breakfast there. We enjoyed our meal very much after the bad fare we had on board ship.

After breakfast we sallied out, got a cab and guide and started off on the warpath. We bought excellent cigarettes on the Strada Reale for 2/- per 100 and good oranges 8/- for 12 dozen. We sent some cases home to England, and a lot more on board ship. After making our purchases we went first to St. John's Church and saw everything to be seen there, next we went to King & Co. to get a glimpse at the latest English papers. In one we read with great interest an account of Stanley's departure from Charing Cross Station ...

1 February [1887]
... Passed a very quiet day reading, walking, etc. Am still reading *Through the Dark Continent* and got as far as where Stanley reached Uganda. Mtesa, the Emperor, seems to have been an open-minded sort of man, ready to take in all the information Stanley could supply, though apparently his earlier days were spent in murdering his chiefs and creating general discomfiture to everyone he met.

His successor, Mwanga, appears to be a blood-thirsty young man, but perhaps some day we shall meet His Excellency, and then find out more of his peculiarities. Went to bed early ...

♦   ♦   ♦

3rd Thursday
Very fine and enjoyable weather all day. Had some more [deck] cricket in the afternoon. Finished *Thro' the Dark Continent*, this making the third book of Stanley's I have read on this voyage.[3] At noon to-day we had 290 miles to run to Port Said, so that if all goes well we should get there [the Suez Canal] by 7.30 or 8 to-morrow evening ...

Although Stairs was no neophyte to long voyages – at twenty-three he had already made several transatlantic and trans-pacific crossings – he concentrates in his early diary entries on details of shipboard life. He offers no speculation about, and makes few direct references to, the expedition and provides no comments on the first of his new companions, Jephson and Nelson. It is only on 6 February 1887, when Stanley and Surgeon Captain Parke join the *Navarino* at Suez, after having spent a week in Cairo, that Stairs begins to write more consistently about the expedition. It is as if, for Stairs at least, the expedition took on real meaning only whenever its determined and forceful leader was present.

Upon his departure for Suez, Stanley had been accompanied to the Cairo rail station by Baring and several leading Egyptians. But Wilfrid Scawen Blunt, the English author and controversialist, who happened to be on the platform, was not impressed by the "evil-looking" explorer. "I hope to Heaven he may leave his bones half-way ... All that Europe has done by its interference of the last thirty years in Africa has been to introduce fire-arms, drink, and syphilis."[4]

6th Sunday
... in the [Suez] Canal. Shortly after breakfast we entered the Bitter Lake and steamed across it at full speed. Passed several steamers drawn up on the side of the Canal. Sighted Suez at 1.30 and at 3.30 we were abreast of the landing stage. Shortly after we anchored, a steam launch with Mr. Stanley, Dr. Junker* and Dr. Parke (who goes with us) came off. Mr. Stanley had been waiting two days at Suez. He looks very fit. Bonny, Hoffman, and Stanley's boy, Baruti, also joined us here. Took on board 61 soldiers for the expedition. They are chiefly Soudanese and most of them know something about drill. They are a

---

*The Russian Wilhelm Junker, a noted African authority who knew Emin well, took the occasion to warn Stanley that he did not believe that Emin would want to leave Africa.

very fine looking set of men, tall, well knit and deep chested; their uniform is kaki [*sic*], armed with Remingtons and sword bayonets.*

7th Monday

... started drilling the Soudanese soldiers. Some of them understand a little about drill but the major part of them know almost nothing. It is a hard and trying job teaching them, as I have to use an interpreter to make known what I want done to the Sgt [sergeant] who in turn gives the word of command in Arabic. Started the men at cleaning their rifles and gave them another drill for an hour and a quarter in the afternoon, turnings and forming fours. Gave them manual exercises in the morning. After a while I shall repeat the English word of command and use the short rifle drill of the English army. Am picking up already a few Arabic words of command.

Read in the latter part of the afternoon and sang songs on the deck after dinner ...

8th Tuesday

... Gave the Soudanese soldiers an hour and a quarter drill in the morning and one hour in the afternoon. They are very willing and do their utmost to pick up the different terms. It is my first experience with native soldiers but we seem to get on all right. All the movements have to be first explained to the instructor and then by him in Arabic to the men. At the end of the drills I give the words of command in English. The men were remarkably quick in picking up the words. They do not seem to understand the rolling motion of the ship and complain of being "giddy" in their heads. Some of the men are very well put together and will make good soldiers. We have two or three of about 6' 3" in height and a good many over 6 feet.

The men are dressed when in full "war paint" as follows. Their frocks and breeches are of kaki of a sandy colour, they have the ordinary Tommy Atkins' ammunition boots and their calves are covered with putties neatly fastened off with tape at the knees. The frocks are quite plain with the exception that the buttons are of brass with a star on them. They wear the ordinary red fez for head dress. One of the most serviceable articles of kit in their possession is the water bottle. This is made of some sort of skin on a pliable frame and will hold say two quarts; the bottle is shaped so as to fit the body and is worn on the left hip. They carry kaki haversacks of a good pattern. The whole of this kit was issued out to the men by the Khedive [of Egypt]. Our soldiers are armed with Remington rifles and appear to take a certain amount of pride in

---

*Several veterans of the Gordon relief expedition recognized Parke from their service together two years before on the Nile.

keeping them clean. They also have a sword bayonet with brass handle – this completes their equipment.

The men are all Mahometans to all intents, though evidently not very fervent ones I should say. Very few of the men smoke pipes at all but almost all are cigarette smokers. They will have to drop down to pipes though very shortly. Their pay comes to about 1/- *per diem*, with a two months advance; the head under-officers get £4 per month, the three next £3/10 each ...

With the help of our Arabic interpreter, I am gradually picking up a little Arabic and can now give a few of the commands in that language ...

◆   ◆   ◆

10th Thursday
Very hot and stifling day, thermometer at noon registered 85° in the shade. We had some good drill throughout the day, the men improving wonderfully. I feel confident that if one could drill these men for a month on shore one could make good soldiers of them. The words of command are given in Turkish but have to be explained in Arabic. I am getting on swimmingly with my Arabic and with three months' constant intercourse with these men should get hold of it pretty well ...

11th Friday
Wrote a letter to the Governor [Stairs's father, John Stairs]. Packed up ready for shipping my things into the other steamer at Aden. To bed early.

12th Saturday
Reached Aden roadstead early this morning. Got up at 6 a.m. and made the soldiers pack up and get ready.

Mr. Stanley went ashore to breakfast with the Governor, [Major] General [George Forbes] Hogg. Nelson, Jephson and I had our breakfast and then got into a steam launch and went on board the *Occidental*, our new steamer [its name was in fact the *Oriental*].* Left our things and went back to the *Navarino*, saw the soldiers safely on board the lighter, said good-bye to all and started for the *Occidental*. Got the men safely on board by lunch time.

The *Occidental* is a small coasting steamer of 1,200 tons or so, belonging to the British India Steam Navigation Company and trading between Bombay, Aden and Zanzibar; she is a slow boat and evidently not a steady one. We have

---

*Presumably, when Stairs came to transcribe or rewrite this passage from his rough notes, his memory failed him (although later still he recognized his error and crossed out *Occidental* and substituted *Oriental* on the fly page of the first volume of his diaries).

now seven of the Expedition in the saloon and have a table to ourselves.* We have also a German expedition proceeding to the German territory to the west of Zanzibar, to colonize and explore.

The soldiers are a bit seasick this evening.

Left Aden for Zanzibar about 4.30 p.m, the old *Navarino* starting for Colombo an hour before and giving us a cheer as she steamed out ...

13th Sunday
At sea, making about 8 knots. Got vaccinated to-day by Dr. Parke. Vaccinated some of the Soudanese soldiers. They were in a great funk at first and wanted the Doctor to start on me first, so I bared my arm and the doctor waded in ...

14th Monday
... I forgot to say that at Aden we took on some twelve Somali boys as servants, cooks and tent pitchers. They seem to be a very nice lot ...

15th Tuesday
Made 220 miles to-day which is not bad for such an old tub. The ship seems to swarm with red ants, cockroaches and rats, the cockroaches are regular mastodons and look very much like mice as they run along the floor [deck] of our cabin.

"Satan", Barttelot's dog, had some fun to-day. A rat was caught forward in the ship and we let it go on the deck. Satan took about 10 seconds to despatch him.

Read up some more Arabic to-day but it will take some time before I can manage to speak in an offhand sort of way. Jephson is learning Swahili, the language of the east coast or rather the one that most tribes on the east coast of Africa understand. Finished reading *The Bridal Eve* to-day. Not a bad sort of a yarn.

The doctor of the ship is an Edinburgh man and an old High School boy. He was at the High School at the same time that I was at Merchiston and knows all the old celebrities in cricket and football. He is going back to Edinburgh in a few months and is to see Mr. Rogerson and remember me to him.

---

*Stanley, Stairs, Nelson, Jephson, Parke, Jameson and Barttelot (who joined the others at Aden after an earlier passage to Alexandria) were "in the saloon". Not being officers, Bonny and Hoffman were not. Rose Troup travelled directly from Liverpool to the mouth of the Congo where Ward was already. Also aboard the *Oriental* was W.J.W. Nicol who was travelling to Zanzibar to join the steamship agent, Smith, Mackenzie and Co. Ltd., in which William Mackinnon had a substantial investment.

16th Wednesday

... We sleep every night on deck now as the heat is too great in our cabins. We have not struck up much of an acquaintance with the Germans going with us to Zanzibar. Each party preserves its own secrets apparently. Most of them, however, speak English fairly well. Our crew on this ship is composed of lascars as on the *Navarino*. They do their work slowly but well, but have to be handled with "firmness" as the Captain says. We should cross the Equator to-morrow night if the wind remains favourable as it is at present ...*

♦   ♦   ♦

22nd Tuesday

... got into the Zanzibar Channel about daylight. Sighted Zanzibar shortly after breakfast and pulled up opposite the town about 11.30 a.m. A lot of people came on board at once to see Mr. Stanley. Met Mr. McKenzie [*sic*] and Holmwood, the English Vice Consul here.** Saw the Sultan's Prime Minister. Had lunch on the *Oriental*, and went off to see our new ship, the *Madura*. Got our light baggage aboard. We then started getting the small powder magazines out of the hold and took a couple of tons or so of powder from the *Madura* to the Sultan's magazine, where we housed it for the night. Got back to our ship about 7 p.m. in a perfect lather. It has been very hot all day and one perspires frightfully. Zanzibar appears to be a very pretty place from the sea, but the illusion is dispelled on landing and moving up into the town.

---

*Whenever they could, both the *Navarino* and the *Oriental* hoisted sail to supplement their limited steam power and to conserve coal.

**Frederic Holmwood, who had been in Zanzibar since 1877, was acting British consul general pending the arrival of the successor to Sir John Kirk, the long-time consul general, companion of Livingstone and antagonist of Stanley. It was Kirk who had forced the Sultan of Zanzibar to end slavery in his territory. Holmwood, who continued in the consular service to 1920, consistently urged a British protectorate in what is today Kenya (perhaps not surprisingly since he was an investor in the British East Africa Company). E.N. Mackenzie, Mackinnon's associate in Mackinnon, Mackenzie and Co. of Calcutta, was a principal in Smith Dawes (which had contributed £1,000 to the expedition) and in Smith, Mackenzie and Co. of Zanzibar who were the East African agents of Mackinnon's British India Steam Navigation Co. and provisioners of expeditions to the interior. See Smith, Mackenzie and Co. Ltd., *The History of Smith, Mackenzie and Company Ltd.* (London, 1938).

23rd Wednesday
At work all day at the Sultan's magazine, loading up boxes of powder and caps. Loaded 4500 pounds of powder and left 1730 pnds. in the magazine. Worked from 6 a.m. to 6 p.m. steadily.

24th Thursday
Very hot. Jephson, Jameson, Nelson and I went on shore and looked over Zanzibar. Bought some books, etc., at Sousa's store. Went and saw the Sultan's palace and some other sights. It was frightfully hot, the perspiration simply poured off us.

At 12.30 the 600 Zanzibaris commenced to embark on the *Madura* and by 5 in the evening they were all aboard. The scene on the decks defied description: donkeys, goats, fowls, sheep and 700 men all strewn over the deck in every direction. The Soudanese look with disdain on the Zanzibaris but will have to knuckle down to them.

We [officers] all went on shore in the evening and dined with Mr. Holmwood, the English Vice Consul ...

25th Friday
Started to-day to organize the Zanzibaris into companies. Each European officer has 111 Zanzibaris to look after, train, drill and supervise as an English captain would do with his company. Mr. Stanley has the 12 Somalis and 43 Zanzibaris as a bodyguard. These will be armed with Winchesters. Barttelot has the Soudanese to look after. I have very good [under] officers in my company, as far as one can at present judge.

26th Saturday
Had the lower decks swept and disinfected this morning. Finished organizing the Zanzibaris into companies. Selected two little boys as my gun bearers ... We issue rations each morning at 5 o'clock, 10 men from each company coming up for them.

Tippoo Tib has 8 wives and 60 or 70 men on board. He is a sagacious sort of chap according to Stanley's stories, and worth a great deal of money. His wives sleep aft just near the saloon. He has the second class saloon for himself.

◆   ◆   ◆

4th March [1887] Friday
Running down the East African coast. Sighted the Durban light about 8 p.m. Heavy sea all day.

The head man of my company and also of all the Zanzibaris is Rashid. He gets $14 per month. Rashid was born at Muscat and is now 37 years old. He has been in Uganda several times and knew Mtesa, the late king, and has also seen Mwanga, the present one. Rashid has never been on the Congo before, but has been five times up to Unyanymihi and at Ujiji [where Stanley had first encountered Livingstone] with a Mr. Howard, an Englishman. He was with Mr. H. some three years.

◆   ◆   ◆

8th Tuesday
Came into False Bay [at the Cape of Good Hope] early in the morning. Had heavy fogs and were delayed till 6.30 when the fog lifting we were enabled to get into Simon's Bay. Anchored opposite the Admiralty Yard and started getting coal on board.

9th Wednesday
... Brooker of the Sappers [Royal Engineers] came off to see me this morning. I took him round to the men's quarters and Tippoo Tib. Dewing and Drummond of the Sappers [Royal Engineers] called yesterday but I was ashore ...

The fellows seem to like Simonstown as a station, though I should think myself one would get very tired of the monotonous life here. It is a two hours' journey to Cape Town, one hour by cart and one by train from Kaulk Bay. There is a little shooting to be got here at the back. Then there is tennis, cricket, boating and riding. These are the chief amusements.

We started off from Simonstown for Cape Town about 1.30 p.m. to continue our coaling ...

◆   ◆   ◆

10th Thursday
... After lunch, a lot of people came down to the ship to see Mr. Stanley and Tippoo Tib [including Rear Admiral Sir Walter Hunt-Grubbe, commanding the Cape of Good Hope and West Africa station, Lady Hunt-Grubbe and their two daughters]. They seemed delighted with Tippoo and his wives. Weston and Phillips of the Medical Staff came down and we had a long yarn; in the morning Perry of the Sappers and some Gunners called on us and we were asked to dinner at the R.A. [Royal Artillery] Mess tonight, but of course could not go. The English mail due this morning has not yet come in, so we have been deprived of our letters, and thus missed the last chance of hearing from England.

We got the decks clear about 5 p.m. and cast off our lines from the wharf; soon after the "audience" on the wharf gave Stanley and the Expedition three cheers, to which we responded. Half an hour later we steamed past the lighthouse and stood out for the open sea and for the Congo ...

11th Friday
At sea. By means of Hassan, our interpreter, I got the words of the "Khartoum song." It is something as follows, though most of it is lost to the Soudanese we have on board:

Gordon the Hero

His words will be heard by all the Powers
The troops are coming for his relief,
Since he governed Berber and Khartoum
Send tidings to Gordon.

Gordon sent word for guns to crush the rebels
This all in vain.
Now Gordon is dead and we must accept God's will.

Tofik [the Khedive Twefik of Egypt] our Governor why do you forget us?
Khartoum once a beauty is now destroyed,
All your chiefs are dead
And all your men are scattered,
And the owl cries loud in the midst of your ruins.

This is what the Soudanese sing; with very little tune and in a drawling manner without regard for any sort of time.

♦   ♦   ♦

14th Monday
One of the Zanzibaris ... died to-day of exhaustion after a severe attack of dysentery; we buried him over the ship's bows, using two iron bars to sink him. About 15 minutes before he died we saw a shark in the wake of the ship, the brute followed us for some miles. This makes the first death. Who can say how many are to follow him? ...

♦   ♦   ♦

18th Friday
Sighted the land at daylight and stood in for Banana [Point on the north shore of the mouth of the Congo River]. Took on our pilot about 8.30 a.m. and went in ...

Mr. Stanley went ashore directly after breakfast and found out that the Congo Free State people did not expect us till the 24th and consequently had not made any arrangements about getting steamers ready to take us up the river. Cable communication with Europe is cut, the cable being broken somewhere off the Congo mouth. Soon afterwards some of the English Trading Company came off and we had a long talk and found that the state of affairs on the upper Congo is pretty bad. The steamers appear to be in a sorry plight. The *Stanley* is said to be worn out, another is ashore and another somewhere away up the river and perhaps cannot be got down to Leopoldville for us in time. Mr. Dennet of the British Congo Trading Co. and Mr. Cobden Phillips came to see us and offered us the use of their steamer, the *Albuquerque*. We have also been promised the *Serpa Pinto*, a Portuguese steamer lying in port.* We also expect to get the *Heron* of the C.F.S. [Congo Free State] and hope to make a start to-morrow. Of all the men who came on board to-day I did not find one who had been higher up the River than Vivi – and most of them seemed very ignorant of the country above Stanley Pool.

The river opposite Banana is of a very dirty colour and runs about two miles per hour I should say. There are factories [trading posts] at Banana, Dutch, Portuguese, French and English. The only trees in the station are some palms (coconut) planted some few years back and getting on very well. The Portuguese Consul came on board this afternoon and offered us the use of one of his government's gunboats at present lying in the stream. The mail service between here and Europe is good, as many as four steamers going per month at times, though generally one steamer leaves per fortnight.**

Another Zanzibari died to-day, making the third. We buried him on shore in the Banana cemetery.

---

*Named after Major Alexandre-Albert de la Roche de Serpa Pinto of the Portuguese army, a noted traveller in southern Africa whom Stanley had first met in Angola in August 1877. Like Stanley, Serpa Pinto offered a two-volume account of his African explorations, translated into English as *How I Crossed Africa* (London, 1881).

**On 9 March 1887, in a letter mailed from Cape Town, Stanley described for an unidentified friend in Britain the experiences of the expedition to date and commented briefly on his officers. If the text of the letter given in *In Darkest Africa* is reliable, Stanley wrote of Stairs, "... a splendid fellow, painstaking, ready, thoughtful and industrious, and is an invaluable addition to our staff" (vol. I, p. 74). Almost three years later, on 30 January 1890, Stanley recorded that he had written to William Mackinnon from Banana Point about the progress of the expedition and had included an enthusiastic passage about Stairs.

Chapter Two

At two o'clock in the afternoon of 19 March 1887, Stairs noted, the expedition "got underway, saying goodbye to all ... and started Up the Congo".

The initial stage of the expedition's long journey inland was the two hundred kilometres of navigable river from Banana Point to Mataddi. Although the expedition had disembarked from the Madura at Banana Point a few days before it was expected, the Congo Free State officials, at Stanley's urgings, were nevertheless able to put together a small flotilla of river steamers to carry the expedition up the river to Mataddi.

There, however, the cataracts of the lower Congo – there are thirty-two between Mataddi and Stanley Pool – required the expedition to leave its river steamers and begin the second stage of its journey, making its way along the banks of the Congo to Stanley Pool where another flotilla would, it was hoped, be available to carry it up river on the third stage of its transcontinental route.

Stanley knew the terrain intimately – he had spent more than two years from 1879 to 1881 laboriously building a track around the cataracts for Leopold, but the real obstacle was the dearth of carriers. If the expedition was to cover the four hundred kilometres from Mataddi to Stanley Pool, local porters would be required in great numbers, a need compounded by the refusal of the Sudanese soldiers to carry anything but their own equipment. They had been recruited as soldiers to help rescue Emin, if that proved necessary – and they would not lower themselves to being porters (they were also less likely to desert or join the porters in causing trouble). To recruit porters – who were increasingly reluctant to accept the brutal life of expeditions – Stanley had sent the experienced Rose Troup direct from Liverpool to the mouth of the Congo. Following the expedition's arrival, Rose Troup was joined in his difficult recruiting task by Herbert Ward (who brought the total number

of Europeans on the expedition to eleven). Ward was eager to join and Stanley
needed little persuading when Ward arrived with three hundred badly needed men.

Depending upon the terrain, an African porter could carry on his head up to
one hundred kilograms and walk as much as thirty kilometres in a day. Much of
what was carried was necessarily food. Few tribes grew surpluses. In any event,
long stretches of a typical trek were uninhabited. Where food could be bought, the
bulky currency of the bush – heavy brass rods or copper wire, beads or cloth – had
to be carried, along with the ammunition, tents, bedding, medicines, and other
paraphernalia of the white man. The costs and other difficulties of carrying such
impediments across a continent were a spur both to enslavement and to the seizure
of food en route.

The brutality inherent in such a system is obvious. And it was compounded by the
arduous and hazardous nature of the enterprise itself. Discipline was essential, but
imprisonment being out of the question, flogging was the principal means of en-
forcing it. Floggings were frequent and even the bullet was used to warn other
wayward porters. Margery Perham, in her perceptive description of Frederick
Lugard's contemporary expeditions, has well described the impact of all this on the
white man:

The imagination can suggest how easy it was for white men, away from all the restraints
of their own society, ignorant of local language and custom, pushing a mass of
uncomprehending black men through strange country, to lower their standards to their
surroundings. There were many such numerous moments when it seemed so much more
speedy and effective to kick than to argue, to flog than to reprimand, to push on faster
than the more weak of the loaded men could stand, to abandon the sickly when hands
could hardly be spared to carry them as well as their fallen loads. Easy, too, to be slack,
not to look carefully after the health and food of the men; not to allocate loads fairly or to
settle quarrels patiently.

If this were true of relations within that little moving society of the caravan, how many
more temptations there were to harshness and violence outside it. Why wait, when bullets
were so convenient and effective, to see whether the warriors peering through the bushes
were friendly? Why endure palaver over hongo, the levy some tribes would ask of passing
strangers? Why barter at length with unintelligible savages whose grain or cattle were
needed and needed quickly? Add to this the strain of tropical life, with its fever, danger,
and loneliness, and the bursts of almost ungovernable rage that could master even the
best of men when faced with what seemed the inexplicable stupidity or malice of Africans.[1]

The first weeks were a nightmare for the expedition. As it began its ascent of the
Congo, the rain seldom ceased. The riverside track was transformed into seemingly
endless, slippery mud. Despite Stanley's repeated floggings, the pace remained slow.
Even with Ward's recruits, there were barely enough porters for minimal needs.

The expedition took from 24 March to 21 April to make its way overland from
Mataddi to Stanley Pool. It was never far from the Congo, but was barred from

using it by the frequent cataracts. However, the portable steel boat brought from Britain, the Advance, *soon proved its value as the means by which the expedition could get its supplies across tributaries of the Congo, swollen by the rainy season. The* Advance *became the responsibility of Jephson who was especially adept with boats (having spent part of his youth, in the immortal words of* The Wind in the Willows, *"messing about in boats").*

At several points along the four hundred kilometres from Mataddi to Stanley Pool and again farther up the Congo the difficulties were from time to time made easier by encounters with Europeans, whether officers of the Congo Free State, traders, or missionaries. They were of various nationalities, but all shared with the officers of the expedition their shelter, local produce, and imported provisions – occasionally even a bottle of wine or a cigar. Nevertheless, Stairs generally regarded the employees of the Congo Free State with something of the same misgivings and even distaste which his fellow army officer, Frederick Lugard – eventually to become the greatest African proconsul – was simultaneously experiencing as he made his initial foray into Africa through the Portuguese territories. In the view of both Stairs and Lugard, Africa was not well served by the type of Europeans it was attracting in the wake of the great Livingstone. *

◆   ◆   ◆

19th March [1887] Saturday
Started early this morning to load up the first of our flotilla, a Belgian steamer called the *K.A. Neiman* of about 380 tons. We put 200 men on board under Nelson and Jameson and about half past 8 she cast off from the *Madura* and started on her way up the river. The next steamer that came alongside was the *Albuquerque*, rather smaller than the former one. On her, after a lot of hard work, we put about 50 tons of cargo consisting of arms, rice, beads, etc., and lastly the doctor and 120 Zanzibaris. We started her off amidst yells from the Zanzibaris on the *Madura*. Shortly after this steamer left us, the *Serpa Pinto*, a Portuguese steamer, a paddle boat, came alongside; into her we put about 75 tons of cargo, I should say, 94 Zanzibaris of my company, 31 of Parke's, 40 of Jephson's, the Somali boys and 18 or 30 donkey boys; my two

---

*Joseph Conrad's description in *Heart of Darkness* of the Europeans whom he met on the Congo parallels that of Stairs and Lugard: " ... these chaps were not of much account, really. They were no colonialists; their administration was really a squeeze ... They were conquerors, and for that you want only brute force ... They grabbed what they could get for the sake of what was to be got. It was just robbery with violence, aggravated murder on a grand scale, and men going at it blind ..."

servants ... At two o'clock we got under way after saying goodbye to all, and shortly after this turned in the stream and started "Up the Congo." The *Serpa Pinto* is a small paddle steamer of the P.C. [Portuguese Congo] trading company. She is officered by Portuguese and has a nigger crew. We make about 5 or 6 knots against a 4 knot current.

We are packed like herrings. I sleep among Tippoo Tib's people. They are devils to talk; all night long they kept up their brainless chatter. After a while, early in the morning I called them a lot of hyaenas. This shut them up pretty sharp as they apparently don't hanker after that noisy animal ...

◆   ◆   ◆

21st Monday

Nelson and Parke reached Mataddi this morning. Jameson and Barttelot and Jephson came along in the afternoon. We arranged the men as well as we could in camp and then started them on fatigue work, carrying up loads, etc. The Portuguese station here is very badly chosen, being on top of a steep hill and difficult to get up to from the River. The chief trade is in ivory and india-rubber, hardware, merchandise, clothes and gin being given in return. Trade through here, as at Boma and Banana, appears stagnated. The various trading houses, Dutch, French, English and Portuguese, all along the River unite in crying down the Free State. There appears to be a lot to be said against the State, though probably most of what we heard was just business squabbling.

22nd Tuesday

... The River here is about 650 yards wide and runs say about four miles per hour and is very deep. There are any quantity of crocodiles, though none of our men were taken off.

Two more Zanzibaris died to-day and were buried near the camp. They suffer a great deal from bad feet and [skin] ulcers.

◆   ◆   ◆

24th Thursday

Left Mataddi early this morning to march over to the Mposa River [a small tributary of the Congo about thirty metres wide]. One of my men died shortly before starting. We had a little trouble crossing the river. We put together for the first time our galvanized steel boat and in three hours or so passed the whole of our force over the river, swimming the donkeys beside canoes.

◆   ◆   ◆

26th Saturday

Left the Umposa River camp at 6:30 a.m. and commenced our second day's march to Parabella. Sickness among the Zanzibaris is on the increase, ulcers and bad feet are very common. Poor chaps, they have to struggle pretty hard to get along with their loads under a broiling sun. I reached Parabella mission station* at about 9:30 and started getting up the tent and making the men comfortable.

To-day's march was very trying on the men; some of them did not get into camp till 5 in the afternoon, quite played out. We sent 20 men from each company back to the Umposa River to bring on loads to-morrow. The mission people here are very hospitable and kind to us. They appear to be very comfortable, having a couple of very good plantations to draw from. Barttelot is back to-night at Umposa with some of his Soudanese and 150 or so of Zanzibaris.

I am writing this in our tent under many difficulties, though we are still very comfortable. Nelson, Barttelot, Parke and myself sleep in the large tent. Jephson and Jameson have each one of their own. Mr. Stanley's is a most elaborate one [Stairs says that fifty-five men were required to carry it] ...

27th Sunday

One of my men died to-day on the road – a straggler brought up by Barttelot. He was buried on the roadside.

◆   ◆   ◆

30th Wednesday

... I left the river at 4 o'clock and by dark we had got to some thick bush on a very steep hillside. This gave us a great deal of trouble, the men slipped and fell continually, their loads coming down "flop" and shooting down the hillside. It was 9 o'clock before Parke and I reached camp, viz. Stanley's tent. We bunked it as best we could, our blankets being behind in the bush. One of the men dropped my iron box in the river this morning, containing all my books, matches and small things. This book was among some of the things that got ducked.

31st Thursday

... Mr. Stanley had an attack of dysentery and had to be carried into camp. About 1½ hours after passing the Lufu [a small tributary of the Congo], we

---

*A Livingstone Inland Mission station staffed by a Mr and Mrs Clarke and a Mr and Mrs Ingham.

came to a halt beside a stream, the men are very tired and hungry so we stop here till to-morrow.

1 April [1887] Friday

Up early and away on the march ... Barttelot and I brought up the rear and had a frightful time. The march to the mission station is only supposed to be 3½ hours, but we were 8½ hours at the rear of the caravan, bringing up the stragglers. We reached the mission about 2 p.m. and had a good meal.* Mr. and Mrs. Richards were very kind to us. There was also an American doctor there named Small, a very decent sort of chap. We had tremendous rain showers at night with thunder and lightning.

My Governor's birthday.

◆   ◆   ◆

3rd Sunday

Up and away early on the march, crossed two decent sized rivers with very clear water in them. To-day we passed a caravan with 25 tusks of ivory. We are continually passing these caravans for the coast loaded with ivory and india rubber. We passed another caravan under the charge of a Mr. Davey of the Gen. Sanford expedition on the upper waters of the Congo.** Reached camp at 2 p.m. after a hard and trying march.

---

*Another station of the Livingstone Inland Mission.

**During the weeks immediately ahead, Stairs was to encounter several employees of the Sanford Exploring Expedition. Henry Shelton Sanford (1823–1891) was a United States diplomat – and dabbler in Florida real estate – who served in various European legations between 1847 and 1878 (the title of "General", which he much favoured, was no more than an honorary designation in return for his gift of a battery of guns to the First Minnesota Regiment in the US Civil War). As US Minister at the Court of King Leopold II and an ardent advocate of the Congo Free State, Sanford played the key role in obtaining its early recognition by the United States (in April 1884) by urging the allegedly philanthropic and humanitarian purposes of Leopold. In return, he received major – and unique – trading and land concessions on the upper Congo (which breached the king's own monopoly). However, the Sanford Exploring Expedition never realized its vaulting ambition to control the upper Congo ivory trade; within two and one-half years of its establishment in June 1886 it was near bankruptcy and was merged with a Belgian company in December 1888. Sanford had first met Stanley in 1878 as an emissary of Leopold to recruit the explorer for service in the Congo. Sanford and Stanley had been at the Berlin Conference of 1884, the latter attached briefly to the United States' delegation. For additional details, see "The Sanford Exploring Expedition", *The Journal of African History*, vol. VIII, 1967, no. 2, pp. 291-302.

4th Monday
... The camp we have just left is the site of an old native village, now quite
deserted owing to the action of the Congo Free State in punishing the niggers
for hindering caravans ...

Our camp to-day is in a small grove of trees on top of the hill above the
river crossing. We hear plenty of guinea fowls near at hand but no one has
enough time to go and shoot a few. A great many of the Zanzibaris are
suffering from the effects of drinking huge quantities of bad water. We
Europeans drink nothing but boiled water or tea. The weather to-day was fine
enough, but there is somehow a feverish feeling of depression after a few
hours marching that is very trying. To stand still in camp near this river for
any length of time would certainly cause very bad fevers and probably dysentery
among the men ...

5th Tuesday
Up early and down to the Kwilu [a tributary of the Congo] to get over the
remainder of the men and donkeys. Started at 6.15 and by half past 12 we had
passed every man, woman and donkey over, except a few sick men following
on a day's march in rear. We passed over our donkeys very quickly, two at a
time by the upstream side of the canoe, and held by the heads and tails by
donkey boys. My donkey, Ned, took the water very well.* He is very small
but active and good at getting over creeks and swampy places. We took all
Tippoo Tib's men and women over safely, though they gave us far more trouble
than our own men. Last of all Barttelot, Bonny and myself came over, and the
800 men had been passed without a single article of any sort being lost. Some
of the men who had been over with Jephson on the Congo caught us up to-day.
The boat [the *Advance*] had not started up river when they left Jephson.

Our men [Zanzibari] are taking a long time to pick up in [physical] condition.
As yet they are not a patch on the Congo blacks at carrying loads. These
fellows can pass our men hand over hand with as heavy if not heavier loads. It
is three days' march from here to ... where the rice of our men is, and owing
to delays the men have already devoured their rations. Somehow or other
they peg out all right, getting guavas, manioc, and papaws along the roadside
and at times too, they buy Indian corn from the natives and roast it in their
fires or eat it raw. After passing all the men over the river, the rain came on
and we stayed in camp, thankful for the rest afforded us ...

---

*From having been Stanley's donkey on the *Navarino*, Ned evidently became at some
point Stairs's donkey.

6th Wednesday

... On the march one of my under chiefs ... strayed from the track searching for food and was shot by some of the natives. One of Tippoo Tib's men was also badly shot in the hand but killed his man with a bullet through the stomach...

♦   ♦   ♦

9th Saturday

... Barttelot started off with about 130 men for Stanley Pool to be one day ahead of us all the way up. He took the Soudanese and all the "goe-goes" or lazy porters with him.

I forgot to say that my stupid boy Abedi led my donkey over a bad place yesterday and broke one of its hind legs. I had to shoot it to put it out of misery and so now am without a mount and will probably have to foot it across Africa.

There are two officers of the C.F.S. at this place, both Belgians and very decent fellows.

♦   ♦   ♦

11th Monday

Our camp last night was chosen in a very bad place as we found to our cost. About 7 o'clock the rain commenced to come down in torrents, flooding everything. Our tent was simply flooded. We stuck to it for a long time but it was too much. I had about 4 inches of water round my bed.

A Belgian officer who was sleeping with us in our tent got all his things soaked. We had a long talk about affairs in general. He is an officer of the Congo Free State and has been out on the Congo for 2½ years; he is not of [the] opinion that the Free State is a success, as in fact not many of the officers are. He intends going on a three months' exploration trip of the frontiers of the Free State and the Portuguese territory; he expects good shooting. There are elephants, buffalo and antelope all along here but they keep well away from the track and we never see anything of them ...

12th Tuesday

Away from camp early, Parke bringing up the rear. After two hours' marching we caught up and passed Barttelot and his men who had left one day ahead of us. His Soudanese are giving a great deal of trouble and are a most insubordinate lot. In addition to this, a great many of them are suffering severely from dysentery brought on by drinking bad water.

Reached camp about 2 o'clock and made ourselves comfortable. Barttelot came in soon afterwards and put up here for the night. Jephson reached here to-day with his men and the boat and goes on with us to-morrow.

I expect we shall have a great deal of trouble with the Soudanese before we have finished. Their officers are not a bit good and they are in the midst of work without having any previous disciplining. On the whole it was a mistake bringing them on an expedition of this sort. On the march they are more trouble to us than 200 Zanzibaris; they are great grumblers about their food, and altogether they are about as unruly a lot of men as could be picked up anywhere...

13th Wednesday
One of our Somali boys died yesterday of exhaustion after bad attacks of fever. This is the first death among the Somalis. It is a great pity as they are first-rate chaps at work, especially where boats are concerned.

Mr. Stanley, we hear, intends taking a chap called [Herbert] Ward with us across the continent. He is said to be a very good chap at his work, namely nigger-driving. Certainly nothing that I have ever seen so completely demoralizes a man as driving negro carriers. One's temper is up all the time, kind feelings are knocked on the head and I should think in time a man would become a perfect brute if he did nothing else but this.

14th Thursday
... Saw in the distance the falls of the Edwin Arnold River* and the Pocock basin of the Congo, the place where Frank Pocock was drowned when coming down the Congo with Stanley** ... Reached camp about noon having quite enough of it, the sun being very trying. A great many of the Somali boys are down with fever. They have no pluck at all, getting frightened at the slightest illness.

---

*Stanley had, during his first expedition to the Congo (in 1874–1877), named the tributary after Sir Edwin Arnold (1832–1904) the deputy editor of the *Daily Telegraph* which had helped to finance the expedition. Arnold, a voluminous poet and translator of Asian literature (Jameson carried a copy of Arnold's *Light of Asia* with him), was one of the few Fellows of the Royal Geographical Society upon whom Stanley could rely for friendly support. In later years it was through Arnold that Stanley met Dorothy Tennant whom he married in 1890.

**Edward and Frank Pocock were the young sons of a Kent fisherman, who went with Stanley on his first crossing of Africa (east-to-west) in 1874–1877. Both died en route, Edward of disease early in the expedition and Frank in June 1877 by drowning when the expedition was only a few weeks from its destination, the mouth of the Congo.

On reaching camp some natives brought in presents of bananas and fowls to Mr. Stanley. He also found a small wooden idol in one of the villages we passed, a most curious looking object ...

15th Friday
... Crossed two small and one fairly large rivers, the latter by means of a log bridge. Saw the Congo glittering in the distance, running between two walls of solid rock. Came upon some natives holding market on the side of the track, most of them ran away as the Zanzibaris came up. They are very much afraid of our men and well so, for a greater crowd of stealing ruffians it would be hard to find. The natives had bananas, fish, beans, roots and various things for sale for which they took brass wire and handkerchiefs as payment.

Close to the market impaled on a high pole we saw the dried up remains of a native who had killed one of his tribe in the market place and so suffered for it by being impaled as we found him ...

We reached camp in the rear guard about ½ past twelve; the day being very hot we felt the march pretty much. Our camp is in a small village of about 12 huts ... Mr. Stanley has one for himself and four of us, Parke, Nelson, Jameson and myself have another. On the outside of our hut the natives have all sorts of charms stuck up to keep away sickness and bad luck; there are fowls' heads, chilies [sic], feathers, rags and all sorts of odds and ends, so we should be well protected. Unfortunately, however, these charms do not serve to keep away earwigs and ants of which there are any quantity.

Jephson is ahead getting the boat ready for crossing the Inkisga River [a tributary of the Congo] to-morrow. Barttelot is camped with his men about 600 yards in rear of us. The Soudanese "bucked up" a bit to-day, but they still are very bad.

Old Stanley is getting a bit worked up now. He is a most excitable man, with a violent temper when roused, but soon subsides. He says and does a great many foolish things when he is in this state for which afterwards he must be sorry. He is not a man who has had any fine feelings cultivated in his youth. I should say, outwardly and to strangers he is most polite and charming, but under this there runs a much different kind of strain. I only hope we shall all pull well together to make a success of the expedition, but he holds such a tremendous leverage over us, that for a single slip any of us might be put down as incompetent and dismissed at once.

16th Saturday
... We hear that the steamers at Stanley Pool are all ready to take all of us up stream but 70. This is very good news as we had been thinking the difficulty of getting steamers would be very great. I believe there are only four steamers all told on the River above Stanley Pool, viz. *Le Stanley* (sternwheeler), the *En Avant*, the *A.I.A. [Association Internationale Africaine]* and one steamer

[the *Florida*] belonging to the General Sanford Expedition, which is now far away up some tributary of the Congo and cannot be got at.*

I met a very nice chap to-day on the road, in charge of some of the Sanford Expedition porters, carrying up river machinery and parts of the hull of a steamer [to be used] for trading purposes on the upper waters of the Congo and its branches; he asked me to breakfast and gave me two eggs as a present which was a most acceptable gift under such circumstances as we are placed in. All these fellows and the officers of the Congo Free State travel from place to place like lords. They have the very best of tinned goods of all sorts: jams, bacon, oatmeal, tea, coffee, condensed milk, tinned fish, besides fruits and whatever else the country yields. They generally have three or four native boys as servants, carry swell tents and beds and generally do themselves up well. In fact, I know one or two officers of the C.F.S. who get carried about by porters wherever they go. These Belgian officers are very hospitable to us as we pass by the different stations, but they appear to us to be the wrong sort of men to have as agents of a young state such as this is. They seem to lack energy and push; to be too fond of staying indoors at the stations and are as a rule very ignorant of the country above [Stanley] Pool.

The Sanford Expedition is a trading company, organized by an American (General Sanford) for the purpose of procuring ivory and india-rubber from the natives on the upper waters of the Congo and sending it down country to Banana [Point] and thence to the Liverpool markets. They already have, I believe, one steamer on the river above the Pool, and one more is now on its way up country as I said before. I believe the manager is an American Naval lieutenant called Taunt.**

What sort of a chap he is I do not know, but a great mistake was made in sending out the steamer in such heavy portions, making it tremendously difficult to get on at all in bad places. Why, the fellow I have just been talking about (whom I met to-day) has been 2½ months coming up from Mataddi, a journey that has taken us but 20 days or so, and done by the natives here in 14 days.

---

*The steamers *En Avant* and the *A.I.A.* had been on the Congo since 1881 and 1883 respectively, during Stanley's tenure as administrator. Both were little more than 40 feet long, shorter than many of the canoes on the river.

**Emory H. Taunt, on leave from the US Navy, endured eighteen months in the Congo Free State as Sanford's principal agent but was discharged in May 1887 for drunkenness. Taunt's sole purpose in accepting Sanford's offer of employment (with payment in shares in the company) was to make as much money as possible in the shortest time in the ivory trade. Despite the fact that he was known to have an African woman living with him and was later court martialled by the U.S. Navy for his unauthorized absence and drunkenness, he was back in the Congo in 1888 as the "Commercial Agent" of the United States.

Jameson gets some very pretty butterflies and beetles now. He must have some hundreds of beauties in his boxes by this time.

We should be at Stanley Pool in five days from this, and are already six days behind time. On the whole though, we have not done badly. It must be remembered that our men on starting were very soft; that their loads were heavy, 65 lbs., with blankets, rifle and 15 days rations besides; that the rivers have all been swollen, giving us much trouble, and that the men have suffered greatly from dysentery and could not be pushed ...

17th Sunday
... Left ... camp at six o'clock and started off on a five hours' march. My men going along well, we reached camp in 5 hours and 10 minutes. The road was very good, the only obstacles being two small rivers and a bad hill. We passed through two small villages, one of which our men looted, taking all the manioc roots and driving off the poor, frightened natives like so many sheep. I sailed in at last with a big stick and drove them off, but not before they had filled their blankets with *chakula* [food].

Tippoo Tib's people travel and camp with us every day. We have great fun with the women on the march. They are a jolly, laughing crew. One passes them every day, as they travel very slowly. We often lift up their loads for them and give them biscuit and in return they offer us manioc roots, beastly things they are too. Tippoo himself is a very good chap and so are most of his followers. There is one fellow though called Salim, who speaks English, a proper brute. We all dislike him, he is such a sneak. There will be trouble with him some day unless he is nipped a bit by Stanley.

On the march I always keep my head man Rashid and my two boys close at hand to help lift up the men's loads on to their heads, this I find to be the best way. The other chiefs I send ahead with the men to encourage them on. Rashid is a splendid fellow, far away and above the best of the men. He is so quiet and yet when he likes he can use the stick very well. All the men like him and would do anything for him. I am very fortunate in getting such a good man for head chief. My boys are both fairly good little chaps, but they take a lot of teaching and get a fair amount of *fimto* (stick) every day ...

Our grub on this expedition is very bad, in fact much worse than bushmen or surveyors in New Zealand or Canada get. Our sugar, of which there is very little, is of the worst description; we get no coffee, none but rock salt, no pepper, and then we have wretched cooks who do not understand how to make the most of things. It is a great pity this state of affairs, as we are only a few days on the road and the chances are that the grub we are now getting will be the best we shall ever get till we reach civilization again. I hardly think Mr. Mackinnon, or any of the promoters of the expedition, intended that we should fare thus.

Our donkeys are getting weaker instead of stronger every day; the pack animals only carry, I think, 100 lbs. all told, and get poorer and poorer every day. One feels that a donkey will be invaluable, especially on the march from the Congo to the Nile.

18th Monday
Up at 5 o'clock. Had a cup of tea and some biscuits as usual and away on the march by 6 o'clock. Jephson and the boat came along with us to-day; the heavy boat loads impede us a great deal at bad places. It would be rather better if they would march a few hours in rear of us, I fancy.

Stanley told me this morning some news which may turn out to be very bad. He had letters saying that the *Stanley* was the only steamer available for taking us up the river and that the English mission had declined to lend their steamer to us. Now the *Stanley* can only take 200 men and loads, and towing two lighters she might take say 100 more, or a total of 300 men. He also showed me a letter from the American Baptist mission saying that pending instructions [from Boston] to the contrary, they would lend us their steamer the *Peace*, taking 60 men and loads. It is by no means certain though that we will be able to get this steamer, as this mail may bring contrary instructions from America. To tell the truth, the missionaries are frightened to lend their steamer to an armed body of men ready to fight any opposing natives up the river, as the natives seeing the *Peace* might fancy it was the missionaries and so the "gospel" would suffer.

We had a 3 hours and 40 minutes march to-day, crossing one fair sized river and camping within ¼ of a mile from the Congo. Two more of my men were shot to-day while marauding in a village close to camp, one through the shoulder and one through the calf of his leg. In both cases, the natives' guns were loaded with small round stones, not bullets. I am sorry for them but it will be a lesson to them and to the others. Several natives came up to the camp complaining to Mr. Stanley of the ravages of our men. Shortly afterwards the stick was being used pretty freely.*

◆   ◆   ◆

20th Wednesday
Away from camp early, the morning being a good one for marching. Passed two native villages on the way and about 11:30 drew up in a third and camped

---

*On the same day Jephson recorded in his diary that he and Stairs spent much of the afternoon by the river. The "rushing water always has the effect of raising my spirits." The more practical-minded Stairs who left Jephson "to sit alone and dream ... was poking about for specimens of gold bearing quartz" (*Diary*, p. 90).

for the day ... An old chief called Makokoro came to interview Stanley. He has a beard six feet long ... is 75 years old and was in power when Stanley came down the River on his first trip ... There are about 15 huts and the usual plantations of bananas and manioc roots. This is one of the few villages that the natives have not cleared out from. Almost all the others we found devoid of natives. They had been scared by the advance of our men ...

◆   ◆   ◆

On 21 April 1887, the expedition reached Stanley Pool. However, despite Stanley's success in laying his hands on every river boat readily available – and even those that were not – he still did not have enough space for all his men and stores. Double journeys would be necessary to carry his expedition to the confluence of the Congo and the Aruwimi rivers.

21st Thursday

... Reached [Stanley] Pool at 12:30 and at once started making a large clearing in the grass for our camp. We were all the rest of the day at this and by night had not finished. Several of the Congo Free State people, some missionaries, and some native chiefs came to see Stanley in the afternoon. He got presents of chickens and goats, most acceptable to the mess these hard times. We fly the Turkish flag over our camp, the reason being, I suppose, that the Egyptian government gave £10,000 towards the expedition.

This is a very pretty place; from the camp we can see a large stretch of water with one or two bush covered islands. To the right there is a large grassy plain said to be a feeding ground for antelopes and buffaloes. Sometimes antelopes are shot within a mile of the station. There are plenty of hippopotami quite close to us and we should get some ribs to-morrow, the meat being very good.

22nd Friday

Up at 6 and off to my camp to start the men at different jobs. Fell them in first and took an inventory of rifles, hoes, axes, shovels and bill-hooks, found all my rifles correct but several of my axes and bill-hooks are missing. Made my men build their huts in rows with parade grounds between and a street in front. Made all the necessary arrangements for a standing camp, built a cookhouse for ourselves and stacked my loads.

About midday I mounted the Maxim gun, I surmise, for the edification of the native chiefs who came to visit Stanley. So far it has carried first rate, but on opening it I found a good deal of rust had collected. It takes five men to carry all the different parts.

More chiefs, officials and missionaries came to camp to interview Stanley. We are to have the steamer *Peace* after all, I believe, so we shall not have to leave as many men behind as we thought. Jameson went away this afternoon with twelve men and two large rifles to try for hippo meat some two miles from camp. We all hope that he will be successful.

The doctor [Parke] has been very seedy for the last three or four days. He has an attack of dysentery and is very much weakened from it.

Towards evening [Roger] Casement* with his loads for the Sanford expedition turned up and pitched his tent close to the Free State station. He is off again to-morrow for Kinshassa, a two hours' march from here. His men seemed in high spirits at getting here, the Kaffirs singing very well as they marched along.

We had a very bad thunderstorm in the evening, with terrific squalls of wind and rain.

23rd Saturday

In camp and hot as the very mischief. Several lengthy interviews between the head of the [Congo] Free State station and Stanley and some chiefs took place in the morning. Food is absolutely unobtainable here for the men; our rice is finished; we can get no manioc for the men, there is no meat, what are we to do? Can we leave 200 or 300 men here to starve and pillage? The missionaries have again and again refused their steamer. Something must be done and we must get out of this as soon as possible to Bolobo where there is food. To-day the C.F.S. seized for us the steamer *Peace*, or rather requisitioned it, so as to avoid danger to the State [i.e., to be rid of men who

---

*Jephson first encountered Roger Casement (1864–1916) on 14 April, but Stairs does not seem to have met him until four days later. The twenty-three-year-old Anglo-Irish Casement – whom the expedition was to encounter again – was later to earn wide fame and, at least in the eyes of the British government, eventual notoriety. As British consul general in the Congo (after service in the South African War), he played a leading role in exposing the incredible brutality and greed of King Leopold's Congo Free State. In 1916, the then Sir Roger Casement accepted German arms and assistance in hazarding the Dublin uprising. He was tried and executed for treason.

Joseph Conrad, who met Casement at Mataddi in June 1890, joined the officers of the expedition in their liking and admiration for him. "He is a limpid personality ..., I've seen him start off into an unspeakable wilderness, swinging a crook-handle stick for all weapons, with two bulldogs ... at his heels. A few months afterward it so happened that I saw him come out again ... quietly serene as though he had been for a stroll in a park" (G. Jean-Aubry, *Joseph Conrad in the Congo* [London, 1926], p.52, quoting a letter of 12 December 1903 from Conrad to Cunninghame Graham; see also "The Congo Diary," *Tales of Hearsay and Last Essays* [London, 1955]).

could not be readily fed] and we have got her now for our use up the river. Again and again they were asked to lend her to us but gave "no" for answer each time. Not a straightforward "no" but a nasty beat-about-the-bush sort of refusal.

We have thus secured three steamers, the *Stanley* (220 men), the *Peace* (160 men and loads) and the *Henry Reed*. We also have got from Mr. Swinburne the hull of the steamer *Florida* of the Sanford Expedition, our own steel boat [the *Advance*], two lighters, and one of the mission whale boats will be towed behind the steamers.* Stanley Pool has now been a station for five or six years, with the very best of rich land on almost every side, yet here to-day there is a famine. Acres of bananas and manioc could have been planted, but no, everything is ivory from morning to night; all are concerned in getting down the greatest quantity of ivory. This will never make anything of a state. The ivory soon will be exhausted, except far up the river and then times will get very bad, much worse than they are now. Things appear to have gone down very much since Stanley's time from all accounts.

In the evening Jameson came down river, having shot two hippopotami, only one of which he managed to get. We had the meat brought up to the camp and distributed as rations to the men. We took some for ourselves and had some steaks which were very good.

24th Sunday

Had a general parade at 6:30 taking a list of hoes, axes, rifles, etc., practised the men a bit at turnings and position drill. I afterwards cleaned up the Maxim and did some other small jobs. Nelson is away with fifty men cutting firewood some distance away from here. Jameson is just going off on another hippo expedition to get meat for the men. He will be away for three days and will send meat back to camp every day. Had several visitors to the camp to-day, among them were two of the missionaries here, most cadaverous looking men.

---

*Arthur (or variously Antoine) B. Swinborne was Sanford's agent at Kinshasa, under Taunt's orders. More important was the fact that years before, Stanley had employed Swinborne (who had been briefly a medical student at Christ's Hospital in London) first as a valet and later as a secretary when he had administered the Congo Free State. Certainly Swinborne was familiar with Stanley's ways. He later justified his loan of the Sanford boat, ostensibly for forty-five days, by saying that if he had not, Stanley would have taken it in any case. Swinborne had adapted to African life by having a black wife in the Congo and a white one in Britain.

I got five or six letters from England yesterday. Two from Mckay [sic] one from the mater and some others and two from Cox & Co.* They had just heard at home that I was going away, having got my telegram from London, but were very much surprised as they could not guess for what reason. I also had one from Mary from Port Said.** She was on her way then to India and was expecting me to follow on by the next trooper.

It is now over three months since we left England and we have only got to Stanley Pool. Nelson has been away all day in the bush cutting firewood for the *Stanley* and at 4:30 I took 100 men over to him and we got out the wood and stowed it away by dark in the hold of the steamer.

25th Monday

Barttelot and Parke started away with about 160 men in the *Stanley* at 9:30 this morning. They go two days up river in the steamer, disembark and march two more to Bolobo, where they await our arrival. The steamer comes down to the Pool again as soon as the men disembark. Nelson is away with 60 men after firewood.

I stayed in camp in the morning, serving out brass rods for the men to buy food with. After this we cleaned and tidied up the camp and made things snug. Stanley went over to Kinshassa to see Mons. Greshoff.*** Jephson was at

---

*Captain Huntly Brodie Mackay, DSO (1858–1891) of the Royal Engineers, a fluently bilingual native of Quebec, graduated at the head of his class at the Royal Military College in 1881, one year ahead of Stairs (they were together on the football team). Mackay spent much of his ten years of army service with the Royal Engineers in Africa, first in Bechuanaland on the South Africa boundary commission and subsequently in Sierra Leone where he was engaged in both fortification works and the suppression of inland slaving. During his second tour in Sierra Leone in December 1888, he served under Sir Francis de Winton. In a letter of 9 May 1889 to Stairs, he described at length his adventures in Sierra Leone (Public Archives of Nova Scotia). Mackay died of disease in Mombasa (see note on page 318) when a member of the first team of engineers sent to survey the route of a railway to be built across Uganda to Lake Victoria Nyanza. At the time of his death, he was also acting administrator of Mackinnon's Imperial British East Africa Company in Mombasa.

**Mary Stairs (1857–1939) was Stairs's third sister. She married in 1883 George Deane Bourke, a British army surgeon who, like Barttelot and Parke, had served in the Gordon relief expedition in the Sudan in 1884–1885. In 1887, when Stairs received the letter from his sister, she and her husband were passing through the Suez Canal en route to India from where, during the next two years, Bourke was to serve in the campaigns in Burma. Colonel Bourke spent many years in India before being posted to Ireland in 1910. He was knighted in 1917 and served in Britain until his retirement in 1920.

work at the boat which has gone off in tow of the *Stanley*. Jameson is still away after hippo meat and as he has taken his fowling piece we should get something good for our pot. Our cooks mutinied to-day. This is a good job as we can sack them and perhaps get better ones, as we certainly cannot get worse.

26th Tuesday

Had a hard day's work, Bonny and I were away all day in the bush with 50 men cutting wood. We got 216 cords cut and Nelson came in in the evening and brought the loads out to the *Peace* and *Stanley*. The wood is very scarce, the axes bad and the men very inferior axemen, so we did not get as much as we otherwise should have.

27th Wednesday

... Jameson came back having shot five hippopotami. We brought up two of the beasts in the evening and one in the morning and distributed them among the men as rations. Some of the Zanzibaris will not eat hippo meat for some reason or other, but most of them devour it greedily, especially when food is so scarce as it is at present.

28th Thursday

Started away for the new camp as soon as we could manage to get the loads arranged. Stanley took 37 loads of ammunition in one of the boats and Jephson took 50 round by water to Kinshassa. The rest of us marched over by the track. Nelson took 100 men to the bush to bring out firewood to the steamers. After about ¾ of an hour's march we came to a small river in heavy flood. This took us 2½ hours to cross and we did not arrive in camp till pretty late. I had breakfast at the Dutch House with Mr. Greshoff and Jephson and Stanley. We all enjoyed it very much. The river is very pretty just here and is quite one mile wide.

On Monday 24th one of my men, and on Tuesday one Soudanese, died.

The Dutch firm has got a very nice station here, with a fine lookout on to the river, good water and all round a first rate place for a station. At every

---

Stairs may have been seeking an engineering appointment in India as did several graduates of RMC (see footnote on pages 32-33) when he spent Christmas of 1886 with his sister at Portsmouth.

He volunteered for the Emin Relief Expedition only in early January 1887 (and evidently did not tell his sister before his departure from Britain on 20 January 1887).

***Antoine Greshoff, another old acquaintance of Stanley, was the Dutch agent at Stanley Pool, soon to be appointed Dutch consul in Brazzaville in the neighbouring French Congo.

point on the Congo where there are Belgians and Dutch, one notices the superiority of the latter over the former as a colonist and trader. The Belgian officers on the Congo are about the worst class of men that could be chosen for such work.* We were invited to dine this evening with Mr. Greshoff, the head of the Dutch House here. We had a very good dinner and the comfort of a chair and table and having glasses to drink out of and cigars to smoke is simply unknown to those who have not roughed it on bad grub and meals in the dark.

I put up my "Edgington" bed to-day for the first time. Before this I had slept on grass on the ground or on a Zanzibari *kitanda*, or native bedstead. The beds Edgington sent us are rottenly conceived affairs, difficult to put together and crazy when they are, besides they cannot possibly last any length of time as the legs are bound to break.

We ought to make a start up river on Sunday... or at any rate some of us should be able to go then. Stanley goes on the *Peace*; Tippoo Tib on the *Henry Reed* ; Nelson, Jameson, Jephson and myself go on the *Stanley*, with about 245 Zanzibaris. We also tow the *Florida* which is to take about 75 or 100 I think.

Several natives visited Stanley and brought gifts to him of fowls and goats. The money here is brass wire or *matako*. These are cut into lengths of about 22 inches, the diameter is about 1/10th of an inch ... They are valued at about 3½ d. each at Stanley Pool, and we issue 1½ per day per man to buy rations. Higher up the River different currencies are in use, blue beads, cloth, etc.

29th Friday
... Jameson and Jephson went over to Leopoldville in the boats to bring over some loads that we had left. They got back in the afternoon and we stacked their loads in Stanley's tent, he using a room in the Dutch House to sleep in. Nelson and I stayed in camp in the morning and in the afternoon Nelson went over to Kinshassa to see Swinburne and take some ropes for the *Florida*. In the evening we stacked and classified all the loads in Stanley's tent. The plans for going up river are now definitely fixed. Nelson, Jephson, Jameson and I go up in the *Stanley*, with our men; Bonny ... in the *Henry Reed*; Stanley and his servant [Hoffman] go in the *Peace*, we tow the *Florida*; the *Henry Reed* tows the State lighter; the *Peace*, the *Plymouth*. Tippo Tib and all his followers go by the *Henry Reed*.

---

*In fact, the majority of officers in the employ of the Congo Free State were not Belgians. Stanley recorded that of the 263 agents engaged between 1879 and 1885, only eighty-one were Belgian (an equal number were British): *The Congo and the Founding of its Free State,* vol. II, p. 306.

30th Saturday

Nelson and I went over to help get the *Florida* off the stocks. We succeeded after about three hours' hard work, getting her off about 11:30 . Casement and Swinburne of the Sanford Expedition then stood us "fiz" in their house and we celebrated the event. The *Florida* is of galvanized steel, built in three watertight compartments, a stern wheeler, about 75 feet long and 13 feet beam, with a 3'6" hold. As yet she has no boiler or engines. In fact we are using simply the hull. We got back to camp, had breakfast with Greshoff of the Dutch House and then started cutting grass and making our loads ready to receive the *Stanley*. She and the *Henry Reed* came to the landing about 3:30 and we immediately started loading and by dusk had almost finished. Just as we were finishing, Troup and Ward whom we expected would have to stay behind turned up. Stanley took Ward but left Troup to stay behind to look after loads. This is a beastly shame, as Ward is quite an outsider to the expedition, having been picked up by Stanley on the road up from the coast, while Troup was taken on at the very start of the expedition in London, and signed the same articles as all of us ...

Chapter Three

Following the twenty-eight-day trek from Mataddi to Stanley Pool, the expedition's third stage was the much longer but easier river journey from Stanley Pool to the cataracts at Yambuya on the distant Congo tributary, the Aruwimi. Almost two thousand kilometres separated Stanley Pool and Yambuya, but at least that stage could be done with relative comfort on steamers – that is, if steamers were available. Stanley managed to commandeer three small steamers from among the limited resources of the Congo Free State, the Sanford Exploring Company, and from a decidedly reluctant American Baptist Mission: the Stanley, the Henry Reed and the Peace. Although Stanley gathered five barges to be towed behind the three steamers (including the American Baptist Mission's incomplete steamer and his own portable Advance), this hastily improvised flotilla was insufficient to carry the expedition and all its supplies to Yambuya.

The ruthless Stanley accordingly decided that he must divide his expedition. First, Rose Troup would be left at Stanley Pool with a large quantity of stores. Then additional stores and the sick would be left with Ward and Bonny at Bolobo, a few hundred kilometres up the Congo from Stanley Pool. A few hundred more kilometres up the Congo at Bangala, Stanley ordered Barttelot to detach himself from what remained of the expedition and to proceed in the Henry Reed farther up the Congo (beyond the point at which the expedition itself would turn into the Aruwimi tributary). Barttelot was to deliver Tippu Tib, his many wives and followers to Stanley Falls. He was then to return with the Henry Reed to the confluence of the Congo and the Aruwimi and rejoin the main body of the expedition at Yambuya.

At Yambuya itself, Stanley would establish a major camp. Once the camp was organized, a steamer would be sent back down the river to bring up Rose Troup from Stanley Pool and Ward and Bonny from Bolobo, along with their stores, to

Yambuya where Barttelot would be left in command. Meanwhile, Stanley, with a small advance column including Stairs, would make the final march on Lake Albert Nyanza. As soon as the whole of the rear column had been consolidated under Barttelot's command at Yambuya, it too would move toward the lake, assuming – and it was a very large assumption – that sufficient porters could be mustered.

Such at least was Stanley's intention. Reality proved to be substantially different.

All in all, the first weeks were not a promising beginning. Jameson began to sense what was happening to the officers. On 29 March 1887 he recorded:

The work we are doing is not fit for any white man, but ought to be given to slave-drivers. It is all very nice for Mr. Stanley, who rides ahead straight on to the next camp, where we arrive hours afterwards, having done nothing all day but kick lazy carriers, and put the loads on to the heads of those who choose to fling them down.[1]

Roger Jones, in The Rescue of Emin Pasha, *has caught well what had insidiously begun to happen on the lower Congo: the European officers were gradually being brutalized by their daily efforts to drive forward their recalcitrant porters.*

... perhaps the most depressing fact which emerges from the records of these first weeks is the almost immediate disillusion of the young Englishmen who had volunteered with such pathetic eagerness, and been so proud of being chosen, for what was to have been a glorious adventure and now revealed itself as a squalid nightmare. It was not the physical discomforts of their situation – heat, rain, insects, sickness and fever, sore feet, wet clothes and poor rations – which produced this effect. It was rather the moral degradation of the work they were called on to do, work which all too often seemed to consist solely in cajoling, bullying and whipping groups of sullen, bewildered or disorderly Africans into a semblance of orderly movement.[2]

◆   ◆   ◆

1st May [1887] Sunday
Started loading the *Henry Reed* with Tippoo Tib's people and goods. At 8:30 we sent her off up river and this made a start on what will probably be a journey of 40 days. We next loaded up the *Florida* with Jameson's and my men and made her fast to the *Stanley* . We then loaded the *Stanley* and *Peace* and the whale boat *Plymouth* and State lighter ... We started in the *Stanley* about 11 a.m. and had a great send-off. There were the missionary and his wife, Mr. Greshoff, another German gentleman, Troup, Swinburne, Casement, Baron Steinworth and an engineer of the Dutch House. They gave us a vociferous cheer, which we returned. Soon after we left, the *Peace* followed and we lost sight of her after ½ an hour or so, apparently she returned to Kinshassa. However, a day or so will tell. At last we have started and all are

glad, the men especially, as their rations of *matako* [brass] rods were not nearly sufficient for the famine prices at Stanley Pool ...

...We are taking just over 600 men up river, those with Parke and Barttelot amount to about 160 more. We should therefore have about 600 men to take up to the Falls and will probably leave 100 of these there in an entrenched camp we are to form.

We are very much crowded on the *Stanley*. The men simply cannot move but stay in one or nearly the same position all day. Of course we shall land late in the afternoon to cut firewood, the men will then get a chance to cook and make themselves comfortable. I fancy we fellows are much more comfortable here than any of the others are. There is a single spare cabin on board, this we tossed for and I won, so I have a very comfortable little room with two windows, a good bed, washstand, table and chair and plenty of hooks to hang my things on. The other chaps sleep in different parts. Jephson sleeps in the saloon and Nelson and Jameson in the wheelhouse on the upper deck. They all have very comfortable beds. Then we have a good table and chairs; to eat our meals in comfort is thus assured to us.

Going up the river we dodge about, crossing from side to side of the channel to miss the rocks and sandbanks. Just now we are not more than 10 yards from the bank, here covered with long grass and small bushes and infested by crocodiles. The mosquitoes are said to be very bad along the river banks but we should be safe with netting rigged up. We landed the mails at the Kimpoko mission station ... and camped about 300 yards above. Kimpoko is an American Baptist Mission station, self-supporting to a great extent. There are no less than three white men I believe. These shoot meat, cut their own wood, build their sheds, farm, etc., in fact employ little or no paid labour on the station. We had a visit from some of them, long, tall, bearded Americans, all keen for news about the expedition, some of them took a great deal of interest in the Maxim gun which we keep mounted ready for action.

We all slept on board and found it very comfortable and free from mosquitoes. The men camped within 200 yards of the steamer and as usual talked all night. At 6:00 we started the men off for firewood, having 45 axemen and others to carry the wood out. By 8 o'clock we had about enough wood for the *Stanley* and we lit large fires and split up our wood and stowed it away in the hold. The *Stanley* burns a tremendous quantity of wood every day. It takes nearly 200 loads of 60 lbs. each for twelve hours' steaming. This wood cutting will get to be very tiresome work I should say. In the dark one cannot watch the men as in day-time and so prevent them getting away ...

2nd Monday
... We have heard nothing of the *Peace* yet. We suppose something must have fouled her screw and so delayed her. How Stanley must be swearing! At 10 a.m. as the *Peace* had not yet turned up, the captain of the *Stanley* and I went

down stream in the *Stanley* to look for her. After steaming about 12 miles we saw her in a small by-channel. Catching up to her, wc found that yesterday, soon after starting from Kinshassa, she had broken her rudder. We offered them help but they declined, so we came on, loaded up the men, took on some more firewood, and now as I write, all these steamers are on their way up stream. We should get out of Stanley Pool by dark ...

3rd Tuesday
Up at 5 and started the men on board as soon as it got light enough to see ...

Tippoo Tib's people are sadly wanting in discipline, as can be seen every day. They seem quite indifferent to the passage of time. I suppose they have always been used to take things easily and so now do not see the use of hurrying up. Certainly now is the chance to make up time, if ever we are to do it. Our captain estimates that it will take us nearly 40 days to get to Stanley Falls, loaded up as we are. This is nearly a week over Stanley's estimate ...

4th Wednesday
Up at 5 and got all on board, steamed into the stream and drew up along side of the *Peace* and handed over some rice and a goat. Soon afterwards, went on our way and left the *Peace* and *Henry Reed* astern....

I fired a few rounds from the Maxim this morning to try some ammunition that had fallen into a creek. The gun worked very well and showed that very accurate shooting could be made with it. The ammunition was some of the 3400 rounds of R.L. 45 Gardner that we got from the English Government just before starting ...

We split the big logs by the light of a large fire close to the steamer and got all the wood on board soon after. Some of the men went back to a manioc field two hours off and robbed the natives of their food. There were great rejoicings in camp when they came back as every one had plenty of *chakula* and felt generally happy. The people here are ... apparently a quiet, docile set, otherwise I should think they would retaliate and attack us.

5th Thursday
Up shortly after 5 and by 5:30 had "all aboard". We found that the *Stanley* was fast in the mud and so had to get 50 or 60 men out to push her off. We started at once up river ... having seen nothing of the *Peace* or the *Henry Reed* since yesterday afternoon.

Jephson was a bit seedy yesterday, but feels much better now. We all thought it was another fever, but quinine and "Livingstone's Pills" made him all right again.

One begins now to feel the dimensions of the Congo. Here the river is about twice as wide as the "Arm" at Halifax, or say slightly over ½ a mile, but deep and swift, closed in on both sides with high, bush-covered hills and grassy slopes, and stretching up and down till lost far away among the hazy blue hills. Far up from here ... the River widens and shallows are studded with numbers of small islands, but here it flows on in one solid mass, hardly broken in its shape at all. We see plenty of natives in their dug-out canoes, paddling along close to the banks and keeping away from the steamers. The Congo natives all paddle standing up and not as the [North American] Indians do (viz., kneeling down) ...

The people in this village are ... quiet, harmless duffers they seem. Our men have bought large quantities of maize, bananas, plantains, manioc and fish and seem very well satisfied with themselves. There are plenty of goats, fowls and yams besides the above mentioned sorts of food, but the natives will not take *matako* for goats, they must have cloth.

6th Friday
Up early and away by about 5:30. The *Peace* led the way at the start, but we soon passed her and in three hours were out of sight of both steamers ...

At half past four in the afternoon we were going along splendidly, congratulating ourselves at the way in which we were leaving the *Peace* and *Henry Reed* behind. We were all on the bridge talking or reading, when smash, bump on to firm rocks went the *Stanley*. The water immediately rushed into two compartments and things looked very bad. However, the Zanzibaris kept very quiet and in about two minutes we had all the men on board the *Florida* and stood ready to cast her off. We soon found there was not much immediate danger as the rock we were on was of a flat, table-shape, reaching out over the stern and sides of the *Stanley* and having about 3'6" of water at the stern. While we were shifting the cargo aft and moving men to weigh down the stern, a very bad squall came up and blew us clean off the rock and probably proved our salvation. We steamed full speed ahead, kept bailing as fast as we could and in ½ an hour managed to run her slowly on to a sand bank on the shore and disembark the men. We then made cables fast and with 300 men tried to pull her up, but only managed to get about one foot of the bow on shore. We then let the men camp and examined the leaks. The engineer reported five holes and water was making in three compartments; the holes are very jagged and vary from 1" to about 18" in size. The men behaved very well, though they knew of the danger. The captain kept his wits about him, and all worked well, the only sheep were some of the crew of the *Stanley*. At one time the danger of driving holes in the rear compartment *was* very great. Happily this was avoided, otherwise we should have gone down just over the edge of the rock into very deep water and so lost a tremendous lot of ammunition and stores, not to speak of the lives of the men and the loss to the expedition of the *Stanley*. At 11 p.m. we started the men cutting wood and cut nearly all night by moonlight and finishing about 2:30 a.m. When we got back to the steamer we found that the engineer and the captain had stopped three of the holes but had found another, making six holes in her altogether. We got to bed very tired after a good cup of hot tea and some biscuit and feeling very glad that we had escaped so easily.

7th Saturday

Up early and worked hard at mending the holes in the steamer's bottom. About 9 o'clock the *Henry Reed* turned up and two hours afterwards the *Peace* came up with Stanley. On learning what was the matter he at once got into one of his mad, passionate outbursts, slanging everyone, whether right or wrong. I have come to the conclusion that when he is in this state he cannot be responsible for what he says. In half an hour his temper subsides and he is a rational being again. One thing in Stanley is that he never will see when he is wrong, but sticks to what he says first with bull-headed obstinacy.

We started afresh on the holes, and by evening had finished three more, leaving several more which we discovered to-day. The three engineers and our captain were at work all the rest of the day putting tin plates over the holes, but there is yet a good day's work before we can go on. We all went to bed early, glad to get some hours sleep after staying up for so long.

◆   ◆   ◆

9th Monday

At work again on the holes and are getting pretty sick of the job. The *Peace* and *Henry Reed* left us at one o'clock and shortly afterwards we finished putting the cement on the inside of the plates and starting filling the boiler with water and putting on board the loads. We will finish by dark and should start tomorrow morning.

A king has just died in a village close to where we are lying and they had commenced to kill off some of the men as a death gift, when one chap rushed away and made for the *Stanley* for protection. I took him on board and as Stanley himself had gone up river decided to take the wretch on to Bolobo, not that it will do much good, but still there is a chance. This interfering with native customs and laws is a dangerous thing to do and on the Congo has been the cause of a good many troubles and was the primary cause of the loss of Stanley Falls to the State. Everyone out here gives a good opinion of Deane, the Englishman who was in charge of Stanley Falls when it was attacked and taken by the Arabs under one of Tippoo Tib's head men.* Tippoo Tib now is governor of Stanley Falls and so has practically full power there.

---

*Captain Walter Deane of the Indian Army and a Belgian companion, Dubois, had barely escaped with their lives when Deane had attempted to protect an African woman from seizure by the Arabs. Deane was killed by an elephant in 1888 (see Ceulemans, *La Question Arabe*).

10th Tuesday
As soon as we could see we started off. About 10 o'clock we sighted the *Peace* and *Henry Reed* far ahead of us. We gained on them very fast, and at 1:15 passed them within about 50 yards. Something had gone wrong with the *Peace*'s boiler and in an hour we had left her far behind ...

♦   ♦   ♦

13th Friday
... Stanley decided to-day to leave Ward at Bolobo instead of Barttelot. This is a great improvement as Barttelot is certainly the best man for the command of the entrenched camp at Stanley Falls. It is certainly rough on Ward but not nearly so rough as would be on one of us.

14th Saturday
... I served out the Europeans to be left here (Bonny and Ward) with provisions. Left tobacco with Ward for himself and Troup. About 5 o'clock in the evening, the *Stanley* returned..., bringing Barttelot and Parke, and the Soudanese and Parke's company. Barttelot is looking very bad and Parke has just got over another attack of fever. He told me his temperature yesterday ran up to 105°. This is very high. They had ... stopped ... at the house of three French priests (the French mission station) and had been waiting some five days for the *Stanley* to pick them up. Barttelot was very much pleased on hearing that Ward is to be left here instead of himself. Ward, of course, is very much disappointed, but he has less reason for being so than any of us ...

15th Sunday
... loaded the *Henry Reed* and the *Peace* with men and at 10:30 both steamers got away. After getting the donkeys and goats on board, we put the Soudanese on the *Florida* and shortly afterwards I embarked my men also on the *Florida*. We now have companies of 85 each, every man armed with a rifle and all the sick, bad men and "goe-goes" picked out and left behind at Bolobo. We are now much better prepared for fighting than we were formerly. At noon we started away upstream leaving Bonny and Ward on the banks looking very sad, and in a few hours had caught sight of both steamers ahead of us. ... At Bolobo we left about 125 men, with 50 rifles and 2000 rounds of ammunition. We calculate on their being there for about 50 days. The *Stanley* will by that time have come down river to the Pool, will pick Troup up, come up to Bolobo and take Bonny and Ward on to the Falls. It is to be hoped that Ward and Bonny have no trouble with the natives.

We had great difficulty in getting any wood and on landing for the night at a small village, the natives ran away after first threatening to fight us and soon after our men commenced to loot in the dark and took a tremendous quantity of food and spears. We had to knock off getting firewood very soon after 8 o'clock and will have to get more in the morning. The spears our men took are very fine ones with long, straight hardwood shafts and a broad blade say 4" wide at the swell. They are bound with brass bands, lapping over each other for about 9" below the head.

16th Monday
Started the men off for more wood at 5:30 and managed to get away by 8 o'clock. The villagers commenced to come in as we were starting. They were horribly disgusted at the looting done by the Zanzibaris but did not dare to attack us, as if they had done so we should have made small beans of them. Silly fools to run away from their village when they knew we had done no harm at Bolobo only 20 miles away. The Congo here is about 6 or 7 miles wide, but there are so many islands in the river that one only sees a channel of say ½ or ¼ mile wide. From Bolobo we have kept to the channel on the left Bank as being the best. Grenfell is said to have tried all the channels and pronounced this one the safest, though it takes some "handling" to run the steamer even here.*

We get on very well on the *Stanley* with the captain and engineer. Luckily for us they are very good chaps. We share our grub together and find it to be to our mutual advantage, they give us sometimes condensed milk, flour-pancakes, salt and such things, while we supply biscuits, rice, goat meat and other things. Now and then too they give us sugar.

Now that Barttelot has come on board, I sleep up in the wheel house and manage to make myself very comfortable. Parke is on the *Henry Reed* and I expect is not having much of a time of it. Tippoo Tib's many women lounge about the cabin all day, making the place smell horribly. Then the white men have to eat their meals there after the women go ashore, and spend the day perched on the cabin roof like so many fowls.

I had some splendid shots to-day at hippos lying on the banks in the river, some of them will allow the steamer to get within 300 yards before they enter the water. With a Remington one can make very fair shooting. Besides hippos there are crocodiles, eagles, geese and all manner of birds to shoot.

17th Tuesday
Got the men on all ready for starting early and fired up as usual when we noticed that the boiler and pipes were getting very warm. In fact some

---

*George Grenfell, a Baptist missionary, had arrived in the Congo in 1878. He was also a tireless explorer, his achievements evoking the admiration of Sir Harry Johnston in his *George Grenfell and the Congo*, 2 vols. (London 1908). Another biography appeared the following year: G. Hawker, *The Life of George Grenfell* (London 1909).

woodwork round the funnel caught fire. Then the engineer noticed that the water had escaped from the boiler, and we soon found that a great deal of damage had been done by the overheating of the boiler. Had we started and water been pumped into the boiler, we should certainly have blown up. We got all the men on shore again and started off cutting firewood. In the meanwhile the fires had been put out and the boilers allowed to cool and the engineer reported that we should be able to start to-morrow morning at the usual time. This has delayed us another day and old Stanley will be ... tearing his hair out and swearing at the incapacity of Congo River captains and everyone in general.

There are any amount of hippos about here, but they sink when one kills one and the body taking four hours to rise to the surface [and then] drifts away down stream. We had again great difficulty in scraping together enough wood for the day's supply. By nightfall, however, we had got enough for twelve hours steaming and very soon after we got back to the steamer the usual daily tropical tornado came on us, making it pretty precarious work dodging the forked lightning.

18th Wednesday
Up early, fired up and ran the steam in the boilers up to 100 lbs. on the square inch; found that they stood it all right and then embarked the men and made a start about 7 o'clock.

... We fired at hippos for practice and hit some of them pretty hard in the ribs and head but did not stop to try for their bodies.

... there never yet has left England any expedition so wretchedly provided for as this one is ... Now we have no sugar at all; we are issued tea at the rate of 1/5 oz. per day, per man. Our soap and candles are exhausted, or nearly so; we have only a few pounds of salt left, and when this goes we shall be put on rations of what really will not be 1/5th enough. Certainly we have tea, sugar and flour in the Fortnum and Mason grub boxes, but we shall not get much benefit from them, as they are calculated to last for twenty months for six men, whereas there actually are eleven whites to draw from them. No, Mr. Stanley has certainly broken faith with us in not getting more European provisions. He has had plenty of chances to do this, but has not availed himself of them.

Nelson and Jameson have both been very sick for the last two days. Poor Jameson is very much pulled down and looks like a ghost. I hardly think that Nelson is a strongly constituted chap. His liver seems to be touched.

I often wonder how Nanton, Twining and Joly are getting on, where they are and what they are doing.* By this time they should all have settled down

*For details of Nanton and Twining, see p.32. Major General Alain Chartier Joly de Lotbinière, CB, CSI, CIE (1862–1944) was the brother-in-law of Nanton. He was for

to the "long, long Indian day," I should think. It is a very strange feeling to be absolutely without any news of the outside world.

19th Thursday
... The wind soon sprang up and we had to lay fast to the bank. We saw two elephants quite close to the ship and while we were waiting Barttelot and I went off after them, but they dodged us and got away into the bush before we could get a shot and soon had to come back as the wind had died away. These are the first wild elephants I have seen ...

As early as May 1887, relations between Stanley and his officers had seriously deteriorated. Although the expedition had by then been on the Congo for only two months, it is evident from their diaries that the officers had growing reservations about their leader. The worst confrontation between Stanley and Stairs and Jephson came on the river bank on 20 May.

Stairs and Jephson were ashore and Stanley on the Peace *when the carriers complained to him of hard punishments to which the two officers had subjected them. The punishments were for looting native villages, something both Stairs and Jephson had striven to prevent (later, in their desperate search for food, they would encourage it).*

Upon hearing the Zanzibari complaints, Stanley summoned the two officers to the Peace *to account for the charges of abuse and violence. When neither officer recanted, Stanley lost his temper. This is how Jameson recorded it:*

He attacked them in a frantic state, stamping up and down the deck of the Peace. He called Jephson all sorts of names, a "G-d d— son of a sea-cook. You d—d ass, you're tired of me ... I've done with you. And you too, Lieutenant Stairs, you and I will part to-day, you're tired of me, Sir, I see. Get away into the bush." Then he turned round to the men (about 150) sitting down, and spoke Swahili to the effect that the men were to obey us no more, and that if Lieutenant Stairs or Jephson issued any orders to them, or dared to lift a hand, they were to tie them up to trees. He had already told Stairs that he had only to lift his hand for the men to throw him into the sea. He lastly offered to fight Jephson. "If you want to fight, G-d d–n you, I'll give you a bellyful. If I were only where you are, I'd go for you. It's lucky for you I'm where I am." Mr. Stanley was on the deck of the Peace, Jephson [and Stairs] on shore. All this was said before the missionaries, Tippu-Tib, and every one.[3]

---

more than two decades with the Royal Engineers in India on major irrigation and hydro-electric projects, eventually as chief engineer and secretary to the government of Bengal. During the First World War, he served with distinction both on the Western Front and as chief engineer to the Anzacs at Gallipoli alongside another RMC graduate who commanded the Anzac artillery, Brigadier General George Johnston, CMG, CB, DSO (1867–1947) of Halifax, the husband of Stairs's sister, Hilda.

Stairs and Jephson were subjected to the ultimate humiliation of being forced to apologize to Stanley for something they had not done. Only then would the mega-lomaniac Stanley permit the two officers to rejoin the expedition. Barttelot was "astonished ... especially in Stairs' case, for no kinder officer to the men, or more zealous or hard-working officer, is there in the Expedition, besides being most efficient and capable. The missionaries, two of them, who heard the disturbance, and the captain and the engineer of the Peace, *never heard such language, or witnessed such a disgraceful scene before.".[4]*

Following this altercation, Stairs's attitude towards Stanley was never the same. Never again would Stairs write in his diary of Stanley with anything approaching regard or respect. Stairs might thereafter occasionally note Stanley's qualities of determination, boldness and perseverance, but he could seldom rid himself of dis-dain for him. In their diaries Jameson, Stairs, Parke, and Jephson all record the exchange on 20 May which no one involved would ever forget, even if later it seemed expedient to put it aside. Roger Jones has described well the deterioration.

Bad relations between the officers and Stanley made things seem far worse than they might otherwise have been. For all the qualities of drive, determination and decision which he so eminently possessed, Stanley's behaviour was not always that of a man who knows how to get the best out of his subordinates. In previous enterprises he had been accustomed to dealing directly with the men under his command and had no talent for exerting his will through the medium of subordinate officers ... Stanley, in his account, is eloquent on the subject of his own "patience" and "forebearance"... such an assertion is pure eyewash ... for all his talk of patience he was subject to outbursts of violent – and frequently misdirected – anger. He was prone to favouritism, moody, inconsistent, secretive ... Finally, though he handed out blame in plenty, for real or fancied blunders, he gave no praise at all for work well done; and his distribution of blame was sometimes wildly unfair.[5]

Against that unpromising background, the expedition made its way up the Congo.

20th Friday
It is just four months to-day since we left England and we have now been two months in Africa.

To-day there was a big row with Stanley and after many high words he dismissed both Jephson and myself. Of course we are powerless to do anything or retaliate and had to bear a great deal. After his anger had subsided he took us back, but as it was before the men and about [i.e., concerning] them that the row took place, discipline must suffer and the men think less of us and become incited to mutiny. I am awfully sorry this has happened as it destroys all harmony among us. At the same time, I will never admit being in the wrong, and consider myself fully justified in doing what I did, viz., throwing away looted food of the Zanzibaris, food looted from a friendly village. Of course, some innocent ones suffered but they must blame the guilty ones for this. I threw away the looted food for two reasons. First, to show them that we considered it wrong to loot from friendly natives. Second, to serve as an example to the looters and to show them that if we could help it they would not profit one iota. I have stood more swearing at, heard more degrading things and swallowed more intemperate language from another man [Stanley] to-day than I have ever before...

♦   ♦   ♦

24th Tuesday

To-day is the Queen's birthday. This time we are under the flag of the Congo Free State ...

We reached the Equator station in the evening, much to the astonishment of the Europeans here who had not heard from down river for six months and of course did not know what to make of us. They at first thought we were a force coming to retake Stanley Falls from the Arabs. Equator is now abandoned by the State as a station and its buildings have been handed over to the Sanford Trading expedition. There is also an Anglo-American Baptist Mission station here, with two missionaries and a very nice earth house.

Though the State has abandoned this place, still an officer has been staying here for some time, looking out for Stanley Falls. Unluckily for him, he does not know as much about the State affairs as we do as we brought news from Zanzibar... about which he knew nothing. His name is Van Gele [sic], a lieutenant in the Belgian service.* There is a chap here called [Ernest J.] Glave, a young Englishman who formerly was in the service of the Congo Free State, but now is in the Sanford Company, buying ivory from the natives here. He seems a very decent sort of chap. Quite a different cut from the usual milk-watery Belgian officer one meets on the Congo.**

---

*Alphonse Vangele (1848–1939), an explorer and employee of the *Association Internationale du Congo*, was in command at Stanley Falls and had negotiated in 1884–85 with Tippu Tib the recognition by the Arabs of the claims of the association to the territory from the mouth of the Congo to Stanley Falls. Something of a favourite with Stanley, Vangele had also worked with Herbert Ward at Stanley Falls. See Z.P. Cuypers, *Alphonse Vangele 1848–1939* (Brussels, 1960).

**Ernest Glave (1863–95) had been a station chief under Stanley on the Congo in 1883–84 and was also a friend of Ward. Before his early death, he wrote an account of his Congo service: *In Savage Africa: Six Years of Adventure in Congo-Land* (London, 1893) introduction by H. M. Stanley. See also R.H. Russell, "Glave's Career," *Century Magazine*, vol. 28, no. 50 (1895) and "Cruelty in the Congo Free State; Extracts from the Journals of the late E.J. Glave", *Century Magazine*, 32, no. 54 (1897). (*Century Magazine* had employed Glave to write articles about slavery in Africa, especially in the Congo.)

The names of the two missionaries I do not know. I suppose they do some work but the natives are not of the right sort to take in Christianity easily. This is a bad place, taken all round for food. All that is used is obtained from villages some distance off. Some day there will probably be a famine here, owing to the same reasons that caused one at the [Stanley] Pool, viz., that no one plants roots or fruit here, or seems to provide in the slightest for the future.

25th Wednesday

... We all went to dinner with Glave and Van Gele in a very comfortable mud and bamboo house of one story. We had hippo meat, butter, palm wine, cabbage, bread, coffee and tinned peaches, a regal repast after goat, rice and weevily, stale biscuits and insipid tea ...

26th Thursday

We left the Equator station at 6 o'clock this morning ... We now have orders not to go ahead of the *Peace*. This of course delays us very much as she is such a horribly slow tub. It is a very pretty sight to see the three steamers with all their boats in tow making their way up river and steaming up some narrow channel with bush covered islands on both sides. Now and then we lose sight of each other and then all of a sudden a steamer shoots out from behind another. It would make a splendid photograph from the shore if we could get the three steamers close together.* Parke is now a passenger on the *Stanley*, Jephson having gone on to the *Henry Reed* last evening. This is a most sensible arrangement, as most of the sick men are with us on the *Florida* and now Parke can always be near them. Once seen, this part of the Congo will never be forgotten. The Thousand Islands of the St. Lawrence are nothing to this.

◆   ◆   ◆

29th Sunday

The *Peace* passed us (fast to the bank) about 5:30 and soon after this the *Henry Reed* also went by.

What noisy devils these Zanzibaris are! All day long and far away into the night one hears the same unceasing jabber-jabber; the same yells from one comrade to another, shrieked out with a fiendish, searching sound. The same subject occupies all minds at nearly all times and is dinned in one's ear till one wishes that some sort of safe would turn up in which one could hide

---

*Stanley appears to have been the only member of the expedition with a camera, but none of his photographs have survived, apparently having been either over- or under-exposed.

away and find peace. This subject is *chakula* (food) and whether there is no food, or whether there is abundance, it is always the same. The Zanzibaris, though fine fellows in some ways, have many petty faults. They are also the most unsympathetic set of men I have ever seen. They will see a comrade dying, one of their own blood, without turning a hand to help him or relieve his sufferings. On the other hand, they are quick, willing workers and this on bad grub and very little of it. They are patient, can stand hard work and at making themselves comfortable under difficulties would be hard to beat.

I should think Mr. Stanley must own now as to the questionability of this route to reach Emin Pasha at Wadeli. There have been three main routes proposed by different travellers. The first is Joseph Thomson's, starting from Mombasa, through the Masai country past Mount Kenya and Lake Baringo and on to Koro or Fadfulli, the estimated time is four months. The disadvantage of this route is that Mwanga, the present king of Uganda, would hear of the expedition's approach, probably attack it and wipe it out in one or two big fights.

The second route is that advocated by Dr. Felkin. He claims it as the safest, most rapid and most practicable of all. He would start from Bagamoyo to Mkumbiro, thence along Stanley's track to Nyagoma; thence west to Lake Alexandra; thus missing Uganda; he would then pass up by the shore of this lake to Muta Nzige, go up its western shores and strike for the south end of Lake Albert, where he would pick up with Emin Pasha's steamer. The chief disadvantage of this route is that it passes through 300 miles of unknown country, but then this also applies to all the other routes.

The third is Stanley's, or the route we are taking. This will take probably six months from the mouth of the Congo to Lake Albert, and will go through nearly 400 miles of absolutely unknown country; but the passage of the expedition up the Congo in steamers is an immense advantage. Probably, therefore, the choice lies between Dr. Felkin's and Stanley's route.

30th Monday

Started away from our camp at 5:30 ... About 12 o'clock we made fast to the bank opposite the State station [at Bangala] and were received by the officials, a salute from a Krupp gun. We were in luck as regards getting wood, as the State always keeps a supply cut and ready for use. We dined with Mr. Baert and the other Belgian officers and enjoyed getting decent food very much.*

---

*Parke noted in his diary entry for the same day that Bangala "is the furthest station on the Congo at present occupied by white men ... The small Congo Free State station – where Lieutenant Baert and Lieutenant Linant, with four other white men, live – is surrounded by a strong earth-fortification, and includes a brick factory. There is a small Krupp gun here, which was fired three times in quick succession in honour of our advent" (*My Personal Experiences*, p. 57).

31st Tuesday

Up early, getting Barttelot and the *Henry Reed* off. Barttelot took 40 of his Soudanese and all Tippoo Tib's men and has rations for 18 days. They go on straight to Stanley Falls, leave Tippoo Tib there, try to quiet the country and then Barttelot and his men come back to the mouth of the Aruwimi where we ought to pick them up. It will be an interesting piece of work, as the Arabs will of course imagine it to be an expedition of the Congo Free State for the retaking of Stanley Falls station and will probably attack, if they do not recognize Tippoo Tib ... This station at present is the highest one on the River, we, therefore, have said goodbye to everything that appertains to civilization and in all probability none of us will see a white man again till we meet Emin Pasha.

We have now seen the whole of the working of the Congo Free State. We have seen how it treats the different trading houses under its jurisdiction. We have also seen a fair portion of the country it governs and the natives under its charge. Our unanimous opinion is that the State as now constructed is one huge mistake. It was originally intended to be a Free State open to all, welcoming all honest trade, countenancing all open dealings with the natives and doing its best to establish postal and other communication between its different stations. Instead of this, what does really exist? Why a Congo Independent State, open as regards its officials to all Belgians, continually at variance with all the trading houses, English, Dutch, French and Portuguese alike, hindering instead of aiding trade, and lastly absolutely ignoring the importance of even a rough track with bush bridges on such a thoroughfare as that between Matadi and Stanley Pool. Certainly the Congo Independent State is a huge, unwieldy mistake (as managed at present), worked purely in the interests of the King of the Belgians who takes the best of care that outside influence is excluded, and apparently imagines that some day this place will form a safe deposit for Belgian capital and manufacturers.

The officers at Bangala were all very good to us and invited us to breakfast and dinner, but underneath everything one could easily see there ran a vein of jealousy which required pretty strong effort on their part to conceal. They imagine, I suppose, that an expedition coming up *their* river in *their* steamers should be composed of Belgians, instead of Englishmen, as it is, but this is only what one expects, as everywhere on the Congo the English are cried down and excluded from billets owing to the unpleasant fact some day the English will control almost all the import trade to this river, and also that the Belgians cannot help seeing that those English officers they have had out here have been far ahead of those of any other nationality in the way of managing the state and dealing with the natives.

The station at Bangala is fortified to a certain extent by means of a palisade and ditch. At the salients are placed gun banks, elevated above the palisade and mounted with Krupp guns (of which I believe there are two). The grass and scrub have at one time been charred in front but now has been allowed to grow up again and will form very good cover, should the Bangala ever attempt to attack the station houses.

They possess also at Bangala an excellent French brick maker, who makes the very best of red building and fire clay bricks. He is a very decent fellow to talk to and well informed on most matters concerning his everyday life. Of the other fellows little can be said, Lt. Baert of the Belgian service is outwardly a nice chap, but he has done some very nasty things here with the natives ...

The country about Bangala is very thickly populated, but none of the white men we met appear to have seen anything of it, but that part which adjoins the River. Capt. Shakerston, our skipper, is a very amusing fellow in a quiet way. He has the funniest collection of Congo stories one has heard yet. He tells of an adventure with a hippo that occurred ... on the lower Congo. Some Belgians and natives had wounded a hippo on the river bank close to the station house and were all up quite close to the beast, plugging it with all sorts of missiles from rifles, muzzle loaders and flint locks, when all of a sudden the beast charged them. Like rockets they all bolted for the house and clambered helter skelter on to the roof, just in time, for the beast kept straight on, burst through one wall, passed clean through the house and out the wall on the far side and escaped amid a shower of bullets to some bush close by. I should imagine it would be a very funny sight to see a huge hippo piercing the walls of a mud hut, with a lot of men perched on the roof like so many turkeys roosting ...

1st June [1887] Wednesday
... What a subject of conversation that dinner at Bangala has been. How we have talked it over and laughed among ourselves and imagined again and again we were eating butter, meat and vegetables and drinking Portuguese wine and champagne, but alas, it is farewell to these little comforts now for some time. I'm afraid the Belgian officers must think us all frightful gluttons, for certainly none of us spared the grub. We played havoc with their cigars and champagne at dinner and just as they were opening a fine bottle of brandy as a liqueur, Stanley rose and we had to adjourn. This was our farewell dinner with white men and Stanley rising to the occasion made a long speech exposing the dangers and adventures before us and, referring in "glowing terms" (that's correct!) to the King of the Belgians, stated that it was owing to His Majesty that we were comfortably "roomed and dined" 800 miles up from the sea, and hoped that His Majesty would be spared many years of useful existence and remain "the protector of the Free State" (I hope the young man will) ...*

---

*In 1887 King Leopold II was fifty-two years old. This diary entry, if to be taken literally and not ironically, contrasts starkly with Stairs's animadversions about the king and the

2nd Thursday

... Last night one of the Soudanese who had been ill for some time died in great pain. We buried him in the bush close to the steamer, giving him an eighteen inch grave. At Bangala ... a Somali boy died. He was one of the best of the Somalis, always ready when well to do his work, quick on his pins and a good man in a boat or canoe ... He died of exhaustion after an attack of some form of dysentery.

Unfortunately, the Somali boys all suffer very much in this country. The climate is too moist for them, used as they are to their dry, arid Somaliland. They are constantly having severe attacks of fever and dysentery. In fact, since we crossed the Kwilu River the Somalis have hardly done a stroke of work. To some extent this is owing to their not getting meat of any sort and somehow the native food does not seem to agree with them.

On board we have some nineteen of the Soudanese. The rest have gone on with the *Henry Reed* to the [Stanley] Falls. Of the 19 some six or seven are suffering very much from ulcers and other complaints. They are very poor material for such an expedition as this, at making themselves comfortable in camp and in foraging for food they are not a patch on the Zanzibaris. Why, when we draw up to the shore at nights to camp, the Zanzibaris in 15 minutes have their fires going, their shelters made and pots a-boiling, one sees these Soudanese wandering aimlessly about, bemoaning their fate, and cursing themselves for coming. In fact, doing anything but making themselves comfortable. Often I feel sorry for them in that they do not get the food they may have been used to in Egypt, but not for long, as one cannot sympathize with men who will not help themselves in a struggle such as this is.

... Jameson is still ill with the same trouble he had before ... The grub is so bad at times that it requires a cast-iron stomach to digest it. This, unluckily, Jameson does not possess.

◆   ◆   ◆

4th Saturday

... Abukir Mahommed died this evening from exhaustion and despondency. He was a Somali boy from Aden, formerly in the police there and was married. He always seemed an idle, sulky fellow to me, though at times he has worked well enough. The other Somalis are worked up into a terrible blue funk. They pray most of the day and lie about between times in a comatose state, utterly indifferent to their surroundings.

◆   ◆   ◆

Belgians in the Congo in several diary entries in May. More likely the entry of 1 June reflects a cynical amusement about the king's obsession with his "Free State."

6th Monday

... About 11 a.m. we made fast to the bank at Upoto, after a long and weary palaver with the chiefs we were allowed to land. The head chief and I made blood-brotherhood by cutting our arms and then rubbing them together.

Stanley turned up in the *Peace* about 4 p.m. having, he said, been looking for us for a day and a half. He was in a very bad humour and slated us on landing.

We had men out cutting wood in the evening. Goats are expensive here but fowls, corn, bananas, sugar cane and a lot of other things are plentiful and cheap. I shall be awfully glad when this river trip is over and we are once more on the march. The men get demoralized doing nothing all day. They have any amount to eat and are getting lazier every day. This state of affairs will terminate as soon as we start on the march again. Wood is hard to get for a steamer such as this. Our boilers are those as used in locomotives and require an immense amount of fuel to generate a sufficiency of steam ...

The chief of Upoto and I became great friends. He asked me to come back to Upoto and stay with him awhile, but I had to decline. He is a fine-looking man, but a great coward.

7th Tuesday

At 10 we commenced to get up steam and at noon both steamers started once more up river. I had another small palaver with the chiefs this morning. The head chief presented me with a small goat and some palm wine. We drank the palm wine together and then I gave him a present of some *matako*. Before going, I asked him if any of our men had stolen or done any damage to his property or people. He answered, "No, you are a good brother" and we part friends. This chief was also a blood brother of a Captain Hansen of the Congo Free State, now dead.

The money here is Kowrie [cowrie] shells. The *matako* has almost ceased to be of use. Empty bottles or tin boxes they will readily take, but handkerchiefs do not seem to be in much demand. We are now drawing near the "Zone of Opposition." At Upoto we might have expected to be attacked but the palaver did away with that. Now, however, we must expect a great deal of opposition and all the men ashore; we got a fair supply of wood but were out till 7:30 and did not finish splitting until 11:30. My New Zealand bush knowledge came in handy here.

Chapter Four

On 12 June 1887 Stanley's flotilla turned eastward from the Congo itself into the tributary of the Aruwimi. Three days later it had steamed the 150 kilometres up the Aruwimi to the village of Yambuya. There, where cataracts blocked any further navigation, Stanley had determined to establish his base for the final stage of his advance on Lake Albert.

A week after the arrival of the expedition in Yambuya, the Stanley *steamed back down river to bring up Rose Troup from Stanley Pool and Ward and Bonny from Bolobo – and the supplies left with them. The* Henry Reed *was at the same time to bring Barttelot from the much closer Stanley Falls.*

On arriving at Yambuya, Stanley had made a fundamental decision about the future course of the expedition. He had decided to divide it in two : the advance column, which, travelling lightly, would accompany him to Lake Albert, and the rear column under Barttelot which would follow with the main supplies as soon as sufficient porters could be found.

Within a few days, Barttelot, having deposited Tippu Tib at Stanley Pool, arrived at Yambuya. There he learned from Stanley that he was to be left behind in command of a camp opposite Yambuya.* Once Rose Troup, Ward and Bonny had joined him, Barttelot and the rear column could overtake Stanley at the Lake – if Tippu Tib had provided enough porters to carry all the supplies. If not, Barttelot could stay at Yambuya and await Stanley's return from the lake.

---

*For some reason, Stairs did not include in his diary entry for 17 June 1887 any description of Stanley's decision. Parke noted: "In the evening, Mr. Stanley called his officers into his tent and informed us that he intended marching to the Lake Albert Nyanza, relieving Emin Pasha by handing him over the ammunition, and returning to Yambuya

Stanley was in a hurry. He would not wait at Yambuya for the arrival of Rose Troup, Ward, and Bonny and their supplies (most of which had been intended to succour the beleaguered Emin). In his Autobiography, *Stanley offered his explanations:*

It should be remembered, that the last news from Emin was an urgent appeal for help. The last solemn injunction to us was to hurry forward, lest we be too late. Hitherto, we had been dependent on the fortunes of the sea, the skill of ship captains, and safe navigation by ocean and river ... Now was the time, if ever, to prove that our zeal had not cooled. Six weeks, probably two months, would pass before the entire force could be collected at Yambuya [i.e., the remainder having been brought by the *Stanley* on her second voyage up river]. If Emin was in such desperate straits as he had described, his total ruin might be effected in that time, and the disaster would be attributed to that delay ... To avoid that charge, I had no option but to form an Advance Column, whose duty would be to represent the steady progress of the expedition towards its goal, while a second Column, under five experienced officers, would convey after us, a few weeks later, the reserve stores and baggage.[1]

The departure from Yambuya would mark the last time that Stairs was to see Barttelot and Jameson. Stanley was leaving them in a highly ambiguous if not impossible position. Stanley had promised Tippu Tib that he would pay him in gunpowder for the additional porters who would be essential if the rear column were to overtake the advance column, but Stanley, having inadequate steamers to carry all his supplies, had left the powder with Rose Troup.

On 23 June Barttelot arrived at Yambuya to report to Stanley that Tippu Tib had, in the absence of the powder, refused to provide the 600 porters which would allow the rear column to rejoin the advance column. Stanley blustered that Tippu Tib should produce the men and accept his promise that he would be paid the powder at some indefinite date in the future. However, it was becoming increasingly evident that the rear column, in the continuing absence of Tippu Tib's additional porters, would needs await at Yambuya the return of Stanley from Lake Albert, presumably with Emin in tow.

A few days later, Stanley departed for the lake. Six weeks later, Ward and Bonny joined Barttelot and Jameson at Yambuya. In the absence of Tippu Tib's porters, all four remained at Yambuya. Stanley and Barttelot had agreed that the rear column should follow the advance column to the lake if Tippu Tib provided all the porters. If he provided only some, the supplies might be brought forward in relays. What was left unclear was what Barttelot was to do if Tippu Tib provided no porters at

---

about October or November. He would leave the entrenched camp here in charge of Barttelot and Jameson. He went on to say that Barttelot was not sufficiently forebearing, but that Jameson's experience of Africa would, he thought, correct his [Barttelot's] impetuosity" (*My Personal Experiences*, p. 66).

all. Barttelot certainly hoped to rejoin Stanley, but Stanley, apparently realizing that he himself had already made it unlikely that Tippu Tib would ever deliver the porters, left the implication that he did not believe that the rear column would succeed in moving from Yambuya before he himself returned in November. It would, in effect, be relegated to a debilitating and likely pestilent camp while Stanley was away at the lake.

Later Stanley attempted to convey the impression that he had given Barttelot clear written orders to follow him to the lake. In fact, Stanley left it to Barttelot to decide whether to follow or not, in light of whether Tippu Tib provided sufficient carriers. Jephson, for one, assumed that Barttelot, Jameson, Ward, and Bonny would remain where they were until the advance column returned from Lake Albert. Parke's diary entry of 24 June reflects something of the ambiguity in Stanley's orders. "Barttelot received his orders from Mr. Stanley. He is to march, when his men are collected, so as to meet us on our return journey, although he is allowed the option of remaining – if he does not consider himself competent to move, after he has discarded a quantity of his impedimenta."²

◆   ◆   ◆

On the morning of 28 June 1887, more than three months after disembarking from the Madura at Banana Point, the advance column of 389 men began its overland trek, entering upon the eight hundred kilometres of unexplored Ituri rain forest between Yambuya and Lake Albert (which forms part of today's border between The Congo Republic and Uganda). Ill with malaria, Stairs had apparently been oblivious to the several discussions Barttelot had with Stanley about what the rear column was expected to do. Stairs recorded laconically, "we all said good-bye two or three times to Barttelot and Jameson and started off on our march ..."

In his later account of what he had told Barttelot on 24 June 1887, Stanley stated that he had given a "written order to Lieutenant Stairs a few days ago, to rake his settlement with the machine gun upon the least sign of treachery."³ If such a written order did exist (there is no other record of it) and if Stanley wrote it about 18-20 June, it may have been when Stanley assumed that Stairs was so sick that he would have to be left behind at Yambuya camp.

In fact, Stairs left for the lake with the advance column, but he was so feverish and debilitated that for almost a fortnight he had to be carried in a hammock or in the Advance, the portable steel boat. The majority of the advance column marched along the Aruwimi River while the steel boat and a few small wooden canoes (seized along the river) carried some of the supplies. One biographer of Stanley has written of what awaited the advance column as it entered the rain forest as "the most dreadful ordeal any European explorer of nineteenth-century Africa ever faced".⁴

◆   ◆   ◆

12th Sunday

... Late in the afternoon we sighted large numbers of canoes and soon afterwards came to the junction of the Congo and Aruwimi, and turned up into the latter river. Stanley took the *Peace* close in to the bank at Basoko, a large village and held a palaver with the natives, using his boy Baruti as an interpreter. The result was that we went across to the opposite side of the river and the natives promised to bring us food there in their canoes. They were distinctly averse to our landing and no wonder. Basoko has been twice burned, once by the State and then again by Tippoo Tib's Arabs. Baruti, Stanley's boy who has been in England for some time, is the son of the chief of this village. His friends were there but his brother failed to recognize him till Baruti had told him the names of his father, mother and sisters, even then the natives were sceptical, but Baruti said, "See, here is the mark of a crocodile's teeth that I got when a boy here" and showing his brother the mark was welcomed by all, but not allowed to land.

All through the night, the natives created a great din, banging their drums and yelling ...

13th Monday

... We steamed on till 5 o'clock and camped on the left bank at a small village, all the natives running away as soon as we came near the bank. We found no food of any sort as the banana trees had just been planted and the natives apparently had only just come there. All day long we passed village after village, with scores of people. Sometimes we went within ten yards of the banks. The natives all appeared valiant at first, but ran like deer as we approached their village, and then came back again when we had passed. A great many of the natives were painted with white and red clays. They all have distended ears caused by wearing small bits of wood stuck through the flaps.

Most of them have their hair done up in different shapes ... The men wear little or no clothing. The women absolutely none. All are cannibals of the worst kind. Their spears and shields seem to be superior to those at Upoto. Their food consists of Indian corn, *chaquanga*, bananas, plantains, *mahogo* [manioc], fish and birds they snare. Now and then they get a hippo or elephant.

14th Tuesday

Left camp at 5:10 and steamed across the river and then worked our way slowly among the sandbanks in a thickish mist. Towards the afternoon we came upon a very large village, probably one of the largest we have yet seen. Here we began to notice a change in the shape of the huts and for the first time saw the conical palm hut of which there are so many on the upper part of this river. For miles we passed this village, seeing hundreds of natives in hideous head dresses and gaudy with red ochre and white clay ... During the night the natives made a great noise but did not attempt to attack us. After dinner we issued ten rounds of Remington ammunition to each man. There is sure to be some accident soon as most of the men know little or nothing of the danger of playing with firearms.

15th Wednesday
Away at 6 o'clock. This should be the last day we are to spend on board, as we hope to reach our destination this evening, if all goes well. This morning we noticed the banks generally got higher than those we have been passing. We stopped for the night just opposite to the village of Yambuya, where our entrenched camp is to be. The natives made a tremendous noise all night and canoes came close to us, the natives yelling frantically for us to go away ...

16th Thursday
Left last night's camp at 6 a.m. and put out a bit and made fast to an overhanging tree where we could see every movement of the natives. Stanley then went across to the village with the *Peace*, upon which all the niggers ran away. Soon, however, they came back and a long palaver was held, Baruti being the interpreter. It was no use though. The natives would not permit us to land. We in the *Stanley* came over, all our men being ready to land and my Maxim ready to murder them if they should dare to attack us. We made a landing soon after and frightened all the natives out and took possession. Unfortunately, they had such a long warning, that all the fowls and goats had been driven out. We got, however, all sorts of curios, paddles, chairs, work tables, charms, drums and dozens of different things. We portioned off the men to different parts and mounted sentries. There are over 180 huts in this village, almost all conical ones. Adjoining this are two villages (small ones) on the down stream side and four or five upstream.

We at once started clearing the bush behind the camp and by evening had cleared to a width of about 30 yards. This will give us some chance of preventing a rush on the part of the villagers. In the meantime, I got Nelson's and my tent up and thus once more we are under a canvas roof, after 46 days' life on board steamer, and back once more to rough work and living. It was in this very village that sometime ago a caravan of Arabs who had been raiding and looting ivory stopped here, getting drunk on *malafu*. At night they were attacked by the natives and 100 of them massacred. Stanley estimates that there must be at least 4,000 people living about here. Now not one is to be seen.

17th Friday
Up early and all hands occupied on different jobs ... I had about fifty men clearing the bush in front of the camp and finished about 4 p.m. I then got a lot of men with hoes and shovels, and having first traced the faces we commenced digging the ditch for the palisade. The general shape of the camp

is to be lunar or semi-lunar, with the river bank as a gorge. The palisade will be about 12 high, every 30th pole cut away to within 4'6" from the ground. At the salients the banquette is raised 4' to 5' so as to give greater command. In the front face to the right is a high tower 12'6" high which will hold six or seven rifles. From this point the ground on every side can be swept. A white man with a Winchester would create immense slaughter among the natives as here he would be quite safe from spears and could single out and pot any skulking nigger behind a tree or bush.

◆   ◆   ◆

20th Monday
All hands off after wood again and by 10 a.m. we brought in our wood and stowed it on board the *Stanley*. Shortly before noon the *Stanley* got off. We all stood on the bank and saw the last of her. Well, Nelson and I have spent some pleasant days on the old *Stanley*, with tables, chairs and plenty of books. One feels a pang at losing her and her jolly skipper Shakerston and Engineer de Manis. Good luck to them and may they return swiftly upriver again with the rest of our stores and men!*

21st Tuesday
... This is the anniversary of the founding of Halifax, N.S. What a day they will be having of it out there! How every one will rush off trout fishing and then set fire as usual to the bush and burn up several square miles of good timber!

Stairs does not record the arrival of Barttelot at Yambuya on the *Henry Reed* on 23 June; nevertheless, he must have been relieved to see him. The day before, Stanley had written to Stairs a long letter (although they were in the same camp) in which he said that he was "terribly anxious" about the safety of the *Henry Reed*. If Barttelot had not appeared on 22 June, Stairs was to take a steamer and search for him.

24th Friday
Both steamers [*Peace* and *Henry Reed*] got away between 6 and 7 o'clock this morning.** Thus we have seen the last white men till we reach Emin

---

*Scandinavians generally supplied both the skippers and the engineers for the river steamers; Shakerston was an exception.

**Jephson notes that the two steamers left on the morning of 25 June (not 24 June) carrying the last letters which members of the expedition would be able to send until they had crossed the continent and neared the Indian Ocean.

Pasha. As soon as the steamers left, we went at the boma [fort] but at 4:30 I had to knock under to the fever and went to bed.

25th Saturday
In bed all day with fever; the rest at work on the *boma*.

26th Sunday
Stayed in bed all the morning, fever still high. To-day the Soudani who was wounded by the natives died. Alexander, the Soudanese interpreter (a Syrian), died yesterday from general exhaustion. He was the most helpless individual I think I ever saw.

I got up at 11 and did up the Maxim ready for the road but had to go back to bed again feeling very bad.

27th Monday
All at work getting the different loads made up. Stanley gave the men a holiday. The *boma* is now fairly complete. The main gate was built partly by Parke and partly by myself. I was kept again in bed all day and now find I am so weak that I shall have to be carried.

Suffering as Stairs was from a severe attack of malaria, it is hardly surprising that his diary entries are mere notes. The entries for much of June 1888 are cryptic rather than expansive about the ordeal that awaited the advance column as it parted from Barttelot and Jameson at Yambuya on 28 June. Until its departure, Jameson remained doubtful that Stairs, prostrate with fever, would be able to accompany the advance column: "Stairs is really very bad with fever; in fact, so bad that Mr. Stanley warned me to be ready to go instead of him at a moment's notice."[5] On 27 June Jephson recorded in his diary, "Stairs is down with fever and it is doubtful if he will be able to go tomorrow – it will be a great loss if he isn't for, after Stanley, he is the most valuable man in the expedition."[6] Parke was equally doubtful, but he had a particular incentive to declare Stairs well enough to go: Stanley had said that if Stairs had to be left behind, Parke would need to remain with him. "... I recommended that he should come with us; and it was accordingly arranged that he will be carried by ten men especially told off (daily) for the duty. I must confess I was very anxious to go myself also."[7]

Stanley, for his part, was apprehensive about what awaited them. On the thirteenth day after arrival at Yambuya, the advance column, consisting of five Europeans and three hundred and eighty-four natives, "entered the great Equatorial Forest ... We were absolutely ignorant of the character of any portion embraced within this area."[8]

28th Tuesday
All were ready to start at 7 a.m. and soon after this the order to march was given. We all said good-bye two or three times to Barttelot and Jameson and

started off on our march of 60 days through the "unknown". I started very badly, having to be carried in a hammock ...

29th Wednesday
Carried in a hammock again, am frightfully weak to-day.

1st July [1887] Friday
Away early. I am still obliged to use a hammock. The jolting is very trying and the stretcher sticks are constantly fouling in the vines on the side of the track. It is very slow work but I suppose it cannot be helped.

To-day is my 24th birthday. This time last year I was in Canada [on leave from the Royal Engineers].

We camped for the night in the bush and made a *boma* round the whole camp. The usual method of marching is as follows: advance guard under Stanley of 40 proceeds at the head of the column; each man has a bill-hook and these men cut the track and clear away natives under the direct orders of Stanley. Next comes the remainder of Stanley's company; then my company; then Nelson's and lastly Jephson's; then a rear guard of 30 under a white man. We stop every day about 11 a.m. for 1½ hours.

◆   ◆   ◆

3rd Sunday
Carried all day. Still very weak, but I hope that the fever has left me.

4th Monday
Away 6:15. About 10 a.m. the advance guard had a brush with the natives and I believe killed two. I rode my donkey this morning for the first time. I have been carried six days in the hammock.

5th Tuesday
... Just as we were going to stop I spotted some canoes made fast to the north bank. We made for them, the natives fled and we captured thirteen canoes, loaded with *mahogo*, chairs, beds, pots and all sorts of things. This and some new huts being built made us think that the natives had just fled from some village up river. This we found afterwards to be the case. I got a very good stool, some oil, charms, spoons, etc. Sudi, one of our men, shot two natives, one through the thigh and one through both calves, breaking both leg bones.

◆   ◆   ◆

9th Saturday

... I am gradually getting stronger, going in the boat every day, but my legs and arms are still very thin and my face bones are sticking out almost through the skin. In three or four days I hope to go on with my regular work. There is plenty of corn and *mahogo* [manioc] in the village we are camped in and our men have tremendous blowouts every night. We whites have *mahogo* greens, *mahogo* cakes and corn and sometimes rice for grub, but no meat of any sort.

◆   ◆   ◆

13th Wednesday

Parke picked up another canoe. This makes five canoes and one steel boat in our river flotilla and we should take say at least 130 loads, thus making the column on the march lighter and the marches longer.

We captured a native boy trying to paddle a large canoe all by himself. He seemed to wish to be caught rather than otherwise. His story is that he was a prisoner in a village up river and he was on his way downstream to his own village when captured by us. My idea is that he is a spy and after finding out our movements he will make back to his own people and tell the news.

◆   ◆   ◆

15th Friday

Our river flotilla now numbers five canoes and one boat, enough to frighten all the natives from here to Zanzibar.

I feel much better to-day, even though one has to get strong and pick up fifteen pounds on Indian corn, *mahogo* and greens. Of course we have a little biscuit but not much.

A Soudani soldier put in chains by me for losing rifle. Ordered by Mr. Stanley to be kept so for one month.

16th Saturday

... We just got our tent pitched in time, for a heavy thunderstorm came up about 7:40 and the rain came down in torrents. Camp in a heavy rain is a pitiable sight. The men have no tents and in the bush as a rule make no shelters. Some spread their blankets over a ridge pole and keep a fire going, but most of the fires go out and the men stand about till daylight; then if we march the men are in low spirits and shirk their work or try to dump their boxes in the bush. I felt very tired about 4 p.m. but luckily I had some brandy of the doctor's and had a good strong mixture of brandy and coffee and so got on to camp feeling a new man. We feel the want of meat very much at times, as marching for eleven hours over bad tracks takes it out of one and *mahogo*, rice and greens cannot supply the place of even goat meat.

17th Sunday

I have been with the advance [guard] now for two days and can say that the work is no fun. We are on our legs sometimes for 11½ hours in wet bush and on bad grub. By evening one feels a bit played out. We have a Soudani and a Mshensi chained together. Poor beggars, they have a rough time of it with the chains and wet bush. How improvident these Zanzibari are! Why to-day they got heaps of corn, [?] and other things and on the 19th two days after they were all starving with hardly a root among the whole lot.

What I have seen of the bush here I cannot say much for. It is the same very much as the ordinary New Zealand bush, but not so bad to make one's way through. Here there are but few large trees, none worth cutting for timber. We have as yet passed through no forest proper.

Am getting much stronger but still at night I feel quite worked out, which is not generally the case.

◆   ◆   ◆

19th Tuesday

... Towards evening some men came in and reported plenty of *mahogo* about two hours up river, but the boatmen did not manage to get any where they went. We had a grand feast to-night, *mahogo* cakes, roast corn, greens, rice and a crane that Stanley shot on the river. This is not bad, taking it all round, but the absence of meat we all feel at times.

20th Wednesday

It is just six months to-day since we left England and I suppose now we are about 45 days from Emin Pasha.* We left camp early and marched on to a village about 2½ miles and halted for the day to allow the men to get *mahogo*...

After we had been in the village for a few hours, the natives commenced to come round us in their canoes. With the help of the native boy [whom] we have in chains we enticed them to a point about 100 yards above camp and then sent out a few men. These were successful in getting about a dozen chickens for us. After this the natives kept off all day for some reason or other. We got plenty of *mahogo* and greens here, but very little corn. The native tobacco is but poor stuff with very little strength in it. The sugar cane we find first rate stuff when one has nothing sweet to eat.

---

*In fact, Emin and Stanley met in April 1888, nine months after Stairs's estimate that the expedition was a mere forty-five days from Emin.

21st Thursday

We started off to-day about 7 o'clock, Stanley going with the cutters, Nelson in advance and I in rear. I tried to catch some natives by hiding 20 or 30 men in the village the column had just left. We lay in the grass without stirring or making the slightest noise for ½ an hour when four canoes made for the village and after a good look round three of them came ashore directly opposite the village. Presently three men, well armed with spears and shields, crept up to have a look about the village to find out if all was quiet. From our hiding places we watched their movements and were almost making for them when one ass of a chief of ours showed his head over the side of a hut and a native being quite close poised himself for throwing his spear. This fool immediately got in a terrible funk and commenced to yell for help. Of course the other two Washenzi heard the noise and made for the river like lightning. We dashed after them but they dived into the river along with a lot of other natives who had just come up and we lost them. We had a few pot shots at them in the water, but our object was to catch men to derive information from them about the country ahead and not to kill. One or two men who could tell us how far from the river the bush extends, what sort of country lies ahead, etc. would be invaluable.

Two of our men who went out early yesterday to get *mahogo* had not returned to camp when we left this morning ... They both had their rifles with them, poor chaps, but probably had put them down on the ground to pluck the roots and were stabbed from behind by the natives who watch our every movement. This will be a lesson to the other Zanzibari who in future will go for food in bands of six or seven and thus run less chance of being surprised ...

◆   ◆   ◆

25th Monday

... We marched on after crossing the river and thank heavens struck a large village about 5 o'clock (rear guard) and seized the huts. It is ever so much more comfortable camping in these villages than in the bush, one has a good hut to oneself and there is plenty of room to move about, dry firewood is in plenty and the *mahogo* fields and banana plantations near at hand. Directly opposite to us is a long island with numerous villages and plantain groves. The men also say that they can see lots of Indian corn. If so, I wish we could get some. Stanley tells me he intends staying here to-morrow to allow the men to get food ...

◆   ◆   ◆

30th Saturday
Stayed in camp. The natives began to come to sell corn, *mahogo* and fowls ... Very soon the prices ran up and they asked 1 *matako* [brass wire] for three [cobs of] Indian corn and soon after three and four *matakos* for one fowl. This of course we could not give. The men were giving clothes, buttons, empty cartridge cases, knives, anything to get food.

Stanley went up river in the boat to have a look about and came down to camp shortly after 11 a.m. Stanley made a plan to seize one of the natives, which was that ten men should offer cloth, beads, etc. to the natives and entice a canoe in and then grasp five or six healthy individuals and make them prisoners. The plan succeeded in that one man was caught. This fellow I put in chains almost at once and Stanley succeeded in getting a lot of information out of him. As soon as the men seized this unfortunate, all the natives commenced to yell with funk and rage and paddled about close to our camp for half a minute or so. All of a sudden Stanley fired a shot into the air, when like lightning, every man, woman and child dived into the water and swam off in every direction down stream like so many wild ducks. Besides the native, we captured two canoes. The specimens we have caught so far are very fine looking men of 5'8" or so in height, say, well shaped and with powerful muscles in the arms and back developed by the use of the paddle.

The bush to-day wet, cold and miserable in every way, brings back to my mind the many wet, wintry days we used to spend in the 70 Mile Bush in New Zealand. Here one's hopes are higher and mind easier than in the old days, when one could see nothing but steady, hard plodding to gain even a small pittance of success. The want of meat here too reminds me forcibly of our attempts to cook different sorts of grass and roots as something to supply the want of beef or pork. What feeds of damper [an unleavened pan bread] we used to have [in New Zealand] on rainy days in our flying camps, everything drenched with rain, blankets, clothes, tools, everything. The one small satisfaction we had was that our tobacco was dry and good and that we could smoke as much as we liked.

31st Sunday
... During the firing yesterday, some five or six natives were disabled and three killed ...

♦   ♦   ♦

2nd August [1887] Tuesday
One of Jephson's men died this morning and was buried near the camp.

Stanley went on in the boat and we caught him by lunch time ... In the afternoon he went on far ahead of us and do all we could we were left far behind. Parke was leading and kept us on the move till 6:30. We then had to stop in the bush all night without tents or boxes. Luckily, some of us had blankets. These we shared and getting a fire started we made some soup out of a soup tablet we had with us and then turned in. We were twelve hours to-day on the march, this through thick bush with very bad tracks is quite enough for most fellows ...

3rd Wednesday

Away early and soon caught up to Stanley and Parke in advance. I had a slight attack of fever and had a rough time of it getting along. We made camp about 4:30 and on nearing it were welcomed with the news that the boat had captured *two goats*. Just fancy how pleased we must have been, gentle stranger, after marching long, rough marches for thirty days without one mouthful of meat to at last sit down to a chop and some soup! Ah, those who have not been without meat for a month on hard work cannot know what its absence means. To-day we are smiles and full of hope. Yesterday we were grumpy, surly and despondent. This all on account of the gentle goat.

Two of Jephson's men strayed away from camp yesterday. They came in this evening and got 180 each with good sticks. This is the only way to prevent our men straying away and getting killed by the natives. We lost the rifles. In this country our rifles are our lives. Our camp is opposite a large village. This we looted but only got a little corn and some odds and ends.

4th Thursday

A day of accidents. Soon after the flotilla and column had started, my double canoe upset in 12' of very swift water. Some 15 rifles, 15 boxes of ammunition, 5 boxes of cowries, 3 of beads and a lot of sundries went to the bottom. We rigged up a canoe, got what good divers we could collect (as the column was far in advance of the canoe before we could do anything) and started to work. Hassan, a Somali boy, did splendidly. We tied a rope around his waist and he took another under water with him. This one he tied to the boxes. The men in the canoe then pulled him up and afterwards the box he had secured. It was perfectly astonishing to see the way he worked under water in such a swift current ...

◆   ◆   ◆

6th Saturday

... Stanley went away up river ... in the boat and was away three-hours. He saw two villages, both on islands, but got nothing. All the natives had fled as usual, taking everything with them. Nelson took 50 men from his company. I gave him 50 or more and Parke took a hundred. They went out in different directions to look for food, but only got some *mahoga* and wild fruit. Our men will starve soon, if food does not turn up ...

As usual in the evening, I placed the sentries for the camp and we all gathered then round our fire and yarned till pretty late on in the night. How at times we prospect [*sic*] as to what is going on at home, where our people are and if any of them are dead and so on.

Arguments we of course have and many. Parke sweeps the tray for sheer bullheadedness, though Jephson pushes him closely. What surpasses everything though is the way in which we quarrel with the cooks. They are the greatest blackguards one could find anywhere ... the head cook knows little enough about cooking; all the under sweeps [*sic*] fight him, we fight him, while he lies and grows fat on our miserable pittance of food. Truly cooks are strange animals!

7th Sunday

... I wonder what they are doing at home now. Playing tennis, drinking gallons of tea and eating cakes by the score as usual, I should say. Now is the season for the wily sea trout in the streams of Nova Scotia and New Brunswick. Many a fisherman will now be driving out to some farmer's house away by the side of a sparkling stream as happy as the day is long, and dreaming as he drives along of the many fish he has taken out of such-and-such a pool he passed by on the roadside. Oh, those are the times one feels oneself, nothing to think of but your rod and gear, with a good chap beside you of kindred spirit, yarning of old times and the different places you have fished over together. Gentle angler, there's nothing like being far away in the quiet bush beside a stream in which you know there are good fish. Upon my word, I would sooner be back far away in the Nova Scotia bush, camping out and trout fishing, than engaged in any single sport or pleasure I know of. Look at the happy days ... I have spent at the Sambro Lakes, at Preston, at the Magdalen Islands, Musquodoboit and scores of other places, why they are the best days of one's life and ones we all will look back on with feelings of pleasure as long as we live. Well, enough of this, back to Africa and the gentle twistings of the Aruwimi and to our friends the Zanzibaris and Somalis.

♦   ♦   ♦

9th Tuesday

... There is very little food close at hand though to-morrow we hope to be able to get *mahogo* for the men and ourselves. *Mahogo* is the staple food of the natives all along this river [the Aruwimi] and the Congo, with us it means everything; if we strike plenty of *mahogo* our men feed up and march well; if we get none for five or six days they go down at once ...

The *rugga rugga* [raiders or marauders who were sent out to seize food or anything else that they could find], while passing through a clearing to-day, fired on some natives and killed one, a man of say thirty years of age.

A goat strayed away from camp this afternoon and men were sent to search for it. These men found the goat with its head cut off and three Zanzibaris preparing for a feast. They were brought up before Stanley and got a very heavy dose of the rod.

10th Wednesday
... To-day gives one a good idea as to what life in an African village is like. The burning hot sun shooting down its rays into every nook and corner forces all indoors; some talk and smoke; some and mostly all, sleep away the hottest hours. On one side I hear the squalling of the baby of the captured woman, on the other, the infernal, incessant bleating of a nanny goat. All life, except that of insects, seems to be at a standstill outside the village. The very wind has gone down to allow the sun to work up to its full blast. The birds have all gone to seek the shades of some favourite tree. Everything is hushed. One often feels how dependent on our rifles we are at present, 1,700 or 1,800 miles up from the west coast, 1,300 from the east and right in Central Africa, with 1,000 miles of bush on one side and the almost unknown on the other, a chap feels that rifles will play a very important part in the future. So far they have got us all our food, canoes and allowed us to get where we are. The bush buffalo is evidently to be found here, as in the huts we have found a great many boleros [sic] used by the natives for catching them. They must sneak up to a beast in the bush and in some way or other throw this affair over the head or horns. There are elephants in any number quite close to the village, but our column makes so much noise that they all get scared and we never get a shot.

◆   ◆   ◆

12th Friday
Parke took 100 men and I took 90 more and started off to scour the country for food ... I ... struck away to the eastward of a large track while he went straight on. We got plenty of bananas, a little sugar cane, some melons and tobacco. Go where we could, we failed to find any traces of *mahogo*. The old woman our guide has turned out to be a liar. Parke threatened to cut her throat and give her to the men to eat. She was terribly frightened at this and then took them to a very good banana plantation. Parke got back to camp about 3 o'clock and I came in an hour later. Stanley reached the camp about 9 o'clock this morning and said that they had to pass 13 rapids and had come 12 miles by water since yesterday.

On nearing camp we passed on the track the body of ... one of my men who had evidently been foully murdered. The doctor brought on the body to camp where we buried it. This murder has caused a great stir in the camp, all the men are keen on finding out the murderer. Stanley offers $100 reward for any evidence which will convict the murderer.

Another of my men failed to turn up in camp this evening. He was seen last on the march yesterday and complained of dysentery. This makes another gun lost to me ... One of the Soudanese soldiers was lost on the march yesterday. He has not turned up as yet and most probably has been caught and cooked by the natives. We left a sick man of Jephson's company in a hut ... He was wasted away to nothing and would probably die in an hour or so.

The pumpkins we got were quite small ones, but very good eating.

13th Saturday
Left camp about 7 a.m. with the object of making a large village some four miles ahead. I was leading in place of Jephson who has a bad foot. On nearing the village we met some Washenzi, [the local tribe] one of whom we shot.

After we had settled down in camp and made ourselves comfortable, Stanley sent off some men to search for food. While crossing a small river near the village (in the boat) these men were attacked by a large mob of natives armed with spears and bows and arrows. At once our men opened fire, but the natives stood. Hearing the noise, I rushed down with my rifle to try a shot or two. The arrows were being rained down on us, we dodging them behind trees and the boat. I had fired two shots, the second of which killed a man, when I was struck in the chest with a poisoned arrow, the arrow breaking and leaving about one inch of the point inside. The wound is just below my heart. The doctor says no vital spot has been touched, but perhaps the tip had entered the pleura. The sensation at first was as that of a knife being stuck into one, shortly afterwards my side stiffened and acute shooting pains set in my back and sides. Of the evening, under morphia and opium, I remember nothing.*

---

*Both Jephson and Parke were deeply concerned about Stairs's chances of recovery. Jephson recorded that "The doctor hopes to pull Stairs through, but it is bad that the arrow head is still in the wound and he dare not probe for it as it is so near the heart" (*The Diary* of, p.136). Parke was more clinical in his description than was Jephson, but he was no less concerned about the effect of a poisoned arrow. "I found a puncture wound on the left side of the front of his chest ... close to the apex of the heart. Just as he was hit, he had struck the arrow with his arm, this had the effect of breaking it off in the wound, leaving a couple of inches within the chest, and well concealed behind the rib ... Accordingly, I could not reach the broken fragment with the probe, and I considered cutting down and hunting about for it as — under the circumstances — unjustifiable surgery. As the arrow was a poisoned one, I regarded suction of the wound as offering the best and only chance of his life ... Acting on the idea, I at once sucked the edges of the wound; till I felt sure that I had extracted the greater part, if not the whole, of the adherent poison ... He was now very faint ... In the evening he had a severe attack of intermittent fever ..." (*My Personal Experiences*, p. 91).

14th Sunday

... Once more I am travelling by river, this time in the big canoe. My wound is very painful to-day. Last night I got no sleep at all, owing to the shooting pains running through my back and chest. In the fight this morning and that of yesterday our men killed some 15 natives. We in turn had about five wounded with poisoned arrows, some of them bad cases.

The natives here have shown unusual pluck even after they had learnt the hurtful power of our rifles. At first, at the time I got hit, they stood up in the open glade, fired their arrows and then would dart like lightning behind some bush or tree and then again emerge, each time taking deliberate aim at us and being exposed to our fire, every minute growing hotter. Gradually, however, they learnt, as man after man was wounded, that the rifles hurt as well as spoke and so grew more careful in their movements.

15th Monday

All the afternoon we were anxiously looking out for the erring ones, but by night they had not turned up. What can be the matter? Have they lost themselves? Have they had a fight with the natives and got scattered? Or where in the mischief are they? This is what Stanley and I said to each other as we talked things over in the evening. Our sick (of course the very worst ones as they are carried in the canoes) are getting worse, the wounded men commence to experience agonies as the deadly poison from the arrow-tips works its way through their systems, one or two with bad ulcers are doomed, I'm very much afraid, to early deaths.

Across the river from our camp is a large village hidden from us by thick trees, but well marked and easily located by the infernal yells and horns of the savage inmates ...

One of my men, a lunatic wasted away to nothing, died this morning.

16th Tuesday

We are getting anxious of our sick and I certainly am of myself. I am no better. We have no medicines of any sort and the doctor is far away, meandering about in the bush somewhere within six or seven miles of us. Last night I sat up in a chair most of the time and did not get one single wink of sleep, the pain is at times frightful.*

---

*Parke remained uneasy about his patient, a concern not lessened by Stairs's evident dislike of being regarded as ill: "he has the greatest loathing of being looked upon or treated as an invalid ..." (*My Personal Experiences*, p.94).

17th Wednesday

Five men were sent up river to explore and were attacked, but killing five Washenzi, the rest ran off. One native was posted in a tree with his bow and arrows. This man was shot and fell to earth.

I am a little better to-day though I got no sleep last night at all and had to sit up nearly all night. Our other wounded are rapidly getting worse, spasms coming on.

[Our] men killed three natives to-day.

18th Thursday

... To-day the two men in camp who were wounded with poisoned arrows are rapidly getting worse, the spasms are growing more frequent and of longer duration. Their agonies are frightful. One suffers from lockjaw. One of them was wounded as far back as the 11th. Stanley administered 20 grains of chloral and ¼ grain morphia (in injection). Even this would not quiet the man.

19th Friday

The two wounded died to-day in terrible agony. Truly these poisoned arrows are the most miserably, despicable missiles ever thrown against an enemy. I am getting very anxious now about my wound, the poisoned arrow is buried away in my chest and I have no way of treating the wound. Then seeing these poor chaps die in convulsions quite close to one makes one feel a dread of the same thing happening to oneself ...

20th Saturday

... Late in the evening Jephson came up to camp in the boat. He and Stanley at once had a long talk, Jephson getting the slating he deserved. He is a most stupidly conceited chap, most bull-headed and probably in a few days will be as bad as ever, though this has been rather a check to him.

21st Sunday

... About 10 the doctor turned up, a most welcome sight. He at once commenced work on my wound, probed, got a sight of the arrow, and though he cut the hole much larger failed to get out the arrowhead, still his presence relieves one ...

The men appear very much worn out though not hungry. Three have died and been killed on this erratic march. One of Nelson's men died to-day in camp of dysentery ...

22nd Monday

I am getting better slowly but still am very stiff.

23rd Tuesday

... To-day I walked with the column as the rapids were bad and the distance short. I did not feel much the worse for it, though one got several bad wrenches. At the halting place, a large clearing was made for the men to fall in and allow us to count our healthy and sick ones and examine loads, etc. ...

For the last four meals we officers have lived on five green bananas apiece per meal. Gentle stranger, don't imagine when I speak of bananas that they are the luscious yellow things one finds at home and other places. Oh no, they are small, green wizened things 40 of which would make a square meal for a man. These we roast on hot coals and wash down with weak tea or coffee. They are, at the best, but poor things to work on. I sent out a man to get bananas and shortly afterwards he returned with 30 or 40 small things.

We have now been 56 days out from Yambuya and are about half way. On parade to-day I had 14 men incapable of carrying loads.

24th Wednesday

... on the 22nd my donkey, which had wasted away to skin and bones, fell down and died on the march. This is a great blow to me just coming as it does when he will soon be needed. Want of sustaining food was the cause. He was a Muscat donkey and would not take kindly to eating bush as the Zanzibar beasts do.

All the canoes and boat got safely over the rapids and reached camp by dark. The river here is changing from day to day. The cataracts are becoming more numerous and one notices the decrease of volume. We can see no traces of hippo or crocodiles, in fact no life seems to exist here at all, the sole food of the natives appears to be bananas.

25th Thursday

... My wound, I'm afraid, is closing up at the surface and the arrowhead, which is 1¼ inches long, will probably remain inside. This is a very bad piece of luck altogether.

◆   ◆   ◆

27th Saturday

Stayed in camp all day. Luckily we got a fine, bright, sunny day of it, allowing us to dry all our clothes again. One's things are all mildewed from being so long in the damp bush. I cleaned the Maxim gun up thoroughly and fired some 20 or 30 rounds at some howling natives on the opposite bank ... They dispersed at once amidst yells ... This long dreary bush march now of nearly two months' duration, day after day through rivers by scores and with food in scanty supply, is taking the very lives out of the men. One notices that every day the number of sick men becomes greater and very few who get in poor condition really, rarely survive. A few days' halt does wonders, especially so if the halt is in a village, for there the men have a roof over their heads at night, food and firewood are near and their general comfort is much greater than in a wet bush camp. One wet, cold night in the bush takes it out of the men far more than a heavy day's march. The number of men with bad ulcers on their feet is astonishing. Why, I have 83 men in my company and I should say quite 35 of these have bad feet. Five of my company have died or been lost since leaving Yambuya.

... Late in the afternoon, some men carried into camp ... a very nice little chap ... with a terrible wound in the foot caused by a bullet from a Winchester rifle some fellow had fired, accidentally or otherwise. All the ankle and foot bones were crushed to pieces. Parke found it necessary to amputate at the ankle joint. Poor chap, it must be a terrible blow to him ...

28th Sunday
... Nelson and I had only our wet rubber sheets and clothes to sleep in and I in addition a wet blanket. However, we ... somehow or other eked out the night ...

Our food now consists solely of bananas, cooked in different ways. The nicest way to my fancy is to roast them on hot coals, though done this way they are not so good for one as those boiled. One eats eight or nine for each meal and then feels very much like a football afterwards. The absence of meat is more serious than most people would imagine ...

29th Monday
... While moving up the river a canoe with a single native in it shot out of a small creek and paddled down towards the boat. In an instant this fellow saw his mistake, but it was too late and Stanley made an attempt to capture him. However, he seized his paddle and tried to make off; the boat nearing, he dived, but not before he got a ball through the back. In the canoe the men found a bow and 12 newly poisoned arrows, any one of which would be sufficient to put an end to a man in 48 hours.

Miserable, contemptible bushmen, lowest form of man, the only weapon you can devise is one which inflicts a protracted, agonizing though certain death. You have made yourselves our enemy, so look out!

30th Tuesday
Struck camp and sent the column off by 6:45. We had to wait till the fog lifted off the river a bit before starting and finally got off by 7:30. Jephson was in advance, Parke in rear. Nelson's donkey to-day is looking very poorly. It is suffering from the same skin disease as the others had, brought on most probably by the want of sustaining food. I am very much afraid it will succumb in a few days. The River since we left the Nepoko now averages only 325 or 350 yards broad, though swifter on the whole than before.

31st Wednesday

... My wound is much better but still I can do no work and have a deadly pain at times under my ribs ...

1st September [1887] Thursday

... At 11 a.m. we stopped at the foot of a bad rapid and here Stanley decided to take the boat out of the water and travel overland, for what distance I do not know, or whether he will abandon the river for good or not. However, I expect his actions will depend on the nature of the river above this ...

I was at work all day, the first work I have done since the 14th August ... Jephson was busy taking the boat to pieces. Nelson was so seedy that he could do nothing. We took all the rifles from the men, as a precaution against desertion. All of us are more or less seedy at present. I fancy the banana has a great deal to do with it ...

2nd Friday

... I was at work all morning on the ammunition boxes, Jephson on the boat. Stanley was taken ill last night, but this morning was much better. He suffered from the same trouble as we did, viz. diarrhoea. Parke feels very seedy, his temperature was 104° to-day ...

Late in the evening the *rugga rugga* (who were sent out last night to capture the deserters) returned, having seen nothing of the men. At night the whole four of us suffered from the effects of either bad water or improperly cooked banana.

3rd Saturday

... Our men are generally getting very low spirited, already within the last few days we have lost eleven men through supposed desertion. Stanley has had all the Munipara up and given them long dissertations and otherwise we have adopted every possible precaution ... I have put no less than five men in chains, some of them attempted deserters and other men who threw down their loads.

4th Sunday

Had all hands up early, separated the effectives from the non- and extracted the hammers from all non-effective men's rifles ... The discontented feeling is growing among the men. No wonder, bad food, heavy loads and then the long, dreary marches through the bush, the men doubting greatly that we shall ever get out of the bush. Placed another of my men in chains this evening for attempted desertion. He is rather a poor sort of chap and not the man one would imagine a deserter.

5th Monday
... The Somalis have broken down altogether; two are carried every day in the canoes and the others can barely get along from day to day. The Soudanese are very little better. They suffer very much from [skin] ulcers.

Chapter Five

By the end of its second month in the Ituri rain forest, the advance column was gradually disintegrating. It began to starve. In their increasingly debilitated condition, the men were yet more susceptible to disease.

Back at Yambuya the rear column was in almost equally unhappy circumstances. Jameson wrote despondently to his wife on 6 August 1887, "I do hope Tippu-Tib's people [i.e., the six hundred porters] will come soon, and then we shall be able to start for the Lakes at once, and save some months. Had the wonderful fleet of steamers of the King of the Belgians, which Stanley spoke about before leaving England, really existed, we could all have gone on to the Lake at one time, and saved six weary months, which have been added on to this trip."[1]

7th Wednesday

... My wound apparently is going to heal up altogether and leave the arrowhead inside. Parke thinks now there is no chance of it ever coming out.

The way in which we are fed and looked after in this Expedition is simply disgraceful. Stanley does not care a jot about our food as long as he is well fed. He never by any chance interests himself in his officers' behalf in any way. We come in wet after a long march as yesterday and have then to pitch our tents perhaps in the dark and rain, when all this time his men have been in camp, having come by river.

We were told in London that we should each have a canteen and candles at night. All nonsense and lies. Only one canteen large enough for three men was brought and one has great difficulties in getting a frying pan or pot out of this as over one-half of the utensils are used exclusively for Stanley. One never has a candle at night; for two months we have had just the light of a fire to sit by and smoke before turning in. Stanley has taken all the candles for his own tent. Why there was not enough of European provisions to last five men nine months. More fuss has been made about these too, than the hanged things are worth. Fancy one lb. tin of arrowroot being brought for the use of six people for six months!

The Committee of this Expedition ought to be deuced well slated for allowing provisions for six Europeans to be sent out and then ten people coming with their knowledge, and then not obtaining more at the Cape or on the Congo. Stanley, however, is far more to blame as he was far better aware of the state of affairs.

... We passed through three small villages out of which the natives had decamped for some days. They were of the usual style, each hut encased in paling *bomas*. Nelson and I got some goodish tobacco close to one of the villages, but the average tobacco here is not worth curing. Nelson has finished all his English tobacco and now resorts to green native and biscuit paper for cigarettes ...

... one of my men, whom the rear guard had to carry yesterday, died this morning. He had one of the worst ulcers in his ankle I ever saw. He had two others on other parts of his body and had wasted away to nothing ... another one of my men failed to turn up last night. I am afraid he must have strayed off the path, intending to come on afterwards to camp and then lost himself or else became too weak to come on to camp ...

◆   ◆   ◆

11th Sunday
Sent off eighty men to bring up the boat and some cutters to widen the track for her. Stanley rode his donkey back with the men to the canoes. We have decided to abandon the canoes here altogether and try for others above the rapids. I cut a track from camp down to the river and made a place there for putting the boat together ...

... The boat reached here by 10:15 this morning and was launched by 12:30. About one o'clock, Stanley went upstream to have a look at the rapid ahead. He says he thinks it possible to get the boat over by water. The second rapid of yesterday was the most imposing one we have yet seen. A huge mass of water simply tumbles down between two masses of rock on either side; when half way down this slope, the water strikes against a central boulder and shoots up into the air and is divided into two rearing streams. The gorge where the water rushes down would be only about 80 yards wide, I should say, whereas immediately above this, the river is quite 450 yards wide ...

12th Monday

We started off as usual but much later owing to an inspection of the sick by Stanley. I started from Yambuya with a company 88 strong. This morning I had 49 men capable of carrying loads, nine men having died or been lost. The other companies have suffered equally badly.

I left in camp [two of my men] and one of Jephson's men. We could not possibly take them in as already the list of men being carried by the rear-guard is swelling visibly. They had all wasted away to nothing from the effect of different diseases. We had been carrying them for some days and there was no room in the boat or canoes. This was my only course. Poor chaps, they will be all chewed up by the natives before nightfall ...

... While Stanley was coming up river they saw an elephant close to the left bank and fired at him. The elephant turned and waded across the river, here about six feet deep all over. All this time Stanley poured bullet after bullet into him but the beast managed to crawl up the other bank and in spite of a long search the men could not find him.

One of Nelson's men made off yesterday with a box of ammunition ...

13th Tuesday

I was leading again to-day and got off by 6:30. Parke took the rear-guard. We made good progress and kept up with the boat and canoes. They, however, had two rapids to get over ...

... made camp at 2:30. While we were clearing a place for camp a Washenzi canoe sailed quietly by without seeing anything of us. All kept silent for a few seconds, till Stanley and I opened fire with our Winchesters. We each killed one and wounded two others. There is some satisfaction now in shooting one of these chaps after getting plugged by one of them.

◆   ◆   ◆

16th Friday

Last night the rain came down in torrents for hours, flooding up every hole and cranny the water could find for itself. Nelson's and my tent was on the path in a hole. About midnight I was awakened by Nelson wandering about the tent in the dark in 24 inches of water and then found everything was floating about in the tent and the water within 2 inches of my bed. Luckily the water soon stopped rising and we just waited patiently till daylight to collect our scattered things. My watch was under water all night and is done for completely. My aneroid is very sick and two compasses refuse to turn on the pivots at all. Every book, knife, all my small things and clothes have been soaked.

We are now 141 geographical miles from the point on the Lake [Albert Nyanza] that Stanley intends striking. Our latitude is 1° 24' North and we want to make 1° 22' on the Lake ...

I was rearguard to-day and had fever all the time, sitting down now and then to get up strength again to go on. This fever is a frightful thing to take it out of one. One is strong and active say in the morning and by night you may have to be lifted into bed almost senseless ...

17th Saturday

Made an early start, Parke leading. Had a fairish track in the morning but bad towards afternoon. About 3 the rear guard came up to a fairly large river of say 40 yards wide ...

Here we could hear the sound of much firing a short distance ahead and on coming up to the noise found it was a detachment of Arabs in our camp having a parley with Stanley. We had a long pow-wow of two hours or so and found out a great deal of the country we should have to go through ahead. The name of the chief is Ugarrowwa;* his camp is one day up river. Here he has about 50 guns and a good number of women ... The chief presented Stanley with 3 goats, 20 lbs. of rice grown up river, 6 fowls and a lot of very fine, ripe plantains. He went off to his camp in a very fine canoe, amidst the beating of drums, singing of women, blowing of horns and the excited yells of his fat followers. Everyone seemed pleased and we had rice for dinner and turned in well pleased.

From this fellow we learned that another detachment of Arabs had occupied a village permanently some four or five days up river and were occupied in getting ivory and improving this village as a standing camp. Twenty days farther ahead of this, was stationed a very large body of men [another Arab camp] with 600 guns and rich supply of cloths and goods. This party is on the edge of the bush and grass country and game abounds in plenty, so we should be right for food when we get there. If Ugarrowwa speaks truly, then in 30 days we should once more see green grass and breathe fresh air after (by then) over 100 days almost what may be called imprisonment in the bush. Reached spot opposite Ugarrowwa's camp.

18th Sunday

Fell all the men in early, weeded out the sick, took away their guns and prepared them for deposit at the Arab village.

Stanley paid a state visit to Ugarrowwa land. William [Hoffman, Stanley's servant] presented a clock later on. Everyone seemed delighted, except myself.

---

*The real name of "Ugarrowwa" was Uledi Balyuz. A Zanzibari, he had been employed by Speke and Grant as a tent boy on their expedition of 1860-63.

After some work on repairing boxes, I put up my Maxim gun and got her ready for the formal visit Ugarrowwa was to pay us in the afternoon.

About 12, just as we were having breakfast, we were startled by a loud report and then all of a sudden the Arabs burst forth from their village, letting off guns, beating drums and yelling like fiends. Presently the canoes stopped and the women commenced a very pretty chant keeping it up till they reached our landing place. Ugarrowwa then led the way to Stanley's tent and a long palaver ensued. They all then came down to where I had the gun mounted on the river side and I fired 150 or 175 rounds off for their edification. (By the bye, I used both Arsenal C Gardner .45 and Maxim .45 cartridges, keeping the sights of the gun at 700 yards. The superiority of the Maxim over the Woolwich ammunition was very much marked.) I used two belts and find the newest kind, viz., that with prolonged clip, to be the best. This also I found to be the case on the Congo. The old chief seemed very much pleased with the whir of the bullets and the numerous splashes in the water. He departed to his village happy.

Ugarrowwa was once a ... porter on Speke and Grant's expedition up from [Lake] Tanganika [sic] to [Lake] Victoria Nyanza. He is a great admirer of Speke and says he was one of the finest hunters he ever met. He [Ugarrowwa] has the reputation of being very cruel, but most probably this is what has made him what he is at present. He can now muster 300 guns, I believe, and is gradually working his way up to become some day a white bearded old father whose name will be well known over all Central Africa.

In the afternoon I took over to the village the 56 sick men we are leaving behind us. I had a palaver with Ugarrowwa again, shook hands all round and started back to camp. I left at the village 5 Somalis, 5 Soudanese, 46 Zanzibaris.

What a great relief this getting rid of the sick will be to us. All the old crawlers with rotten limbs who took six hours to do a two hours' march are gone; those *goe-goes* who were the curse day by day of the rear guard are in peace and will not feel the ... stick for some time and lastly those whom the canoe men have cursed at so loudly and longly, those absolutely unable to crawl. have found a resting place for their weary bodies. Thank heavens, we who toil along day by day through rivers, swamps and mud, will have a little work thrown off our shoulders, and perhaps the column will make better marches to the promised land, "the grass country".

19th Monday
... The Arabs paddled 1½ miles up river and said good-bye to Stanley there. Three of our men ran away to-day, went back to camp, were caught by the Arabs, got 50 each, were brought on to us and I made them fast to a tree for the night ... Desertions have been so numerous and threats of death so common, that if anything is done to these fellows it will be the rope.

20th Tuesday

All were fallen in a hollow square. The three condemned men were brought out and Stanley addressed the men, telling them he would hang one man to-day, one to-morrow and one next day. The men then drew lots and Mabruki's lot was cast for to-day. Accordingly he was tied up and run up with the help of the prisoners in charge and died without a struggle in 2 or 3 minutes. This is the first execution we have had. The example will prove of great value in preventing further desertions. All the chiefs agreed that it was good and of use. This finished, we all started off ... I made the remaining two deserters fast to trees for the night, placed the sentries and turned in.

We had a violent thunderstorm toward evening, making us uncomfortable and the men wretched in their miserable shelters.

21st Wednesday

Osemi, one of the doomed men, escaped during the night. I at once put the soldier in charge of the men under guard and tied him to a tree. We all fell in again. Mohandu, the other man, was brought out, tied, and the rope made fast round his neck. The men were all ready to hoist away when Stanley started away on a fiery speech, treating of the great number of desertions that had taken place, of the many times he had threatened to shoot men for losing loads and of the great importance it would be to us to have a large body of men to repel attacks in the open country.

"I have come here not to lose men and ammunition, but am sent by one Queen [Victoria] and two Kings [Leopold of the Belgians and presumably the Khedive of Egypt] to rescue the Muzungu. Don't think I'm afraid to go on, even if you desert me – Said Bargash [the Sultan of Zanzibar], and the Sultan [sic] of Egypt will say I have done well to kill this man" and so on. The Muniapara then went in a body and asked him to forgive the wretched man. Stanley then spoke a bit longer and then ordered the ropes to be cut. I'll bet this was the nearest shave that Mohandu ever had ...

By the last week of September 1887 the advance column was starving. In the rain forest, it could not live off the land. Despair was increasingly evident. Stanley recorded:

To add to our desperate state, several of our followers who had not sickened, lost heart, became mad with hunger and wild forebodings ... Even the white man does not endure hunger patiently. It is a thing he never forgives ... When hunger begins to gnaw at his stomach, the nature of the animal comes out ... Despite education and breeding, the white man is seldom more than twenty-four hours ahead of his black brother and barely one hundred hours in advance of the cannibal ... He will never be so civilised as to be independent of his stomach; so it must be understood that we also exhibited our weakness during that trying period ... [2]

"Trying period" is a major understatement. The advance column was literally dying of starvation as it pushed its way through the rain forest where the natives destroyed their food rather than let it fall into the hands of the invaders. Stanley's servant Hoffman later recalled vividly the wretchedness of the column. "Many a time, wracked with hunger and with scarcely enough strength left to stumble along, we would come upon a village clearing, only to find it abandoned and its store of food in ashes. And the long weary trek would begin again."[3]

24th Saturday

To-day I started with this book on account of the old one's dilapidated condition, three times both books having been underwater in my tin box, which is utterly useless as far as keeping out water goes. One did not realize in England what an amount there would be to write about, and consequently one did not bring enough blank books as diaries. This book is my old surveying and astronomy note book at the Royal Engineers' depot at Chatham.

To-day we fell in as usual but did not march. Almost all the men were sent back to a banana plantation some two miles away to get bananas – poor chaps, they need them. The canoe crew and boatmen we kept at work getting their canoes over or around the rapid. Stanley started by cutting a track round the rapid and making a rough survey of the channels.

The fall of the rapid from top to bottom must be quite 40 ft., and this say in half a mile; a small rocky island lies in the centre, dividing the water into two large channels. On each side of this the water tosses and tumbles in all directions, making a very pretty sight; this is about a quarter of a mile from our camp.

Gradually a few of our men are getting weak and exhausted again even after the recent weeding out they got at the Arab village a few days back. Ulcers on the ankle bones soon take it out of the men. To add to this there is always the trouble and uncertainty of getting food. Men suffering from dysentery, of course, rarely get better, as there is no proper means of treatment provided. The coarse, rough food soon acts on their raw stomachs and does for them.

Jephson and Stanley, who had been cutting the track for the boat and canoes returned to camp about 10:30, having had an easy job, as they found the Washenzi had been taking canoes over from time to time and so had formed a track over which our boat should pass easily. From top to bottom the rapid is three-quarters of a mile long, average width about 250 yds. Jephson started taking the boat to pieces about 1 o'clock, going up river some little distance to do it. We are now about 112 geographical miles from Kavalli on [Lake] Albert Nyanza.

... Towards evening the men began to turn up with small loads of very bad bananas, really nothing to speak of; they will have to work the canoes over the rapids to-morrow on empty stomachs. Had our dinner of a little rice and wretched bananas and turned in hungry.

25th Sunday

... As we were pitching our tents, ... the *rugga rugga* went far ahead to try to see if there were any signs of the Arabs we should now be nearing: they came back, however, and told us that they could see nothing of them but I believe saw plenty of fresh cuts on trees and other signs of their presence.

Some fate seems to be against our getting on; obstacle after obstacle comes in our way. First it is the almost total absence of food, next it is the rapids, then perhaps bad rivers to cross and masses of densely tangled brush to carve our way through. What is it that is acting against us? People in England no doubt are now supposing that we have long since arrived at the Lake, relieved Emin Pasha perhaps, and started to take him out to the east coast. Why, even Stanley himself thought we should arrive in Wadelai by the 16th of July, and gave his thoughts expression in London before starting; but look how it actually is. We have taken ninety odd days to get here, and have still 35 days marching to do, supposing we strike open country in 20 days as we hope; this would bring us up to the end of October.

According to all Arab reports, we are still some 15 days' march from the edge of the bush. From this ahead there are five days of bad marching through some sort of cane brush, then we are told we are to reach grassy, open, rolling country abounding with game of all sorts; may these reports be true is the prayer of us all ...

26th Monday

... Everything looked rosy for a long march, and "push ahead" was Stanley's last word as he left camp. After one hour's marching, however, we received a severe check in the shape of a bad series of rapids. We had to take the loads out of the canoes and the boat and carry them across some distance. By ten we had passed the first rapid and embarked all the loads again. Here luckily one of the men killed a guinea fowl, which we at once put in a pot and had our breakfast off of it. The flotilla went on gaily, but in twenty minutes or so had to stop again and disembark its load once more. Jephson had been sent on by Stanley to this rapid to stop the column and make the men carry the loads to camp and return for more. The *rugga rugga*, however, under Baruku, instead of following Jephson's blazed trail along the bank of the river, struck out in another direction with the column following close on their heels; the result of course was that Jephson was left waiting a long time at the rapids while all the spare men were sailing gaily onwards up the river. The mistake lay altogether with Baruku, and as usual he lied to Stanley and said Jephson had lost his way, whereas in reality Jephson had kept close to the river's edge and Baruku had disobeyed his orders in not doing the same.

Stanley went on by land and camped about one mile and a half above this rapid. Parke and Nelson stayed with the loads, the canoes went on empty. I remained at a point half way between camp and the loads, and all tried hard to get them on to camp. Stanley and Jephson (who had a bad fever) kept sending the men back from camp as fast as they could, I passed them on to Parke who loaded them up and sent them on to camp. Hunger played the very mischief with the men; they would leave camp, work along the track a bit and then strike off into the bush to look for bush fruits. Thus we were prevented from getting the loads on in spite of every exertion. We white men were starving also, having had absolutely nothing to eat except now and then a bit of coarse, tasteless bush fruit.

Parke and I stayed behind and by dark just managed to get up all the loads to camp. On the way up I received an order from Stanley to release the prisoner Mahara from his chains. Poor chap, he is a goner, I'm afraid.

Opposite to camp was a small banana plantation – it was just possible that there might be bananas there so some men were sent over – it was a last chance, as if there was nothing to be got we should have to go on tomorrow with not one mouthful for the men to eat. We officers would suffer also, as the wretchedly small stock of provisions we brought is exhausted and we exist on the same food exactly as the men. Luckily the men got a few small bananas and said more could be got at some distance from the river. This simply saved us, allowing us to turn in with something inside our stomachs, instead of doing so with gnawing pains and low spirits.

The river ahead looks bad, being one succession of rocky rapids. Stanley told me at night to go on in the morning with five men and have a look at the river high up, while the men would have a halt and get food. Turned in after a big blow-out of green baked bananas.

27th Tuesday

Picking five good men with bill-hooks and rifles I started off early to go up river and report on the nature of the rapids and see if any food was to be got. I told all my chaps to be quiet and only blaze a tree here and there when necessary, as we might get a shot and perhaps return amid shouts to camp with some hippo or elephant meat, and so as it afterwards turned out we nearly did.

While we were marching along quietly and quickly and had gone perhaps 1½ miles from camp, we reached a large elephant and a hippo wallowing quite close to the river. Mirabu who was behind me gave a low whistle and beckoned violently to me to look in a certain direction he pointed out. For some time I could see nothing, but gradually, high over the small scrub, the shape of a very large elephant caught my eye. There he was – the big brute – not 15 yards off from the track we had just passed over, standing perfectly still and watching every movement we made. I had only my Winchester and a

Remington military rifle. To use the Winchester would only tickle him up, while the Remington, though of greater penetrative power, would do him but little harm unless a vital spot were hit. However, I took the Remington and sneaked up close, but he saw me and trotted off, turning his head around for an instant. I hit him slap in the side of the head and he bolted like a shot. I put one more bullet between his ribs as he disappeared.

This was the first. The next gave more trouble and nearly finished this child. We found a herd of four or five feeding in the bush about a mile from where I fired at the first one. I sneaked up to one huge black chap busy feeding on the tops of small trees and got within ten yards of him. I could see him from head to tail utterly unconscious of my presence. Kneeling down I put a Remington bullet slap into his side just below the tip of his ears and where the lungs and heart should be. For a few seconds he staggered a bit and then rushed into some thick scrub and vines and stopped. I again sneaked up to this spot to get another shot at him, but could not see him properly and was just moving to one side to get a better view when he gave out a fiendish yell and charged straight at me. I ran like a shot behind a big tree and had my rifle ready but he stopped on his side and I on mine and keeping quite still. He did not seem to know where I was and simply stood looking about him with his huge ears straight out like a schooner coming down wing and wing. After ten seconds or so in which I nearly died of funk, he turned sharply round and bolted into the bush and got away. It was deuced near shave as he could have very easily put his trunk around the tree and squashed me flat. He must have been quite twelve feet high and had huge yellow tusks. The men ran like deer with the exception of Mirabu who also got behind a tree close to me, but for some reason or other did not fire.

We marched on till one p.m. seeing fresh signs of elephant, hippo, deer, pigs and buffalo but did not get a shot at anything else though we heard buffalo crashing through the bush close at hand.

On the return journey we saw the tracks of more elephants and where one I had shot at had torn up saplings in his rage. We got into camp at twenty minutes to six and found the men had been most successful in getting bananas, each man having as his ration 50 to 75 fair sized bananas. We each got 70.

28th Wednesday.
... On we marched, trying to get opposite to an island on which there was said to be a village still inhabited. About 3:30 we heard the natives pounding their cloth and bananas, and shortly after this we caught sight of some huts and saw the natives peacefully at work. We had no canoe nor could we find one. Stanley was far behind us and could not get up by dark. If the natives saw us they would bolt taking everything with them; we had thus no means of cutting off their retreat from the opposite side of the island. What could we do?

I sent word to Stanley to send a canoe if possible quickly up the eastern channel to attack. The natives would thus rush out on our side with their goats and everything while we, hidden in the under growth, would grab everything. For three hours we waited till darkness was coming on and something must be done. At last, seeing no canoes could reach us to-day, I decided to fire on the village from three places, one at the top of the island to sweep the other channel, one at the bottom for the same purpose, and one directly where we were hidden. I opened the game by shooting one chap through the chest, he fell like a stone and was seen next day, stiff as mutton. Immediately a volley was poured on the village. At first the natives ran, but rallying, they peppered us well with their iron-tipped arrows but without effect. For some minutes we took pot shots at the heads as they appeared above the grass and huts and managed to drop a few more and then gradually they made off one by one till all was quiet. At the bottom of the island the doctor managed to drop two as they were making off in a canoe – above also some were knocked over. After all was quiet, some men swam across the channel, say 75 yards wide, and ransacked the place. The only things they found were some spears, dried bananas and smoked elephant meat ...

... It was most interesting, lying in the bush and watching the natives quietly at their day's work; some women were pounding the bark of trees preparatory to making the coarse native cloth used all along this part of the river, others were making banana flour by pounding up dried bananas, men we could see building huts and engaged at other such work, boys and girls running about, singing, crying, others playing on a small instrument common all over Africa, a series of wooden strips, bent over a bridge and twanged with the thumb and forefinger. All was as it was every day until our discharge of bullets, when the usual uproar and screaming of women took place ...

29th Thursday
About 9 o'clock Stanley turned up with the boat and landed on the island opposite, to look at the scene of the recent battle. They found some bodies in the grass and saw a lot of blood in the canoes.

One of No. 1 Company... had quite an adventure to-day. He endeavoured to catch a Washenzi and the beggar grappled and took hold of the muzzle of his rifle. Another man standing near them took hold of the butt and shot the native through the foot. He then let go... and ran off and was shot through the back just as he dived into the bush.

30th Friday
... We had a great streak of luck this morning. I had just left the track with the intention of trying to get a shot at a hornbill or some other large bird and had gone perhaps ten yards or so, when I saw a native elephant pitfall and looking

down it saw a fine bush doe. We speedily cut her throat, dragged her out of the hole and cut the shoulder off for Jephson's and my breakfast. This was a great stroke coming just as we are almost starving. Stanley also got a few fish out of a native creel, so that for once we should have something to eat besides bananas without a vestige of anything in them.

About four o'clock Jephson and I heard firing ahead and after twenty minutes or so came up on the camp and found that five Arabs had come down from their village some four days off to meet us. From then we learned something of the country ahead ... We are four days off from their camp, which they say is many days from the big Arab camp on the edge of the bush.

They are all young looking wanderers, plump as butter and seeming perfectly content with their position. From here to their camp they say there is nothing but a very few banana plantations with but wretchedly small *uchangu* bananas in them. From their camp onward they say there is plenty of food to be had, and beyond the big camp, rice, *mtama* [sorghum] and plenty of cattle and game.

Our men, already reduced to eating anything they can pick up in the bush, will have a terrible time of it for three days in the wilderness. The Arabs brought a few bananas to sell, but no present for Stanley. They would only take cloth, of which we had none, so I got a man to give cloth while I gave him tobacco for the bananas.

Stanley never bought one for us, tho' practically we are starving on one meal a day. After I had bought these bananas, the doctor went to Stanley and told him that the other three fellows were under an obligation to me for having used my own tobacco for food when Stanley himself should have bought it. Stanley offered Parke tobacco and told him to give it to me, but William, who was near, told him that I had plenty of tobacco, on which Stanley withdrew the tobacco and said, "Oh, then it's all right."

Just fancy what a caddish thing to do, his not buying bananas for us at a very critical moment shows his meanness of character and is a breach of our agreement with him, viz., "that he would provide us with a due share of the native produce of the country"; all along this has been disregarded by him, and one has to give shirts, tobacco, etc., to allay one's hunger.* For fellows working ten or eleven hours every day, trudging through mud and bush, wading over rivers, and urging on spent men, forty bananas of the sort we are now getting are none too many. Instead of this we get on an average say twenty-five

---

*Stairs may have believed that his less than adulatory attitude toward Stanley was well disguised, but Stanley sensed what Stairs was thinking. In his journal for 15-16 October 1887 Stanley wrote of Stairs, "I do not quite believe him to be friendly. Sometimes I catch something in his looks which forbids me let myself go in overpraise" (quoted in McLynn, *Stanley: Sorcerer's Apprentice*, p. 199).

wretched little things with nothing in them. Of course one cannot stand this long and has to buy bananas out of one's own tobacco or clothes. To people living say in England and used to big ripe yellow bananas, they would say, "Oh, thirty bananas should be quite enough to keep up a man's strength". Not at all, the average banana is almost seven inches long with little or nothing in it and green, besides their having very little sustaining power. The Expedition has treated us all disgracefully, both in the matter of native and European food. What we have got so far has been mainly owing to our own exertions.

Once more we find that Arab reports are not at all to be relied upon. They told us yesterday it was four marches to their camp ahead and after that many days on to open country. To-day the chief coming in says it is four days right enough to his camp, but only five or six marches on to grass lands and game. Just fancy if this be only true we should reach open country in say ten or twelve days from now after over one hundred days in the bush. To those who have ever worked in the bush for any time, this blessing will be apparent ...

1st October [1887] Saturday
... Late in the evening two men ... came in with the report that there were plenty of bananas to be got down river. To substantiate this they brought in some very good ones and each of us got fifteen or twenty.

Felt fever coming on.

2nd Sunday.
... In the afternoon the hills got much worse and getting along with the loads became a most despairing job. The two donkeys, Stanley's and Jephson's, did some wonderful feats of climbing. At last as it was getting dark Parke and I who were in rear heard the welcome shouts in camp and soon afterwards we came in perfectly played out. Stanley had not reached us and made camp about half a mile below us. This was a very trying march, probably the most trying we have had for over a month, we made in all about five miles.

◆   ◆   ◆

4th Tuesday
... Here we are stuck in a hole, ahead no passage for the boat, hills rising to 300 ft on each side of the river, and last but most important of all was the fact that the men possessed not one vestige of food. Our sick may be numbered by tens, of loads we have more than men, no food except bush fruits can be obtained; something must be done.

Well, Jephson took the boat to pieces in the evening. We had grub and a long pull of brandy and turned in. Parke started cutting the path ahead for tomorrow and got up in the hills half a mile from the camp. For 92 days we have possessed a flotilla on the river, to-day it seems as though it were coming to an end. Of course there is every chance of our being able to place the boat once more on the river, but the canoes will be sunk here and probably we shall not be able to procure any higher up owing to the absence of natives.

The condition of the expedition is becoming deplorable. This route has turned out to be the most difficult one that could be chosen. For two and a half months, our people, though at times getting plenty of bananas, have not had three days running in which they have had enough food to eat ...

Nelson's feet are getting worse, though every possible care has been bestowed on them. We have say ten men who cannot stir – these will certainly have to be left behind to die.

◆   ◆   ◆

6th Thursday
This morning things came to a crisis. Our sick men could not march and keep up with a hungry column in search for food. Our loads were too numerous to be carried by the men we possessed, so Stanley held a *shauri* [conference], all the men and chiefs being present. His plan was to leave a white man here with the [fifty-two] sick and what boxes we could not carry, press on with the column to the Arabs or to any place where we could get food, load up men with food there and send them back to bring on the boxes and what sick they could. To this the chiefs added consent, and Nelson proposed that five or six men should be sent on quickly ahead of the column and try to communicate with the Arabs. This was at once done, five Muniapara started off with orders to press on. Nelson being unable to walk was ordered to stop. We left about eighty-one boxes and say fifty-four sick. With Nelson we left what little European food we could, a tent, and five or six good men to procure what food could be got in the bush. Parke left him a supply of medicines and of ammunition – he had about fifty or sixty boxes.

In the morning the canoes were all sunk close to the camp and the boat [the *Advance*] sent on in pieces. Stanley marched on at about 10 o'clock and told us he would cut ahead as fast as he could. We (Jephson, Parke and myself) did not get off, however, till noon or after owing to the boat not being ready. After a "Good-bye, Nelson", we started on a march to get food for these fifty people we have left behind. What is in store for us nobody can say. Nelson is in a very tight box where he is. We will do our best to get him out of it. Food, food is what we want. We travelled on till dark, could not catch Stanley and camped one hour behind him, in one tent, without blankets.

7th Friday
At eleven we stopped for breakfast, mine consisting of some fungus given one by one of the men and two or three small brown beans one picks up in the

bush. They are poor eating, but the fungus is good if only one could get enough of it.

As the boat was said to be very far behind, I stopped for it to come up as all my things were being carried by men in the rear. Stanley went on at noon or a little after. Taking my rifle I went off into the bush to try for a shot at something. After two hours walking I could see nothing and came out back on to the track just in time to see Jephson coming up with the boat.

Parke has a slight fever and was coming on up slowly. The men occupying the boat were quite exhausted and wanted to camp at once, so that they might stray off into the bush and picked up a little food. They have had nothing now for two days but bush fruits. These are simply nothing when men have to work hard for ten hours. We went on another half mile or so and camped, all hungry and tired.

8th Saturday

This is a day one will not forget in a hurry, I should say. To start with our boatmen, who are now in a pitiable state, almost refused to work; some intended to abandon the boat altogether and march on quickly up to the front. They all feel their position far in rear of the advance is a bad one, and so it is, as they, poor beggars, have not the same chance of picking up food as their brothers in advance have. After speaking to them and telling them we could not get across to the Arabs without the help of the boat they started off again. In three-quarters of an hour or so, a man came down to us with a note from Stanley saying he had marched on ahead for an hour or so and camped, had taken a small village on an island here but found no food and that yesterday he had shot an elephant and that it had got onto a small island near his canoe and probably would die there. We were to put the boat together, search for the elephant, bring him on to camp and come on with the rearguard to camp.

It was very weary work putting the boat together; the men hungry to despair ... and it took three hours to get the boat ready for the water. Parke went off to try for a bird or anything he could lay his hands on but returned in an hour or so without anything and quite done up. Soon after he had another attack of fever. I also went off in another direction and got a shot at a large monkey, but failed to hit him. Jephson then went down with the boatmen to the scene of yesterday's elephant shooting, and I took in the rear guard and some other men to camp, distant three-quarters of a mile or so.

I had a long talk with Stanley about the condition our men were in and the chances of food. It certainly looks very black, especially with Nelson behind us. If only Jephson would bring the elephant, all would yet be well, the men then would get two good days' rations and we would be saved. All waited with open eyes and ears for the boat to come. At last about nine o'clock we heard the oars, and soon after the boat came up. "Have you got the meat?", we yelled. "No," came back the answer. We all felt sick, and quietly one by one the men left the landing place and with hardly a word turned in for the night.

This is a terrible blow to us, as if we had got the meat, we should perhaps have been able to get on to the Arabs or some place where food could be got. Far and wide the men searched the bush for food, but only managed to pick up a few fruits and fungi.

Two natives were killed and some ten taken prisoners at the taking of the island. No food was found ...

9th Sunday

... Towards evening Feruz Ali, who was cutting grass with two other men across the river, was set upon and badly cut across the head by a native hidden in the grass. The other two men immediately ran away and yelled for help. The boat was sent over and brought back ten prisoners, mostly women taken by our men out getting food.

Some fifteen men returned late at night without a particle of food except the ordinary bush fruits they could have got on this side of the river. The major part of the men, however, came to the river's edge, and apparently after a *shauri* among themselves decided to go back again to the bush tomorrow morning and try again to find out where the natives had got their food planted. I myself believe that these natives have really little or no supplies or regular food, but exist simply on bush fruits and fruit with an occasional elephant or bush deer they may catch in their pitfalls. The natives we captured made a deuce of a row in the night yelling and screaming, and some had to be gagged.

No news from Muniapara yet. They should have reached the Arabs by this if any Arabs are on the river. Three things Stanley must have learned by this time:

1. It does not pay to drive ahead into an unknown wilderness without stores of food;
2. Do not go anywhere in this country without a guide, even if a bad one;
3. The information derived from the Arabs amounts to so many lies.

He may have known of these before, but he certainly did not practice them, nor act according to them.

Nothing turned up in the evening, no food.

10th Monday

The men are still on the other side of the river searching for food. We on this side have strange feelings all the time as to whether food will be got or not. We are simply existing now on bush beans ground up and boiled or baked. It is about the lowest form of food I have ever tasted and has very little sustaining power, I should fancy.

To-day it has been a question whether the expedition will have to be abandoned or not. Things are looking terribly black for us. We do not know now whether some of the men on the other side of the river have deserted or not, it is an open question. To leave a white man here with loads would mean certain death for him and the abandoning of the loads. Stanley, I half fancy, had some idea of this, but imagined he would lose his loads. I don't think he is the sort of man to care whether the white man is left behind or not.

I took out the shotgun, my own rifle and Stanley's express [*sic*] and was away for five hours but could get nothing and returned quite exhausted. After some food I started fishing, and managed to catch three small ones after a great deal of trouble and time. Jephson and Parke remained in camp in the morning and Parke took a stroll towards evening for a bird but saw nothing. Everything seems against us. Towards evening the men began to come in, most of them without food and a few with bananas and fungus, a mere drop in the ocean. They have scoured the country on the other side of the river for miles and captured some natives, but food in any quantity does not exist. We were able to get enough bananas for a feed and take twenty or thirty each on with us. Though we felt brightened a bit at the sight of the bananas, still our position is not one whit improved. To-morrow we shall have to go on without food as before.

11th Tuesday

... Jephson and I went on with the rear guard and from morning until we got to camp in the evening had one series of difficulties. The men, tired, hungry and despairing would put down their boxes every few minutes and collect the brown bush beans to be found there. Others just simply dropped their boxes and had to be well beaten or encouraged before they would go on. A man crossing a small stream on a fallen tree dropped his box of ammunition into the water and though we tried hard, we failed to get it. Rarely had either of us been so tired and hungry as when we reached camp about 5:15. We found out in the evening that ... two of my men and two of No. 1 company had not turned up ...

As Jephson and I, our boys and a few men were marching along close to the river bank, one of the men espied a large elephant feeding on a grassy island 150 yards from shore and quite unconscious of our presence. I seized a Remington rifle and fired at him, hitting him just above the eye. He dropped like a shot but soon got up again and turned round to move off. Just as he turned I again hit him in the head and once again in the side. He made off slowly to a small island and we lost sight of him. One could tell just where the bullet hit him by the small puff of dried mud that was knocked off.

12th Wednesday

Stanley decided this morning to send Jephson back to the boat [the *Advance*] to repair and bring her on. He [Jephson] has about 15 bananas to take back with him, and it will be some days before he can catch us up. He was very much against going back and no wonder, as under the present circumstances a white man going back may never see the column again. Stanley and Parke remained an hour or two in camp before starting the men off. A *shauri* was held and the men were asked straight whether they would march forward to get food, or whether they chose to go back. To a man they said, "Let's go forward". Accordingly, the march commenced about 9.

Again early I went far ahead of the column with the big rifle and shotgun, hoping against hope that something might come in the way. For three-quarters of an hour or so I followed an elephant and two or three times managed almost to cover him, but at last he broke away altogether and I lost him. The next thing I saw was a large ape. This chap I knocked over but he sprang up again and ran away. We caught a native woman from whom I captured [*sic*] a small basket of wild bean flour.

Stanley went on at about one. I waited until Parke came up with the rear at two o'clock. Together we marched on having great trouble with the men, and at last reaching camp at about five.

One of the men ... while swimming across to an island to secure a canoe he saw there, was drowned. He had his rifle slung across his back, and getting into a whirlpool was sucked under and never again seen by his comrades on the bank.

Men of Jephson's company who came to camp about 1 p.m. reported the boat had difficulty in getting over rapids. [one man] of No. 1 company and two others died of starvation on road. Jephson himself turned up about 3 p.m. having captured two baskets of Indian corn from natives. One he gave to the men and one was divided in equal shares amongst the white men, each of us getting twelve small cups full. This will be a perfect godsend to us at this critical moment when we have absolutely nothing but these infernally rank, nauseous bush beans. They had a very hard time of it, the men being perfectly beaten up. The corn revived them a bit but so little that it was a mere drop in the ocean ... The corn and tobacco they had got from the natives who had fled from us on to a small island, on seeing the boat come on towards them, all fled, and jumping into the water many were drowned in the rapids.

... a man of Nelson's company died on the road yesterday from sheer want of food. Numbers of the men get in such a low state of exhaustion that they cannot get off to the bush and search for food and so must perish unless we get bananas or other food soon ... one of my men has not yet turned up nor will he probably ever. I fancy he was left on the other side of the river from camp of 8th or 9th and got lost in the bush or killed by natives.

... The men cower round their fires at night, gloomy, hungry and despairing of ever getting food. Poor chaps, they are suffering a great deal and are slowly going down hill to miserable deaths should we not soon strike food. To give an idea of how things stand, I left Yambuya with a company 88 strong, 11 I left with Nelson, and to-day I have only 48 men and five of these sick.

... the boat's crew went off up river in the boat, while we left with the direct intention of finding some Arab track which might lead us to the Arabs or to food. All day long Parke, Jephson and I trudged along keeping the loads up and having a wretched day of it. Men were down and could barely get up, others were off in the bush looking for food and we would have to wait for them to come out and get on again. Oh, but this is exhausting work, ten hours every day with little or no food and no comforts at all. How one would relish a little good food or something really.

Some men ... turned up about 2 p.m. and said they had found an Arab track leading N.N.E. This they had followed some distance and then turned back another way and met us. This is good news, for supposing it will take us on to the Arabs, as three more days without food will probably mean the abandonment of the whole expedition.

Stanley stopped at five and made camp and soon after killed his donkey for food. We divided him up and distributed rations to all the men, keeping a leg, liver and heart for ourselves. Each man's share should be about one half to one pound, not bad at all. As soon as we got ours, we made soup, stew and roast. These with bush beans gave us the first fill up we have had for fourteen days. Oh the blessedness of being able to sit down after dinner at night with a good pipe and feel full! The men too seemed much more cheery in their camp, one even heard singing. Poor chaps, a pound of meat will not go very far with them in their present state; what they want is meat in quantities or bananas for ten or twelve days with a good rest in camp: this would do them all the world of good.

One of my men, worn down with ulcers and starvation, died on the road this morning. Poor chap, he had worked well up to the last few days, and then suddenly wasted away and died.

... We all thought the donkey to be very good eating, the meat is dark but I fancy more juicy than goat, the liver especially is very good.

Where we are camping is an old native retreat. The natives were driven out by us. Stanley got about twelve cups of Indian corn. The natives here are the lowest specimens we have seen yet. Their food consists of grubs, those nauseous beans, and a ground nut. Driven away probably by the Arabs they have not had time to cultivate anything and consequently we are unable to obtain anything in the way of food. Either this or they make no attempt at all to grow anything.

♦   ♦   ♦

17th Monday

Away 7:30 and made good marching for an hour or so on Arab track. We were then stopped by hornets and delayed two and one half hours, the advance meanwhile going on ahead. Some of the men were very badly stung and a great many boxes thrown down ...

At 5:15 we fetched camp perfectly played out, wet, hungry and no food ready for two hours, wet and no tent ready for us to move into; gentle stranger, this is our work now, on, on with nothing comforting to body, soul or mind. A pipeful of tobacco being one's only solace. Some of the men are getting desperate. Stealing is frightfully prevalent.

Chapter Six

On 18 October 1887, almost five months after disembarking from the river steamers at Yambuya, the advance column finally reached Arab slavers whose small plantation afforded the men some desperately needed – if expensive – food. Death had been near them all. Now their survival cost them dearly.

During the second fortnight of October 1887 Stanley decided upon his dispositions for the final march on Lake Albert. Parke was ordered to remain at the Arab encampment to care for the sick from the advance column. Stanley and Stairs would push on to the lake (estimated on the basis of information from the Arab slavers to be about a fortnight distant). Jephson was sent back to retrieve Nelson who had been unable to walk and was to catch up to Stanley and Stairs in about a month or so. With Nelson had been left the sections of the steel boat, the supplies which the dwindling numbers of porters could no longer carry, and fifty-four sick. Along with Nelson and the invalids, Jephson was to bring the steel boat – if he could find enough sound men to carry its sections.

The expedition in October 1887 was dispersed as it had never been before. It was, in fact, unravelling. The Rear Column of Barttelot, Jameson, Bonny, and Ward had been left at Yambuya, where Jameson recorded in his diary on 24 September his doubts that the expedition would ever come together again. "I feel more and more every day what a waste of life it is being left for months in this miserable camp. If Mr. Stanley has all the confidence in Tippu-Tib which he says he has, he could easily have left all his stores at the Falls, and taken us on with him." Two days later, he added, "I have very grave doubts as to whether we shall ever see Lake Albert Nyanza, and it is a pretty ending to our share in the relief of Emin Pasha."[1] It was only Stanley and Stairs who were to press on to Lake Albert – until Jephson could join them. Worse, supplies had to be left with Parke, supplies in-

tended to succour Emin. Worse still, the scarcity of porters was such that Stanley decided not to wait until Jephson could bring up the Advance. *Contact with Emin would accordingly depend upon whether native canoes could be found at the lakeside – unless of course Emin was awaiting Stanley at exactly the point where the advance column would reach the lake.*

18th Tuesday

This morning started off with hopes of hearing or seeing something of the Arabs. Stanley left camp say at 6:45, we three in rear did not get away till 1½ hours later, holding a sort of court martial over some boys who had been stealing our supply of corn. Stealing is now the order of the day – no one can be trusted, even William, Stanley's white servant, was flogged the other day for stealing his porridge. Hunger plays the devil with everyone.

Just as we were leaving camp we heard shots, horns and a bugle mingling in confusion ahead, and then knew that Stanley had struck the Arabs. Hurrying on we soon came up to them, and found that they had settled in a large clearing three hours distant from the river. We had a long yarn with the Muniapara in this house of meeting, the head man ... being away at present on a journey to Muscat. Stanley was given a house and we three got another with three rooms and verandah and should be very comfortable.

The Arabs came here about seven months ago, took the village from the natives, enlarged the clearings greatly, planted rice, beans and Indian corn, and weeded out and planted more banana trees and on the whole are in a fair way of having a very fine station. The name of the head Muniapara here is Khamis, an open chap with a pleasing face. He is helped in his work by five or six others. They have come right through the bush from the Lualaba [River] above [Lake Albert] Nyanza in five months and have only got twenty tusks to show for it. They have, however, captured a great deal of ivory in the shape of slaves. One sees them in all stages from the newly taken one who has to be watched to prevent running away, to the fat jolly wanderer who speaks his Swahili with just the slightest tinge of Washenzi intonation. One sees great numbers of different bush people gathered together from different parts, those with disfigured lips from far away Manyuema, those from the huge forest between the Aruwimi and upper Congo, and lastly one finds the Washenzi of these parts. The Arabs attack and capture a village, kill the grown up men and make prisoners of all the boys, girls and women they can. These then can carry on with them on their marches, selling women where they can for ivory, and bringing up all the boys for raiders and the girls for their harems. Their system is a good one, though one which destroys the country they pass through; this has been one of the causes of our suffering so much from hunger.

Unfortunately for us, the rice they have planted has not yet had time to bear fruit. Indian corn they have in great quantities, bananas are scarce as yet but bye-and-bye they should have any quantity. We are absolutely without money of any sort, a most dangerous position to be in.

So far we have taken anything we could see owing to our strength, but here where we are friends we must pay for things. Our beads, wire and necklaces were all lost by the upsetting of a canoe, we brought no cloth for trading from Yambuya, and in fact our only money is *matako* or brass rods which really are not currency in these parts. Now that we have passed through the desert and got to food, Stanley will find the problem how to buy food a difficult one to solve. To add to this, food will have to be got to send back to Nelson, now in a desperate state, and food for eighty men who will have to be sent back to him for the loads ...

Went on a stalk after some birds in the cornfields in the afternoon, but was stopped by the Washenzi Arabs, who imagined that I was trying to shoot fowl. Rather than offend them I turned back and got to camp just in time for a huge feed of "GOAT ", corn porridge, *mahoga*, indian corn and tea. By George, how good everything tasted and how one's spirits rose with each successive spoonful of porridge or bite of meat! One cannot realize the satisfaction it is to get one's stomach full after fifteen days or so of gnawing hunger.

19th Wednesday

Slept till nearly seven o'clock in our comfortable house and once more feel this morning that life is worth living. We had a good breakfast too of porridge and meat, corn and beans, and all felt better for it. As the men had a holiday to-day we also took one. Directly after breakfast the people came to us with splendid looking corn flour, beans, corn, fowls, etc. to sell. We have nothing to buy these with, but I gave a kumerband [cummerbund] of red flannel for two baskets of beans, say about ten cups full. For a small tin I got nine heads of green corn, for three empty brandy bottles we got thirty cup fulls of beans.

Stanley, who is supposed to feed us, has sent us *nothing* barring giving us twenty-seven heads of corn each and our share of goats. It is simply scandalous the way in which we are treated. He [Stanley] for his meals has fowls, goat, porridge, beans, corn and bananas, while whatever we eat we pay for out of our own miserable supply of necessary clothing. The men got no rations to-day at all, and consequently have been stealing the Arab corn and been tied up to trees. After being promised quantities of food on their arrival here, they have so far only got four heads of corn apiece, a beastly swindle. Stanley may say he has no money to pay for food; well then, he should give ammunition and rifles.

Jephson had a long interview with him [Stanley] in the evening, the result being that he is to go back to relieve Nelson with seventy Manyuemas and ten Zanzibaris to carry goods and bring up the loads. He [Jephson] will in all probability on getting back to this place remain here with Nelson. He is to start the day after tomorrow and will be away say fifteen days, Stanley in the meanwhile going on. Our position is critical in whatever light one looks at it. There are at least seven days with no food at all ahead, our men will not get any here, and will thus have to start with empty stomachs and faith in Stanley lessened tremendously. Stanley proposes to return from the Lake ... pick up Barttelot and perhaps thence strike direct across to the Lake. The expedition is now so frightfully cut up that I doubt if these plans will ever be realized.

20th Thursday

... Rifles being lost or stolen to give to the Arabs for food, took all rifles away from the men. The men were again given four ears of corn, a mere drop in the ocean.

Mofta Myaiga was badly wounded by one of the Arabs for stealing corn. He got a spear through the back going into the pleura. One could hear the wind rushing out when he talked.

Discontent is more rife than ever, one heard the men complaining bitterly to-day. One Jephson heard saying, "What use is there going on? We are told again and again that there is plenty of food ahead. We never get any of it, all is finished."

... In the evening I went down to Stanley's tent and had a long talk with him. At first he was despondent to the very lowest degree. "The whole expedition is broken up now, there is nothing for us to do but return. Perhaps we may make it back to the [River] Nepoko, follow up its course some distance and then slant off eastwards. But we must be prepared to loose one half of our men. These Arabs have wrecked us, had I known them to be on the river I should never have come this way. I can come to no terms with the Manyuema, they are playing a destructive game with us, by not giving us food they are inciting our men to sell their guns for corn and gradually will work our men over to their side. To go ahead without fixing terms we cannot, or they would steal every load we left here." He [Stanley] looked very bad over it and has had a rough time since reaching here.

The men have had no food. Tonight all that we had for food from the expedition was *tea*, everything else we purchased out of our small store of clothing.

I suggested returning as far as Ugarrowwa's, send back for Barttelot, bring him on, then strike N.N.E. for a while, afterwards true East, and work on to Kavalli or some place north of this as before; we would then be out of the radius of destruction caused by the Arabs and at the same time would not lengthen the course. To go up the Nepoko would perhaps be easier, it certainly would be a month and a half longer. We also would have to pass through the wilderness between Azarown and the Nepoko, which would prove fatal to a great many of our men.

By 22 October the expedition was on its last legs. Behind there was no news of the rear column. Ahead there was no news of Emin. In between, Parke, Nelson and Jephson were scattered. Disease had not only reduced sharply the number of porters, but the survivors were severely debilitated. Few stores could be carried and, in any event, were so depleted that they would not prove of much succour to the pasha who was still thought to be *in extremis*.

In both *In Darkest Africa* and in his *Autobiography*, Stanley passes lightly over the dangers that confronted him. Stairs in his diary is more explicit. Basically the decision had to be made whether to gamble that the expedition would find food along what remained of its direct route to Lake Albert or whether it should turn back to its newly established Fort Bodo or even beyond to the confluence of the Aruwimi and Nepoko rivers. There Stairs hoped that Barttelot and the rear column – and their desperately needed supplies – could join them. Thus reinforced, the expedition could turn up the Nepoko River and attempt to make its way northeast – instead of directly east – to Lake Albert Nyanza. Most important in Stairs's view, the expedition "would then be out of the radius of destruction caused by the Arabs ..."

◆   ◆   ◆

23rd Sunday
... Stanley changed into his tent from his hut. He is looking seedy and says he has bad fever ever since he has been here. This is bosh and one of his funny ways to enlist sympathy ... He came to see us at dinner and made the remark that, "you don't appear to be starving at any rate." We at once jumped at him and exclaimed that *he* had given us *nothing* [that] we were eating, barring the tea. He at once shut up. Upon my word it is scandalous the way he is treating us ...

24th Monday
... Parke is to remain here with Nelson, look after the sick ones, and afterwards, when a caravan comes here from the Lake, either of Emin's or our men, he is to go on to the Lake. Nelson will, however, remain in this place till two and a half bales of clothing are in some way delivered over by Stanley to the Arabs to pay off the debt incurred by the expedition staying here. (Thus Nelson is simply a hostage and may remain here for years, a most cruel proceeding and only necessary on account of Stanley's failure to bring more money.) Jephson, after leaving Nelson here, will take the boat to pieces, store it here and come on after Stanley and myself with the boatmen and some fifteen others. I am to go with Stanley to the Lake with a company of seventy-two men. Other plans are not yet decided on. The marching plans are, fifty per cent unloaded, seventy-two men carry one day, and seventy-two the next, Stanley in front, I in rear. For fifteen days or so we are shown a good route through the wilderness. Deserters are to be apprehended and handed over to Nelson or

Parke. One tent (Stanley's) is to be taken. I am to sleep in the back part of it, a most wretched place, and have only fifty pounds of baggage. One box of provisions, almost empty, and one of medicines Jephson and I share. Parke and in fact all of us were rather staggered on our hearing that he was to be left here. Stanley had, we fancied, decided on Jephson. It is perhaps useless to try to estimate how long he will be here, but giving two months to the Lake [Albert Nyanza] and two and a half to communicate, organize a caravan from Emin Pasha and reach here would make it four and a half months. But should [Stanley] descend the Nepoko, bring up Barttelot to the Lake then send to relieve Nelson and Parke with the cloth, they would both be here quite twelve months. Fancy a deadly existence of twelve months in a place like this.

Now take the question of food; Stanley has shown himself a cur on this. He has simply arranged with the Maurezuma [the local tribe] that his men should, as soon as they get well, work in the fields and receive provisions. They are to receive no meat at all, and on the doctor's asking Stanley about this he said the Maurezuma had no goats or fowls and told him to try and win them (the Maurezuma) over with smiles. This is all the money he has left the doctor, "smiles," no *matako*, no right even to claim meat and with a clause in his agreement, I hear, that the Maurezuma have a right to punish our men who offend, instead of the white man alone possessing that right. The result will be that some of our men will get their throats cut for stealing corn, as this is the unalterable custom here now. He [Stanley] has left it to the chiefs to provide food for Nelson. This will amount to something quite insufficient I have no doubt. As the caravan for Nelson does not leave for some days, no doubt I shall be able to write more about these arrangements. The Arabs (one calls the Maurezuma "Arabs") will show Jephson the way back to Nelson and will be crossed over by us in the boat ...

Of course I am glad I am going on with the rush ahead, but I feel a sickly sensation at parting from Parke. He is a ripping chap to get along with, always cheery, ready to help one, a great chap to have on the march to brighten one up when things are going bad, and lastly of course, the danger of sickness is much increased by his absence. We shall have no one who knows anything about treating wounds and will not, perhaps, for another year.

◆   ◆   ◆

26th Wednesday
Fell all hands in, took twenty men from each company to go back with Jephson, gave them thirty heads of corn each and sent them down to the river to be ferried over by boat. The Maurezuma were ready by ten and got off soon after. Jephson left about noon. He had 110 corns for eleven days, not much, and takes some corn meal and two fowls for Nelson. Parke went down ... to issue ammunition and take numbers of rifles of men. Jephson bought and

took some things for himself or else he would surely starve. I bought four fowls for the road, but expect they will be stolen from me. Parke made up a medicine chest for me, or in fact for us, as Jephson will catch me up after say thirty-five days.

Parke and I had one last meal together this evening, and to me going on through a wilderness it will probably be the best one for some time. We had soup and meat, fried liver and kidneys, a stew of goat, beans, corn, bananas and tea. After dinner we sat by the fire for quite two hours talking the whole thing over. At last I produced some whisky from a small bottle I put up when we were on the *Madura*, and we drank each others' healths in a good stiff nip. Poor old Parke felt very sad over being left, and no wonder, as the conditions under which he stays are by no means understood by him.

27th Thursday
Up by five a.m., dressed and had a good breakfast off things bought by my pyjamas and shirts, and then fell in our companies. After some talk gave out rifles, then loads and made a start about 12:15. Parke and I had lunch for the last time, and then getting my rear guard together and boys ready, we said good-bye ...

On the march again now, only I am the only white man in rear till Jephson comes up. I felt very lonely at times, especially so after just leaving Jephson and Parke and starting as we are through the wilderness.

... Marching on we passed several plantations ravished by the Arabs and reached camp shortly before five o'clock. Some natives came to camp shortly afterwards with some bananas and corn. I doubt if I shall ever see any of it. Stanley grabbed it and generally keeps it all for his own use.

I left my bed (the Edgington) behind with Parke and now sleep on banana leaves or grass. The bed was one of the rottenest contrivances I think I ever saw, heavy and unhandy and of bad design, it was of the very worst kind to bring on an expedition of this sort.

I should think we made seven and a half or eight miles to-day. The huts here are quite different to anything I have yet seen. The isolated ones are circular in shape like the Eskimo ice huts, the doors too are in the same style.

◆   ◆   ◆

31st Monday
... After lunch the track was again good, and by three we reached camp having made nine miles, the best march for a good long time. What is better that all day we were going due east and did not wander about much. The bush to-day was of a much lighter description than that we have been accustomed to pass through. Here and there we would come unto small clearings or collections

of native huts ... It is astonishing how very much a wet track affects the marching. In a ten or twelve hours march it would make three hours' difference whether the track was wet or dry.

I got another bunch of bananas from Stanley this morning. They were a little better than the last but still not up to much. Everyone is saying that we should reach a village the day after tomorrow where there is plenty of food, bananas and sweet potatoes and *dhoora*. The porridge made from *dhoora* is said to be very good. I hope so.

I wonder how they are getting on at home. By this time tennis will be cold, windy work and any outdoor pleasure will have lost its charm. How a good cup of coffee and some bread and butter would be these mornings in England, but how still a greater treat it would be here. Fancy sitting down to a breakfast of bacon and eggs, coffee, toast and good butter with some honey or marmalade or a good chop to finish off with. "Oh, ye Gods!"

1st November [1887] Thursday
... Shortly after reaching here the chief of the place came and presented Stanley with a goat and some corn. I should say we made some eight and a half miles to-day.

Upon my soul, the way I am treated is disgraceful! To get food I have to ask several times for it and then get a few bananas thrown at me. Last night it got dark, owing to the storm, at 6:30. I had simply to lie in the dark with no light or comfort of any kind till it was time to go to bed. While all this time there was Stanley in the front part of the tent, with a big candle burning and comfortable as a bug in a rug ...

... There is with the expedition a family of seventeen, all carriers, ranging from ... one of my boys of about eleven years old to men of forty and forty-two years of age. Of this family, nine left Yambuya on the march to the Lake, six have died, three are left and one is in a fair way now of going under, his legs are simply rotting away. My boy's leg is not yet well, he keeps constantly kicking it against something, stumps and roots, and will not wash it properly, and so the thing never can get well without a long rest.

Ulcers pay the mischief with our men. One breaks out, say in a man's ankle, gets worse day by day till he cannot carry his load, he goes down hill and has hard work to keep up with the column at all, and at last has to be left behind to die or perhaps find shelter with the Arabs somewhere. This is a constant occurrence ...

By this time Jephson should have reached the spot where Nelson was left and have found out whether he was there or not.

♦   ♦   ♦

6th Sunday

... The chief of the guides gave me two very good bunches of bananas, a most thoughtful and welcome gift, as I should only have got twenty or so from Stanley. As it is I am able to put forty or fifty away to get ripe or use on the road ahead. From the back of my hut, which by the way is a very good one of the circular type, I can see for quite twenty miles. It is like being back in New Zealand where we used occasionally, at a [?] station, see country that we had not been in for six months or so. Here the country is broken up by hills of 300 or 400 ft. high all bush covered, and far away one can see the clearings, many in number, of the natives showing that there is a good number of people in these parts. The men are all building themselves good huts as the chances are we shall have to be here for several days. We must be quite 3000 ft. above the sea level now ...

The natives ahead are reported as being cannibals and very fierce. These people here eat their own kind should one be killed in a fight. Their bows are much larger and more forceful than those of a week back.

◆   ◆   ◆

10th Thursday

Off at 6:45, marched one hour and then reached the village. We then found the Manyuema had been successful in getting great quantities of dry Indian corn. At once we issued twenty-five to every man and boy, this being rations for two days. Stanley, William and I took three hundred cobs each, while for Jephson I took 150. Over and above this, I portioned off 1300 for the 52 men who will come on with Jephson. We then had left some fifteen large baskets over, say enough rations at the same rate for fifteen days.

This is the first time since the expedition started that we have seen food in any quantities. William [Hoffman] had secured a first rate hut for me and into this I put all the reserve corn and unissued rations, so that it looks now very much like a granary. Immediately after we had finished issuing rations, ... the guides ... with some fifty or sixty of our chaps went off to sack a village some few hours off, especially to try for the goats, fowls and corn. Three goats were brought in in the course of the afternoon from another direction, one of these we killed for ourselves which proved to be a beauty. Each of us got about three pounds of meat, this with roast bananas is very good.

This village is the largest, best kept and I should say richest we have come to for many a long day. On every side the banana clearings extend for quite a mile or more; corn the natives appear to have also in any quantity, and tobacco one sees in every direction. The number of goats and fowls is said to be very great. However, this is open to doubt as the natives invariably take these off to the bush on the arrival of a caravan.

The hut I have got is ... on the whole is a very good one. It is quite forty feet long I should say and ten feet broad; at one end sleep my two boys and cook ... while I occupy the other.

... We shall remain here now I fancy until the arrival of Jephson and his men; it is of course impossible to say how long that will be, but I make a shot now at the 19th or 20th. Our stay here with plenty of food and rest will do our men an immense amount of good. Those with ulcers will have time to pick up a bit, while those utterly worn out will of course start away fresh men once more. Perhaps here I too shall get fat.

11th Friday.
... One of the No. 1 Company killed yesterday seventeen fowls. These he decapitated and concealed in his hut but was found out by some of the men who told Stanley, the result being that I tied him up to a tree and distributed the fowls among the sick men.

I had Marazoon at work all day pounding corn meal. It is a most laborious and tedious job, then he eats about as fast as he pounds. The corn is boiled say for an hour to make it soft, it is then put into a *kinu* or pounding pot. After this is finished, it is put into a flat basket or plate and tossed up, the chaff being blown out and the unpounded corn coming to the surface. This is skimmed off with the hand and the finest flour which is below is put into another vessel and so on. Of course the corn must be ripe and cured, though at a pinch one can make a sort of mash out of green corn, but this preparation ferments if left for a day or two.

Some of the pounders are on a most elaborate scale of ivory, cut and scratched with all sorts of devices. The *kinu* [pot] is made of a hard wood and is generally plain without any ornaments.

The fleas are numerous here in the huts. In mine one has only to bare one's arm and in a minute or so one can count five or six great whoppers hard at work ... In Stanley's hut they were so bad that he had to decamp and pitch his tent. Cockroaches, beetles and ants also infect all these places, while as for the rats in my hut, they move simply in droves, being attracted by the quantity of corn stowed in it ...

12th Saturday
... In the afternoon some four or five men who had been out on the raiding expedition returned and reported that the natives had all fled in every direction, the men had decided then to sally round all the villages and take what they could get by shooting down every native they saw. The result of this is sure to be that our men will get scattered in groups of two and three and some of these will get cut off and shot by the natives.

13th Sunday

Again in camp waiting for the return of the raiders. Last night I had a regular picnic of it; I turned in after the pipes hoping to have a good night's rest, everything promising it. It turned out, however, it was not to be so. In a very few minutes the fleas settled down to solid feeding on me, they were simply in dozens all over my body. At last I got up, went outside and had a smoke and cooled off by the fire of the night watchmen, thinking after a while things would be better, but it was no use; again and again I tried to get to sleep but first it would be the fleas, then the rats or the heat and so on right through the night. It ended by my going up to the other end of the hut and talking to the boys and cook, who alas were troubled by the same cause. It is simply wonderful, I think, how the natives manage to stand these animals and insects.

A native dog came into my hut last night as I was trying to get to sleep and commenced lapping some soup on a plate that I had intended for breakfast this morning. Rushing out with a stick I caught him well across the ribs and knocked him into Heri's hut from which he was at once promptly expelled and disappeared amidst roars of laughter into the bush.

These native dogs have developed into a regular breed in the same way as the so-called wild dogs of New Zealand. They are very small, say about the size of a Skye or Yorkshire terrier, of a slight build, have very long pointed ears are of all sorts of colours; they have, however, not the foxy tail that the N.Z. wild dog possesses.

Without loads and with fresh men, we could march from here to Kavalli on Albert Nyanza in seven days, and find open country in three days from here. But having to wait for Jephson and carrying loads as we do I should say we would be at the Lake about the 5th or 8th of December.

One of the Manyuema was shot yesterday in the stomach by a Washenzi and died shortly afterwards.

A skin of a small crocodile was brought in last night from some village ahead, and the "sultan" (whom I tied up to a tree) said it was got from some creek near the Lake. Our men all want to kill this sultan as he holds great sway over several large villages. Stanley was content, however, with tying him up. This is the same sultan that we made friends with two days ago.

14th Monday

Our enemies the fleas and rats were again hard at work last night doing their best to keep us awake. As it was much colder, however, we all managed to get a little sleep. Stanley had apprehensions that the natives might make some attempt at an attack on the village last night; these proved to be false though and all of us survive this morning as fit as ever.

Our friend, the sultan, whom we have as a prisoner amongst us, is a most sour looking brute, quite the "correct card" as a man-eater, I fancy. He objects very much to the hard cords he is fastened up with and would like very much,

I have no doubt, to be let loose. From him we learnt that the Ituru and Eturi rivers approach each other closely a short distance ahead and then separate, the first going northward, the second southerly. On the other side of the Lake he says there are men (good men) who wear clothes the same as ours and use guns to fight with. Perhaps this is Casati, the Italian* who is now imprisoned on the eastern shores of Albert Nyanza, but still more likely it is that the old man lies.

Just a month ago to-day we crossed the column over the Aruwimi to try our luck in finding the Arabs, then we were all weak, desponding, and in grave doubt whether we should be able to go on or not. To-day, a month later, our hopes are high and our stomachs much fuller and though we still do not know what has happened to Nelson and his men, yet we 115 in advance feel that after all life is worth living. The men now have actually so much corn that they never come for rations. Ahead the villages are said to be full of dry corn.

Yesterday for breakfast I had ripe, roasted plantains, banana cakes, *mahogo* cakes, sweet potato cakes, cold leg of goat, corn bread and tea, not a bad meal for these parts. There is only one thing wrong and that is that when one has plenty to eat one wants something dainty, and the absence of salt makes everything lack in taste – however, plenty after a long starve is a godsend.

Books are things that would now be worth their weight in gold. Stanley is so mean that he never offers the loan of any of his, and does not like being asked for them. In the same manner, he is so devilish mean that he sticks to all the candles, never giving me one, whereas ... I am entitled to a share of one by rights. Mind you, he uses the major part of these candles in reading at night in bed, not in working out his calculations or anything of the sort.

Off to cut up the goat into three equal portions so must stop. With a little meat one could buy almost anything from the men, they are very keen just now in getting anything in the shape of flesh. All the men returned about ten [o'clock] with half a dozen goats and a lot of fowl. The fowl for some reason were all given to the Manyuema and in the afternoon we distributed ten goats among the men, keeping five for ourselves. A large goat and a young one, broke away and made for the clearing. We had an exciting chase, but at last I shot both after a regular stalking match. They are as active as deer, these native goats.

---

*Gaetano Casati (1838-1892), the son of a physician, was born at Lesmo, near Brianza, Italy. As a young man he served in the Bersaglieri, eventually reaching the rank of major before resigning his army commission to join, on behalf of the Milan Geographical Society, an experienced fellow Italian explorer, Romolo Gessi (1831-81). A year before his death, Casati published *Ten Years in Equatoria and the Return with Emin Pasha* (London, 1891).

15th Tuesday

... Yesterday morning we again got some more information out of the old sultan. He says on the big lake is a big canoe as high as the houses in the village only very long (probably a steamer) and also he says, "The Ituru and Eturi rivers join, *run up* high hills and then when they get to the top fall straight down into the lake." Pretty good this, rivers running up hill and then over the other side! The maps that Gessi got up for Gordon places Kavalli in long. 30°12' East about, whereas another map that Stanley drew up puts it in 30°30' East, eighteen miles difference this. I fancy Stanley's is the more correct as Gessi, I believe, worked only with the compass and other men's data to get up his maps.

In their raid the day before yesterday, the men got a large iron hoe ... they also got a large brass ring, such as are used in the upper Nile for trading purposes. Finding these had a great effect on our men who by this time were beginning to doubt the white man's capability in showing them the way to the Lake.

Perhaps now we shall wait for Jephson after all, though I think it hardly probable as the Maurezuma are getting restless already to go back and would like to finish their contract to take us for 15 camps as quickly as possible.

The sick men do not appear to be picking up as fast as they might, in fact one or two have gone back a bit (on account of their ulcers) which no amount of farinaceous food with a rest [?]. They require meat and strong sustaining food.

These Maurezuma chaps are awful spongers. They will come into one's hut and squat themselves down for hours, never uttering a word, but merely sitting there and waiting for the chance of a present, however small. They are mean, grasping devils, never returning a gift, or else sending a few heads of indian corn or something of that sort in return perhaps for a shirt. One has been in here all morning hoping to get a little English tobacco out of me. I know them too well now and after letting him get tired, I told the cook to tell him to get out, which he speedily did, much discomfited.

A long *shauri* occurred this evening in which the Maurezuma endeavoured to persuade Stanley to allow them to return to their settlement. He was firm though, and told them, "No! if you choose to go back I will not give you the letter I promised you" (i.e., a letter to Parke to hand over a rifle, ammunition, and gold watch, as their reward for guiding us for 15 camps). Again and again they tried to persuade him, but no, he would not. Their real reason for wanting to go back now is that they have more goats and fowls than they can readily take forward and then return with them. Thus the matter dropped for a while and we all turned in.

16th Wednesday

During the night some of our men observed the Maurezuma loading their guns, making up their loads, and generally preparing for a start. This information was made known to Stanley only this morning. About 6 o'clock these fellows again came and asked to be let off their contract but met with the same answers as they got last night. Directly after that, Stanley ordered some of our men to take away the guns ... This they started to do and confusion followed. There was a great deal of loud talking, and at one time it looked as if a fight would occur, but at last we got seven of the nine guns into the tent, the remaining two men making off, and evidently going in the back-track towards the settlement, where doubtless they will give tongue to the effect that Stanley had made all their friends close prisoners. Fearing this, ten of our men and a Manyuema were sent off at once to go back and put the chiefs' minds at ease on this score. However well this affair has blown over and friendship been established again, still these brutes will make the doctor and Nelson pay for it, having them as they have, so completely at their mercy. To add to everything, Stanley hit one of the men and then tied him up. I was deuced glad of this, he was an awful brute, one who went about bragging of what he could do with his gun and calling us cowards behind our backs and that sort of thing. He evidently must have thought differently when made fast to the house, I made the rope pretty tight, too. One of No. 1 started to-day to the Arabs, he probably will have made his way back this morning.

About 3:30 Jephson and some more Manyuema reached our camp. Everyone was burning to hear of Nelson and his men, and for some hours Stanley and I plied Jephson with questions of all sorts.

Nelson, thank heaven, was alive when he reached the camp where we left him, just alive though and no more. He had only four men left out of the fifty-six, twenty had gone off for food and had not returned and ten had deserted in a canoe ... Nelson had simply been living on fruits that his two boys had gathered for him in the bush, he was in a desperate state of despondency and fairly broke down on seeing Jephson and his men. All the rest of the men had died from starvation and sickness.

Jephson said no one could realize the privations we had gone through until one returned over the track we had come and saw the numbers of skeletons on the road-side. In one march he counted six, and many others at different times.

On reaching Nelson one of the first things he [Jephson] did was to throw the bodies of four men who had just died into the river. Nelson, of course, had formed all sorts of conjectures as to what had become of us, and finally decided that the column must have been delayed through hunger, as in fact was the case. Day after day, with his men dying around him, and nothing but a most scanty supply of food of the most wretched sort, Nelson must have been in a terrible state of mind, especially with such a man as Stanley for a leader, who thinks far more of his boxes than of his officers.

Jephson made a very smart job of it, leaving the Arab camp on the 27th and reaching here on the 16th. From Kerin to here he marched in seven hours – this took us two days and a quarter to do. Nelson's feet were very bad when he got to the Arabs, and he could not sleep at night on account of anxiety. Fifty-six men and boys were left with him, of these only four reached the Arabs. This is a catastrophe that ranks pretty high in African travelling.

Jephson was still in a hungry state when reaching here, but I put him to rights on that point, giving him a good blow out on meat and porridge.

17th Thursday
Started off early with 56 men to go ahead and search for open country said by natives to be two days ahead of us. Stanley had only given me two days to make open country and these would be up this evening, so I resolved to march forward till noon tomorrow and then return.

◆   ◆   ◆

19th Saturday
... the natives either got confused as to the right track or else did not wish to show us the way on. Three times we followed tracks and then had to return, and at last, sickened by their actions, I punched the old chief's head and we started on the return journey. We reached the village we had left this morning and camped for the night. In our march yesterday we must have crossed over the border of the Congo Free State.

◆   ◆   ◆

21st Monday
Off again, and after quickly marching reached camp (Stanley), about 11:30. We then delivered our yarn, and found that in our absence the Maurezuma had skipped, leaving their guns and other effects, and made back to Kelima. They thought Stanley was going to cut their throats, I suppose.

... one of the men, while drawing water, was shot by a native, he got one arrow in the shoulder and one in the stomach, this last being barbed, caught in the muscles of his stomach and could not be withdrawn. He returned to his hut, and during the night shot himself through his head, dying at once.

During the night our friend the sultan escaped, and now no doubt is safe in the bosom of his family. He bears the mark of my stick on the back of his neck, and I have no doubt he would make me into stew pretty quick if he got the chance.

22nd Tuesday

Here to show the scandalous way in which Parke and Nelson were left provided without food at the Arab camp I copy a letter which Parke sent me ... Upon my word it is disgraceful the way Stanley cares, or does not care, for the wants of his white officers, the most useful and loyal men in his expedition.

My Dear Old Stairs,   Arab Camp, 10th Nov/87
I should have written by Jephson as I promised but now I send this letter by Ulidi, who has been away foraging since the 29th October and only returned to-day. This is a fearful place for everything unpleasant, from [?] to Manyuema chiefs. Bana Ismail is the only one here since you left and we can hardly get enough food to keep off semi-starvation. For the first few days until they discovered I had no presents for them, they sent me ... just enough to appease the agreeable promptings of appetite, but now we get disgracefully little. Nelson is much improved by the [?] and freedom from anxiety, but he is far from well. He cannot sleep at night and is much pulled down in condition. Out of the whole crowd who were left with him, only he and three men and two boys reached here, six to four on the white [?] any day.
We are troubled night, noon, and morning by thieves, already they have taken two Remington ordinary boxes and set the hut on fire with the intent to destroy all the explosives, ammunition, arms, and effects left behind. Now, however, we have everything in the net, but it was from the tents that one of the boxes was stolen, and as we have not a soul to assist us and plenty to frustrate us, and we have not been able to make a house as yet. If we ask for a [?] Ismail won't feed him, and as we have not enough food for ourselves we cannot feed him. My donkey has been speared twice. Everything they see these people covet and all round it is a hell-upon-earth life. You will hear from Jephson what sort of a time we are having.
Nelson and myself have written to Mr. Stanley to send us two bales of cloth to pay for our food and the food of our three servants. As the chiefs say that I am living on their charity, and that they were told by Mr. Stanley that Nelson would make his own arrangements about food, they refuse to feed our boys.
Good-bye until we meet, which I hope won't be too long, and wishing you pleasant times and every success,
            Yours very sincerely,
            (signed) T.H. Parke
(I must conclude as it is growing dark.)

Just fancy the position these chaps are in. Grabbers of the lowest and fiercest on every side, in the midst of plenty and yet hunger assails them every moment, left with great responsibility and no power, all this simply because Stanley, in his desire in leaving Yambuya to make every load a box of ammunition, neglected to bring cloth as being rather a hindrance and taking up carriers, and this really has left these two fellows as hostages or guarantees for the price of the corn advanced by the Manyuema to him during our stay amongst them.

◆   ◆   ◆

24th Thursday
Off on the march again, and from the very first the improved state of the men was visible. Still, with fourteen day's rest and plenty of food there are some seven or eight men in my company who cannot carry loads, it would take a couple of months though to set them up ... we had made six miles and caught up to Stanley. Jephson and I again brought up the rearguard as before the days of starvation. It is much more pleasant than walking along by oneself with no soul to talk to ... The men leading the goats to-day carelessly let two of them get away into the bush, so our flock is now reduced to five. It does rile me so to have a thing of this sort happen, the more so as goats are really hard to get at present. The next raid we make may not be for a long time yet.

25th Friday
Stanley pitched his tent in the open space in the village, but Jephson and I took a hut, and a very dirty one it was too. This village is a most irregularly built one and kept in a filthy state, the best of the huts are but poor, tumbledown affairs, and filth of every sort abounds in every direction.

Stanley was seedy all day to-day, but I do not fancy there was much really the matter with him. He gets the very worst state of funk in the slightest illness. Several times we have noticed this.

It is just a month to-day from Xmas, where we shall spend it is a matter of uncertainty as yet, but probably not far from the shore of [Lake] Albert Nyanza, I should say.

26th Saturday
Our elevation above sea level is nearly 4,000 ft. or about 1,300 ft. higher than the Lake [Albert Nyanza] ... We need not therefore expect to have to cross a range of hills but should simply come to a series of cliffs or hills dropping down to the level of the lake.

A stranger to the trials and tribulations we have experienced during our 130 days march through the bush, with not a vestige of anything pleasing to the eye, can hardly realize our feelings on finding ourselves so near open grassy country almost within a day's march of the Lake within a few days of this camp. To feel the fresh morning breezes and see open plains will seem new life to us altogether.

◆   ◆   ◆

30th Monday
Got off about 6:15 and soon struck plantations and had very bad marching over fallen logs and scrub. We sighted and reached a village on a high hill about 10:30, and there away to the E.S.E we could see the open country. By Jove, how our spirits rose and how good we felt after nearly two hundred days of it in the bush with nothing to see but sky and then to see open country makes one feel a different chap altogether! Tomorrow we shall reach it, I hope, if all goes well.

The appearance of the country (about four days' march from here) is very much like that of Kent, undulating hills with here and there patches of bush on the hilltops and gullies. The grass from here looks just like wheat within a fortnight or so of ripening. In places it is quite green though, looking from the distance like English grass fields in spring.

We made our camp at 11 in this village and from our hut Jephson and I can feast our eyes on the welcome scene, run out now and then to have a glimpse and make sure it is a reality.

◆   ◆   ◆

2nd December [1887] Friday
All left camp this morning with the certainty of reaching open country to-day, as last night one of the men had in his wanderings reached the edge of the bush and reported it was but a short distance off and so it turned out to be. We had lunch in a village where we got the most splendid bananas, some fowls and a few goats ...

Leaving about 12 or so we marched for an hour and three-quarters, and then struck a long patch of long grassy country, but enough to say we are now out of the bush. There may be more patches of bush to go through, but still I fancy we have left the main bush behind. We have thus been since leaving Yambuya 158 clear days in the bush, a dose quite sufficient for most men, I should say ... We again secured a couple of goats and the men a good many fowls. All along the line the natives have fled from us, taking what livestock and everything portable they could in the short time allowed them. Off to the bush they go until we are again at a safe distance ahead of them, when I suppose they steal back and occupy their homesteads. Evidently they value their lives more than their homes.

It is wonderful the way in which the men are fattening up, one hardly recognizes them as the same lot of men that left the Manyuema settlement some five weeks ago. Still, though in good condition, many still have ulcers and sore feet and a few chest complaints. Everyone's spirits are up at the thought of leaving the bush grave we have been in so long and, as food is now plentiful, the men are quite frisky again.

... Jephson and I then went out with some men, and after less than an hour's work, by following down a small stream, we found ... a very good crossing. We stripped, and I took my rifle and a man and crossed over. On the far side we found a belt of about 400 yds. of bush, and passing through this at last reached real "open country". No mistake this time. Short jolly green grass rolling away to the east and north east, far away to the blue hills forming our horizon. The bush ends quite suddenly and very much as the native women described it to me, viz, on the west side of the Aruwimi the bush comes close up to the river's edge and on the other side it is all open country.

It would have made an excellent group for a photographer to see we three out on the grass dressed as we were. Barati Ulidi, our man, was stark naked but wore my white helmet and carried my stick, Jephson had his shirt on only and I had a shirt and rifle, and there we were, stalking about this grass, talking to each other like mad on feeling ourselves once more where one breathes free air and can see more than trees and sky. Game seemed plentiful by the number of fresh tracks we saw. We returned to camp and had a good feed and talk over our bush experiences. We had been 160 days in this almost interminable graveyard and now to get out of it seems more than one can realize.

◆   ◆   ◆

4th Sunday
... The whole country to the south of us to-day was one huge English scene, rolling hills divided by patches of bush in the gullies; every shade of green that one could imagine is to be seen, here and there one sees the patches of burnt grass that have been burnt by the natives. As a game country, it appears to be all that one could wish. We saw fresh signs of different animals and actually fired at buffalo and eland and saw springbok. The only sign of natives we saw was a village to the south of us on a high hill. To the N.E. is a range of high hills that we could just dimly see through the haze. Back of us to the N.W. is the dark green bush graveyard we have passed through and left so many men's bones in. I only wish that Parke and Nelson were here to enjoy the pleasure of being out of prison, in fact the whole expedition.

5th Monday
... We got quantities of very good ripe bananas and sugar cane, some fowl and goats. I don't think I ever saw such quantities of splendid bananas. Jephson and I got as many as we really wanted and the men were simply loaded down with them. The natives here build their houses in groups of three or four among the banana trees, and not in one big village as the bushmen. Their plantations are beautifully kept and as a result the beans and bananas are very fine. In appearance they look very much like the bushmen we have recently

caught, but they have not the peculiar intonation in speaking that the latter have.

Stanley and Jephson saw the footprints (fresh ones) of a lion this morning quite close to the village we took. He was evidently lurking about for deer or some sort of game at the watering place we passed through. We left the village about half an hour after I came up with the rear guard ...

... we again came on some more plantations and in one of them a chap ... was shot through the loins and in the side by a native concealed among the bananas. Shortly afterwards, I saw one sneaking along the edge of some long grass and fired at him twice, the second bullet hitting him as he partially stopped in his running and turned off into the long grass at once ...

♦   ♦   ♦

7th Wednesday
... To give an idea of the number of natives there must be here, I could count sixteen separate collections of villages with their numerous plantations ... we discovered a fenced-in place where the natives herd their cattle at night for protection against the lions, of which there must be a good number judging by the footprints we see. When one fired at the natives at long ranges, instantly they heard the report they at once dived into the [?] like lightning and then appeared again making insulting gestures and yelled at us ...

My feet are still very bad and it gives me great pain to walk any distance, one is afraid they will not be well till we reach the Lake, where rest and plenty of cold water should work wonders.

... Far up on each side of the valley almost to the tips of the hills we could see the *matama* glistening in the sun, the whole thing was a sight well worth travelling miles to see, and strongly reminded me of [what] the five starving men in *King Solomon's Mines** must have met with when they crossed the range overlooking the promised land. Stanley decided on going up on one side of the valley, not caring to risk being attacked in the centre where the natives hiding in the *matama* could come on us and perhaps cut off our column. On all sides the natives were collected in groups and whenever we fired at them the shots would be followed by loud jeers and war-like shaking of spears and shields. Many shot arrows at Stanley. I bowled one "swollen headed" chap over like a nine pin, the others near him putting off like to mischief to tell their friends of the "dreadful things that shoot out smoke and iron".

A native driving a bullock along the track was surprised by us and made off, first killing the beast with his spear. We collared the animal, dividing it up

---

*A year before, Rider Haggard had published his popular adventure novel set in Africa.

among the men and keeping the heart for ourselves. By the bye, this is the first fresh piece of beef we have tasted for over eight months.

We made our camp in a flat saddle between two hills, occupying both of these latter with *bomas* [forts] and were closely watched by the natives gathered on the hills around us. Occasionally they would gather courage and come closer and then getting fired at, would make off amidst hoots and yells from our men. The whole thing was most amusing if it had not been that we dreaded a night attack from them. We worked hard at the main *boma* and got it finished by night and posted ten men on each of the hill tops on either side of the camp. After darkness came on, the arrows came in by ones and twos but our sentries being on the alert promptly fired in the direction from which the arrows came, and the natives withdrew and left us in peace for the night. We are now in a country where evidently the natives have some pluck and determination, and where any time we may be attacked and suffer considerably.

Our men, to put it plainly, are frightful funks, and will run first, sure as the mischief. Our hope lies in building good, strong *bomas* at night and placing plenty of sentries in good positions to prevent surprise in the dark.

◆   ◆   ◆

10th Saturday
Again this morning we endeavoured to make friends with the natives, but gathering together in small groups on the hills, they came closer and closer to us, hooting and menacing us beyond safety. Accordingly at 10 o'clock I took fifty and Jephson took fifty men, and falling out in different directions we cleared the natives from before us and burnt every hut and granary over a large area of country, returning to camp about 2 o'clock. The natives now were standing in groups high up on the hills watching their houses burning away but kept quiet for a while. Towards evening they again got too noisy and again we sallied out and burnt more houses and cut down a lot of plantations of bananas. No attack at night.

11th Sunday
Out again at the natives, burnt more houses and cut down more bananas; this time we went further up the valley and devastated the country there. In the afternoon Jephson and I went up to some high hills at the back of the camp and burnt all we could see, driving off a lot of natives like so much game. I managed to capture some six goats and yesterday I also got six, which we gave to the men. The natives now must be pretty sick of having their property destroyed in the way we are doing, but it serves them right as they were the aggressors and after taking our cloth, fired on us.

Jephson and I are pretty hard worked now pushing things on and keeping off the natives, we rarely get our food at nights till long after dark and then after a smoke turn in in our boots and clothes thoroughly tired out, perhaps soon after to be awakened by the reports of rifles and have to get up to see what is the matter.

12th Monday

At last, thank heaven, we got a start and managed to get off and put in three hours' marching before we had to stop the column to drive off the yelling natives who had collected in numbers on the hills, and getting bolder every minute would have at last attacked us. From this time forward all day I had a rough time keeping these chaps at a safe distance from the rear of the column. Stanley managed to drop one or two yelling devils on a hill top some 300 or 400 yards off and towards evening I got one chap at about 350 yards.

... After a sharp brush with the natives in sight of the whole column, we ascended a hill and made camp in a small village making a strong *boma* of brush and odds and ends, placed my sentries and turned in. Feet are still very sore and much swollen. Again at night we turned out several times to false alarms and went back to bed amid many cursings.

Jephson and I get on much better with Stanley now that we are by ourselves. He takes our advice on many occasions and there is none of the old talk of conspiracy that he used to rave about when we were all together on the lower Aruwimi and Congo.

We should, if all goes well, see the Lake tomorrow. What a welcome sight it will be to our weary eyes! Even yet though all streams run west and make their way into the head streams of the Aruwimi, but ahead we see a range on gaining which we should see the Lake and find it to be the watershed separating two of the mightiest rivers in the world, the Congo and the Nile.

Our men are living like fighting cocks now; they have corn, sweet potatoes, beans, and fowl in quantities, and besides a great many goats are served out to them every day or so.

Jephson and I had a first rate hut which turned out to be our salvation as towards midnight it turned bitterly cold and this with only a tent fly is not at all pleasant. We are now about 4550 ft. above the level of the sea.

13th Tuesday

... After lunch we were plodding along in rear as usual driving along the lazy and sick and hoping perhaps by the evening to get a sight of the Lake. This was about 25 minutes after lunch and ahead of us there was a long, even ridge beyond which we could see nothing. On the *rugga rugga* reaching the summit of this we heard loud ... cheers mixed with wild yells and could see men rushing about madly as if the devil possessed them all of a sudden. Then we knew that the Lake was in sight, and pressing on like steam engines we also in turn caught a glimpse of Albert Nyanza between the saddle of the range we were on. All of us then went on a little farther and ascended a slight rise and there we saw the Lake 2200 ft. below us, stretching far away to the horizon ...

Any person not present at the time cannot realize our feelings on getting at last a glimpse at what seemed to be our final destination. Day after day, month after month, have we looked forward to this, plodding along through the wet, dreary, interminable bush, often without food of any sort as our death roll plainly tells, bursting to reach the open country and once more to see green hillsides and the open sky, ever and always our talk has been, "When shall we reach the Lake?" Are our chronometers keeping up to the mark, or are we much out in longitude? Each observation we Europeans, Jephson and I and William [Hoffman], watched with the keenest interest, while our black chaps pegged away patiently with their heavy loads trusting to Stanley and the sea watches [chronometers by which longitude can be estimated] to get us safely to the Lake.

Imagine then our feelings on seeing the dark blue waters of Albert Nyanza nearly 2500 ft. below us and only some eight miles over a sloping park-like country below us. Now we thought we should soon communicate with Casati and put at rest the question burning our brain as to whether Emin Pasha is at Wadeli or not.

After a short stop to feast our eyes, we commenced the descent and then began our worst piece of fighting ever since we landed in Africa. Every inch down this desperately steep hill the natives pushed us. From behind the huge granite boulders they would shoot out, rush down to shooting distance and let fly their arrows. Again and again and again I took back the rearguard and pasted them but still on they came and not till we had reached the plain below and crossed a largish river late in the evening did they give us any peace. Shortly after this we made camp in a village and surrounded ourselves with a *boma*.

Never shall I forget this day's work as long as I live, my feet swollen to almost bursting with marching, then the anxiety lest we should be cut off from the main column, and to add to this the hot sun and jagged rocks — I tell you at night I was fairly well done up. We had only one wounded, but it was a miracle as the arrows kept flying about in all directions. At lunch at 11 we drank water which, running into the Aruwimi, at last finds its way into the Congo and so on into the Atlantic. Forty minutes after, we drank from a stream running into the Albert Nyanza and so on down the Nile to the Mediterranean, and these two streams are not more than twenty minute's good walk from each other.

We should be somewhere near Kavalli's as we see the river running into the south end of the lake.

Chapter Seven

When the now depleted advance column reached Lake Albert Nyanza, it found neither Emin nor any news of his whereabouts. Stanley, without canoes to carry his small force up the west shore to search for Emin, made another momentous decision: he decided to return from the lake "to the bush" to fetch more men. Stanley was convinced that, having failed to purchase canoes from the hostile lakeside natives, he did not have enough men to ensure the safety of his small force if he attempted to seize them. Hence the need, in his view, to fetch more men and the steel boat:

> *... no amount of guessing [about the whereabouts of Emin] would feed two hundred hungry men, stranded on a naked lake shore. I therefore resolved, after three days' halt, to retrace our steps to Ibwiri, and there erect a small fort [Fort Bodo] for the protection of the ammunition, and as a resting-place for my sick; after which we could return once more to the lake and, launching my boat on its waters, sail in search of the missing Pasha.[1]*

14th Wednesday
Got away early, all anxious to make for the lakeshore. After two hours' marching towards the Lake and when within ½ mile of it we struck a large path leading to a village, and following this were soon close to the huts. Here we sent the interpreter, Fetteh, out and managed to talk with the natives. For two hours we sat in "parley" doing our best to obtain their friendship. At first it seemed as though they were afraid of us and desired friendship but afterwards they became bolder and at last we said we should retire. All we wanted was a canoe, we said, but this they refused, so at last we moved and marched along the grassy plain northwards along the lakeshore.

Here for the first time we saw game of all sorts in any number, springbok, hartebeest, eland and buffalo, besides the signs of leopards and other large animals, making it a perfect paradise for sportsmen. Again and again we started them up from the grass and they would run off a short distance and then turn and stare at the column as it made its way slowly onwards.

At three we camped on the plain about three-quarters of a mile from the Lake to give ourselves breathing space to form plans as to future actions. In this huge park, though game abounds, still there is no food of any sort, not a square yard of it has been turned over by the natives for planting, no *mtama* [sorghum], no corn, no bananas, nothing. The natives all along the shore live on fish and make salt which they sell to those living high up on the plateau and in return get corn, beans, bananas, etc. This absence of food makes it quite impossible for us to build our fort close to the Lake (within nine miles, say).

Then there is the canoe question. To buy a canoe we twice found out of the question, to take a canoe means making enemies of all the natives ... This Mr. Stanley says we are not strong enough to do – both Jephson and I, however, think we are. How then, now that we are at the Lake, are we to communicate with Casati who is at Kibiro across the Lake? If we had our boat, then well and good, the problem would be solved at once, if we had a large canoe even, it would be all right, but neither of these can we get, what then? Jephson advocated marching up the west side of the Lake till some good food-producing district was reached and then seize a canoe and build our *boma*. To this Stanley replied that it would be impossible, first as we should lose half our men fighting our way up and secondly as no canoe could possibly cross over the Lake there so wide and reach Casati in safety.

My plan was to seize at once the biggest canoe we could find close at hand, send back a strong force, seventy men, say, back up the hill to collect food for ten days for three men and then start the canoe south to the end of Lake and up to the Unyoro shore to Casati ... when the canoe was dispatched retire the whole column to plateau, build a strong *boma*, collect plenty of food, and then set to burn all the natives' huts, destroy where it would not hurt ourselves their property, raid their goats and cattle and endeavour to draw them into some position advantageous to ourselves and then kill as many of them as possible. If this did not seem feasible to Mr. Stanley then to send the canoe up the west side of the Lake for two days or so and from the natives perhaps learn something.

To-day I took some men out to the village of Kavalli and endeavoured to shout across the channel to the natives on the island but it was no use and after two hours we returned to camp sickened. What tremendous quantities of birds there are on the shore of the lake here, duck, teal, gull, herons, cranes, storks, geese, plover, snipe, singnecks, clotterels, fish hawks and eagles and other birds one does not know the names of.

In the afternoon Jephson tried the natives of another village for a canoe but it was no use. These natives knew that there was a white man (Casati) across the Lake ... and that another white man (Mason)* had shot a hippo here many years ago. They told us we had better go away, as death from starvation would be our fate here. We got some shots at buffalo in the afternoon but did not bring down anything.

Again at night we thoroughly thrashed out the question of what could be done to get news to Casati and it was then I fancy that Stanley fully made up his mind to retire back to the bush and bring up more men. Stanley stood Jephson and I [sic] a couple of bottles of "fiz" and we drank success to our return to the Lake. We all felt pretty sick at having to go back after such trying work getting here.

◆   ◆   ◆

17th Saturday
Away before daybreak, struck the foothills in three hours, sent on an advance guard to clear the hills, and had breakfast. We were so early that the pioneers met with no opposition from the natives and soon afterwards the whole column passed up the hill without firing a shot. Never shall I forget this march up the hills, for five blessed hours I toiled in the rear to get the *goes goes* up the hills, cursing, beating, imploring, everything. At last on reaching the top I was perfectly done up. We marched westward another five miles and made camp. We got our last sight of the Lake from the top of the hill and with sad hearts turned our faces westward, perhaps not to see Albert Nyanza again for ten or twelve months.

People in England will wonder why after coming so far we did not make a dash for Casati. Stranger, so do I now. I think a greater mistake was never made. It is all very fine to say, "Oh, when we return we shall have plenty of men and the boat". Perhaps so, but all the same it may then be too late. This is not a caravan. It is an expedition and should be expeditious ...

18th Sunday
... All day long Jephson and I stayed in camp mending and trying to make shoes and other such jobs. At respectful distances we can see small groups

---

*Lieutenant-Colonel Alexander Mason, one of many former Confederate and Union officers who served in the Egyptian army following the US Civil War, had been a lieutenant in the Confederate Navy. He had administered Equatoria under Gordon (before Emin's appointment), discovered the Semliki River, and circumnavigated Lake Albert in 1877 (see W.B. Hasseltine and H.C. Wolf, *The Blue and the Gray on the Nile* [University of Chicago Press, 1961]).

of natives collected on the hill tops, but they have learned by this time to keep out of the range of rifles and to duck like hell-divers at the sight of the smoke. Every night we adopt the precaution of making the men build their shelters in a circle in the centre of which are the tents, loads, goats and cattle. We also throw out sentries in a circle about 60 yards from the camp to prevent surprise.

◆   ◆   ◆

24th Sunday
... Well, here is Xmas Eve, and all day long nearly, I, Bill Stairs, have been sitting out in the grass watching the rear and guarding the flanks of the Emin Pasha Relief Expedition, now returning to the bush graveyard to pick up the stragglers and Barttelot's column far away down the Aruwimi. Here in Central Africa sitting under my mackintosh spread over the tops of three spears stuck in the ground to shade us a bit from the sun, around me are the cattle and rear guard, all or nearly all lying down in the long grass trying to get away from the scorching sun. Jephson is at work on the bridge. At lunch we meet and talk over our last Xmas Eve's experiences. This time there are no plum puddings, no mince pies and brandy and no Xmas cards and "Merry Xmas to you", nothing but work. Happy enough we might be though were it not for the bitter thought always coming up that we are returning to the terrible bush without having accomplished anything of our mission to Emin Pasha. This at times give us the blues.

To-night our friends at home are having a good time, no doubt. Xmas in one's own home cannot be called a good time, no doubt, to grown up people, though to youngsters, of course, it is the very essence of all that is joyful, but it is a good thing this keeping it up, as I think all one's hot feelings against others are cooled down for the time, and one feels open hearted and inclined to be generous to everyone and consequently feels better for it afterwards.

This time last year I was in Portsmouth staying with my sister [Mary]. Two years ago ten or twelve of us had a very lively dinner together at Monico's in London. One's thoughts, of course, go back to home and all one's people at this time, as this is the thirteenth Xmas running that I have spent away from my own home, one has merely dim recollections of what it used to be.

At times one gets very much disgusted with the men. They are brutes. As Gordon says of his Khartoum people, when they are not eating they are sleeping, when not sleeping they are praying, and when not praying they are sick. Sickness is the most perfect cover for them. Who is able to tell whether a man is sick or not? Of course one can detect glaring shams, but still it is the inevitable "Sewezi Bwana" (I am sick, master), that worms its way into one's very soul and drives out all charitable Christianlike feelings and making one a perfect demon at using the stick. Again and again and again have I tried to explain that work is work and that no feelings of brotherhood can exist unless work is done and done thoroughly. No, it is no use, and every now and then I am horrified at myself and almost driven crazy as I in a frenzy cut a man's head open with a stick. Control myself I cannot as my work would remain undone. The chiefs are absolutely useless to a man ... , belly and sleep are their gods, loafing their indigenous talent, to stir them up is more even than Stanley is able. No, as I said many months ago, the Zanzabari as a rule is a good porter, can exist where other men would perish, is a good forager, and as a rule has a generous disposition, but he is naturally lazy, shirks his work terribly unless forced up to it, is a liar to the very entrails, has no idea of "sense of duty" and [in addition] to all this is not faithful or loyal to a man who does him a good turn.

25th Monday, Xmas day

Well, here is Xmas, 1887, at last. Many a time have we wondered where we should put on this day, and here we are to-day crossing our force over the bad water of the Ituri, all hands hard at work all day. This time there is no stopping in bed till ten or eleven o'clock to get up to a good breakfast of grilled bacon, poached eggs, sole, and chops, to finish off with good butter and toast and honey, but up before the sun as usual and off to our work.

No doubt our people all this time are thinking of us and wondering where we are and what we are doing as they go to church or drink our health at dinner, but it will be yet many a long day before we can be heard from, in fact our stay now in Africa cannot be much under three years.

... Jephson and I sat down to our dinner, hungrier than we would often be at home at Xmas, but we had pretty plain food to masticate. We had one small helping of goat meat each, left from this morning's breakfast, green corn, bananas, coffee and goat milk. For a long time after dinner we talked together over "old Xmas", and what our friends would be doing, and finally I produced my small little bottle of whisky and we each had one nip and drank "A speedy return to the Lake and good luck to our friends in England and elsewhere."*

I am sorry to say the animals in our hut kept up pretty nearly all night and several times I got up, went out and walked around for a smoke to get relief

---

*One year later, Jephson, by then a prisoner of the rebellious garrisons of Emin's Egyptians, recalled the Christmas of 1887 with a certain nostalgia: "Stairs and I were quite gay over our frugal dinner, especially when Stairs produced proudly from the depths of his box a medicine bottle wrapped in a bundle of old rags, and containing about a gill of whisky, which he had secretly saved through all the starvation days for that festive occasion" (*The Diary of*, p. 356).

from these tortures. All my boots that I have with me have given out and one has no resort to *Feldtschoons* or shoes after the pattern made at the Cape for use in grass country. My pens also have rusted, so have to write in pencil, which is most unsatisfactory.

Well, a Merry Xmas and Happy New Year to all, and may 1888 be more friendly to us than 1887 was!

26th Tuesday
Jephson and I both have slight fevers, but to-day out of the sun will put us to rights again. All day long we talked of our return march, and have both come to the conclusion that Stanley will not go right back to the Major but will merely go to the Arab settlements, bring on Nelson and Parke, and then bring on the boat and ammunition to the Lake with a column say 190 strong.

We have now twenty-seven head of cattle and nineteen goats, a pretty good stock for a force moving as we are through a country we have just passed over ten days ago. We get milk twice a day, about four and a half quarts each time.

27th Wednesday
Stanley determined to punish the natives for their determined opposition to us, and especially those of the village near at hand, where [one] of my company was wounded by an arrow as he sat by his fire cooking. Accordingly I took out some sixty men, and make straight for this village. I cut down some five acres of bananas and burnt down every hut and granary we could see. We did this to about eight or nine villages ...

◆   ◆   ◆

29th Friday
Away again, through plantations, villages and bush and out on to the open plain. Far before us we could see Mount Pisgah as Stanley named the high, bush-covered hill from which some twenty days before we had viewed the *promised land from afar*. Straight towards this we steered and about 11:30 we entered the bush ... "Quaheri" to the open country, *good-bye* to all our prospects of game and pleasant scenes, once more we are in the bush to remain in it for goodness knows how long, once more we shall meet the mean, cunning, low-class bushman with his poisoned arrows and pointed sticks stuck in the ground. Once more we are to encounter and deal with starvation, ulcers, and sore feet, and go through the weary old game of rear guard with half-starved carriers.

After crossing the Ituri and getting all the cattle over safely, we turned to the east and made camp in the village we had stopped in for two days on our way to the Lake. Here we found the natives had burnt down three or four of their huts and had not been living in the village since we left. They have evidently got the funk pretty well installed into them.

30th Saturday

One realizes terribly plainly on the march this morning what a backward move we are making in thus retiring without having done anything to find out whether Emin Pasha is still on the Nile [i.e., north of Lake Albert] or not. Why, supposing Emin Pasha has decamped, well then we are here slaving our very lives out in the bush to get ammunition up to the Lake absolutely for no purpose. Then again, suppose he is there, well then, shall we not be too late?

Here is New Year's Day almost upon us. How long are we to spend in Africa? Why, as things turn now, I should say in all probability we shall see two more New Year's Days before we leave the country. As we are all growing more and more crabbed every day, by that time we shall have eaten each other up like the Kilkenny cats. Recollect, we have no books to read, nothing to draw off our minds from our endless everyday work. Very little brain work except at times, and nothing but indefinite subjects to discuss in the evenings. As the sun goes down, so are we in darkness, with no light except the glimmer of our fire in front of the tent to smoke by, nothing cheering or homelike greets us on our arriving in camp tired, hot, with sore feet from constant marching, and generally cross with everyone and everything, so in every way this is far more trying on one than any campaign with a British force would be.

Here, for instance, is the sort of thing that greets one constantly on getting into camp, "Well, Maragook, have you got some boiling water ready for tea?" "Yes, master," he will answer, "the water is boiling." Mind you it's on first arriving that one feels like a cup of tea, half an hour afterwards is no good. "All right, put in the tea, Oh, no, hold on, just see if the water is all right, no, by jove, you old fool, it's full of fat, mucky stuff you have been boiling meat in." Then follow cursings and sticks, and you feel as though you could just slay that cook, but it's no use. This goes on day after day till one despairs of ever getting anything to eat without personally superintending the cooking. All the cooks that we have tried are the same. An average cook in this part of the country I should say for every three months he worked for you would take off quite a year of your life, such brutes they all seem to be.

31st Sunday

... Just fancy, this is New Year's Eve to-night, and here Jephson and I sit yawning over the fire with hardly a thought of it, our conversation being mostly about Jephson's school-boy and tutor life ...

This time last year I was orderly officer at Chatham & Broughton Barracks, I remember in the ante-room at the former we had three huge bowls of rhum punch and some of the chaps had pretty sore heads next morning. The year before last at this time I was also in Chatham, and then two years before that in New Zealand. Next year on the 1st, we shall still be in Africa, I expect, with something done towards the relief of Emin Pasha ...

◆   ◆   ◆

3rd January [1888] Wednesday
Stanley's fever is much better to-night. He is the worst hand when sick that I know of. On the slightest attack of any illness his spirits at once go down. Jephson says that all the way along the road he was groaning and rolling his eyes about in a frightful manner. One's fears are at once quelled, however, on seeing the meal that he puts down on reaching camp and then one realizes that the sickness amounts to nothing. Several times one has heard him say that he is dangerously ill, when all the time he and everyone else knows that it is only side or fright that causes him to get in such a state.

4th Thursday
... Had a long chat with [Stanley] about the Arabs ... It is wonderful, upon my word, how depressed he gets or seems to get at times. Really I fancy at times he appears depressed just for "side." I have read him pretty well by this time and find that there are two men: the hard-working, keen Stanley as he appears at times when there really is need for him, and then again Stanley as he would like to appear before English people of the very highest circles. The two Stanleys contend against each other at all times in a most confusing manner.

He told me the other day that I had lost some men near the Lake – so I had, no doubt. I left two men to fall into the hands of the Wasomboni, but if I had not left these men and pushed on, my whole rear guard would have been cut off and destroyed, or partially so, so that to prevent losing the track and being cut off with my twenty men I gave up the lives of two sickly feeble men who could hardly crawl to the natives. I may say too that ... one of the men was quite stark, staring mad. Recollect that the natives were pushing the rear guard at every turn, and that my orders were to keep close up and protect the rear of the column. Well, as I said, Stanley told me that I had lost these men, and that if I lost another he would have to lose me too. Just fancy what a brutal thing to say to one like myself, whose whole soul is for the success of the Expedition, and who is willing to work twelve hours, and in fact does, every day for him for nothing. Brute!

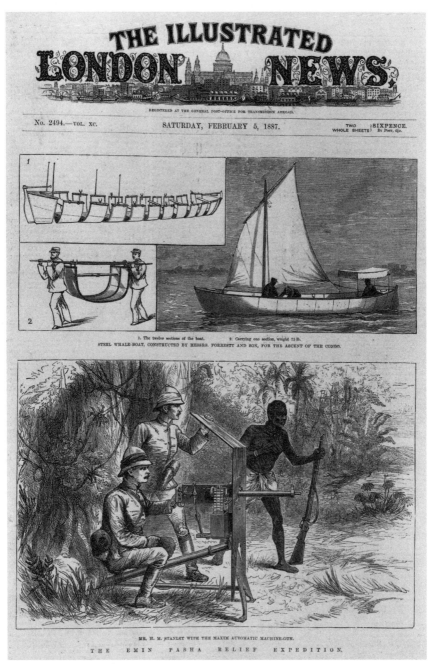

The Illustrated London News of 5 February 1887 marked the departure of the Emin Relief Expedition by depicting for its readers two of its more mechanical features: the portable boat and the Maxim gun.

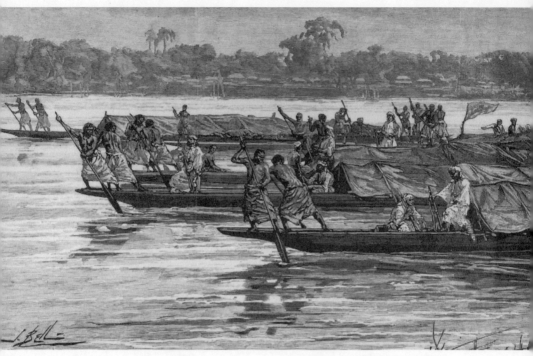

Several of Tippu Tib's great canoes on the Congo, typical of the larger boats on the river. (*Illustrated London News*, 21 December 1889)

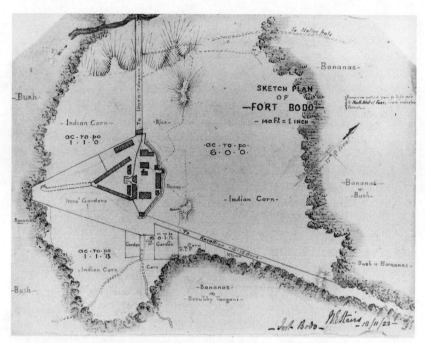

A drawing of Fort Bodo by Stairs which he signed and dated 18 November 1888.
Stairs spent a frustrating six months in command of the small palisaded fort.
(Public Archives of Nova Scotia)

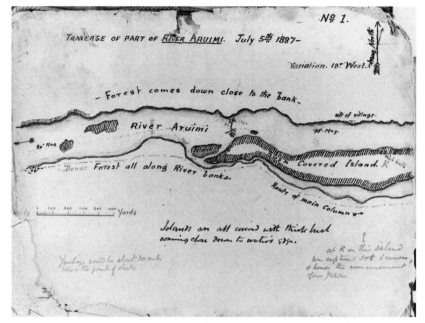

Stairs's sketch of 5 July 1887 of the Aruimi River from his journal of the Emin Pasha Relief Expedition. Stairs's diaries are replete with such skilful sketches, as befits a well-trained sapper. (Public Archives of Nova Scotia)

A sketch by Herbert Ward at the interview at Stanley Falls in February 1888 between Major Edmund Bartellot and James Jameson and Tippo Tib. What exactly the motives of the slaver were at any time remained uncertain, but his unwillingness or inability to provide Bartellot with adequate porters resulted eventually in the disintegration of the Rear Column. (*Illustrated London News*, 7 December 1889)

The Victorian public was always eager to follow the latest adventures of African
travellers, a fact indirectly reflected in advertisements, commemorative pottery,
and popular engravings and photographs, as well as in a myriad of articles
in journals and books. (*Illustrated London News*, 22 February 1890)

A life-size statue to Surgeon Major T.H. Parke (in safari kit) stands outside the Natural History Museum in Dublin. On the granite plinth below the statue is a bronze plaque depicting Parke sucking the poison from the arrow wound in Stairs's chest, 13 August 1887.

Chapter Eight

Although Stairs makes no special mention of the fact in his diary entry for 6 January 1888, it was on that day that Stanley, Jephson, and he returned to the site of Fort Bodo from their futile trek to Lake Albert. Stairs did not stay long at the Fort. Between January and April 1888, he was constantly on the move. He made two arduous trips back along the Ituri River to collect the men who had been left behind during the great march of the advance column toward Lake Albert.

8th Monday

... I am to go back with ninety men in a few days and bring up Nelson and Parke with all the loads to this place. At least this is Stanley's order, but how it is to be carried out is hard to see. Mind you, we are in debt still to these people for food supplied by them to us, and the loads of rifles and ammunition there are our pledge that the debt will some day be paid off (it is 3½ bales of cloth). How to go and say we want to take away our pledge and your guarantee from you is simply childish. What other guarantee Stanley is to give I cannot see nor do I think it possible he can give any. The statement that we are soon to go down to Barttelot and bring him up will not wash with these people. They are the most infernal liars and swindlers themselves and so of course believe every one also capable of the same things. Once we could get Barttelot's column and the beads and cloth up, why of course there would be an end to the matter, but this is very far from being accomplished yet.

In a talk with Stanley he thinks we should reach Barttelot about the end of April. I said the end of May. He has given me twenty days to go back to the Arab settlement, make up the loads, and bring them and the boat back here. I want twenty-seven days to do this, as the track for seven days out from the

Arabs is very bad, being in places a tangled mass of fallen logs and scrub, over which the heavy boat loads will take a long time to pass.

◆   ◆   ◆

17th Wednesday
Worked nearly all day at my clothes, mending and changing one garment into another as a makeshift. Really, Jephson and I are in a desperate way as regards boots and clothes and there are yet many months to go through before we can get any addition to our bags of rags.

The work on the fort still goes on, done by those who are to remain here, say fifty rifles. To-day Stanley started the poles for a granary he is to build in the square in front of our houses. This is to do away with the rat nuisance. Jephson also was building towers and putting on roofs all day. Later this evening the *rugga rugga* returned having captured some native women and seven or eight goats. They said they had been a very long march off and had seen plenty of signs of the natives but everything indicated that they had moved off a long distance and taken all their portable stock with them. No signs of corn were seen at any of the camping places they passed on their way out. Two natives were shot by them.

I am to leave for the Arabs' [settlement] the day after tomorrow.

◆   ◆   ◆

19th Friday*
Left about 7:30 for the Arabs' settlement, Stanley saying we should be back in twenty days' time. I said 29 days to Jephson last night ... all told we are 97. I hope there will be no trouble of any sort with the Manyuema as it would lead to most unpleasant after results at Zanzibar and elsewhere ...

20th Saturday
Left camp early, lost the track several times as the elephants had obliterated all signs of it in places by tearing up trees and messing up the vines in such a way as made it a difficult job to tell which was the traffic path and which the elephant ... At 2 p.m. we drew up cold, wet and miserable, made camp there and soon got comfortable in the huts. The Washenzi have all fled into the bush.

Just one year ago to-day Jephson, Nelson and I left old England, thinking we should be about fifteen months in Africa. We shall be quite two years

---

*Jephson records 17 January as the date of Stairs's departure, noting that the porters had voted for Stairs over himself as their preferred leader.

more before we see the last of this country, perhaps more than this. When shall we stroll down Regent Street again or have another fight with the War Office people or when shall we join the festive dance again or the still more festive mess supper? Oh ye Gods, just fancy grilled kidneys, snipe, salmon, ices, jellies, fiz, and the many other luscious things one gets at home! Just at present my diet is corn and bananas ...

21st Sunday

The above is all rot, of course, but any and many a time as one trudges drearily along close to the back of some wretched, ulcerous creature striving hard with his load, one forms menus by the score that one intends to have on reaching England again. Even coffee and tea are now things of the past, though I have a very little I am keeping till some rougher time, perhaps in the rainy season.

I am wondering more and more day by day how Nelson and Parke have got on with the Manyuema. They were left in a disgracefully false position by Stanley and under a Washenzi with a most repulsive character and one whom I feel was the cause of most of the trouble among our men during our eight days' stay there.

◆   ◆   ◆

24th Wednesday

... Marched very fast all day, must have gone twenty miles by 4 p.m. Should reach Arabs tomorrow. Men in great spirits. Should the Manyuema be unwilling to give us food, we will fight them and give them a deuced good licking. I hope this will not be the case, as though I have verbal, I have no written orders and great trouble would afterwards arise with Zanzibari people. Then Stanley would be sure to say I had disobeyed, and some other such things.

25th Thursday

Reached Manyuema settlement at 11 a.m.

Nelson and Parke both looking well but still suffering from poisonous sores brought on by the poison inoculated by flies. The place I found a reeking mass of filth and Nelson and Parke squatted right down just where the filth was worst. They have had a regular hell on earth life of it with these brutes of Manyuema; at every possible turn they would be frustrated by some paltry excess of Ismail's (the chief) or some other equally brutal chief ...

26th Friday

... All ready by 2 p.m. and made a start ... Of the twenty-three sick men at the settlement some thirteen elected to come on with me. The other ten were away on *rugga rugga* with the Manyuema.

Starvation exists to a terrible extent at Ipoto, and all those able to move at all have gone off into the bush to raid native villages and thus get food. Those in the place simply exist on *mahogo* and are as thin as the pictures we used to see in the *Graphic* of the famine in India. Some of our invalids will never be able to reach [Fort Bodo]. One's spirits rose at once on getting out of the hell Nelson and Parke spent so long in.

27th Saturday
Off early, Parke leading ... Made camp at 10:30 a.m. I stayed behind with the boat and had great difficulty in getting the rear section along. Changed the men several times but with no advantage. Reached camp, the men quite done up, at 4 p.m.

I had to shoot Parke's donkey on the road to-day as we could not get him over the *gogos* (logs) and had no time nor men to make a track for him. Poor Neddy, he was the last of the donkeys we brought from Yambuya, the bush is too much for these brutes. Food is very scarce along these roads, the Manyuema having eaten everything up.

28th Sunday - 3rd February [1888]
Nothing of any event occurred to-day except that we had trouble more than ever with the rear section of the boat, from this on to the 4th of February the days went by, food scarce, work hard, men tired. On the 3rd of February we reached the big village east of Mabunza.

4th February
The doctor left this village to-day with all the odd loads and boxes and reached Stanley at Ibwiri on the 8th without mishap.*

5th February
I halted to-day to give the boatmen time to collect a little food. They got some bananas and flour for two days.

6th–12th February
I started off the boat, reached Kilimani on the 7th and Stanley on the 12th, thus being 25 days out from the fort. I found then that Jephson had gone away with some men foraging. I was very glad, of course, to get back to comfortable quarters but all the same one enjoyed being on the march and one's own boss and away from the constant naggings of Stanley.

---

*This entry is typical of several in which Stairs describes events that actually took place in the future. The repetition of the information in the entries for 6-12 February and 12 February may simply reflect rewriting.

12th February

Reached the fort [Bodo] ... at 1:30. Found Jephson away with *rugga rugga*. During the month I had been away great improvement had been made. Jephson and Stanley had cleared four acres and planted corn and beans.

Nelson's feet are still very sore. He and Parke have got their systems thoroughly poisoned from the filth at the Manyuema camp.

The next question is, are we to go on to [Lake Albert] Nyanza or to go back to pick up the major? There is a lot to say for and against both plans. I am for going on to the lake as fast as we possibly can.

All the men who remained at the station are in splendid trim, as fat as butter and cheery.

Slept for the first time in the "officers' house" which seems very comfortable in the daytime, being nice and cool. Nelson says, however, that the roof leaks a bit.

13th February

... I cleaned and packed up all the bolts and nuts of boat (221) and handed them over to Stanley, cleaned five rifles I brought on, and oiled eighty-three breech locks.

Parke and Nelson indoors. Nelson spends all day lying in his bed and shouting to his boys. Stanley has built a long sort of a walk fenced in on both sides; this he calls Avenue Nyanza. It is not of much use except to give us safe exercising room. The huts are white-washed with a wash made of white wood ashes, which looks and acts very well. The men's quarters look first rate. The one bad fault of the place is the tops of the houses, they are made without pitch, and in these heavy tropical showers leak like the mischief. The grain has been all stowed in a granary in the centre of the fort raised about eight feet off the ground, thus rats are avoided.

We fly the Egyptian flag, one of the rottenest flags we could possibly fly. Nothing good every came out of Egypt, their ammunition was bad, the boxes bad, powder caps done up in rotten boxes, the men useless to a degree, the boots also that the men wore were bad.*

14th February

Yesterday we had a lengthy *shauri* about our next move. [Stanley] is evidently determined to thrash every side of the question out. His last scheme is that I should take twenty men, go through to Ugarrowwa's, send on the twenty men with letters to Barttelot, bring back the men who were left there as invalids,

---

*It was, however, the Egyptian government which had put up the initial £10,000 that had made possible the expedition.

come on to him somewhere near the edge of the bush, then united go on to the lake.*

One officer and a garrison of say thirty men to stay here. I am against this on account of the following:

1. I don't believe that twenty men can be trusted to make their way down the river even as far as Yambuya;
2. I don't think Ugarrowwa will give over the men and rifles *to me*;
3. I don't think that a month's delay is worth the few men we will get from Ugarrowwa. Really fifty-six, but only thirty of them would be fit to fight.

Whether I should ever catch Stanley or not I do not know. The journey for at least ten days would be through unknown country as on account of the famine we never dare go back by the same roads we come. Jephson will be for going on to the lake.

To-day is St. Valentine's day. This day last year the Expedition passed Cape Guardafui on the Africa coast [i.e., the Horn of Africa]. Then we had good cigarettes and not too bad grub and were generally happy with books, chairs, etc.; now, however, things are changed ...

On 15 February 1888 Stanley wrote a long letter to Stairs directing him to take twenty-five men to Ugarrowwa's camp, send fifteen of them on with letters for Barttelot and then return with the remainder and whatever stores they could carry to Fort Bodo. Stanley wrote, "Before proceeding to the lake, I have thought it best not to leave this place without attempting to open communication with Major Barttelot. There is no doubt that the major must be sorely tried, encumbered as he is with all that mighty mass of baggage and stores, and yet we dare not tell him to destroy any quantity until we have clear and authentic news of Emin Pasha."[1]

---

*The rear column was still at Yambuya. Having received no porters from Tippu Tib, Barttelot was convinced that he could not yet move the rear column forward. Isolated as it was, the rear column was vulnerable to the hostility of the natives goaded to despair by the maltreatment by the Arabs. The behaviour of the Europeans cannot have appeared very different to that of the Arabs. In one encounter with Africans, the Arabs shot several as they attempted to escape across a river. Jameson, to his posthumous denigration, noted in his diary for 4 February 1888 that "A number of natives were shot, but I cannot tell how many, as most of them sank in the water; however, they ... brought back one head with them which Ward and I sketched. Afterwards I skinned and preserved it [i.e., the head] and shall try to get it home with me." (*Story of the*

15th February
Got my orders to go back to Ugarrowwa's.** Jephson came in last night with ten or eleven goats and other loot. I am to take twenty-five men down and twenty of them go on to Barttelot [presumed to be still at Yambuya]. I have to join Stanley by the 25th March. Can't do it.

16th February
Started off from the fort amidst cheers from those remaining, on our long, dreary trip back to Ugarrowwa's. In one's heart one knew the thing could not be done quickly. One felt very much incensed at Stanley for the limit he imposed of thirty days to go and come. Though now it is nearly three months after this date that I write this, still in my rough notes I remember putting down that I told Stanley that there would not be thirty men below fit to come on. He said, "Nonsense, why I expect fifty." My spirits are high, though, and one cannot tell whether the rope is going to pull one or draw one back. I am ashamed of this book as it is such an eyesore, and certainly looks as if it would break up soon like the ice in the Canadian lakes in April.

Made Stanley's camp in the bush about 4:30 and camped. Men heavily laden with corn for the road got in 1½ hours afterwards. My escort is twenty-three men, twenty of which go on to Barttelot, my two boys and self. Total 26.

17th February
Here is Stanley's timetable, all nicely cut and dried and beautifully worked out marches, accompanied with a rough chart showing the route I am to take! Very nice to sit down in a comfortable room and tell one to go 250 miles or so down river and return, sixteen days or so of which would be through unknown country, and return in thirty days to the fort. In his letter to me he has either not considered, or absolutely ignored, the following very important items: 1. Has the rainy season commenced down there yet? (it had) 2. Was food to be got on the traced [?] routes he ordered me to follow? 3. Are the men at Ugarrowwa's now quite strong, or are they weak yet from disease and famine? 4. Will there be canoes ready for us to cross the Ituri or will there be delays in crossing?

Rear Column, p. 204). Jameson hoped to have Messrs. Rowland Ward, the Piccadilly taxidermists, mount it. On a yet more notorious occasion, Jameson had been the passive observer as cannibals butchered and ate a young slave girl, whom he had allegedly bought. He sketched the scene.

**Stairs's report of his journey to Ugarrowwa's village, dated 6 June 1888, is at appendix I.

NO, I was to go ahead without a break, marching the 250 miles in 15 days or an average of 16¹/₃ miles per day through unknown bush tracks to a great extent, not forest, mind you, but tangled, vine bound bush. Is this generalship? Is it rational ... ?

18th February
A desperate day ... Marched very fast N.W.,W.N.W. and W. till 10:30 over this very large track, passing three old villages from which natives had fled. At 11:30 had gone all told some 10 or 12 miles, then difficulties commenced. The big track struck north and we wanted west nearly, so followed a track leading in that direction for nearly two hours, then lost track, it ending in nothing as nearly all bush tracks do. Afterwards they may be found again a mile or so ahead, but one must have a guide for this. Returned, followed big track, took advice of captured native woman and tried another track. No good, and had to return. Made altogether four attempts. By evening had walked twenty-five miles and at last struck blazed road which natives said led to river. Decided to camp and follow tomorrow. Found an occupied village and got plenty of tobacco and bananas ...

19th February
Off again but blazed track stopped at some old huts and had to retire. Then began to dread we should go on in this way till we had wasted four or five days. Held a *shauri* and after much deliberation decided to follow up an old road to Ipoto and then get guides for some short road on to Ugarrowwa's ...

◆   ◆   ◆

1st March [1888]
Marched hard and fast. At 2:30 crossed the Lenda [River] on a native pole bridge, a very tumbledown affair. At 3:30 we fetched a village on a hill and there camped. Caught some eight or ten women in the bush as slaves and guides. Lenda here very rapid, descending near bridge in a series of cascades each 15 feet high.

◆   ◆   ◆

3rd March
Made camp again 10 a.m. as the [Manyuema] got into trouble about the road, so had to stop and catch natives for tomorrow. Caught some women in the evening.

◆   ◆   ◆

9th March

... This place ... is really under the care of Ugarrowwa who lives some three marches off on the Ituri at the place where we met him before. Immense quantities of rice and corn have been planted and substantial clay houses put up. All this will be abandoned though very shortly, as owing to the scarcity of ivory Ugarrowwa ... will locate somewhere down the Aruwimi in quest of more elephants. Kalunga is found to be a first rate and most agreeable manager...

The Manyuema have been here nearly two years now and have exhausted all the supply of native goats in their raids, and as the Manyuema men never breed goats or fowls, the supply of meat ... is very small. Here there are two cattle [*sic*] the remains of a former raid to the open country. It is sixteen camps to open country and three to Ugarrowwa's though it has been done in one.

In a former trip eight days down the Ituri, Kalunga told me that he got over one hundred splendid tusks; certainly they have a splendid collection here now, and some eight months ago they had cleared out every tusk and sent it overland to Ugarrowwa's ... All the Ugarrowwa's and Kalunga's ivory will now go down the Aruwimi in canoes and thence up the Congo (or Lualaba). Thus it is seen that we have been the means of opening up a new road which these people have availed themselves of. Who can tell? This may alter in time the importance of the Ujiji country and end by the ivory going down the Congo to Banana Point instead of up river and then across the continent to Zanzibar ... ?

Bad reports reach us from Ugarrowwa's, twenty-six or twenty-eight out of fifty-six said to have died and the remainder very weakly. Kalunga sent a fowl and some rice. Long yarn with all the chiefs. Decided to stop tomorrow and go on next day with some of Kalunga's men.

Gorillas here very plentiful but very wild. Natives here all fighting against each other.

10th March

Arranged to go tomorrow morning and only spend two days on the road. Lenda is two days from here ... Have a slight though troublesome fever, cannot keep down the quinine.

◆   ◆   ◆

12th March

Got off early, and shortly after starting rain came down in torrents. At 1 p.m. I came up on the Manyuemas seated down in a large village (deserted) and as everyone was nearly dead with wet and cold, decided to stop and make camp...

13th March

Marched till 4 p.m. ... My bag, food or tent did not come up by nightfall and after thoroughly exhausting myself in the cold, wet bush my fever became much worse and by midnight the attack was very violent.

14th March

Fever bad. Waited for men to come up and then gave them a deuced good flogging. At two made our old camp opposite to Ugarrowwa's and crossing over were soon talking to Ugarrowwa and his chiefs. Ugarrowwa I like better than any of the other chiefs of all the Manyuemas in these parts. He is a Zanzibari and knows the ways of the white men as witnessed by his taking bills of exchange on Zanzibar to the tune of $900, as we afterwards arranged. The place looks much the same as it did before except a few new houses have been put up. Rice and corn in plenty but not fully grown ...

Found twenty-nine men out of the fifty-six we had left were dead, and some fifteen of the remainder were away out on *rugga rugga*. Cannot possibly catch Stanley now as I shall have to wait here at least four days for the absentees. What a tough blow this is! Fancy now I shall have to stay at Ibwiri and do [words illegible] work and miss the very cream of the Expedition and what one has looked forward to during one's many weary months of toil. Oh by Jove, it's too rough altogether!

I found that all the Somalis except Duallah had died, two having been speared by natives while after bananas. None of the Soudanese had died, but two died the first day after leaving Ugarrowwa's ... the man with the amputated foot was able to walk about quite briskly with the aid of a stick.

For two months, while the rice and corn lasted, our men fed up like lords. After this, however, starvation ensued and many died off from disease and famine. Nearly all food was got by the *rugga rugga* and brought into the settlement. Some of the men I met were in poor order through laziness, but most were in good trim for short marches. Our men were quite differently treated to those at Ipoto. I made Ugarrowwa terribly disgusted with Ismaili and Kalunga by telling him of this, and assured him Abed bin Salim and Seyyid (the Sultan [of Zanzibar]) should hear every detail ...

15th March

Fever raging. My head is almost bursting. One cannot keep down food or quinine. I am suffering also from bad diarrhoea. I must have lost a good many pounds in weight during the last few days ...

Visited the graves, twenty-eight or so, of all those who died and were buried here, a most melancholy sight. Just fifty per cent of those left here. Deaths more from sickness than starvation, ulcers, fevers and chests [?] took off this number.

16th March

Sent off ... nineteen men to search for the rear column and carry off letters for different officers in it. All went off cheerfully. Hope they will find the major soon and bring us up news. Vomiting, diarrhoea and fever all day, spent time in bed ...

17th March

Closed with Ugarrowwa for $870, being pay for twenty-nine men at $5.00 per month for six months. Two men away *rugga rugga* [whom] I did not close for with him. Gave him bills of exchange in Arabic, Swahili and English, payable at the English Consul's at Zanzibar. Each was signed by Rashid and the English ones have my signature attached. Gave Ugarrowwa 100 lbs. ammunition ... two rifles and about fifty rounds Rm. [Remington] cartridges. Two more men ... came into camp about 11 a.m. Also told Major to give Ugarrowwa $60 if he got the two men now absent.

18th March

At last got off once more on the march and return journey to what one calls home, viz. Ituri. I knew from the very start I would lose a lot of men and endeavoured again and again to dissuade ... some six or seven ... who were really weak and ill from following me. However, they were all struck by the reports Abdullah's men brought down of the paradise the open country was and so would not listen to me.

Felt good at moving on but my thoughts are not good when I think of losing Stanley [i.e., arriving back at Fort Bodo after Stanley had departed for the lake].

◆   ◆   ◆

9th April [1888]

Am perfectly played out with this constant fever. No one helps me on the road at all. There is no one fit to carry me, and so I have to walk. Quinine will not work as one cannot keep it in one's stomach. This lonely, helpless feeling depresses a chap terribly, added to this the disappointment of not getting on to Stanley and the lake, and you can form some idea of the time I had. Reaching camp I fall on my rubber sheet already laid on the ground by Abedi, and then crawl into bed. Rashid is the only one who helps me at all with the men. He is a good fellow, Rashid, and one who obeys what is told him.

Reached Ituri and made camp. What a welcome sight this old river is again after such an absence, though all hope of seeing Albert Nyanza this time is destroyed. What a state of weakness my men are in, it is terrible. We left with 26 men and I have only got 16 now, ten deaths. Found no canoe and had to wait in camp. How is Kilonga Longa to know we are here unless we send a

man to swim over? Two men tried in evening but failed. Lay on my back all
night in agony, simply burning up. Could not get a sweat up.

10th April
Got ... a Manyuema, to swim the Ituru River early this morning. He reached
Masumba and re-swam the river at night saying there was a canoe one hour
lower down.

I am simply burning up inside, I feel. One's heart and pulse go like
racehorses. No thermometer. Toothache again.

11th April
Left camp, simply crawling from tree to tree down to canoe, crossed all over
and reached Ipoto at 3:30 worn down to nothing and as thin as a stick.

Found all chiefs but Ismaili had moved down to the new village they have
built. At last for the first time for eleven days I managed to keep the quinine
down, and now hope for better times.

◆   ◆   ◆

13th April
... I bought some salt for a goat's head, but very bad stuff, all alkali ... My
fever is going away, but it is leaving me terribly weak and light headed.

Stanley will be well on his way, now perhaps at the lake. I wonder if he will
take the Maxim with him. I think not.

14th April
Camped near village (camp of Stanley). Estimate about ten camps more to
Ipoto. Weak as mischief. Toothache gone.

15th April
Short march. Camped near Uabunga. Washenzi planting bananas. Do not seem
to think we are near.

◆   ◆   ◆

17th April
Decided to go on to Ibussa and camp as there are bananas to be found there.
Marched over in two hours. All out of food, condition of men desperate.

18th April
In camp. Sent back men to look for the two missing men, but in afternoon
they returned without seeing any signs of them. Caught two women.

... Death now for all if we stop for sick.

♦   ♦   ♦

21st April
[One man] died just before we left camp. Made camp for day in burnt village.
Got good bananas. All of us weak.

22nd April
Remained in camp for men to get food. This was our salvation.

♦   ♦   ♦

25th April
Made the next boat camp and should reach the Masumba tomorrow. Astonished
Washenzi on road. All fled but took their baskets with them.

Chapter Nine

Upon recovering by the end of March 1888 from more than a month of dangerous illness at Fort Bodo (caused apparently by an impacted gall stone), Stanley departed a second time for Lake Albert Nyanza. Quite simply, Stanley was increasingly determined that he would, if necessary, force Emin to accompany him to Zanzibar. He would need, in any case, the addition of a substantial number of Emin's soldiers to help force his way through hostile tribes. However, even with such reinforcements, Stanley would not have the resources to establish Emin in east Africa as Mackinnon had hoped, but he was not going to abandon his trophy on the shores of Lake Albert. Whatever Emin's wishes, Stanley was determined not to be deprived of the additional fame of "rescuing" Emin.

Once recovered himself, Stanley was unwilling to delay his second departure for the Lake until Stairs returned to Fort Bodo or news arrived from the rear column. Stairs would simply have to wait at the fort until either Stanley returned from the lake (with or without Emin) or sent for him to join him there.

On 2 April 1888, while Stairs was still away at Ugarrowwa's village, Stanley, Parke, and Jephson set out on their second trek to the lake, taking with them 126 men and, this time, the portable boat, the Advance. *More than three weeks later, on 26 April, Stairs arrived back at Fort Bodo having been absent sixty-nine days. He found, as he had feared, that Stanley had already departed for the lake, leaving the invalid Nelson in command at Fort Bodo with forty-nine other sick.*

Stairs was deeply disappointed. His worst fears were being realized. He would miss the long anticipated rendezvous with Emin. "I would have given anything to have gone on with the saffari." Instead, Stairs was effectively immobilized at the Fort. "Stanley said that he could return in two and a half months from the lake ...

He will in all probability be longer than this" (in fact, Stanley was back on 8 June, a week less than he himself had forecast).

Meanwhile, all that Stairs and the sickly and now querulous Nelson had to oc- cupy them were the mundane tasks of improving the defences, the internal arrange- ments and the plantations of Fort Bodo and warding off both human and animal marauders. These and other pedestrian tasks Stairs was to know well. He was to spend a total of eight months (April-December 1888) at the fort.

The excitement, the challenge, the danger of the expedition had gone with Stanley and Jephson. At best, Stairs and Nelson could only join in the modest diversions of a sort of Robinson Crusoe existence, as the weeks and months passed without word from either Stanley or the rear column. What had become of Stanley, Parke and Jephson? Had Emin been found? "Is the Major's saffari still extant?"

Unknown to Stairs, the rear column of Barttelot was still stranded at Yambuya. Surrounded by the piles of supplies, alternating between hope that finally the car- riers would be sent by Tippu Tib and despairing that they would ever come, the rear column became daily more despondent. On 17 March 1888 Jameson wrote darkly in his diary, "It is a sad, sad sight to see men dying round you every day and not to be able to put out a hand to save them. Without a single fight we have lost close upon seventy men out of our small force and there are many more who, I am sorry to say, will never leave that camp, or, if we leave it, must be left there to die."[1]

26th April
Started off early and at 4:30 reached Fort Bodo. Here I found that Stanley, Jephson and Parke had started for the lake on April 1st (at once I felt all the old disappointment again). Nelson was left in charge of the fort. Stanley in a letter was to follow our old road and make his fort on the small island near Kavalli. Jephson was then to go on even as far as Wadelai if necessary, and Nelson tells me that Stanley gives him fifteen days to do this. Rot!

Parke will be of great use to them all. Stanley was very ill for over a month after I left with gastritis, he seems to have suffered a great deal. I believe he was very mad with me when he heard ... that I had followed the Manyuemas instead of crossing the Ihuru and swore terribly. By George, after all my hard work and after deuced near getting left with fever I reach here only to find that I am to remain and do *masumba* [settlement] work. It is a terrible blow. I would have given anything to have gone on with the *saffari*.

I only brought fourteen men into the fort of those from Ugarrowwa's, and all these are weak and tired. Nelson is living in Stanley's house, I will live in the Officers' House which I now call mine. We agreed to mess apart as this would undoubtedly save many a row.

Fancy plantation work right on the equator! We work here from seven to eleven a.m. and from one to four p.m., plenty long enough under such a hot sun, but one hour and a half shorter than Stanley's hours. Stanley and Jephson, before they left, built more houses and planted great quantities of Indian corn. The beans we planted are a failure. Fortunately, Stanley left some of his books to while away our spare hours. I found some eight or nine goats left here, but five are only kids. Killed a large goat for my men and Nelson gave all some very good meat from a kid he had just killed. There are four fowls, two of which lay eggs. I suppose one must just go in for this work with a light heart and try and do the most possible, but at present one's feelings are anything but pleasant. Corn, beans and tobacco are the only things worth growing, as we have no seeds of any sort.

27th April
Spent the day in resting, eating good meals and looking about the place. Nelson is a first rate hand at making good things out of very little.

For dinner we had: soup – goat kid stew and flour (Indian corn) sauce with vegetables, roast goat – (leg), sweet potatoes, green corn, *mboga* [pumpkin], Indian meal porridge, and milk (one cup each, goat's), banana fritters, potato cakes, Indian corn toast, red pepper and salt.

All very well cooked, the roast leg and beans were really well done. More about our meals later on. Nelson has had *pombe* (banana, beer made from sorghum and sugar) and oil (castor) made, but the latter was very impure. What I made some time ago was much better.

28th April Saturday
Nelson had bad fever. Temperature ran up to 106° this afternoon.

The old heron that was a prisoner when I left for below has disappeared and gone into the bush. Others say it died of hunger.

The *masumba* [settlement] has been very much extended since I left. Several acres more of corn have been planted, fences built, ditches dug, a wattle *boma* added to the old board one, the water draining place much improved, avenues, Stanley's mania, made, and many other improvements, many quite useless, such as clearing roads to 12' to 14' wide for man traffic.

As the place is so complicated I shall have to wait a bit and make a prismatic compass sketch with all the fields, etc. It will be a very funny life here, I can see, situated as we are away from any white men, absolutely cut off from the world in every way, without a bit of European food to eat, even tea or coffee are things of bygone days. It is different to what one has been accustomed to, even on the march. Here we have our little troubles and trials, here we have just to sit and wait patiently for our friends to come to us. Stanley said he could return in two and a half months from the lake, this would make it about the middle of June. He will in all probability be longer than this.*

---

*In fact, on the following evening, 29 April 1888, Stanley finally met Emin on the shores of Lake Albert Nyanza. Stanley returned to Fort Bodo on 8 June, a little less than the two and one-half months that he had forecast.

On all sides of us there are the Wasongora who sneak into our plantations for food and who fire at us and get fired at by our men. Elephants also we dread very much, as in a month or so if undisturbed they will destroy the largest grove of bananas. Why in four months after the Manyuema had driven natives out of village near here, not a single sign of a banana leaf was left, all had been eaten up by elephants and buffalo, even to the roots of the trees.

What a miserable set of chaps we have become, upon my word! No clothes, no boots, no pens, no pencils, ink, our knives lost or broken, no candles or anything in the way of food except what we can get out of the country, very few medicines, and to make things worse, Stanley has taken almost all the quinine, Nelson was only left ninety grains, just three good doses in a bad attack. Mind you this quinine is not Stanley's but Parke's, some that was given to him at Cape Town by a surgeon ... Here we are then without quinine. I have a couple of hundred grains left of my own.

Of all the old women that any of us have seen in the way of a secretary, oh Lord help us, old de Winton sweeps the tray. Utterly ignorant of African life, he recommended this and that and scorned other things, and we taking his advice like fools have been badly left. We have one cooking utensil on an average each, all are scattered. We were told expressly we should have candles and a small canteen each. What a preconcerted lie this was. Old de Winton knew there were forty boxes of grub for five whites. When he afterwards knew there were twelve whites going, why didn't he order more boxes? *Secretary*! What the deuce does an old R.A. officer know about this business?*

Stanley of course would join in and say in quite an offhand manner, "O, they'll manage in some manner, don't order any more, tra-la-la." Then when we have been out fifteen months the quinine, brandy and ulcer medicines are

---

*Major-General Sir Francis de Winton (1825–1901), after being commissioned in the Royal Artillery, had served in the Crimean War. He filled various staff appointments in Canada for a total of twelve years, including three years in Halifax (when Stairs was born). He married a Canadian and invested heavily in the brewery proposed by his Cambridge contemporary, John James Dunn Oland. As military secretary to the governor general, the Marquis of Lorne, de Winton travelled extensively in western Canada and became a ranch owner south of Calgary (the village of de Winton, Alberta is named after him). He followed Stanley in the Congo Free State as administrator general (Stanley and he overlapped for a brief period before Stanley's departure in 1884). In organizing the administration of the Congo Free State, de Winton drew upon his Canadian experience to urge upon Leopold a police rather than military force:

"In the North West territory of Canada over 60,000 Indians in a territory 800 miles long by 300 broad were kept in perfect order by about 450 men. One reason for the power possessed by these few men in so large a territory was that they were called North

out. After this let no one run down military expeditions, they generally allow their officers medicines when sick, and light to see by at nights. What fools we all were not to enquire into these matters before leaving England! But no, we begin to think of this in Central Africa when right on the equator, as far as possible away from salt water.

Stanley treats his officers like dogs, and himself as near like a prince in this country. It would be splendid if we could only march to Zanzibar in company with Emin Pasha – but all this is Gordonizing. Old Gordon was a terrible sneak, he was fanatically stricken by religion, and then called every one he came in contact with a d — d fool. His Christianity must have been something like de Winton's practice of secretaryship, viz. decidedly doubtful.

This day last year we reached Kinshassa ... We have lost over 210 men from Yambuya till now, of these at least twenty have died of arrow wounds ...

The following is the first of several "diary" entries which Stairs prepared for publication in the periodical *The Nineteenth Century* in 1891. They are included here to suggest the degree to which he altered further his diaries from the already revised and edited version which he had based upon his original rough notes.

28 April Saturday [from *The Nineteenth Century*]
... It will be a very strange life this. Here we are cooped up in our own little surroundings, with our trials and cares to grin at and bear as elsewhere. An army corps might be within twenty miles of us and we should not know it. There is now not a bite of European food in the place; even tea is a thing of bygone days. To work hard and wait patiently for things to develop is all we can do. On all sides are the Wasangora, who sneak into our plantations and play havoc with our food-supplies. We are constantly exchanging shots with them, but I do not think a friendship with them advisable; they are too cunning. Herds of elephants seem to hover around us too. They are extremely partial

West Mounted Police and the Red Indian did not look upon them as soldiers. Some such similar name for the Société's force on the Congo would be less likely to wound the susceptibilities of foreign nations, for, while the term soldier implies a standing army, that of police implies only the preservation of law and order."

De Winton's deputy in the Congo Free State was Camille Jannsen whom King Leopold recalled from Canada where he had been the long-serving Belgian Consul General in Quebec (where de Winton had known him). Following de Winton's work as secretary of the Emin Relief Expedition committee, he commanded a small British army expedition to Sierra Leone in which Stairs's RMC friend Huntly Mackay served (see note on p. 60). In later life, de Winton successfully combined several entrepreneurial activities – he was a collaborator of Mackinnon in Africa and a promoter of the Alberta Ranche Company in Canada – with a role at court as a financial adviser.

to banana stalks. In four months after the Manyuema drive natives away from their villages there is not a single banana-plant standing. Elephants complete the work of the slave-raiders ...

30 April Monday [from *The Nineteenth Century*]
Men out cutting poles and materials for new houses; others working up clay. The new granary should hold six tons of corn, so that with the old one we shall be able to store about eleven tons. The beans are a failure, owing to insects, though planted in three different spots.

Natives getting bold; sent out *rugga rugga* ... saw the natives, who decamped, leaving their baskets. A favourite amusement of these people now seems to lie in placing sharp-pointed stakes freshly covered with poison on the paths through the bananas. It takes a sharp eye to see them.

1 May Tuesday [from *The Nineteenth Century*]
Claying up my new house. N.[elson] has a quarter of an acre of healthy-looking tobacco plants (native seed) doing well. Huts in this country must have steep pitches to the roofs; we have no grass, so have to use leaves. After a week's hard work on a roof it is riling to see the way the wind lifts the whole thing off and deposits it half-way across the square.

5th May
Some of the men who came with me from Ugarrowwa's are beginning to put on a little flesh, but the most of them are in very poor condition. I have two men with very bad ulcers and others with bad chests, etc., a fortnight more, though, should make a wonderful difference. Still cutting materials for the granary, slow job, as men will loaf in bush. *Rugga rugga* came in with a lot of lies to tell us.

Stanley made a great mistake. Though I am supposed to be the senior of Nelson, still Stanley never left any order as to what positions we should hold respectively here when I should arrive. Nelson offered me the post, but as Stanley had headed his letter to Nelson commanding Fort Bodo, I refused.

◆   ◆   ◆

13th May
I made a great discovery to-day, finding that the juice of fermented bananas before reaching the *pombe* stage was very sweet, I thought sugar could be boiled down from it. We then filled a *chungu* [pot] of partially fermented liquor and boiled it down, when at last a thick, sweet syrup of delicious taste was the result. This we used on our porridge with great success. I also made a little jam which is grand. This find is just the right thing, and some sweet substance is just what we have wanted for a long time. There is little or no

sugar cane about here or one could make sugar at once. Nelson's attempt at making salt also turned out a partial success. He used a water wad that the natives had planted in the creek ... The process is dry grass in sun, burn in *chungu*, pour water over ashes letting it fall into second pot. This liquid is quite salt and can be used in this way. To get dry salt boil this liquid over hot fire.

One's feelings as to what Stanley and others are doing, and when they will return are almost constantly coming up. Giving all things to be done a fair amount of time they should be back here by middle of June.

Abdullah should also have returned by that time, unless the Major is still at Yambuya. One cannot help feeling that it will be yet two years before any of this expedition ever see Zanzibar. We are now four months beyond the time Stanley said he should return to the Major. Is the Major's *saffari* still extant...?

◆   ◆   ◆

13 May Sunday [from *The Nineteenth Century*]
Killed the big white goat; first day of Ramadan, no books to read. (Mr. Stanley afterwards left his books here, two months later, and the enjoyment we got out of them may perhaps be understood.)

I pass on now over the first two months when the column came through from the Nyanza, and left on the 16th for Yambuya. Our duties were now increased by the addition of many sick men suffering from ulcers, &c., and food became more scarce, owing to frequent tornadoes which destroyed our crops.

In the meantime we had made salt, beer, and banana jam, to add to our comforts. The supply of ripe bananas procurable having given out by the end of July, we had to write off the beer and jam from our diet-list.

We have some amusing characters among us, though perhaps sometimes the amusement afforded by them is not always intentional on their part. Mufta Saramini, having been sent into the bush with some men to cut poles, climbed a tree to get at a nice dry limb of firewood some distance up from the ground. He got at last half-way out towards the end of the limb, and commenced chopping the limb on the inside, or the side nearest the trunk, he sitting outside; when he had nearly finished cutting through the wood the limb he was sitting on broke off, and limb, billhook, and man came all of a heap to the ground. He decided ever after this to cut outside when sitting on a limb. For many days the mention of this was the signal for roars of laughter from the men.

My supply of ink is nearly finished; I have added water so many times that it now resembles picnic lemonade in strength. I will try the Arab plan of making some more from burnt husks of rice.

One often forgets that on every side of us are our enemies, and that we are liable to attack at any moment; of course, when our men meet the Wasongora in the bush, it is bullets *versus* arrows and spears. There are now no inhabited villages within fifteen miles of the camp, but bands of natives constantly come in and raid our *shambas* (plantations); we generally track them and have a scrimmage next day, just to show them we are not asleep.

Tracking is a science: some have a natural quickness and aptitude for it; others are of no use at all at it. The keen way, for instance, in which Farag Ala can follow up a native track is wonderful; the slightest sign is noticed by him. The only other art that resembles tracking is finding your way about in the bush. A clever bush native near his own home, acting as your guide, no matter how much you may have twisted and turned, or gone up hill and down dale, when asked where camp is, will instantly say, There, and point out the direction. He knows where his home is, just as the wild bee does; he has mentally and instinctively been carrying on a traverse, carefully noticing the angles of deflection and the distance travelled over; this he has plotted in his mind, and when asked where he is, he reads the map he has made on his brain, and lets you know the result. It is fatal to interrupt a tracker by unnecessary speaking. If doubts are cast as to the skill of the leading man, and he feels that he is not trusted, most probably confusion will follow ...

18th May
My supply of ink is just about finished, again and again I have added water to it, until it much resembles American public picnic lemonade. How to make more I am at a loss. The Arabs make *fari* ink by burning the stalks and husks of rice in an earthenware pot and then boil the residue down and use this as ink. I have seen some of it but it seemed to be rather watery looking stuff.

Nelson and I are going to try our hand at distilling whisky from corn and rhum from bananas. So far we have made or prepared a good many new things, but the want of a book on the subject places us completely on our own resources. We have made banana beer, banana syrup, and jam which is splendid, tasting like crab apple, or quince if very strong. We also have made salt, soap in a sort of way, red pepper, indian corn, beer, and some other things, then we make banana and corn meal, puddings, cakes, toast, fritters from ripe bananas (when we have fat, which is very seldom) and a lot of minor dishes.

One often forgets almost that on every side of one are enemies, and that we are liable to attack at any moment. Of course it is bullets and arrows and spears whenever our men meet Washenzi in the bush, and pillaging on both sides whenever anything happens. There are now no inhabited villages say within fifteen miles of this place, but still the natives have built here and there rough bush camps generally near some source of food as a plantation for bananas, the women of course carrying the loads. Often enough our men, also looking for food, encounter these parties, and then the rifle speaks up and drops perhaps one or two, the others all running. Then again our chaps sometimes get an arrow which often enough does for them.

No attempt at friendship has been made here by any side, nor in fact do we want to be friends with these people as one feels sure that under the cloak of peace these cunning devils would play back on us and perhaps get the best of it. No, an open enmity is far and away the best. I have on guard in the towers of the fort some eight men every night and two sentries by day. Zanzibaris make the poorest of watchers though, and constantly one had to be out in the night to see that they keep on the alert. We make them shout from station to station (post to post) every hour, and every night I visit them three times. The Washenzi seem to know the difference between us and the Manyuema well enough, they say the Manyuema take women and ivory while we only take goats. The Manyuema kill many more natives than we do, and are much crueller. In the ramble from Ugarrowwa's I just had, the Manyuema stabbed four of their women slaves to death, and cut off the hand of another, letting her go into the bush to die ...

19th May
It is terribly hot just at present, and I should think the temperature was about 95° when I write this, shade imperative. About nine at night, while in the yard, I heard rustling in the corn and went up into the two easterly towers and watched with the sentries but saw or heard nothing more.

20th May
What I heard last night must have been a native creeping through the corn. Some men came in from getting bananas and reported the Washenzi had been again filching our corn. I went out and found that evidently some ten or fifteen had been residing on the outside of the corn fields near the road to the Nyanza. They had broken down very little but had plucked some four or five baskets of ripe corn and then retired. Some three or four men must also have been on the east side, as the corn there had been tampered with and their tracks came to within sixty yards of the ditch and there stopped. Some four men had done up their loads on the little rise on the road 150 yds. from the ditch. It was a bright moonlight night, nearly half moon. This is the second raid they have made, the interval being about one month.

◆   ◆   ◆

27th May
The average yield per acre from the big field was sixty bushels. I don't think it will be safe to put more than ten tons into the new granary. To-day I got about 100 more Wasangora words from the captive boys we have, but it is very difficult work. Plurals, genders, etc., one cannot possibly get yet for some time. In our expedition of a few days ago I got a small brown and white

native dog of the regular Washenzi breed. I should like very much to get her home or cross her with Stanley's dog. I have named her "Mtoro" – the runaway.

Read a lot of Wolseley's pocket book.* What a godsend a few books would be here!

♦   ♦   ♦

29th May
All the men say the corn we are now planting and will plant will never come to anything, as the planting season is now over. This is bad, and I am afraid too true. Clearing up the corn stalks all morning, at Nelson's house and repaired the south tower.

30th May
Cleared out the ditch, hoed the big road N.E. clearing up corn stalks, clearing and burning in field. The boys caught a dozen or two of not bad fish yesterday, they were barbers, or minnows. They all got a dozen or so of crabs and a few shrimps or crayfish.

♦   ♦   ♦

1st June [1888]
In for another month. West winds and dry for last six days. Bad for corn. Little rain last night. The dog is getting to know me a little but still is very shy.

Stanley ought to have left the lake by this time according to his estimate. I don't believe he will be very far out either. One only hopes Abdullah will get here with news of the Major before Stanley comes. He, Abdullah, has now been away three months, or about 105 days, barely time to get back.

2nd June
Nelson building new house for self and his boys.

♦   ♦   ♦

---

*Field Marshal Lord Wolseley wrote *The Soldier's Pocketbook for Field Service* in 1867–68 when, as Colonel Garnet Wolseley, he was serving in Canada. It was an immediate success, passing through numerous editions.

4th June

At work again hoeing and at the two houses, Abedi getting my clothes and boots once more patched up. On each of my trouser legs I have four patches, besides a great many others in various parts. My boots are beauties, patched and repatched all out of shape. The awls and needles I made work very well. If one goes over to the relief of the Major, one will suffer terribly from sore feet.

Military men just note our position. Our front is 600 odd miles from our base, between these two no communication has been carried on for one year. Our supplies at the base cannot follow for there is no communication. The front has to retire to relieve the base, else it can't move! Now in retiring the front leaves behind it (550 miles from base) a detachment of incapables (forty, or nearly so) in an enemy's country and retires these 550 miles to the base. Will it ever advance again to the relief of these forty men?

5th June

At the same work as yesterday. At 11 Rashid and his men finished the upper field and started hoeing in front of the ditch where we are to plant beans. My house for the boys is nearly all clayed in. Work is very slow just now with so many men on the houses. We want three weeks' good work outside yet to put in all the crops we have space for. Probably we shall get fifteen bushels to the acre.

6th June

Stanley should be back in ten days to his calculation. This book now is simply a source of insanity to anyone writing it. To start with, one has just to pick up and collect the many scraps lying about on one's board table. Putting these together they form the book, then one gets quite lost shifting these about till they assume a proper form for writing on. Truly we are in a pretty bad way as regards our supply of the many little necessities every educated European travels about with. I have not a single pen and only one miserable little lead pencil, none of the others have ink, and very little paper. The use of this book for a journal shows up pretty fairly my need for another one.

I had often wondered what it would be like to be left in a detached fort in some black man's country far away from even any of the comforts of the back-woodsman. By Jove, we have it now in right good earnest! On the march one does not mind the absence of tea, coffee, sugar, salt, etc., so much, but in a fixed position with one day's life just the same as another, one feels the want of salt especially, and tea would be positively a godsend. With abundance of coarse food comes satiety and then a desire for refinement, but this one cannot gratify. Our life compared with station life, say on the Congo, is as ordinary prison fare to grub, say, at the Metropole [Hotel in London] or the

Palace Hotel at Frisco, only prisoners get salt, we don't. One eats quantities of red pepper and *mboga* [pumpkin] green, and so keeps in fair order.

I'll back this place against any other in all Africa for the number of fleas to be found here in the yard, in the houses, everywhere they seem to be doing brigade drill. My dog fairly swarms with them and frequently imparts them to me.

Chapter Ten

Stanley and Parke returned to Fort Bodo from Lake Albert on 8 June 1888. After an absence of two months and a week, Stanley arrived back without Emin and Jephson, but he did bring unexpected news.

First, following a dramatic meeting on the shores of Lake Albert on 29 April 1888, Stanley's vanguard, ragged and ill-fed, had realized that the supposedly beleaguered governor and his followers grew splendid crops, produced admirable clothing, and appeared well supplied, with the possible exception of ammunition. In fact, it was, in a real sense, Emin who had to succour Stanley, rather than Stanley who had to rescue Emin.

Second, Emin showed signs of procrastination from the first encounter on the lakeshore. Having spent his adult life in the domains of the Sublime Porte and having become a Moslem, Emin had no interest in returning to unemployment in Cairo or Europe. His scientific interests could be given free rein as governor of a distant province in Central Africa. Further, Emin knew his Egyptian officers and clerks and Sudanese soldiers well enough to sense that many of them, complete with families, were in no hurry to exchange the pastoral pleasures of Central Africa for the uncertainties of urban squalor in Cairo. Emin, in any event, no longer held any sway over his more distant garrisons. They would decide for themselves what their reaction to the Khedive's orders would be (some dismissed them as fraudulent).

All this Stanley had not foreseen. He and his expedition had struggled for thirteen months to reach Emin, only to find that he did not want to leave Equatoria. Stanley's first conversations with Emin suggested that if the garrisons did elect to leave in the face of Mahdist pressures from the north, they might well decide to settle near Lake Victoria, as the "Mackinnon clan" hoped that they would, rather than return to Egypt. For his part, Emin, himself showing no wish to depart, managed to convince Stanley that the opinion of his outlying garrisons had to be canvassed. Some might elect to remain where they were; others might prefer to remain elsewhere in Central Africa. Stanley agreed that Emin should take the necessary time to sound his garrisons (although he may have done so because he himself needed time to determine what had happened to his rear column).

Having ordered Jephson to accompany Emin on his tour of his garrisons to determine their wishes, Stanley returned from the lake to Fort Bodo on 8 June 1888 still hopeful that news had arrived during his absence about the rear column.

Ten months had now passed since Stanley had heard from Barttelot, but no news awaited him at the fort. Stanley thereupon decided that when Emin was travelling to his distant garrisons, he would return to Yambuya in an attempt to determine what had happened to the rear column.

On 13 June 1888 Stanley gave Stairs a long "letter of instruction," appointing him commandant of Fort Bodo (with Nelson as second in command and Parke, upon his return, as medical officer). Stanley charged Stairs with the care and expansion of both the fort and the plantations, but he left him an option. Stanley expected Emin and Jephson to arrive at the fort by mid-August, two months hence. If Emin and Jephson brought sufficient carriers, Stanley recommended that Stairs then evacuate the fort and return to the lake with Emin and Jephson, establish a camp and await there his arrival which he estimated would be no earlier than December, six months hence (assuming that the rear column was still at Yambuya).

On 16 June Stanley left Fort Bodo to march westward to Yambuya. Parke would accompany Stanley as far as Ipoto where he would recover the supplies that had been buried there. He would then part with Stanley and return with them to Fort Bodo. From Ipoto, Stanley would be accompanied by no European (other than his servant, Hoffman). The dispersal of the expedition was now almost total. Stanley and Parke were heading westward through the Ituri forest. Jephson was moving northward with Emin. Barttelot, Jameson, Ward, and Bonny were still at Yambuya. Rose Troup, seriously ill, was on his way to Britain. Stairs was at Fort Bodo confronted with the prospect of several more months of inactivity with the invalid Nelson – at least until Parke returned from Ipoto or Jephson from Lake Albert.

8th June

About 2 p.m. heard shouts and shots and soon after Stanley and the *saffari* came in amidst great excitement. What is the news? Everyone asking dozens of questions and not waiting for the answer. Yes, the white man is there, we have seen him and fought side by side with him. We had very little fighting, all our former enemies are now our friends. Jephson left in boat and in six days brought back news that he [Emin] was alive. A letter had been left by him with the natives and Stanley getting hold of this knew all would be well. Parke looks rosy and Stanley fit.

Jephson remains behind and will go the rounds of the stations with Emin Pasha. Casati was alive and with him [Emin] in his camp.

9th June

Stayed indoors yarning nearly all day with Parke and Stanley. They have discovered a snow mountain to S.W. of lake, perhaps "Gordon Bennett".* Emin Pasha and Casati both willing to come out and in six months are to be ready at south end of lake ... Emin Pasha has suffered very little from sickness and has made an enormous collection of insects, snakes, etc., and has discovered old spades and tools buried away for centuries in the earth. [Alexander] Mackay, the missionary in Uganda, is safe and sent letters on to Stanley and Emin Pasha.

The Pasha was very much pleased at seeing the white men and made great presents of honey, cloth, tobacco, vegetables, cattle and goats. He lives very well and appears quite happy, rather objecting to leave Africa. His followers number 6,000, including two drilled battalions well armed.

Stanley brought 105 natives with him to this place as porters. They are of the Madi tribe at the N.W. end of Lake Albert. Stanley this time made friends with the Wazamboni, our old enemy, and advanced on and drove away an unfriendly tribe. He had 1500 of natives working for him. He, Stanley, looks very much pleased at the success he has achieved. Parke, Jephson and Stanley sent letters through Uganda. There is some doubt yet as to whether they will get through or not, but if they do, people at home will hear then of us about August or September.

Letters from Zanzibar had reached Casati, but not forwarding them to Emin Pasha they were burnt with his home when Kabba Rega, the King of Uganda, drove him out. When Casati was relieved he had nothing on but a loin cloth.

These Madi people will go on down by Yambuya with the column and carry loads. They say the bush is a bad place. Wait a bit! Many of them are bound to die on the road. They gave us a dance in the fort at night, a very clumsy affair, not at all like the Somalis or the South Africans. Poor devils, they have no clothes and don't know how to build quick shelters in the bush and so will suffer terribly at night in the bush and if there is much wet will die off like rats. They will be of great help to us though, as our men can go empty handed.

Who is to go with Stanley yet we don't know. Emin Pasha gave Stanley and Parke each a donkey, first rate little beasts. They will be left here. He has promised to give us all one. He has two hundred of these and a trained elephant.

The report of Stanley's arrival with a big army has I believe frightened the King of Uganda very much. Now with the Major's people and say 1500 of

---

*Named by Stanley after his employer at the *New York Herald*.

Emin Pasha's we could do some pretty good work if any big tribe should attack us ...

10th June
Still yarning about Emin Pasha and talking to the men who all look very fit and bumptious as they always get with full stomachs. All want to stay here, dreading the bush journey through mud and water very much.

Emin Pasha sent Nelson and myself honey, tobacco and salt in good quantities, a perfect godsend. He also gave Stanley quantities of honey and potato whisky, but he [Stanley] has not given us a drop of it yet. The latter is very good stuff though a bit smoky. Parke brought also a present of a basket of tobacco from Emin Pasha for each of us. It is mild and very light coloured and not bad smoking.

11th June
... The newly arrived *saffari* got orders that they would leave here on the 16th and we started issuing rations for 25 days 219 men, or over 32,000 corns. This cleared out our new crop of corn, nine tons. Stanley will follow down the old road practically but will return by another, probably being the old one near Ipoto and striking N.E. and join the Ituri at the ferry where he crossed before.

12th June
Cutting poles. *Saffari* for Major [Barttelot] preparing corn. Stanley gave us fifteen cups of whisky, or rather Emin Pasha did, and some tobacco. The honey is delicious, only it is going very fast. My own crop of tobacco is coming on very well and I am almost ready to top now.

Gave Wadi Mabruki a letter for the Major ...

Stairs's candid letter to his brother officer, Barttelot, was highly disparaging of Stanley. (Stairs wrote an equally derogatory letter to Nelson).* Stairs berated Stanley for needless brutality towards Africans, burning their villages in return for a harmless arrow attack. Further, Stanley had proven himself wholly indifferent to the officers of the expedition, careless of their welfare. Stairs letter read in part:

"Stanley has got the name all about these parts of being the meanest man ever given life. It's pretty well true ... Stanley treated us all from first to last in a perfectly damnable manner as regards food; he has at times had all sorts of things given him, not one of which we ever got unless one of us went and shamed him out of the thing. Emin gave him a devil

---

*Stairs's letter to Nelson was sold at auction in Newcastle Upon Tyne in 1993 and is at writing unavailable.

of a lot of whisky and tobacco for us which we have not seen, and so on, till every one of us have quite given up any idea of ever getting anything from him ... Stanley will chisel like the mischief and want all the provisions for himself at Yambuya; he gives in at once, though, if he is stuck up to on this point."[1]

15th June
Planted an acre of beans near the fort ditch. Men all ready and fell in 5 p.m. to examine rifles and ammunition. Stanley's force 219 men. Nelson has fever and a bad hand and I don't expect will be able to take on the twelve men to Kilonga-Longa's for loads as was intended. Parke will go.

16th June
The *saffari* 211 strong with 14 men under Parke left this morning about 6:30. All were in good spirits and left with the determination to do good work. Parke should be back in about 22 days.

Stanley hopes to reach the lake about January 2nd [i.e., seven months hence he would return with the rear column to Fort Bodo and then march on to Lake Albert with his reunited expedition].

We expect Jephson and Emin Pasha here in about three months and then all will go on together. Stanley's last words to me were, "I hope to meet you on the [Lake Albert] Nyanza before long."

◆   ◆   ◆

19th June [from *The Nineteenth Century*]
At work on garden and N.[elson]'s house, men getting leaves from the forest for the roof of latter all day. Our garden has now assumed quite a respectable shape; we have four large, raised beds, and the whole is secured with a strong fence. Our ideas of planting the different seeds disagree considerably; all we know about it has been gained in early life. We planted the onion-seeds in different 'styles' as experiments; as for the peas, there are so few that this first crop is planted to get seed for another; we shall not eat any of the first at all ...

20th June
Coronation day?*
Last night I fully expected a raid on our corn by the natives. Just about dusk we heard them shouting in the bush quite close at hand and afterwards heard

---

*The coronation of Queen Victoria was on 28 June 1838. Stairs may possibly have recalled that it was on 20 June 1837 that King George IV had died and Victoria had learned of her accession to the throne.

other signs of their presence. Nothing definite, though, could we hear or see, though I watched in the towers till nearly ten o'clock. It was a fairly bright moon and they had everything their own way. I half believe the donkeys scared them off by their braying in the yard near the ripe corn.

Poor old " Randy", Stanley's dog, died in my room last night. He had been left under my care by Stanley on leaving for Yambuya, and here now he only lived four days. I feel certain he died of a broken heart. He ate nothing yesterday, and yesterday evening came up and put his head in my lap several times. At midnight he gave three or four howls, and then turned over and kicked his last. He had been to the Nyanza twice. Stanley will be in an awful way about it and will think I either starved him or beat him to death.

21st June
We have been eighteen months out from England. It was originally to have taken us only eighteen months to reach Zanzibar. Now in time we are about half way. In a few days we shall have been absent from Yambuya a year. Gardening, making fences, cutting leaves ...

22nd June
Nelson is up to-day for the first time since Parke left. He was up for morning parade for a wonder. He is simply maddening, though I should not say so. He is the biggest grumbler I ever saw, always his food. His only talk is about grub, which he bolts with the speed of a hungry dog. Among the men he is an utter ass, too, and picking holes about men insulting him ... I can hardly speak civilly to him now, it's either grub when he answers or, "I've got a pain in my big toe" or something after that style.

Am making a pair of *Veldtshoes*. They require a lot of patches to make them wearable and will not stand the wet very well. We make them of untanned leather.

23rd June Saturday
... Nelson has three more very bad sores. Always the same thing. It makes me mad to hear him talk like this and then press to have a goat killed so he can have a good guzzle. He is a perfect specimen of a *goe-goe*.

Yesterday and to-day we weeded all the roads and cleaned out the drains, and by this evening should have the place ship-shape. I am now certain I was never built for sitting down to this sort of work, it slowly drives me wild, generates a temper fit for an old Indian curried general, makes me notice every little weak point in my neighbours while at the same time one forgets one's own.

Here life is the same day after day almost without a break. The only way to make the days pass pleasantly is to work yourself with the men. I cannot talk cheerfully now with Nelson as, firstly, he is a chap now I begin to despise, on account of his loafing qualities, secondly, if we do attempt to talk the subject always ends in food. Not a bright life is it? Perhaps I had better not talk any more of this, but one alone all the time hardly ever speaking one's own language gets to notice all these things, and I swear at time I go outside of the fort to get away from Nelson's constant nagging of his boys.

How great a pleasure it would be here to know something of botany, all the innumerable shrubs and plants are simply unnamable by us!

24th June Sunday
Parke should be now on his way back with the loads from Ipoto. Sunday here is always a dreadful slow sort of day, one has nothing to do much but write up one's journal, and see that the goats and sheep do not go out into the garden. This is a most trying job and one on which no amount of supervision seems to have any effect ...

24th June Sunday [from *The Nineteenth Century*]
Sunday is always a trying sort of day here; we do no work, and as a result, it is a plot-breeding day among the men. Sentry duty is the only necessary one that is performed; strangely enough, the natives seemed to find this out, and generally choose Sunday evenings for their excursions amongst our crops.

Our calf (from the Nyanza) got into the beans this morning; it took some time to get him out, and we discovered he had been feasting on the bean-tops for some hours, and had wrecked our melon patch. If I had possessed a rifle ready loaded, I feel sure he would have been made into veal on the spot.

We had for some time after this two donkeys, which had been presented by Emin to Stanley. They at first did very well, but after two months at the fort, began to pine and get thinner every day; these donkeys caused us more trouble and anxiety than any dozen natives. Though we told off men to look after them, and built a yard, and tied them up, somehow or other they would break loose and sail wildly through our fences into the melon patches, wrecking and crushing everything in their way. All hands would then turn out to catch them; they generally managed, though, to destroy considerable portions of our valuable crops, before getting them in. We spent two whole days once, in making a yard for these beauties, and the first night we put them into it, they ate the vines off, and kicked away the whole concern. This and poor food gradually took it out of them though, and at last one day, amidst cheers, I told the men to slaughter and eat them; we all had a share in the feast, but it was rather difficult to get rid of the thought of their red skin and generally fly-eaten appearance, even when they were made into stews. This was our last meat for 135 days; after this, neither N., P., [Nelson, Parke] nor I had a chance to get anything in the shape of flesh between our teeth, and not till we moved forward towards the Albert Nyanza did we once more revel in goats and fowls.

25th June Monday

[Two men] ran away yesterday on sentry, and have not returned. Both were under punishment for sleeping on sentry ... My punishments are as follows: flogging up to 100 strokes, and in addition one months stone drill, then of course any combinations of these downwards. Tying a man up till he is repentant. Standing in one position up to two hours with a heavy stone on one's head, this they dislike the most of all. Stone drill means the marching up and down in the square four hours per day with a fifty pound stone on a man's head ...

♦   ♦   ♦

1st July [1888]

My 25th birthday (1863) to-day. One is getting old and feels one is doing nothing in this place, locked up from all the world. On my last birthday I was near Yambuya and bad with remittent fever, thank Heaven it is not so now. Second birthday in Africa. I hope the next will be near Zanzibar.

They must be having a good time of it in Canada by now, sea trout, with trout fishing, with tennis and strawberries and cream and ice cream. By Jove, how good strawberries and cream would go now – hush, don't speak of it!

Yesterday to "save her life" we killed the fatted, only calf and gave rations to the men, keeping as much as we wanted for ourselves. She was badly on the wane, poor thing. Another day would have done for her. She used to go the creek for water and fall and remain in the water till beaten away. She was not the prodigal fatted calf. We are not over particular about the meat we get these days.

To turn to fever, I believe that there is no greater mistake made by medical books when they say, do not eat large quantities of meat in hot climates, if so the liver becomes torpid, the bowels clogged, etc. Don't believe this at all, eat as much meat as you want, do not gorge yourself, but to prevent violent fevers when doing hard work, keep up your system to full power by plenty of good meat and other good [word illegible], if necessary meat four times a day.

The cause of a great many fevers is weakness in oneself, I mean poorness of condition. Every time on this expedition that I have walked and worked hard for, say, ten or fifteen days at a time with poor food I have been attacked with bad fevers. Once I got good food and got rid of the fever I never get another till once again my system becomes weakened by hunger.

No, meat and other good, strong foods are the things to work on in this and every other country. I know that fever itself wears one down violently quick, but what I say is that the primary cause of that fever was weakness, perhaps combined with a chill or effects of the sun. Those coming strong and healthy, built up with good English beef, to this country, are rarely troubled with fever for the first six months, for the reason that their system is well able to knock off malaria, etc.

Drank my own health in evening and had the best dinner I have had for many a long day: soup from the heifer we killed, cold tongue, a steak, the undercut joint, bananas, corn, *ugari* [porridge], etc., and then half a cup of Emin's whisky to finish up with, not so bad?

2nd July Monday

Made another change and tried to dry the corn we pulled last week. For myself I think the best way is to husk the corn, not shell it, and then dry it for a couple of days in the sun and then put it into the bins. The natives leave the husks on it, but dry it over fires. I should like to get at least four tons of good corn in by the time Jephson comes, and a couple of hundredweight of beans. Then each man could get a good ration. Parke ... in three days ... should be here.

I am moving the *boma* [stockade] out some six feet on the S.W. side to give room for a large house should Emin Pasha come here. I will also build another for his officers.

Sometimes the word "I" comes in very often in this part of my journal, but Nelson is a nonentity and hardly seems to count ...

3rd July Tuesday

... Settled down to stationary life such as this place affords. Daily almost with the same things to occupy one's mind and with nothing reaching one from outer sources, one is apt to become rather a "crank" and forget to a certain extent one's pleasanter moods. Strive as you like to against feelings which constantly come up, you cannot get over the feeling of one in prison, or confinement of some kind or other.

Often I wish I could tear away from here and once more get on the march again. Once on the move one's spirits rise and one feels one is doing something; here, ever so hard though you work, ever so much you may think, there is still that buried away feeling which at periods comes up from its grave and lets you imagine you are doing nothing for your own or anyone else's good – narrowness, selfishness and all brother [?] qualities grow on one at a terrible rate. To counteract these one feels that books (and light books) are necessary, conversation in one's own language too would be a counter check, but who can one talk to? From morning till night I hardly utter an English word, all work is done in Swahili. The very greatest comforts are smoking and looking after the garden.

I feel I have become like my father who in seeing a dandelion blossom invariably cuts it off with his stick, I in turn on seeing a weed on one of the tracks stop and root it up ...

3rd July Tuesday [from *The Nineteenth Century*]
We had another exciting time of it last night; about 8 p.m. the ants came in millions (we had these invasions usually once a fortnight).

Silently, deadly and irresistibly move these battalions; out of the forest, down, into, across, and up the ditch, through the *boma* (wood stockade), across the square, and into every nook and cranny conceivable they swarmed. The first notice (they generally came at night) would be a loud yell from some of the men. "Look out! *Siafu!*" [ants] There would be no more sleep that night. After experience gained, we found it the best plan to clear out of our houses, rush into the square, and build rings of fire round our persons. To put on one's clothes was to get bitten by dozens all over one's body, unless they had been first thoroughly smoked over a fire. Every now and then yells and curses told how a lazy one had got caught in his bunk. The sides of the huts, the roofs and floor, were simply one seething mass of struggling ants. They were after the cockroaches, mice, and insects that had taken up their abode in the roofs. Now and then squeaks of young mice told their story. As fast as the ants found their load (generally a cockroach) they would make off down the hill in long lines. Luckily they never touched our granaries; they seemed to prefer animal food. Towards morning there would only be a few thousand lost ones, aimlessly tearing about, apparently looking for the main body which had just decamped.

Usually these raids on us were made after a rain-storm; many of them came into the forest already staggering under loads; these appeared to wander about till the others were ready.

Next day not a cockroach could be found in the place, so that the ants did us a service in ridding us of these pests. The rats had decamped also, and did not return for some days.

We have seen outside the fort armies of red ants two and a half days long – i.e. they would take two and a half days passing a given spot. During the day the march would be incessant, every one marching at his very best; towards night they would huddle up in a seething mass, and if disturbed scatter in all directions.

The width of the stream of ants would be about two inches generally. On the flanks of this were the soldiers, fully twice the length of the workers. On our approach these big chaps would run out and up our legs like lightning. No birds, but of one sort, seemed to trouble them; these were little fellows about as big as sparrows and of a dull grey colour.

4th July
... Men constantly bring in reports of the boldness of the natives in coming close up to the fort for bananas and potatoes. We are helpless till Parke comes to have a slap at them ...

5th July

... I have read so much of Tennyson lately that now I know something of nearly every piece in his works.

What are they doing at home just now? Tennis and tea and cakes, boating, picnics across the "Arm" and in steam launches and all sorts of garden parties. Garden parties are a great fraud; they are given out of kindness to people who have invited one to their dances and in return one gives a garden party – very mean! Just about as mean I always think as in the practice of "presenting a testimonial" to some chap who has worked hard and spent a lot of his money in some public affair ... "

This is Parke's 20th day out; he must be near.

6th July

... About 11:15 a.m. the doctor and his carriers turned up at the fort. One of his men ... died on the road for want of food really. Parke has been 21 days absent. He brought up a good sized box of unhusked rice for us to plant; this will be a great godsend should Jephson be four or five months in coming.

Stanley, he said, was very mournful about the long journey ahead. I rather fancy he would have liked it better had he taken some white officer with him. He did Parke out of a goat with his usual meanness. Kilonga Longa and the other few chiefs who were there were in good "lying" form. Ismaili actually had the gall to say to Stanley that he gave Parke and Nelson food every day during their stay at Ipoto; a most confounded lie. The road Parke said was very bad. Stanley was carried in a chair all the way to Ipoto! Note this!!!

What were Stanley's reasons for going to Yambuya alone? Undoubtedly they were the following: (i) so that afterwards in his book he can say I alone braved the terrors of famine and the bush, found my way down river and by my skill and nerve, saved Major Barttelot; (ii) he knows he will have all the goats and food to himself (don't think this paltry, it is not. On the subject of food Stanley is a perfect glutton; he eats more than even Nelson); (iii) he wants to get out of paying the Manyuema, and does not want us to see the affair ...

6th July [from *The Nineteenth Century*]

P.[arke] weighs 154 lbs., N.[elson] weighs 150 lbs ... S.[tairs]. weighs 155 lbs. Abedi weighs 110 lbs., Mafta weighs 95 lbs.

Abedi has grown like a lion of late; his clothes are a sight to behold; I fancy his present appearance in a London street would awake a certain amount of interest in the passers-by. During meals I have occasionally to order him to take up a hitch in his waistcloth for decency's sake. I was reading Allibone's quotations to-day, and asked him if he thought I was studying my Khoran; he answered, "Yes, master." "Are all the books we white men read Khorans then?" "Why, yes, of course." If simplicity exists anywhere it is this; fancy anyone taking a strong yellow-back [a cheap paperback book] for a Khoran!

If, in describing any bird or animal to the boys – say a swan, for example – one asks, "And are there swans in Zanzibar?" "Oh yes, *telé* (many)." "How many, Abedi?" "Oh, the Sultan has one in a cage, or Mohammed Bin So-and-So keeps one tied up with a string," is the inevitable answer. You cannot get round a sharp Zanzibar boy in that way; fancy a swan tied up with a string. If you pursue the subject further you will probably learn that the swan builds its nest in high cocoa-nut palms, or does tricks, or something equally clever.

As for Farag Ala we have never yet stumped him in his strong point, natural history. There is no use telling him his stories are not founded on fact. The four-eyed story is his great weakness. 'In my country there is a large red and black bird about the size of a *kuku* (fowl); this bird is only seen when a man dies, and then comes and sits on his grave; he has two pairs of eyes, one in front, and one pair behind his head; with one pair he can see by day, and the other he uses at night. For three days and nights the bird keeps watch over the body, lest the *sheitani* [the devil] should come and steal it. After a fit of violent screaming he flies away and is seen no more. He, Farag Ala, has seen the bird, and has also seen giraffes sleeping at night with their heads resting in forks of trees.

The contents of the moon seem to tax his unusually original brain. He makes the bold statement that hyenas are fond of dancing, and will sneak up to the villages while the men are dancing, and then next night can be seen far out on the plains indulging in wild antics similar to those of the natives themselves.

7th July Saturday
The rice will make a good crop I hope. To-day I went over the crop of beans and put in seed where it was wanted; we also planted some fresh beans ...

8th July Sunday
Showers again showing that now is the time for planting corn ... I am now writing with the ink just made, it would run much better from an ordinary pen, this is a stylo and the thick ink catches; if used thin it is of no use. This makes another manufacture turned out by Fort Bodo ...

9th July Monday
... Upon my word some of the things the doctor tells me about Stanley in his dealings with Emin Pasha astonish even me. His petty meanness and selfishness crop up on every possible occasion. He and Emin will have a big row some of these days; [Emin] is not a man to have anything to do with one who practices anything underhand.

When two big men meet 'tis seldom they can work together peacefully for long: each wants his own way in any matter. Emin will not be ready for Stanley when he comes up, and this will incense *Bula matari* [Stanley] very much.* Egyptians and such ilk take a long time to act. It's an open question too, whether this is not the best policy in such a country as this ...

... By the bye, I believe that quinine is of no use at all in *any stage of a fever*. It should be used as a prophylactic or preventative before the fever ... Ulcers of a [word illegible] sort take months to heal up even if absolute quietness is guaranteed to the patient. We have not medicine for them ... water and rest are the best medicines, the water to be applied by means of a strong syringe and injected well in among the decayed flesh and tissue.

10th July Tuesday
... Nelson got in his crop of tobacco, plenty of it but poor quality being second leaves.

Stanley must have heard by this time news of the Major; if he has not yet met Abdullah, then things are black ...

11th July Wednesday
... the Zanzibari is no soldier, and when rough times come up he shews the coward to a degree, his trustworthiness and pluck desert him at the same time, and he wants then to "be off". As the porter though in quiet countries, I should say very few other natives could come up with him - our loads are all over 60 lbs. and many 66, 67 and 68 lbs., these the men will carry *all day* on very poor food and remain cheerful. Besides this load say of 65 lbs. (an average) he carries a Remington 9 lbs., his blanket, or mat, say 5 lbs., then say 4 lbs., of food (for they rarely carry much more), then the hoe, axe, or spade (these are nearly all gone now) say 3 lbs. more and the total would come to $65 + 9 + 5 + 4 + 3 = 86$ lbs. Not a bad load! Though these fellows can carry this amount, I say, 50 lbs. should be the limit. When one recollects the sickening mud, the rivers, swamps and other choice obstacles on the road, one thinks this 50 lbs. would be none too little. Their pay is $5 per month.

As a sentry, where protacted attention to every little thing going on around him must be given, the Zanzibari is an utter failure. I have lectured a man for sleeping on sentry at the same time giving him fifty strokes and 30 days stone drill, yet on his next guard that man was asleep and got 100 lashes. Sentry with us is no playing. We must be on the alert especially towards

---

Bula matari, evidently a corruption of *bula matadi*, the "breaker of rocks," a sobriquet bestowed upon Stanley by local Congolese as a result of his construction work on the railway around the lower Congo rapids in 1880.

dawn; NO, they are not of the right stuff for sentries. Here at night the very slightest snap of a twig, or the faintest spark from the native fire must be heard and seen; both times the Wasangora have come, white men gave the alarm.

◆   ◆   ◆

13th July Friday
... This applies to Stanley very well: "His passions and his virtues he confused / And mixed together in so wild a tumult /That the whole man is quite disfigured in him".

One becomes frightfully exasperated at the old one's [Stanley's] doings at times and vows all sorts of things, but then what can one do? He is a despot of the worst sort. Eaten up with pride, vanity and arrogance, he is incapable of seeing anything good in the doings of others, his own occupy so much of his thoughts. A meaner, more selfish (especially concerning his stomach) man, one has never seen, nor did one think man descended so low. He will borrow food when one is starving and then not repay it. He will borrow or ask for anything that his eye lights on and when asked in return for the same thing he will say he has not got it, when all the time it is "sticking out" before one as a sign board.

To shew the utter rottenness of the expedition, we *received more* from the man we were *going to relieve*, than the expedition ever brought from England. More in clothes and food; that is of course more cloth was brought but for eighteen months *who saw any* of it? By utter stinginess and false zeal for ammunition not a [word illegible] ever left Yambuya. So far not one officer has given him a word of praise: his generalship in spite of all his own praise has been of the poorest. He let 300 native porters slide through his hands at the lake through sheer pride, in not listening to Emin Pasha's word to tie them together.

It is interesting, though not very amusing, to go over the number of lives we have lost since leaving Yambuya. We started with 389 souls and reached the lake twice; on the return of Stanley to Yambuya he had 117 men of those that walked out of Yambuya 18 months ago and we were left 58, a total of 175 men out of 389, making 214 deaths, desertions, missing, etc., in 18 months. This is about 53%. Most of these deaths were from privations in the way of food caused by bullheaded plunging through the bush, not stopping for food when it was to be got.

At times when one thinks of the hard work one has willingly done for Stanley, of his petty and great meanness one has endured, of the (really) four months starving one has passed through, of the crushings one has got in being called deserter, and other choice epithets, one's whole soul burns again to think I ever had anything to do with such a man. One's good feelings for everyone at the start and for him have been swept away as clean as a corn broom sweeps a marble floor and in their place feelings of the bitterest, the most intensely acute have crept in and take the place of the former. What is the reason for this? Why every day seeing this man [Stanley] jealous of any little popularity his officers get, jealous of any petty little thing they may do which will bring them up in the eyes of the men, every day seeing him secretly talking with his men against some officer and breaking down discipline as he would break down his officers' hearts, ever day hearing his constant bickering really about nothing, seeing his paltry borrowing fits, being treated like dogs in not getting a due share of provisions, hearing his false voice in his conversation on official work, seeing his bullheadedness in not taking the advice of such a man as Emin Pasha. These and the many other qualities he possesses all tending in the way of petty, mean jealousy kill one's good feelings, crush one below par and make one's inner feelings bitter as gall. Examples one could give by the dozen but it is doubtful if such would do any good. Bitter are the feelings of some of his officers against the brutal way they have been treated! Ingratitude is treason to mankind.*

14th July Saturday
Mater's birthday ... It is very strange one is forgetting all the tunes or snatches from operas one knew in England; for instance *Patience*; slowly but surely the airs from this are fading away as well as those of the *Mikado, Olivette, La Mascotte*, etc. One is constantly whistling the same few old stale things and has forgotten others more recently come out. Fever again today (102°).

14th July Saturday [from *The Nineteenth Century*]
It is very strange how one is forgetting all the tunes one ever knew; all the "airs" of [Gilbert and Sullivan's] *Patience* have completely left us, and we only remember now such things as *Bonnie Dundee* or old waltzes that we

---

*None of this tirade against Stanley appears in Stairs's "diary" entries published in *The Nineteenth Century*. As an example of what other officers thought of Stanley, the following diary entry by Jephson for 5 March 1888 is illustrative. Stanley "told me he had been just as impetuous and rash as I am when he was my age but that time etc had taught him to curb himself and a whole lot more rubbish. He made himself out to be a St. John for gentleness, a Solomon for wisdom, a Job for patience and a model of truth. Whereas I do not suppose a more impatient, a more ungentle, a more untruthful man than Stanley could exist. He is most violent in his words and actions, the slightest little thing is sufficient to work him into a frenzy of rage, his sense of what is honourable is of the haziest description and he is certainly a most untruthful character ..." (*The Diary of*, p. 229).

have heard hundreds of times. *Grandfather's Clock* still remains in all its original purity; I doubt if fifty years would drive that out of us.

Our men are getting more restless day by day as the time goes on; we are looking for Jephson and the Pasha to come, and then all of us will go on to the lake. How the Pasha will revel in the beetles and bugs about this place! There are enough to stock ten British Museums. In the huts too, there are selections to choose from, but perhaps not quite of the kind the Pasha would derive much amusement from. We constantly find ourselves talking to each other in Kiswahili; being with the men all day and working with them encourages this, of course. All work is done in Suahili [*sic*], but now and then we would break out into English expressions to encourage the men. "By the Soul of the Prophet" and "By the shade of your grandfather's brother" are but unsatisfactory expressions.

♦   ♦   ♦

16th July Monday
... Nelson has slept steadily for the last three days, not a bit sick. He sleeps from 9 p.m. to 4 p.m. as a rule, hardly going out of the house during this time.

17th July Tuesday
... How one's feelings tend towards England and home ... In Nova Scotia (by George, I should like to be there now) one would be somewhere off in the bush or along the shore after trout and sea trout, perhaps putting up at some farmer-fisherman's place, where for breakfast they would give you both farm produce and fish of the best kinds. How very many happy days has one spent in this way, fishing, canoeing and yarning with these old bluenoses ...

♦   ♦   ♦

21st July Saturday
... Gave rations of ten [corn cobs] to each man. In afternoon when giving rations Shaban deliberately walked up the line out of turn and was going to snatch up a bunch of corn, I stopped him, he replied in an insolent, insubordinate manner and I punched him; at once he ran out and got a thick stick to hit me I suppose, but I sent him off again. This is the second attempt made by some of the worst characters here to stir up the loyal men to a general desertion of we [*sic*] white men and march away on to the plain and Emin Pasha where they will get better food and plenty of beef. Long before I punished [one] I knew that some ten men or so were trying to poison some good men into desertion *en masse* and leaving us and the loads; in both cases did those two men act badly so as to try and draw the sympathy of their comrades to their side... No wonder they want to go away; here the work is

irksome, the food poor and the hope of getting out soon very thin. On the plains they would have good food and little work, the Zanzibari idea of a true heaven.*

What this will come to in the end one cannot say ... My every effort here has been to make the men's lives happy and as easy for them as possible. Food I cannot give, as what corn we now have must be kept for rations on the march with Emin's men. The sentries I have punished severely when caught asleep, a proceeding any even rational-minded savage must see is advantageous to all; if the sentries sleep why then we are in the hands of the Washenzi.

My blood boils at times over a thing like this, as it is all owing to Stanley's conduct every bit of it; his lack of treatment of his officers in every single detail tended to lower them in the eyes of the men; if one of the officers justly beat a man and that man went off and complained to Stanley he would take the man's part to a certain extent, or at least sympathize with him and so the officer lost prestige; in a thousand ways he has tried to belittle his officers in the sight of his men and so to atone to them in a measure for his *own cruelty*.

I want to stick through this expedition a comrade of the men, not their enemy. I should like to bring my company to Zanzibar and be able to say, well, I know that there is not one man in it who dislikes me or thinks me capable of any brutal or unkind act. If so, I should be happy. But how can one treat with such dogs as some ten of these men are here. With one's hand one helps them, and in return they endeavour to extend a mutinous spirit among their comrades. Liars, creeping afterwards to kiss one's feet to save a licking. Ungrateful dogs to treat us so after the kind treatment they have received, fools to think they can get to the lake by themselves in such a small number, double fools to forget Jephson and Emin will put everyone of them in irons should they desert this place; one's every good feeling for them is quenched and hatred as one hates poison takes its place.

True and nothing truer is it that the *idle low loafers* are always the *energetic chief mutineers*; the sullen, lazy growler will in the end show himself up to all when he thinks he has power in his hands. Wait my boys! Wait till I have

---

*Parke recorded in his diary that the day before (20 July) Stairs had demanded that one of the Zanzibari release a native woman whom he was holding captive. When the Zanzibari delayed in doing so, Stairs punched him between the eyes and struck him on the shoulder with a stick. On 21 July Stairs struck another man, further fuelling the various discontents among the restless porters. Parke warned Stairs of the need to give the men a hearing: "I can see that mutiny is rife and unless the men are properly handled we 3 white men will be left alone [at Fort Bodo] to look after the boxes." (Parke's diary entry for 21 July 1888, quoted in *Surgeon Major Parke's African Journey*, p.107).

more power; then as sure as my name is Stairs if I don't warm up your cowardly hides, I am much mistaken. Just now you have [us] in a hole but I hope some day we shall be on the [word illegible] and you in the gutter. To be your slave, to pander to you, to avoid every punishment when punishment is due, to sympathize with your little whims and be all smiles and chaff is what one will have to endure for a season but when the time comes you will find once more that the white man must either have the reins or get out of the trap.

As yet one cannot say what is going to happen, I intend using my wits as well as possible and to try and reason with them on any point they may bring up. To say who is loyal and who is disloyal is more than any of us can say ...

22nd July Sunday
Parke takes a hopeful view of affairs and his judgment is generally better than that of most of us. Nelson, I suppose, has his own views but sleeps so much one hardly ever sees him or takes him into account. One's hopes lie in Jephson coming with a good strong force, enough to take all the loads ...

... Stanley knows not what this word "discipline" means; his method of enforcing "obedience" is solely with the rod; he reigns by terrorizing his men, not by expostulation, reason and then force. Any one of us could teach him lessons in treating men.

23rd July Monday
Addressed the men this morning. Told them how mad they were in thinking of running away from here, how they would get eaten up on the plains, etc., and said if they would only play fairly towards me I should do the same towards them. After this I gave them a holiday for to-day. No work done at all to-day...

Will have to feed some three or four men now as they are too weak to go for bananas ...

24th July Tuesday
... Jephson should be here in three or four weeks. This is giving him plenty of time ...

◆   ◆   ◆

26th July Thursday
Still feverish. Temp. again 103°. Although both Parke and I have got fever and to-day I am in a perfect lather, still Nelson keeps in bed sleeping and reading, a lazier chap I never knew or saw or one more utterly useless to this expedition. Surely it would not hurt him to get up for five minutes or so and just go and see the men working. I get in a regular frenzy over his idleness, especially when I have fever ...

Saturday 28th July
... Reading Baker's *Nyanza* again ...

◆   ◆   ◆

4th August Saturday [from *The Nineteenth Century*]
Last night an elephant came into the plantation; it was pitch dark. I could just make out a black mass, and blazed away into the centre of this; as usual he made some passes and then bolted straight for the bush. He worried a patch of forty yards by twenty of green corn and trampled down some of the beans. I hope there are no more of them.

Finished the roof of Emin's house, claying up N.'s [Nelson's] cook-house, weeding paths, repairing stockades, and various jobs. P. [Parke] thinks Emin and Jephson will be here in ten days. I give them a fortnight; perhaps they will not come at all, who knows? P. and I had a thorough look at the crops and talked about home; we both agreed that a good ham and some bread wouldn't go bad just now. Stanley away just fifty days to-morrow. I find discontent among several of the men; it is deep. They want us, I fancy, to abandon this place and march on to the lake, which means thirty men to carry seventy-five loads and fight too.

Bootmaking and tailoring going on. P. is by far the best bootmaker of the three of us, he is so patient and makes small stitches. Abedi is a *fundi* (master) tailor and has made me a pair of trousers out of Emin's cotton cloth.

5th August Sunday
One gets sick of such utter brutes as these Zanzibaris are that we have got here; mean, low, stinking skunks, almost to a man cowards.* I should like to be able to say "go your way", I'll go mine, never again after I reach Zanzibar do I want to see you and your tinpot island and pasteboard Sultan, palace and army. You know just enough about white men to possess their vices yet not enough of their ways to follow them and serve them faithfully; I hear people like Stanley saying they are splendid fellows, heroes, models of virtue, faithfulness, courage, etc., yet no man ever born up to now hates Zanzibaris from his inner heart as much as H.M. Stanley; one judges by his constant venomous imprecations and his sorry dry [?] treatment of them.

---

*During the month of August 1888 the Zanzibaris hanged a small native girl by her arms until she died for having allegedly stolen a fish. Another child they buried up to her neck (*Surgeon Major Parke's African Journey*, p.107). Neither Stairs, Parke, nor Nelson record these events nor state whether they attempted to rescue the two children from their porters.

It is easy enough after reaching home to publish in one's book splendid fellows, martyrs, heroes, tigers, etc.!! But let me hear the white man say all this on the spot, here far away from anyone else with poor food and bad lookout. All this slushy talk will then be altered and the most patient, godfearing Englishman who at home never utters anything worse than "Oh gracious" will become such an adept in the art of "swearing" that the tallest blasphemer on a Canadian or Yankee canal would turn green with envy and import a few Zanzibaris to work up his declining talents.

◆   ◆   ◆

9th August Thursday [from *The Nineteenth Century*]
Last night the sentries reported natives in tobacco plots. Sneaked into the tower with P.[arke] and listened; remained till 10.30; no result. People do not know what listening for natives is; you cannot see in the dark or smell, so you must listen. Were they near in the darkness the slightest move on your part might be fatal; all you can do is to keep absolutely silent; those who cough or sneeze had better stay at home. One hour is all we expect a man in the towers to listen, it is too fatiguing for more. We knew that natives were near the forts on five occasions; in four cases they were heard, in one a fire-stick was seen.

◆   ◆   ◆

12th August Sunday
This is the day Parke *divined* that Jephson and Emin would come; it is one o'clock and no sign. I say about the 5th of September ...

13th August Monday
To-day means death for a good many grouse on the Scotch moors ... If Jephson does not come soon we shall have absolutely no meat. Our diet will then be a purely "grazing" one. How one curses at times at being left here ...
    ... Food is getting scarce and I am very much afraid there will yet be trouble with the men; some day I fully expect them to move off on their own hook and make towards the plain. Consider our position – all the loads left here, we deserted by the men who would tell all sorts of stories and perhaps we should never be believed at all. Bah, the whole expedition has been trampled up right from the start to finish till one is sick of it.

◆   ◆   ◆

16th August Thursday
Two months since Stanley left for Yambuya; it is six months also to-day since Abdullah left and I left and yet here I am – six months and not one inch forward. I say by now Stanley has established communication with the Major, that is, if the Major is there?
... We are all wearing boots of our own make now. They do very well about the place but on the march, especially in the bush, they would soon give out ...
Parke has got erysipelas again. He says it may not be much, I only hope so. The 13th was the anniversary of being wounded with an arrow ...

17th August Friday [from *The Nineteenth Century*]
Two months since Stanley left for Yambuya; he has already established communications with the Major. I wonder if Abdullah and the couriers ever reached Barttelot. All three of us are now wearing boots of our own make; they do very well about the fort, but would not be up to much on the march. Anamari's ulcer is growing at a terrible rate. P.[arke] thinks he will die. Khamis Feredi, who came from Ugarrowwa's, is worn away to a shadow; he will have to be carried should we march. P.[arke] has a bad leg.

17th August Friday
Repairing *boma*, weeding road; dug up my late tobacco field ... Now would be the time to learn a little Swahili grammar, but unfortunately I left my two books at Yambuya ...

18th August Saturday
Weeding up corn. Weeding pumpkins. Cleaned up yards. This time last year Jephson and the [Advance] Column were promenading about the bush endeavouring to find the river.

19th August Sunday
... Ulcers instead of abating are becoming more numerous. I feel sure this whole basin of the Congo is nothing but a pestilential prison to us. Fever, ulcers and sores of all sorts are the lot of any men who may have to sit down for any length of time in this deadly area. People who praise up the Congo and its grand future, forgetting its deadly fevers, and want of natural production to keep up trade, always seem to my mind as those of not knowing the essentials of a good trading community or the necessities of a good opening for colonization. Perhaps on this the Congo Free State has fallen through: it certainly will when Leopold II dies. If it were not for the shame of the thing he would give up his subsidy at once. It is such men as Stanley that have blinded him.
Stanley by this time has found out the state of affairs down below, I should say, and in another month will be on his way back ...

20th August Monday
Men away for bananas ... It no doubt would seem strange to English people that here in 10° 20' lat., all of us have fires going every night; it is true that we have them partly as lights to go to bed with and partly to keep off the myriads of bats. Still leaving these considerations out, the warmth from a fire at night is very cheering. We find that here the nights are rarely warm, in fact the only heat we experience at all is that from the sun about noon; constant thunderstorms and violent rains cool the atmosphere almost daily.

21st August Tuesday
Last night the same gang of Wasangora who stole my tobacco returned with the object of looting more. This time they also found us awake and ready. The moon, though almost full, was partially hidden by drifting clouds when ... one of the sentries, came to my hut and told me he and his companions on guard had spied natives in Nelson's tobacco. I at once seized my Winchester and went up into the watchtower ... and from there we could dimly distinguish some twenty Washenzi all busily engaged in plucking Nelson's short new tobacco crop. At a signal we all three fired, reloaded, and gave them three rounds each. Like men possessed with the devil they ran, dropping bows and arrows, baskets half filled with tobacco and making for the bush like deer; we only heard one yell from them. In an instant all hands were ready and out we sallied; we found one dead in the tobacco, shot red-handed with his tobacco close beside him, another boy wounded and was quieted with a bullet through the head, a most horrible looking wretch; a regular man-eater. This made two dead. We also feel certain that the one who yelled so much was badly wounded but managed to get away into the bush. Bows, arrows and baskets we picked up (all told 18 baskets).

This morning, also in the bush, we found their hiding place before emerging into the open; all sorts of wild roots and potatoes had been cooked by them and two baskets more of roots, etc., were brought in by our own men this morning.

This will be a most salutary lesson to them I hope. The sudden surprise at night when fancying we were all asleep and harmless will have great effect on the savages' brain.

This morning I cut off the heads of the two men and placed them on poles one at each exit from the bush into the plantation. This may prevent further attempts of the sort for some time and so save life ...

21st August [from *The Nineteenth Century*]
Anamari's ulcer is terrible; from almost the kneecap down to the toes is simply one poisonous mass of decaying flesh. To fight against this with meal porridge is hopeless. P.[arke] is untiring, though ill himself. Last night the same gang of Wasongoro who bagged my green tobacco returned with the

object of getting more; they found us ready. About 10 p.m. the sentry came to my window and whispered '*Washenzi!*' (natives). I went up into the tower and in the dark could only make out their approximate position; they were thirty-five yards from the ditch. The two sentries and I laid our rifles on the ledge of the tower, and at the signal from me blazed away and pumped up more cartridges into the Winchester and got off four rounds each. In the dark we could hear them scatter and make for trees; in three minutes twenty men were up, armed, and out through the gates, and the natives fled howling into the forest; we found two dead. It was their intention to try and set fire to us, as we found fire-logs close up to the fence. They would never have dared to carry logs simply for light and warmth so close to the fort. The men killed were villainous-looking specimens, with filed teeth (all the tribes here are cannibals). One was shot in the head and the other in the chest. We picked up bows and arrows and three spears; these had been laid down to pluck the tobacco more easily, I fancy. It will be a wholesome lesson and teach them we are awake at night as well as in the daytime.

Weeding big corn-field, stumping men's yard, others fencing the main road. Ali Jimba and Yusuf Bin Osman rewarded with 5$ each on arrival in Zanzibar, for their cleverness last night. They tell me that for a quarter of an hour they had heard the natives before warning me.

◆   ◆   ◆

23rd August Thursday

... I fancy the feeling among the men against remaining here is once more springing up. One has done one's best to make things as easy as possible for them, not a single case of flogging has taken place for over a month. I have endeavoured to treat them with the most stringent fairness possible. Never in my life at any time have I been in such anxiety [as] at present: anxiety lest Jephson should be *too late*. Food is not over plentiful (the curse of this country is want of food) and when a Zanzibari is not getting plenty of food and sees also that food in quantities can be got at a very short distance off, his whole soul yearns to get to that place. Dangers, troubles, even loss of his own life he considers not but goes on blundering away head first into everything till at last he is pulled up short and then perhaps wishes he had a white man with him to pull him through his danger.

What does the Zanzibari chief conversation consist in? Why, exactly the same topics as I imagine all natives talk about. Food – of how much food they had at such and such a place and how little they get now ... Always the same, on the march, on sentry, in their huts, everywhere it is food and *pombe*. Should they get plenty, it is all the same, delicacies then are talked of. Civilization has done him [the Zanzibari] a lot of harm, he knows just sufficient of the white man's ways to be impudently saucy. In a standing camp the Zanzibari is impatient to get away, frets himself if there is move [?] not the same day by day, magnifies the slightest injury, while on the other hand likes to become bumptious and troublesome. If discipline has not been instilled thoroughly into him beforehand I am confident it cannot be done when he remains stationary; he likes excitement, change, looting and other such pleasures, delights in capturing a woman or two and giving her immense loads to carry besides making her a slave to his person ...

Out of our fifty-four men and boys I hardly think more than twenty-three will be able to carry loads on the march. Seven or eight more might take loads of 20 lbs. but that is about all. *Ugari* [porridge] made from green plantains of a bad type and greens is the now only food of the men. Many slowly fade away under this diet, especially so if they be attacked by bad ulcers. To tell the truth, for the men and to a great extent for ourselves, *it has been one long starve ever since we left Yambuya thirteen months ago*, only relieved by short sallies on to the plains ...

23rd August Thursday [from *The Nineteenth Century*]
Our pumpkins not doing well; they blossom, but no fruit forms. The feeling among the men against remaining here is increasing. Jephson should have been here by now. I have tried my best to make things easy for the men as possible; not a case of flogging has occurred for over a month, and the most impartial justice is given them. Never have I been in such anxiety in my life. What if Jephson is too late! Food is not over-plentiful; for the last gale here wrecked our bananas. The feeling among the blacks is that the there is better than the 'here;' it is always the same story – with the *saffari ya zamani* (former caravan) there was plenty of food, *viazi, ndizi, maziwa, ngombi,* potatoes, bananas, milk, cattle, &c.; with this there is nothing. I remember once getting so sick and tired of this that I was determined to catch a Zanzibari named Abdullah, who was always relating highly coloured stories of a former *saffari.'* Abdullah, I said, you have seen more food and fiercer natives, more cattle, longer marches, and bigger men on other saffaris (caravans); tell me now, have you seen more starvation than on this one?' Oh, yes, he said, it's true we have sometimes starved, but on one *saffari* I was on, long, long ago, we had – and so on. I refused to listen; even in starving the there was better than the here. (This was the same man who, months later in the open country, when we had cattle, sheep, and goats by hundreds, flour, bananas, beans and potatoes by the ton, being spoken to by one of the Europeans who was impressing on him how much better this life was than that at Ford Bodo, said, Yes, master, it is splendid; every night I have a full stomach; but "ah" at Fort Bodo there was *kuni telé* (plenty of firewood.)

This place has few attractions for the men, and as long as they play fair, they cannot be blamed, poor chaps; some of them had tasted cattle and goat meat on the plains and sigh for it hourly.

24th August Friday
... Emin Pasha has had this time to visit all his stations, and if he intends coming at all, should now be on his way here.

Two Zanzibari lie buried within the outer fence of the fort, victims to looting native camps. Two natives also lie buried outside this fence, also victims to looting our plantations. Many no doubt will say this is nothing but a righteous fate ...

... I have a presentiment that Jephson will be here in a few days! I hope so...

25th August Saturday
This morning about nine o'clock after a great deal of suffering Anamari died. He had wasted away to a mere skeleton from pain caused by his ulcer. The diameter of this ulcer, the worst I have ever seen, was about five inches, all his foot bones and sinews were attacked to within ten inches from the sole of his foot upwards.

The native's head placed by us on the road to the lake was taken away last night ...

The flies are very dangerous here, they rest on men's ulcers and then carry the poison about injecting it perhaps inside some other unfortunate's system; one cannot be too careful about keeping the place clean. The Zanzibari is a very dirty animal about camp, if not watched ...

26th August Sunday
Killed one last sheep this morning, two days and we will have no more meat 'till Emin Pasha comes ... How cranky we have all grown here... !

◆   ◆   ◆

28th August Tuesday
We now have peas, onion tops, beans and corn out of our garden ... We have been out of England 19 months and 7 days. From Yambuya exactly 14 months. When leaving England Stanley expected in 19 months to have finished the work and again have returned home.

28th August [from *The Nineteenth Century*]
Jephson has had ninety-four days to go round the stations with Emin; he will not come. Something is the matter, or he would have been here long before this ...

29th August Wednesday
Men at the same work as yesterday ... One understands thoroughly well by this time why it was that nearly all the Belgian officers on the Congo looked pale and unstrung, many indeed appearing asleep all the time; it is the heavy

atmosphere and want of something attractive to the mind; to pursue pleasure out of doors there must be hunting or fishing, to most men this is absent; to the keen there is botany or entomology of course.

♦   ♦   ♦

31st August Friday
Fever all day.

Tremendous hurricane last evening, destroyed the roofs of nearly all the sentry towers, and those of some of the men's huts. Also damaged a lot of corn and other crops. A great many trees blown down and flattened out the corn. Had all these removed and the men's huts repaired today. It will take a week's work to get everything straight again. Bridge again destroyed.

1st September [1888] Saturday
Another month and Jephson not here yet ...

Fever much better. Oh how one wishes Jephson would come quickly! I am desperately tired of this sort of life and long once more to be on the move.

♦   ♦   ♦

3rd September Monday
Men away getting bananas.

This is terribly wearisome work this waiting. One feels it so much more because one is aware that we are absolutely doing no good by remaining here, as Stanley will not pass by us on his way up. Day after day goes by still they do not come till at last one has almost begun to give them up ...

To-day Stanley estimated he should reach Yambuya; in reality I expect he reached there though some time ago and is now on his way east again.

3rd September [from *The Nineteenth Century*]
Khamis Feredi died to-day; we buried him in our little graveyard; there are six there already. Waiting, waiting, it is terrible: cooped up in a place of this sort, the tendency is to become cantankerous and narrow. It requires everything good in one to meet the daily work patiently and cheerfully; there is very little left in one by nightfall.

4th September Tuesday
At work again on these wretched roofs ... In the evening Ali Jimba came to me and said "the men" had asked him to come to me and say: food was getting scarce and Jephson had not yet come, men were gradually losing their strength and that day proposed two *shauris*: (1) That fifteen men and a white man should go to the edge of the bush with a letter; if natives appeared friendly

then these men would work through to the lake and give the letter to Jephson. This letter to say that food was giving out and that a *saffari* should come down soon or we could not hold out; (2) if natives were unfriendly then men return to Fort Bodo, move all loads on and build ahead somewhere. I dismissed Ali telling him I would consider the matter.

Now these things I know: (1) That though *all* want to get out of this place including we whites, yet only some eight or ten would persist in their complaints should I speak to the men and tell them the utter madness of either these propositions. (2) That it is a *muhogo* [manioc] the men want, they are tired of bananas and *ugari* [porridge] day after day without change and want new food. (3) That there are bananas enough here for every man to have two big feeds of *ugari* or porridge every day. (4) That there are some very bad eggs among the men who at a pinch would abandon loads, white men and everything for the sake of feeding. If Stanley hesitated to pass through the Wazamboni country with 120 strong men, well armed and elated with late successes, how much more so should we with 50 wretched men and boys, only 23 of which are effective, the rest all "ulcer" boys, none of whom have ever seen the open country natives in a fight.

No, to neither of these propositions can I give my assent. Stanley's words to me while having breakfast before leaving here were: "For God's sake, don't leave this place 'till you are relieved. Kabba Rega will hear of your coming and you may walk straight into his arms. Then where is our ammunition if Jephson does not come! Wait for me!" My own opinion is that it is death to everyone of us should we leave this place.

The storm we had the other day has knocked over hundreds and hundreds of banana trees, which of course makes the outlook worse. With the bananas I hope we can stand out till the end of September or middle of October, then I should begin to give the men a little corn out of the bins, this would tide us over 'till the new corn came in say about the fifteenth or twentieth November. We could plant again but then *it is the dry season*, and we should get very little yield.

4th September [from *The Nineteenth Century*]

At work again on those interminable roofs; the gales simply play with our efforts; we are putting heavier logs over the leaves this time; and I hope it will work well. Ali Jimba came to me this evening, and said the men had deputed him as their spokesman. I told hm to bring the chief with him (Khamis Pari), and I would listen. He said that food was getting scarce, Jephson had not yet come, and that we should all die here like rats; and proposed that we should move forward to the lake. I said no, for several reasons: if we moved forward with the loads, we had only thirty-three carriers; and we have six sick men who must be carried in addition. The result would be double trips, and two camps to defend every day. The natives would cut us up; we had struggled with the Pasha's ammunition through 120 days of forest, it would be insane now even to risk it. "Go back and reason with the men; tell those who wish to know more, that we Wasungu (whites) will explain. *Lakini si fanya vibaia* (don't do bad things), or there will be trouble."

5th September Wednesday
Had Khamis Pari in today, he ... gives it as his opinion that to leave here is madness ...

6th September Thursday
Had a *shauri* with men; told them that it would be madness to move out of this; we should be killed to a man on the plain; who would carry the loads? Did they want to desert the white man and loads? ... I would rather cut my throat than leave here, at least until another year has passed. I must own our position is critical, but then Jephson said he might be four months in coming and now only little more than three have passed. NO, we must just wait with patience 'till we are relieved either by Emin Pasha or Stanley.

◆   ◆   ◆

10th September Monday
This is the territory of that most "rotten of rotten" concerns, the Congo Free State. You are welcome to your vast extent of wastelands, dear Leopold! You have about the finest empire of water and scrub that the world affords. Bush from Nyangwe to the Niger, from the Atlantic to the 30th meridian east, within ten miles of open country at these parts. No doubt there are still fools who will extol this mismanaged concern, but if I ever live to reach England, it will be my duty to state exactly what exists between Banana Point and Basoko, and Basoko and the 30th E. longitude. Do you know the Arabs (Manyuema) are working north and west, gradually invading your territory and draining every single tusk of ivory out of it? Do you also know they meditate taking Basoko or perhaps by this time have done so? Are you asleep? If you are wise do one thing, abolish the State and once more throw the river open to the unhampered trade of the Dutch, English, and French houses. Waste no more money out here. It is the Zambezi "second edition" managed by Belgians instead of Portuguese.

I am afraid the present state of things cannot exist long: the men impatient at our long stay are becoming more anxious to get on to the lake. I have a little corn but to give it to them now is madness; we must wait till the next crop is nearly ripe – we have quite 30 men disabled from ulcers, we have close on 70 loads. To start means the abandoning of these loads of which some 30 are ammunition: this lost we can scarcely hope to cross Africa, through unknown savage tribes. Nor can we help Emin Pasha much ... Come

Jephson old man and come quickly is our cry ... Never in my life have I been so anxious, never have I turned over in my mind all sorts of schemes and devices; at night for hours I have kept awake thinking till my brain is simply tangled up into a knot ...

It is not for ourselves that all this anxiety is caused. It is for the men and loads. If Emin Pasha does not come out with us through the fighting country and we lose these boxes of ammunition we are helpless and our cause is hopeless. Stanley has told me this, "I will drive my way through to Zanzibar if the devil is in front", and I, knowing how bullheaded and determined he is, feel sure he would attempt it – with a small force you must have ammunition and ours is going to be a small force. If Emin comes we could do with less ammunition in proportion to our numbers. He would, say, bring 600 fighting men or even 850. This is a big force and with all the camp followers and our men would inspire the natives with fear. Truly in this country "in numbers there is safety".

To anyone who say, "Ah, but you lay far too much stress on the importance of plenty of ammunition and too little on what cloth would do", I merely answer with a question: by what means have we travelled over 730 miles of country from the Congo to the lake? Why *by rifle alone*, by shooting and pillaging: about the cloth I merely say Stanley is not a "cloth giver", he prefers the leaden method of securing respect and food ...

11th September Monday [from *The Nineteenth Century*]
Turned out eighteen men to scour the woods for the missing men; fired rifles from the fort at every hour. If caught by the natives their fate will be an awful one, first tortured and then eaten; no signs of them by evening, blew the horn till 9 p.m ...

Come Jephson! For heaven's sake, come!

12th September Wednesday
... Emin Pasha has had time to stop at each of his stations ... One can't help thinking that every day the chances of his coming are getting less and less. Perhaps his people won't let him leave, fearing that it is only a ruse for him, to get away altogether ... These are the sort of propositions one is constantly and impatiently turning over in one's head. All sorts of things may be happening one says to oneself. At nights now with me it is all sleep or no sleep. If I once begin thinking about Emin Pasha and the Major (Barttelot), I cannot get to sleep 'till far into the night ...

13th September Thursday
Planted my ex-tobacco plot with beans. This planting makes the men's spirits

go down terribly as they then say, "Oh *Muzungu* * intends making a long stop here, we shall all starve!"

14th September Friday

... Yesterday among the bananas Farag Ali fired at a native who ran away at once, dropping his bananas ...

Planted small plot of bananas. It is most amusing to hear the men talking about *dawa* (medicine or charms). Many of the men who doubt the efficacy of the doctor's medicines, walk quietly away to one of the scribes in camp and from him get small extracts from the Koran written out on a dried banana leaf, these they neatly fold up and sew up in a small piece of cloth; these then are tied to the affected joint or limb and trusted in as an absolutely certain cure for the disease. Now they will go up to Parke and again get medicine, this time believing that it will do them good. *Dawa* with a Zanzibari, as well as I suppose with an Arab, means almost anything in the shape of medicine, charms, fetish collections of bones, teeth, etc. They have *dawa* for leopards which simply kill the leopard at sight, no force, trap or stratagem of any sort being used, merely this *dawa* or charm. The Manyuema smear their faces over with banana flour, before proceeding on a *saffari,* to protect them[selves] from evil spirits and the enemies whom they may have to fight. Small houses they build on reaching camp and in them place little fires which are kept up till morning; these houses are the ... "houses of the devil", who wanders about the camp promiscuously and would feign sleep with the men in their shelters, but on seeing these nice warm little huts lays himself down by the fire and sleeps comfortably there till morning. Some of the Manyuema also look with dreadful superstition on fire; to allow a fire stick once lighted in their houses to be thrown out means that some evil is to happen to them; all sticks lighted, fires made, or even ashes of a lighted pipe thrown down are to go out by themselves in the hut and never thrown outside. The greatest care is taken not to throw live coals into the ash heap when sweeping up the house.

Meat (beef) in any form is refused by the thinnest and most starved Zanzibari should he be suffering from an ulcer or venereal disease: even the bones from chicken soup made by Nelson were refused by his boy on account of his having an ulcer, this, I have no doubt, has some connection with *dawa.* On the other hand, they will eat goat meat at all times. Abedi, my boy, tells me that in Zanzibar his father will beat him severely should he hear that the boy had been eating either beef or fowl of any sort when he was sick or had sores of any kind ...

◆   ◆   ◆

---

*Stairs's Congolese sobriquet meaning "He of the [Maxim] gun."

16th September Sunday
... If ever I reach England I will have "special" feed of the following things for breakfast: some toast and good butter, stewed kidneys and couple of soles, bacon and poached eggs and mushroom omelette (savoury), buckwheat pancakes, plenty of Devonshire cream and fruit, jam, muffins, coffee, etc. My heavens, I will patronise EATING HOUSES , not cafes when I get back again – five o'clock tea I will make a square meal of. Invitations to dinner I will accept *ad lib*. All are cordially requested to invite the officers of this expedition to dinner and afterwards to the Savoy, Lyceum, Globe, etc. ... I wish I had known in England that we were likely to be kept in a place for such length of time as we have been. If I had known we were to go in for "farming" like this, I should have brought a lot of garden seeds, onions, turnips, cauliflower, lettuce, radishes, cucumbers, tomatoes, etc., and also some botanical paper and a book on botany and zoology. Then one would know what to collect. I find we "graze" on eight kinds of grasses collected near the fort; of these I have made a collection, as well as some edible bulbs, etc., so that if any future explorers desire to know what grasses, leaves, etc., can be got in these parts I will instruct him; five days of this diet and he will cry, "Enough!"

◆　　◆　　◆

18th September Tuesday
... How do you spell vice? I mean the *tool*, vice? I say it is *vyse*, the others say *vice*. So far we have been unable to arrive at a decision satisfactory to all...

Parke and I often wonder if the W.O. [War Office] will give us our back pay for the time we are in Africa ... If they do it, it will be a perfect Godsend ... The Committee of the expedition too ought to give us something, at least those who have volunteered. McKinnon [*sic*] is a Scotchman though and they are hard-fisted boys.

At times one burns to know just what is going on in Europe. Is there a big European war? There quite well might be, say between Russia and England. Have any new regulations about promotion come out? Or any more about service abroad? What has been done about the Alaska boundary? This one expects will have been settled by this time. One's old companions are a source of speculation. Where are McKay, Twining, Joly and Nanton? Joly by this time will be quite a fatherly sort of chap, I should say, burning himself brown in India.

I expect the W. [War] Office will stick me for India on getting back. Life in Chatham after this sort of work would be deadly ... Here all is move, new things to see everyday. There the same old round, the big mess with its expensive living and little trips to town are the only things to see or do. Plymouth or the N. of England would be good stations.

In Canada now the evenings will be getting chilly and people keep now indoors. But they will still be having all sorts of outdoor affairs in the day time. Kingston will be about re-opening again now and all the recruits in their brand new uniforms stalking about the place feeling like fish out of water.

18th Tuesday [from *The Nineteenth Century*]
Have fits of sleeplessness. When one starts thinking at night of Emin, where Stanley and Jephson are, and the ammunition, in twenty minutes all is a hopeless muddle. Again one starts thinking until nearly crazy ...

... Things are beginning to look very bad about Jephson coming at all now; on the 24th he will have had four clear months. Either they have decided not to come at all or some unforeseen circumstance has occurred   ...

♦   ♦   ♦

24th September Monday
... Jephson and Emin have... had four months to get here. I do not think they will come. I have never been so heartily sick of a place or had such bitter feelings as I have at present.

25th September Tuesday
... One wants plenty of medicine in this country for parasites ... it is a standing rule to drink boiling [*sic*] water and abstain from eating half boiled peas, vegetables, etc.; otherwise, all sorts of horrible parasites breed in one's insides. Of these useful medicines we have very few ...

26th September Wednesday
... I wish it were only possible to take a huge, sleeping draught and sleep away the time 'till Jephson comes, that is, if he is coming ... Read *Measure for Measure* ...

♦   ♦   ♦

28th September Friday
... What is causing the delay (in not coming here) with Jephson. There must be some serious trouble or he would be here ere this ...

... One does not mean to be so low spirited or down in one's luck at having to stay here, far from it. It is our duty and all of us know it, to stick to this place to the last. But one puts down every side of the question in one's journal, so that in after days, perhaps on looking over these pages a true story will be depicted.

Returned African travellers appear as a general rule to praise up the countries they have been through without much regard for the truth. This, to my mind, is far worse than those pessimists who run down tribes, climates, etc., *in toto*. For, in the first case, money may be invested and the investors "fooled"; whereas it is a speculator's own look-out should he invest in the second case. Besides, one forgets one's troubles to a certain extent after a relief from them and beside a fire after dinner in England, with a good cigar and a whisky and soda, the pleasant side of affairs only occurs to one, and perhaps listeners do not hear "an absolutely correct" account. This I know and know thoroughly : never [to] believe that any man as you know him in *civilization* will be the same man in mid-Africa. Let success go as it may; no fighting, plenty of food, spare porters, everything – and that man will be as different in disposition in every way, as day is from night. A promise, I find, made in Central Africa is very much like a cloud; you may catch at it, catch at it a thousand times without success and at last you see this thing dissolving before your eyes and stand cursing the one that ever induced you to believe there was any substance in it.

28th September Friday [from *The Nineteenth Century*]
All hope of J.[ephson] coming has been given up. Stanley due in two months and twenty days; elephants, as usual, charged the men not five hundred yards from the fort. We fire blank at them now, but they charge at the noise. Instantly a man fires he clears out like lightning; fires and horns are the safest way of frightening them. We had eighteen fires going this morning and evening, and besides set fire to several old dry trees. I saw seven elephants this morning; they didn't seem to mind Remington bullets much, but just cock up their trunks, let out two or three wild screams, and come straight for the sound of the rifle. Intibu was crushed under a sapling; but the elephant did not apparently see him, or he would have been certainly killed.

29th September Saturday
All of us have now become confirmed gluttons, could the food be provided only. Not gluttons at this sort of food here, but would-be gluttons for good solid English food: beef, mutton, goose, ducks, spuds, vegetables of all sorts, turkeys, gamepies, oysters, beer, stout; these are the sorts of things one pants after. By George (one says), how I should like to be in the Criterion, or the Bristol, or at so and so's. Just for one night would the grub fly! When one gets in this state it shows that present food cannot be up to much.
Read *Henry VIIIth*.

Some five or six of our men will never reach Zanzibar. [They] are, I am afraid, going down the hill very fast, so much so that they now cannot go for food to the *shamba* [plantation] ...

30th September
Another month gone and still Jephson not come ...

1st October [1888] Friday
Since leaving the *Madura* I have lost 21 lbs, my weight now is 142 lbs. On July 6th it was 155 lbs so that since then (three months) I have lost 13 lbs. Both Nelson and Parke have also lost on this grass feeding.

The men's gardens are getting on in fine style: it was my idea thus to give the men ground and seeds and get them to till these and make gardens, as I thought thereby they would have some further hold in the place and perhaps forget a little their desire of "absconding"! To shew the zest with which this has been taken up, I may say that I have given some twelve or fifteen men seeds. The fish baskets have also awakened an interest in the men, every man having now some two or three or more baskets and getting sometimes fish twice a day, generally the small sort, but still even these form a relish to their otherwise dry *ugari* [porridge].

2nd October Saturday
Though we three whites have gone down in weight, as I said yesterday, still our boys have kept up or even put on flesh during the same time , shewing that the food certainly agrees with them.

What in the mischief are Emin Pasha and Jephson doing? What has happened, are we to be relieved at all by them or wait 'till Stanley comes up? Stanley's estimated date for this place is about 18th December ...

3rd October Sunday
... Read *Much Ado About Nothing* for about the sixth time ...

◆   ◆   ◆

7th October Sunday [from *The Nineteenth Century*]
N.[elson] and I started tent-making. We cut up the clumsy old tent and are making it into two smaller ones; mine will simply be a small *tente-abri*. The best tent for this country is one that can be pitched easily and quickly, strong, and with a good fly; it should be low, or every now and then will be blown away. The men continue to get fair hauls of fish in their baskets; it helps them on wonderfully; they call anything of this sort *kitiweo* [relish].

Abedi wants to know why white men leave their homes and come out to countries like this, where the food is poor and the natives bad. I told him that we liked to know what sort of people lived in these countries, and, thinking to impress him, said that perhaps some day the white man would build a railway across this continent. Had he ever seen a railway? Oh, yes, the Sultan has one! (It is a derelict tramway out to his plantations in Zanzibar.)

9th October Tuesday [from *The Nineteenth Century*]

Caught the sentries on the granaries asleep or rather dreaming; they invariably answer on being charged with sleeping, *Hakuna ku lala bwana, macho tu* (Not asleep, master, eyes only); that is, they could hear and see, but had their eyes shut. A Zanzibari has a very odd expression, *kulala macho* ; we have no equivalent; it means to sleep with one's eyes open – always to be on the *qui vive*. If by themselves almost all African natives sleep '*macho*' (with eyes open). It really means they hear or see nothing until some one in the camp is stabbed by the enemy and yells out; then there is a wild seizing of arms and loosing off of rifles. It is most difficult to make natives like the Zanzibaris into good sentries; to listen for hours without talking to each other is a sore trial to them. We have fires for them in the towers and they are allowed to smoke if they like. I do not think the practice of shouting out their post numbers at certain intervals a good one; it teaches sentries a false security, and the natives soon learn what it means. (For actual sleeping on post the first offence is twenty-five strokes, extra duties and up to fifty strokes for second offence, fines of five dollars and ten dollars, paid in Zanzibar, in addition, if caught a third time.)

P.[arke] has fever of a bad type.

◆   ◆   ◆

10th October Wednesday

At this time last year, we were right in the very focus of starvation ... We have now been over six weeks without a bite of meat, it is telling heavily on three of us. The men, I fancy, look much better than they did.

Won't Stanley be mad when he hears of all these deaths! He never thinks for one instant that here as at Ugarrowwa's and Kilonga Longa's he has left nothing but the wreck of the expedition and, of course, will go for me like the mischief. But what of that? Is it not to be expected from a man who has called a faithful, hard working officer of his [i.e., Stairs] "deserter": and who has threatened *to crush him under water* with his Zanzibaris and also to tie him up to a bush in the forest and let him die. Brave man he must be, this leader!

I fancy some bungling has taken place up at Emin Pasha's country. Does not Jephson know this that in the bush wilderness very few places can support the garrison required to defend them. What between "hunger and watchfulness" from day to day can anyone hold up long in such a hell of fever as this is? Not one of we three whites *miss a single week* that we do not have an attack of fever which leaves us as weak as cats and robs us of a pound or two of flesh which we cannot make up on the food we have. Perhaps anyone reading this might say, "Oh, but you talk far too much about these things, your trials". I answer, not one whit. What good are we doing here at all? Is Stanley to call here and get food for his men on his way back? NO. We are just simply farming in mid-Africa under bad conditions, waiting for the time when we shall be relieved.

All this time we should be on the Nyanza, then our men would have a chance to get strong and ready for the road and we should then be doing some good. If there were no strong tribes in the road we should pack up and be off by stages tomorrow: but the Wazamboni are ever there and we should not be justified in moving one step across the plain.

11th October [1888] Thursday
A most unforseen and unfortunate affair happened to-day, tending very much to depress everyone in camp ... About nine o'clock this morning when all hands were at work I took three men and went into the bush to cut some poles of a particular sort which the men by themselves would never be able to do. We had finished cutting our poles and were ready to start back for camp when suddenly we heard several long shouts some distance to the south of us accompanied by reports of two Remington rifles. We naturally considered that our men had met with natives, fired on them and caught a woman, for the yells resembled those of a female exactly. On our way back, however, we found that two of our men had been fired on by natives and had run towards camp and that one of them, Msungessi Idi, a very hard working chap had been slightly wounded in the right breast. We laughed and chaffed about their running away and soon after reached camp. The very first words I then heard were that "Msungessi is dead". Dead, and not 50 minutes from the time he was hit. The arrow merely entered the flesh and muscles; no vital part was injured in the slightest. Death then according to all of us (Parke included) must have arisen from either of two causes, first from apoplexy brought on by fright and nervousness (he was terribly excited Parke says and, in addition, was a short, thick, heavy man), and consequent death from some blood vessel bursting in the brain or, second, from the poison on the arrow which must have been a wooden one.

We were all very much depressed over this as Msungessi was a regular character about the place, always ready for work, noisy, cheery and contented with his lot. One never forgets either that any unfortunate occurrence such as this creates a gloom over the camp for several days, and that during this time a great deal of loose talk goes on among the men and the old question (my bugbear) of going to the lake is once more on the *tapis*. Parke held no post-mortem as after questioning the men a bit I found they did not fancy the idea. These natives must have heard our fellows in the bush, sneaked up to them and then fired a volley of arrows after which they ran, as soon afterwards others of our men came up and explored the bush but found nothing but fresh tracks.

The Wasongora bow-men are as certain of their mark, if they get a careful aim, as one of us would be firing at a big barn twenty yards off. The more I see of these natives the more certain I feel that the "wooden, poisoned arrows" are used for human warfare only; the iron tipped ones being used either for game or men. This reduces our men now to 52 ...

◆　　　◆　　　◆

13th October Saturday
... Parke's state to-day gave both Nelson and myself great anxiety. He has bilious malignant remittent, a very bad type of fever. Recollect, gentle stranger, our position should one of us get really bad. We have *no proper medicines*, we have no fowls to make chicken broth of, no meat to make tasty soups, no beef tea, no sugar, flour, even not a drop of tea or coffee; once a man's condition gets down very much, and a fever attacks him it is the very mischief to build him up again even with good food, but think how much greater the difficulty must be when there is nothing for him but preparation of Indian corn which in a great many cases his tired and weakened stomach will refuse: think of this and anyone can then realise our position. When healthy, each of us eats five cups of Indian corn, *flour* (not meal) per day; this to us now has absolutely no taste and very little strengthening power. I gave rations of ten good corn to each man.

Am trying to make a concoction to tan leather. I put great quantities of bark into a large *chungu* [pot] of eight or twelve gallons, and am boiling this for two days, then will soak the hides a week or so in this concoction; I hope it will be of some use in the making of thongs of the donkey's hide, though perhaps it is doubtful.

14th October Sunday
Parke very bad yesterday afternoon, this morning better though and was able to get up and go out to the men's quarters and lance Khamis Pari's bad leg ...

These bush natives must be great snake meat eaters if they all go in for it at the same rate that the Monbuttu [pygmy] woman does. The last snake we got ... we had cooked. Of this she ate about two pounds at night, about the same next morning and still some more during the same afternoon; interlarded with this slippery feast were huge *chungus* [taro] of banana *ugari* and roasted bananas. To finish up with she also made away with about three and a half pounds of the roots of *mayuba* plant, and still she lives. I fancy her legs must be hollow a bit or she could never make away with all this. This is not all either for shortly afterwards she sneaked up to Parke and quietly asked for *mohindi* (corn). None of the Zanzibaris would eat this meat though I feel sure their mouth were watering for it to a man. One chap took a little "just to make some oil from ..."

15th October Monday
Men out for bananas. This time last year we had just crossed the Ituri and were within three marches of the Manyuemas though, at that time, we were not aware of it. We were then all in desperate condition and sacrificed Stanley's donkey to keep up our strength for a further try. A year afterwards (to-day) we are not much in advance, although it is true Emin Pasha has been found ...

16th October Tuesday
Sent men out to look after the elephants. The brutes were gorging themselves last night on the fattest *mijomba* (stalks of bananas) they could find. The men built several fires, these with the smell of the men, may scare off these "probosciden" for a week or so. They are a thousand times more destructive to our food supply than the natives; one elephant in one night will clean, I should say, clear and destroy by trampling under his feet from ¾ to one and one half acres of corn, and I should think quite ¾ of an acre of bananas; the beasts after this heavy feed move into the thick bush, during the day, and then again emerge during the following night and repeat the performance if not stirred up.

Parke moved into Emin's hut today; we feel certain it will do him good; I don't believe the old "barn" he has been living in is at all a healthy place. Should Emin come, Parke will go back, of course, to his old quarters ...*

♦   ♦   ♦

20th October Saturday
There is a great deal of talk going on now among the men about going to the plain, one or two would appear to want to throw over the white men ... ; others wish to have another *shauri* with the white men and endeavour then to give consent. I know exactly the reason these beggars want to go it is "hondo, hondo!!" (literally belly full) with them. These mutineers will be very much "solid" if I can only get my way; I will give them *ugari* every day on the plain, I would persuade Emin Pasha not to give them one ounce of meat or salt or

---

*A diary entry by Parke for 16 October 1888 reflects the degree to which the enforced inactivity and thin rations were wearing on all of the three officers isolated in Fort Bodo: "Nelson and Stairs had a tiff this morning. The latter was rather rude. He said to the Chief Maniapara, Why don't you ask me for things? Don't ask Capt. Nelson but come to me, ignoring Nelson's position, which is very wrong and shows great want of tact and experience ... Nelson then accused Stairs of giving our onions to the men. Stairs admitted to giving two. This is bad taste as he should have asked Nelson and myself as we have very few" (*Surgeon Major Parke's African Journey*, p. 110).

anything that now their tongues clamour for. Those who have acted squarely here I should endeavour to make *their* lot just as comfortable as I possibly could.

Among Zanzibaris in a camp, say, where three or four men are living together: should one get sick and unable to go for food, the other unanimously will hunt him out of their mess. What then becomes of him, I ask? *Ah ta cufa pekiaki* (Oh, he will die by himself). People may not believe this, but it is absolutely true.

... One only hopes that the elephants will go to the bush again and that Jephson will come soon. Five months nearly now and nothing of him! Parke is still very bad, fever every day and bad nights. He is pale as a ghost and very much pulled down in condition. At times now, it is all I can do to control my passion and keep cool. To give the men now any excuse for going away from here would be disastrous to me as Stanley would listen to and believe the men, not me.

◆ ◆ ◆

25th October Thursday
... Read *Ivanhoe* and *The Antiquary* again yesterday and day before ... I only wish that we had the whole of Scott's works instead of only these two ...

26th October Friday
... Parke very bad today, temperature up to 104°. It is real bilious remittent fever he has got. He has now been over three weeks ill.

◆ ◆ ◆

29th October Monday
... Reading Tennyson. If we stay here much longer, we shall all be great authorities on Shakespeare and Tennyson ...

◆ ◆ ◆

2nd November Friday
... The following from Tennyson's *Amphion* suits us down to the ground with a little added:

> And I must work thro' months of toil,
> And years of cultivation,
> Upon my proper patch of soil
> To grow my own plantation.
> I'll take the showers as they fall,

> I will not vex my bosom:
> Enough if at the end of all
> A little garden blossom.

With one alteration, *viz* that we expect something more than a "garden blossom". With this added:

> With hailstorms wild, and native gangs,
> With elephants twelve feet high,
> A chronic state of dreadful pangs
> Proclaims that we should die.
> A thousand rations scooped up clean,
> More "grazing" for us all;
> We plant again with hopes to glean
> Perchance again next fall.

3rd November Saturday

... We all think now that something out of ordinary must have happened up at the lake to prevent Jephson's coming. How we have all cursed Stanley for this blunder! Will people in England after this expedition still believe that Stanley is a capable leader?

◆   ◆   ◆

6th November Wednesday

... Will Jephson never come? Must we again have to reap four months hence and then *sow again*? It is cruel work for us. Every day we hope on and hope on and still he comes not. Plant, plant, fight the natives, treat with brutes of men who see that to a certain extent the white men are in their hands, subject to destructive wind and hailstorms. This is our fate. All hopes are being [word illegible] blown to the winds abut Jephson's ever coming. He has had nearly six months now to get here and if he comes not soon, say by the end of November, it will then be too late for him to move at all ...

◆   ◆   ◆

10th November Saturday

This morning Parke and I were debating as to whether or not I should take chloroform tomorrow and he make an incision to try to get the arrow out of my wound. We went into his hut to go through some preparatory probing just to make sure where the arrow was; after about thirty or forty minutes with the probe and tweezers who would think it but, by Jove, out came the arrow! It had struck one of the ribs and the point had been broken then it lodged across the hole which has been open for 15 months and constantly suppurating. The piece we got out was about 6/10 of an inch long and about 4/10 had broken off and the whole being about one inch long. It was an ordinary native poisoned arrow, made of *mwale* [raffia] palm just as the natives about here make, but owing to its long confinement it is in places eaten away. The relief at getting this out is very great and anxiety now, I hope, will go altogether to the winds!! Fifteen months it is since I was hit. Parke says he is very glad he did not make any incision before as he had intended. The position of the wound was so dangerous, just over the heart and lungs. I must say it was a narrow squeak: had the arrow just missed this rib I should have been a dead man many a day ago ...

Nelson is going down in condition again very fast; he lies on his back nearly all day and will not be persuaded to move about and take a little fresh air ...

♦   ♦   ♦

21st November Wednesday

The doctor got from Washenzi some leaves, etc., to concoct poison with ... Planting big field where former corn did not take. *Rugga rugga* saw nothing, but reported natives had been cutting bananas yesterday at end of N.W. plantation.

I am heartsick to the very core at having to stay at this place, utterly disgusted with the rotten way in which everything has been done in this expedition. Tired of working with such a lot of brutes as we have here and boiling over with rage at them. Upon my word, I often feel like going away into the bush and not coming back again. To keep one's temper down day after day in working with these men is more than ordinary mortal can do. I have acted squarely and fairly with all of them, have eased their troubles as much as I possibly could have done. What is the result? They do not thank one in the slightest, in fact they take everything for granted in the way of helping them: behind one's back they swindle one, lie about one, try and frustrate any little plan one makes about getting birds or fish and so many other "endearing trifles" too numerous to mention. Sick of them I am utterly. I also feel that some day one or two of these beauties will smart for it if I know my name; this is the only consoling part. I am speaking of a clique of some ten or twelve men only. The rest are all right ...

22nd November Thursday

... To-day the Monbuttu [pygmies] made some of the poison for us that the natives use on their arrows: both Parke and I have got specimens of the different plants, etc., used and when I know a little more about it I will try to describe the several plants and method of making the poison.

Planting west field and started hoeing up the old south one. Finished re-roofing old granary. Hoes are nearly all done for, the roots play the mischief with them, we use three native hoes now to help a bit; they are but poor, clumsy things ...

23rd November Friday
Hoeing S.E. field. Cutting pea sticks and doing odd jobs. Poison made by native ready.

24th November Saturday
This morning about 9:30 Parke made an incision about 2/5 of an inch long close to back bone of my dog and together we introduced a quantity of the poison, to see if it will have any effect. We preferred this way to prodding him with an arrow as lockjaw might supervene. We await the result with "much anxiety". If this does not do for him we will make him swallow a lot as well and try what effect that will have.

This poison is a dark-green colour, whereas that made by the Wasongora and Monbuttu in their villages and camps is of yellowish-brown colour (like dirty yellow sealing wax, such as is used to stop the corks of wine bottles).

Sent out *rugga rugga* to hunt elephant. Last night an elephant came to within 170 yards of fort, making great noise cracking the branches and banana stems. I fired a shot as near him as I could judge and after some horn blowing he went off. They are much more difficult to distract at night than in day time. Nothing makes them go off so quickly as the smell of men or fire.

Some of the men saw a leopard the other day, or said they saw one. Perhaps it was only some large type of bush cat of which there should be numbers of, judging from the skins one sees in villages. Whether or not the leopard comes this far into the bush I cannot positively say. At Ugarrowwa's one took off a child in sight of some women and children.

25th November Sunday
Jephson has now had six months to come here; what can be the matter with him? Is it his fault? Is he so wrapped up in the comforts of Emin's country, the good food and easy travelling that he has forgotten his promise to come here? Or is it worse? Is there something more formidable in the shape of obstacles? Perhaps Emin's No. 1 Regiment of which he is never certain about may have mutinied and retain Emin in case he should try and sneak off unawares. This is quite within the bounds of possibility ...

26th November Monday
Men again off for bananas. Boys got a good catch. Peas for dinner yesterday.

The dog died yesterday from the poison.*

28th November Wednesday
The leaves Parke and the native woman got yesterday, for making the antidote, have been collected and dried. To-morrow the woman will make it up. The antidote is applied through the skin ...

29th November Thursday
... With six men I went through and through the plantations looking for marks of elephants. We saw a great many plants broken down near the bush, but on the whole not nearly as many as I had expected ...

30th November Friday
... The dry season is on us too, I think, and I am rather afraid the want of rain will damage the crops very much. The rice is getting ripe very quickly. Next week we should be able to take some of it in.

1st December Saturday
Cutting pea sticks and roding up the peas. Sent out *rugga rugga*, followed up natives but could not catch them. Sent out four men for bananas. Weeding corn near bush. Nearly finished with umbrella. Have two men at basket making ... We are sadly in need of baskets and *chungus*. Parke has made a very good grid iron out of some old wire, the "irony" of it though lies in our having no meat to grill. In the same way, I have no cloth to cover my umbrella frame with.

We have now been over twenty-two months out from England: it is doubtful if we shall reach Zanzibar in another fourteen. Everything now seems to be hanging in mid-air. We know nothing of the whereabouts of Stanley or Jephson. For all we know, Stanley may have gone gaily off down the Congo and left us here. We simply go plodding along day after day here, planting, keeping things in repair, fighting natives and elephants and trust that soon some one will turn up ...

◆　　◆　　◆

---

*Stairs was not alone in intentionally killing his dog. Jephson had done so on the voyage from Cape Town. Jameson recorded in his diary on 15 March 1887 that "Jephson, disgusted with the low habits and appearance of his dog [Bill], flung him overboard in the dead of the night, with a furnace-bar attached to him" (*Story of the Rear Column*, p.8). Stanley also maltreated his dog, Randy (named after Lord Randolph Churchill). According to Roger Casement, "When Stanley was somewhere near three-quarters through the Great Forest, and a great distance in time, from town or village of any kind, he became very hard pressed for food and sick from eating the everlasting plantains,

4th December Tuesday
Parke off with ten *rugga rugga*, came up with six or eight natives to NNW of fort two miles in the plantation. They were sitting round a fire near native hut on the track. Killed one [woman] and caught two children ...

The Monbuttu woman says natives here eat those caught ... The ordinary way is to cut up the body, dry the meat thoroughly over a fire and eat "when required". The bones are roasted on the coals and the marrow eaten ...

... Christmas will soon be on us with the almost certain prospect now of having to spend it here. We have been puzzling our heads what to have to eat. I am saving a poor, tiny, miserable pittance of salt as a present for the other two chaps; a funny Christmas box this! An eggspoon full of salt! If we could only shoot a bird or monkey it would not be so bad. However, perhaps we shall have some fish ...

5th December Wednesday
... This time last year we were getting close to the lake, going strong and with a tremendous supply of spirits. Personally, I cannot say I feel in the same mood this year as I did last, at this time.

Reading *McBeth* [*sic*] again. What a brute "Mrs. McBeth" was and he himself about on a par with Richard III, I think.

The men are eating great numbers of the locust or rather grasshoppers that have been attracted here by the rice fields. I had a few last evening, they are not bad and serve as a relish or "kitiweo" for the men but then in England or where there was food one would not trouble them much.

6th December Thursday
Weighed ourselves. Parke 148, Nelson 138, Stairs 151. Nelson weighed over 12 stone in England, I weighed 11 stone 10 pounds [164 lbs.] when at Chatham...

7th December Friday
Finished picking the rice this afternoon with exception of a little not yet ripe ... Zanzibaris are poor farmers; every one has his own idea about things and

---

wild nuts, etc. In fact, he was so weary of being a vegetarian that had he happened to stumble across a cannibal feast he might have joined in. As he chanced to be fondling his fox terrier, he suddenly looked up at Captain Nelson and said, I believe Randy ... would make an excellent roast or stew! Nelson would not acquiesce, although no doubt he was of the same opinion. But the idea of Randy coming to the rescue would not be downed, so Stanley had the dog's tail cut off and instructed the cook to make soup. Stanley and Nelson ate the soup; then gave Randy his own tail to eat; which he did with apparent enjoyment" (Fred Puleston, *African Drums* [London, 1930] p. 241).

these ideas all differ so widely that one can depend but little on the information; we planted this rice too closely by six inches ...

8th December Saturday
Went off S.S.E with twelve *rugga rugga*. Shot [i.e., killed] two natives and wounded another ...

♦   ♦   ♦

11th December Tuesday
... Have fever to-day. First time for over six weeks. Side where was wounded still pains, there must be a bit of decayed bone in the wound yet as the suppuration is constant ...

It is wonderful how quickly fever prostrates one in this country. If one is doing some work in which one's whole energy is employed and one's nerves strung up, perhaps a fever can be warded off; but sitting down to it with ordinary work it is quite a different matter, it is then impossible almost to fight it off. A man at nine a.m. will be strong and cheery and happy with himself and all the world. At noon he feels slack and tries to fight against this feeling; by three p.m. he has to lie down and then if the fever is intermittent he has three or four [word illegible] hours of wrestling and gets up after this feeling perfectly washed out and incapable of doing anything that entails bodily and other labour.

I hope these attacks will not come on one when in England.

♦   ♦   ♦

13th December Thursday
Fever again. Oh, how heartily sick I am of this place! Jephson now can never come and Stanley probably a long way off. Fever baddish.

15th December Saturday
... My head man ... is simply a great big, hulking, bellyfull thinker, as long as he can get his belly distended to almost the bursting point he is happy. No thoughts of after promotion or emolument affect him. He lives by himself in a hut, the men dislike him so much; he panders to the lowest scoundrels of the disaffected gang and would any day side with them were it not for fear of after punishment.

Oh you infernal collection of belly-worshipping brutes! Glad will I be when the day for marching comes, happy shall I be once more to have you on the trip again my beauties, with 60 lbs. on your heads each of you and 15 miles to march. We'll see then who will work! Curs! I treat you as well as I would any white soldier and you can't appreciate the treatment, you don't acknowledge just dealing in the slightest; what *is* best for you? Why these: unkindness, hard work, forced marches, severe punishment for the least offence, utter unconcern for your happiness, and the very lowest scale of pay possible, indifference to your comfort other than it concerns one to get the most work out of you and prevent sickness. These are a few of the leading maxims to be practised against you. There are men here I should like to chain up to a large stake; give them as much water and flour as they wanted, then watch the results: "a great burst"!

♦   ♦   ♦

Chapter Eleven

What had happened to the rear column finally became clear to Stanley on 17 August 1888 when he arrived at Banalya two months after leaving Fort Bodo. Parke had already returned to the fort from Ipoto. Accordingly, Stanley was the only European present (aside from his servant, Hoffman) when his small force rounded a turn in the Aruwimi River and suddenly realized that there was a white man in the village ahead.

Stanley could hardly believe what Bonny told him:

Pressing his hand, I said,
  "Well, Bonny, how are you? Where is the Major? Sick, I
suppose?"
"The Major is dead, sir."
"Dead? Good God! How dead? Fever?"
"No, sir, he was shot."
"By whom?"
"By the Manyuema – Tippu-Tib's people."
"Good heavens! Well, where is Jameson?"
"At Stanley Falls."
"What is he doing there, in the name of goodness?"
"He went to obtain more carriers."
"Well then, where is Mr. Ward, or Mr. Troup?"
"Mr. Ward is at Bangala."
"Bangala! Bangala! what can he be doing there?"
"Yes, sir, he is at Bangala, and Mr. Troup has been invalided home some months ago."

These queries, rapidly put and answered ... prepared me to hear as deplorable a story as could be rendered of one of the most remarkable series of derangements that an organized body of men could possibly be plunged into.[1]

Stanley had left Barttelot at Yambuya with orders to follow the advance column toward the lake as soon as sufficient porters had been sent by Tippu Tib to carry the supplies. Barttelot had attempted repeatedly but always in vain to obtain from Tippu Tib the necessary number of porters. Whether Tippu Tib had been unwilling or simply unable to provide the requisite number, given Stanley's failure to provide him promptly with promised gunpowder, can now be only a matter of conjecture. Certainly Tippu Tib believed that Stanley had failed to fulfil his part of their agreement. He told Barttelot that without the promised gunpowder he could not hope to find the six hundred porters. Or was the problem that Tippu Tib had been unable to find the men in a district ravaged by Arab slavers? Whatever the reason, the porters had not been forthcoming, despite Barttelot's repeated pleas. The net result had been that Barttelot, Jameson, Ward, and Bonny were isolated for many months at Yambuya in the insalubrious forest.

What, if anything, Stanley had ordered Barttelot to do if insufficient porters were provided by Tippu Tib remains unclear. Many months after Barttelot's death, Stanley wrote In Darkest Africa *that he had given him the option of moving the supplies through the Ituri forest by stages, with relays of porters going back and forth. Such a recollection served Stanley's purposes; it helped to shift the blame for Barttelot's death away from himself, but Stanley, having crossed through the forest three times, must have known that such a supposed option was not really feasible. The only way in which the rear column could have made its way through the forest would have been to abandon most of the supplies at Yambuya, carry little more than its own food and press forward as quickly as possible to the lakeside.*

When Jephson finally learned of the sad story of the rear column and Stanley's near panic response, he recorded perceptively in his diary,

Stanley's stories are never very just in matters of this kind and I suspect that there is a good deal more in the real story than meets the eye in his letters ... Poor Barttelot's death is most tragic and sad, and will create a profound sensation at home where he is fairly well known. Poor fellow, he was so bright and full of life and go – indeed, the whole story is a very dark one, as dark as any of the many dark stories connected with African travel.[2]

Amidst the consternation and sorrow with which the news was received at Fort Bodo, one incident related to Stanley's search for the rear column went unnoticed, but it was to have severe implications for Stairs. Unknown to Stairs, Stanley had chanced upon his letter of 12 June to Barttelot (see pp. 183). In August it was still in the cartouche of the drowned messenger to whom Stairs had entrusted it. From the letter Stanley learned to his deep resentment just how little Stairs thought of him. Stairs, perhaps without ever understanding the reason, was thereafter subjected to Stanley's repressed fury, manifested in assigning him not only to one but to a series of difficult, dangerous, and taxing assignments. Stairs was fortunate to survive them.

The sorry fate of the rear column was now more or less clear. The column was no more. But what had happened to Emin and Jephson remained unknown. No word from them had reached Fort Bodo.

20th December Thursday
About 11 a.m., heard shots and soon after this Stanley and the *saffari* from Yambuya arrived ... The only other whites were William [Hoffman] and Bonny, the sole survivor to us of the Yambuya garrison.

The story of this most disastrous affair I leave 'till later. I only add here that we were all shocked to hear of Major Barttelot's death. Stanley had sent off letters to England [presumably down the Congo] which would of course put an end there to the reports of his [i.e., Stanley's] death which we have read in scraps of paper sent out.

Bonny gave me two letters, one from father and one from mother. The dates were February 7th 1887, nearly two years ago.

Only 36 of the Yambuya garrison ever reached here and twelve Soudanese = 48 and one Somali = 49 ...

Upon my word, I have never heard or read of such a heart-rending story as Bonny brings up. Deaths, desertions, sickness, wholesale swindling and robbing on the part of the Manyuema make up a story that completely hides itself in a mass of such complications that at first one can grasp nothing. All the whites seem to have fought against each other. Later on I give more details.*

In England great interest seems to be taken in the expedition, the news that we reached the Lake had got to England. Reports of Stanley and all our deaths were rife.

The Conservatives have again got in in Canada and the Nova Scotians beaten on their cry of separation from the Dominion.**

---

*Clearly Stairs at some later date re-wrote this account of Stanley's return to Fort Bodo.
**This was Stairs's first news of the results of the election held almost two years before. The majority of Sir John A. Macdonald's Conservative government was reduced, but the results in Nova Scotia were little changed from the previous election. (How Stairs learned of the results is unclear: he says that the letters of his father and step-mother were dated 7 February 1887; the election was on 22 February). Stairs's father had been strongly opposed to Nova Scotia joining in the Confederation of the British North American colonies in 1867 (*Family History Stairs, Morrow* [Halifax, 1906], pp. 62-65).

All were well at home. Georgie appearing to get on well among her friends in New York. From Mary [in Burma] I got no news.*

All of us were delighted at seeing Stanley and the smiling faces ...

Going down country they made good marches reaching Bonny at Banalya on the [blank], Banalya being [blank] days from Yambuya ... On arriving at Banalya of course Stanley was stunned with the news. The Major dead, the goods gone, Troup invalided home. Ward stopped on his way down country, probably at Bangala. Jameson somewhere on the Congo between Stanley Falls and the Pool.

A horrible story of cruelty, misery and death was then told by Bonny to Stanley, the same as he told us. I abstain from making many remarks as I think Bonny's story wants confirmation. One must hear Jameson and Troup speak first. The Major was shot dead by a Manyuema from a loophole in a hut not fifteen yards off the [words illegible] alleging that the Major intended to beat a woman of his. This man was afterward shot by Jameson, Tippu Tib and the white men [Belgians] at Stanley Falls Station after a trial.** Jameson was away when Stanley arrived at Banalya, going down the Congo after answers to despatches. Over 130 men died at Yambuya alone.

Getting his men together and those he could scrape up from Bonny after a stop at Banalya of three days, Stanley started off up country. It must have been a terrible blow to Stanley thus to have his base so demolished as it was. All he brought is simply the wrecks of what was originally left both in men and goods.

All of us are shocked and horrified at what has gone on down there and for some time I'm afraid that we shall not get over it. On his [Stanley's] march up country, the column suffered through terrible periods of starvation. At one time they were eight days in a hole with absolutely nothing to eat. This was ... only three marches from Fort Bodo. Stanley reached us to-day, 20 December.

We will be able to issue 24,000 corns, this will give every man about 66. Accompanying the expedition in the hope of collecting and getting ivory from Emin Pasha is a force of Manyuema. They number 76 souls. Of the 111 odd Madis (as carriers) who left us and went down country to carry our loads, only 21 returned, thus 90 of them have died. Chama is the last and only surviving Somali. Out of over 60 Soudanese, 12 reached here.

The Major had shot one Nubian for continual thieving, whether justly or not one cannot say as yet.

---

*Georgina Stairs married Edward Twining, a prosperous cotton broker in New York. For Mary Stairs Bourke, see the note on p. 60.

**Bodson, one of Stairs's officers on his later Katanga expedition, had sat in judgment of the assassin. In Katanga Stairs was relieved in Bunkeya by the Belgian officer Bia who had executed the man.

The Manyuema have played the mischief with all the country within say 250 miles; new settlements have been opened up, slaves by the hundreds taken and of course the ivory all collected. Tippu Tib has men as far north as the Aubauni River ... Our total loads now number 280, our carriers only 222 and we have reduced everything down to its lowest as far as loads go. In consequence of this we shall have to make double trips as Stanley this evening decided to abandon the Fort.

Of the stores of European provisions that were left at Yambuya, we officers up here who have been 1½ years without anything in this shape, get 6 tins of condensed milk, 3½ lbs. tea, 4 lbs. butter, 165 lumps sugar, 1 tin biscuits, 1 bottle brandy and a tin of arrowroot and 1 of sago among 5 of us, also 1 crock of beef tea each.

Although Stairs does not mention it in his diary, on 21 December 1888 (the day following Stanley's return) he wrote a letter to Stanley, recording his stewardship of Fort Bodo (its text is in full in *In Darkest Africa*, vol. II, pp. 113-14). Its most notable passage relates how Stairs contended against those who had urged that the garrison, making double trips if necessary, should abandon the fort and carry the supplies to the lake to rejoin Stanley. Stairs believed that, without the support of the porters whom Jephson was to bring, it was his duty to keep the garrison at Fort Bodo until Stanley's return.*

◆   ◆   ◆

21st December Friday
To-day all the new arrivals at the Fort received a day's rest – well earned. Many are very sick and feeble and the ulcers of the Manyuema are most horrible to look on. Several are suffering from other sicknesses of course, but ulcers and wounds from pointed sticks swell the list the most.**

Nelson and I were at work making up loads. Stanley has decided to remove all hands from the fort and march on by easy stages to the front.

To-night Bonny told us a lot more about the Yambuya affair. The whole thing seems more like a horrible dream than anything else. Bonny's story I

---

*The text of Stairs's report to Stanley of his command at Fort Bodo, dated 21 December 1888, is at appendix I.

**The same day, Parke noted in his diary, "The men were really in a terrible state from debility and hunger. I never witnessed such a disgusting sight as the unfortunate ulcerated people ... The stench from the putrid flesh and dirty scraps of bandages was sickening and filled the air all around the Fort. Most of the ulcers were on the lower extremities, great gangrenous sloughing surfaces, some of them a foot long and as large as a soup plate... Great pieces of putrid flesh hanging in strings and the stink was simply awful" (*Surgeon Major Parke's African Journal*, p. 117).

am inclined to think must be taken with a "grain of salt"; in his whole story he is most even.* One thing he says tallies exactly with another. Barttelot appears at first to have gone hand-in-glove with Jameson. Afterwards, however, he would appear to take Bonny into his confidence. But now from Bonny's own story Barttelot did everything he could to please Bonny. Yet Bonny says he was a most disagreeable and cantankerous chap. It is very hard to make anything at all out of it. Bonny arrogates a great deal to himself that he has no right to.

What I want to hear are Jameson's and Troup's story on getting to England. Such grave and serious things are said about Jameson and Barttelot that I will not even put them down here.** Ward and Troup fought among themselves. The Major and Troup and Ward fought. Jameson, it would seem, was the best liked by the men, and did his best for the expedition. Till I get absolute particulars from Bonny, I abstain from making any further statement.

One only hopes that the lower [?] English papers have not got hold of a lot of this and are publishing them [*sic*]. It will be a long time before they can be contradicted and a lot of mischief will be done.

Poor old Major, it will be a great blow to his father who I believe was very fond of him. Besides he was a most lucky chap and had a grand chance before him had he only not been murdered.

22nd December Saturday
... Had a long chat with Stanley and all the fellows in the evening. Bonny again repeated his story and told us more about what had happened.

Stanley gave us some cuttings from English papers.*** Reports had been circulated that Stanley and all of us with the advance column had been killed. These, of course, were contradicted by Stanley and other letters. They have for some reason (probably thinking Stanley was dead) sent on almost all the provisions to Bangala. Everyone had most positive opinions that Stanley and all of us would never come back. Stanley's maps and a whole lot of things belonging to different fellows were sent down to Bangala.

By the Halifax papers I see that "at last" the ferry boat company intend[s] getting a new steamer. A cathedral is to be erected and electric lights increased in the city. The Liberals have been badly licked in Nova Scotia, but in the whole Dominion their cause has brightened. Uncle Alfred has been elected

---

*Stairs's wariness at accepting Bonny's story in every detail was justified. On other occasions, Bonny proved himself unreliable, perhaps because he was a narcotics addict.

**What Bonny was alleging about the relationship between Barttelot and Jameson remains unclear.

***Bonny had brought with him from Bolobo the clippings and mail of June/July 1887. There were four letters from Parke, but none, apparently, for Stairs.

as Liberal and Mr. J.E. Kenny as Conservative. J.F. Stairs has been beaten.*
It's just what I always said; the Liberals have only taken up the cry of "separation
from the Dominion" to get into power. Once they get into power I fancy they
will be remarkably silent at Ottawa on this point ...

23rd December Sunday
This morning about 8:30 the *saffari* left the Fort, leaving Nelson, Bonny and
some 40 or 50 men who leave the day after to-morrow. For many, many a
long day I have not felt so light hearted; one was almost crazy at getting away
from the place. At the small hill just where our corn plantation ended, I turned
round and had a last look at the place. Of course I felt sorry at leaving after
having worked so hard at putting the crops into the state they are now in, but
this was quite outweighed by the thought of once more getting on the march
and on to the plains and out of the bush.

Nelson and Bonny (who is very thin) will leave on the 25th. We go ahead,
camp, send men back and then all behind come on. We have to do this as we
have nearly 100 more loads than men and so have to make double trips. The
men as a body are all in the best of spirits, but in poor condition. It is a case
of "the spirit is willing but the flesh weak." The Manyuema people suffer
quite as much if not more than our men, but get along well with the short
marches we are making.

I reached camp with the rear of the Column about 3 p.m., the distance gone
over being about nine miles. Stanley's plans as to what he will do ... are yet
not settled; I fancy though it will end in the sick people and feeble ones being
left in camp just beyond the Ituri River and Stanley and perhaps another officer
go on to the plains then find out news of Emin Pasha and afterwards return
and pick up the sick ...

---

*"Uncle Alfred" was the Hon. Alfred Gilpin Jones (1824-1906) who had married Margaret
Stairs (Stairs's aunt). Jones was a Liberal Member of Parliament from 1867 to 1872,
1874 to 1878, and 1887 to 1891. He was minister of militia in 1878 when Stairs applied
for admission to the Royal Military College of Canada, and Lieutenant-Governor of
Nova Scotia from 1900 until his death in 1906.
Thomas Edward Kenny (1883–1908) was a Conservative Member of Parliament from
1887 to 1896 and a prominent Haligonian businessman associated with Stairs's family.
John Fitzwilliam Stairs (1848–1904) was a Member of the Legislative Assembly of
Nova Scotia from 1879 to 1882. He was a Member of Parliament from 1883 to 1887
and from 1891 to 1896. He became the leader of the Conservative Party in Nova Scotia
in 1897, but was defeated in the provincial election of that year. In 1885 he played a
central part in inducing John Thompson, the Chief Justice of Nova Scotia, briefly premier and future prime minister, to accept the repeated offer of Sir John A. Macdonald
to join his government.

♦   ♦   ♦

25th December Thursday
To-day I took off about 100 men and went off about eight miles to the S.S.E.
I had Manyuema, Lados, Madi, Soudani and Zanzibari, a more badly disciplined
lot of men never stepped on this earth; noisy, heedless of my voice and the
arrows of the natives. I had a pretty hot "Christmas Day." In getting there, the
natives, as usual, ran off and our men captured a lot of women; we then sailed
into a large and newly built village where we got some fowls and a goat. Then
our men raided all the other villages and scattered all over the bananas. Do
my best, I could not get them together till 5 p.m.

Several times the natives collected and threatened the village, but I sent
out men and drove them off. These Manyuema are exactly of the same cut as
those we have had so many dealings with, such insolent, unruly brutes I never
before saw.

Nelson reached camp this afternoon ... having burnt the Fort. He had to
leave [abandon] four sick behind ...

26th December Wednesday
Boxing Day. Returned to camp and had some brandy in celebration of
Christmas.

27th December Thursday
Started off this morning with about 100 men to go on to the Ituri River and
make camp. Of these, 55 will go back to Stanley and bring on loads. I have 48
to remain as garrison till Stanley comes up to the River. It will take us four
days' good marching. Nelson also goes with me, but I am afraid he will be
very far behind when we reach the river ...

♦   ♦   ♦

30th December Sunday
Off early. Reached Ituri [River] at 3:30 p.m. and made camp on west bank.
There are two canoes moored on the other side of the River, but none on this.
Spoke with the natives across the River, they say they will bring a canoe over
to-morrow ...

One wants a few weeks' good feeding with plenty of meat to get strong. At
present one has no strength at all in one's joints. There are plenty of good
bananas within 1½ hours of camp.

[I] am very anxious that Nelson should reach us soon. On leaving Stanley, I
told him that Nelson would never keep up with us and now this has been
realized.

31st December Monday

Last day of 1888. Nelson may come to-day. I hope so. Sent away the 55 men for Stanley. We have thus only a garrison of 28 or so. These collected in a small compass are sufficient but as yet nothing is organized, the men sleeping all over the place.

Nelson and all the men behind came in to-day. Many of them complain of sore feet and ulcers but I hope the rest here will do them good. To-morrow we must get the canoes over, the natives do not seem to desire our friendship apparently.

1st January [1889] Tuesday

New Year's Day. I only hope by this time next year we shall all be out of Africa and once more in old England.

Early this morning one of the men ... swam across the river and brought over one canoe. Four men then went across and up to the village on the other side and found the natives had all decamped and gone off into the bush. The men captured a few fowls and got a lot of ripe bananas, and then returned bringing over the other canoe so that now we have in our possession the two canoes. This is a good stroke. Our men here have completely lost their heads at the sight of the ripe bananas and the taste of the goat meat they got the other day. Last evening five of the men went off and have not yet returned. I suppose they are off at some village filling their stomachs with goats and fowls. When they are full up to the neck they will probably return ...   I suppose one's people are having a good time of it to-day and wondering where we are. In Canada everyone appears to visit everyone else on this day and drink other people's wine and tea.

The provisions brought up from Yambuya though few in number are a great addition to the bush feeding; with a cup of tea, morning and afternoon, one feels quite civilized again.

The authority Stanley has over these men seems to disappear at once when he is absent. The difference between the "big master" and the "little masters" is very great, and one often is inclined to believe that Stanley does not seem to mind it much. This is a great pity as we have responsibility without power if this is not looked to. The men are civil and pleasant enough but they don't care much about the "little masters" to tell the truth. When there is plenty of food the Zanzibari at once loses his head and simply will not work.

2nd January Wednesday

Ituri River camp. This morning I sent off a party of 21 *rugga rugga* on this side of the River. It was not without some inward feelings of uneasiness, however, that I did so. These men, when off raiding by themselves, simply go wild, there is no getting them together when it is time to return. The chief in command of them has absolutely no power and cannot prevent the men scattering in small groups of three or four or so, getting shot by the natives. At times my blood boils over at the careless, callous way in which these fellows regard danger. It is not as if they were brave at all, far from it – if faced they will, I feel sure, run away.

3rd January Thursday

Took some eight or ten men across the river and cleared a place for the new camp we propose shifting to to-morrow or next day. This camp is getting too filthy to live in. The amount of filth in the bush on all sides of us is something astounding. As a matter of course this filth has attracted myriads of flies and midges which alighting on the filth and then on the men's bodies breed sickness.

We made a small *boma* on the east side of the river large enough to hold all the tents and goods. The men will build their huts around and outside this *boma*. I went on ¾ of a mile or so past four or five villages till I reached a hill top from which the plains can be seen.

Stanley intends leaving a force behind with the sick and a lot of the loads and then take a strong body on to the Lake to find out what is the matter there. Should all be right he will at once send back but should Emin Pasha and Jephson be detained there then he will not run the risk of losing his loads at the hands of Emin's Nubians. It is very hard what to think is the reason no news has reached us from Emin Pasha.

This site would be a first rate place for such a station as I have just spoken of, except that I feel sure we can never keep out the elephants. Judging by former experiences, elephants are always numerous near the rivers and here they seem especially so ...

4th January Friday

... Sent ... eight men across river to build a hut for the goods ready for us when we cross. Stanley ought to be here on 8th–10th. I hope to be able to move over to-morrow, but the men are poor hands in the canoes.

The *rugga rugga* came in this morning bringing me four live fowls and three kids. They had gone north and east until they cut our old track to the Lake at the village near where Jephson and I found a crossing of the Ituri. They got a good supply of goat meat for themselves and their comrades which I let them keep.

5th January Saturday

Started early this morning at crossing the column over the river ... In the river here there are quantities of the most horrible looking crocodiles. I fired at a large one the other day just as he was crawling off a log into the water. The bullet hit him somewhere about the tail and he splashed about a bit and then dove. We did not see him again ...

In the evening as Umari Ben Brahim was going to bathe and just entering the water I saw the head of a huge crocodile appear about seven yards down steam from where Umari was. I yelled out, "Mamba! maluba!" "Crocodile, crocodile!" Umari was just in time to get away. Shortly after this, Nelson and I had a shot at him [the crocodile] about 50 yards off in the stream. Whether we hit him or not we can't say. It will be a bad day for any one who falls out of the canoe.

6th January Sunday

Men want to go off on another *rugga rugga* but I would not think of it as Stanley may come any day now and perhaps send me on to the plains. I often wonder what Jephson and Emin Pasha can be at. The news that we are coming must have been carried on from village to village and reached them by this time. Perhaps we shall meet some of Emin's men on the road. I dare say they would not like the idea of coming into the bush; if they don't, they show extremely "good taste."

7th January Monday

Killed a small kid. We are saving five fowls and eight goats for Stanley and the other people when they come.

The soldier ants came into the *kraal* last night in millions. All along through the night till two in the morning we fought them with fires, brushwood and every other means we could adopt. Time after time we had to shift the miserable goats from place to place. By midnight, the fight was general, all hands turned out and at last we turned their line of march and gradually got peace, but very little rest.

8th January Tuesday

... Stanley is camped ... waiting for Parke who is a day behind with the sick. I sent back twenty men empty handed, according to directions from Stanley. These are supposed to help along the sick and weakly ones. [One man] died at Stanley's camp. A Soudani, getting firewood ... was fired at by natives, getting struck with five arrows. He still survives, I believe.

Chapter Twelve

On 11 January 1889 Stairs was again left by Stanley in command of a camp (this time at Kandakore) while Stanley went ahead for a third time to Lake Albert Nyanza. Stairs was again deeply disappointed, knowing that he would miss the final rendez-vous between Stanley and Emin (assuming that Stanley could find Emin and Jephson upon their return from the garrisons).

Upon Stanley's departure for the lake, Stairs believed that he would not see him "for two months or so." In fact, Stairs spent only three weeks at Kandakore before letters and porters arrived from Stanley ordering Stairs to abandon the fort and march to M'swa on the shores of Lake Albert where Stanley was encamped.

On 6 February 1889 Stanley had been joined at Lake Nyanza by Jephson. Eleven days later Emin himself had arrived with a Tunisian apothecary, who was one of his principal lieutenants, and a few followers. Not less than eight months had elapsed since Emin and Jephson had set out on their perilous survey of opinion among the garrisons of Equatoria. That they had survived was a close run thing. The rebel-lious garrisons had rejected Emin's authority and had abused him and Jephson. One garrison had even imprisoned them. Only the approach of a Mahdist force from the north had probably saved their lives. The eight months had been hazard-ous in the extreme, but the intentions of the garrisons with regard to withdrawal remained obscure.

Stairs arrived at the lake on 18 February 1889 to join Stanley and Jephson. That was also the day on which he first met Emin Pasha (who had arrived the evening before), but in his diary he is silent about that long-sought event. For two years Stairs had laboured and suffered to help succour Emin, yet the moment when they were for the first time face-to-face, appears to have been a matter of indiffer-ence to him. Possibly in light of later events he removed, during the editing and rewriting of his diaries, his original description of his first impressions of Emin, intending to rewrite the passage at some later date. In fact, only two years later in The Nineteenth Century *did Stairs offer his initial impressions of Emin.*

Gradually, during the weeks following Stairs's arrival at the lake, small groups from several of Emin's garrisons straggled in, but Stanley was again prevailed upon by Emin to delay their departure for the coast until the intentions of the garrison at Wadelai could be determined. Throughout, Emin remained evasive about his own intentions. Jephson, who after eight months with Emin knew him better than any other member of the expedition, was convinced that he did not want to leave. Junker had been right when, two years before, he had warned Stanley that Emin would not want to quit Africa.

9th January Wednesday
Stanley came up to the river with the rear column about 10:15 this morning. Parke got in about 5 p.m., and behind Parke two days were sick men straggling all along the road ...

Stanley's plans are fairly well matured by this, I fancy. He will leave all the weak and sickly ones at the village of Kandakore on the hill top about twelve minutes east [longitude] from here. From this village he will take on the strongest men, say 90 or 100, and go on to the Lake, taking say two white men and leaving two at the village. Here will be left most of the expeditions' loads, those of Emin Pasha being taken on.

Parke will be left of course to look after the sick and I to look after the Fort and men. Nelson is unable to march, I feel certain, but I had to tell Stanley otherwise.

I am simply broken-hearted at being left behind this time, not because of the fact that I am left, but because I know Stanley did it for certain reasons which I must refrain from giving and because these reasons are absolutely unjust and unfair.*

Have I not always done every little thing possible towards helping on the expedition when under all sorts of difficulties? No man better knows it than Stanley himself that he has not got one white man who does his work more willingly and cheerfully than I do.

In the evening Parke, Stanley and I had a long chat. Stanley decided that Wm. Hoffman, his servant, should be left here ...

---

*To what Stairs refers remains unclear. In *Darkest Africa*, Stanley wrote briefly, "I valued the ready and prompt obedience of Stairs ... painstaking, ready, thoughtful and industrious" (vol. I, p. 5), but Stairs's reference may possibly indicate that he had become aware of the fact that Stanley had read his letter to Parke.

10th January Thursday
Fell all hands in, weeded out all sick; I shall have some 130 men all told, 40 of them can hardly move and will have to be fed. Thirty will be well in 15 days and ten more in say 25 days.

I give about 60 days as the length of our stay here. Knowing the Zanzibaris as I do, I expect some will try to desert me. This position is a fair one as regards defence. The water is about 900 yards off. I am as yet unacquainted with the vicinity, but perhaps later on will have a look about the place ...

11th January Friday
Stanley went off this morning to the Lake for the third and last time I hope. Originally it was intended that Nelson and Bonny should go, but Nelson's ulcers prevented him walking and so Bonny was the only other white man. I have not yet made up the numbers of those to go with him but will do so in a day or so.

I am again left in charge at this place and the garrison. This time I have over 130 men, a lot of slaves, boys, girls, the whole forming a regular second edition of the Tower of Babel ...

Well, here one is planted again for two months or so till the sick are well and we are able to move on the Lake. Every single man, woman and child, white men and all in this camp is suffering from some form of sickness or other. There are three exceptions only: Parke, his boy and myself. We are the only three out of 140 odd souls who are whole.

I give the men to-day and to-morrow to build their houses. This camp on the whole is a better position than that at [the] Ituri. The only one serious obstacle is that the water is so far away, 7 or 800 yards off. We are on a hill top and on a clear day can see the open country. Mount Pisgah lies about 3½ miles west of us, the Ituri River between.

As yet I have not decided as to what precautions I shall take as regards defence, but the men's huts will go to form the outer defence and inside I shall make an inner ring with the goods and a tower inside ...

12th January Saturday
To-day the men were again occupied in building their houses. About forty of our people are in a very bad state; it will be months before some of them could be expected to recover even if in the very best hospital in England. Some three or four will die in a very short time, Parke thinks. We are both determined to do our very utmost to get every man well and strong as quickly as possible. The sick get goat soup, Indian meal porridge and other foods and have all their water supplied to them. Those very bad are in a hut by themselves with a man constantly looking after them.

This is the largest command I have ever had, the responsibility is very great and I only hope every one will try his best to help things on. It was a great disappointment in not getting on the Lake but still I see that perhaps it is for the best that I should stay here. As a result of Nelson's idleness at the Fort and consequent soft feet, the march up gave him six ulcers and he could not go on to the Lake. He now is laid up in bed just at the time there is so much work to do.

13th January Sunday
Building *boma* on west side. I am making this of upright boards 4' high, with pointed sticks giving a total of say 7'.

Terribly hot winds and a scorching sun. The atmosphere is densely charged with the smoke of the plains' fires. The sun has the appearance of a crimson ball, but has the orthodox Central African power nevertheless. The houses are the coolest places one can get into ...

14th January Monday
To-day the natives took off the canoes to the other side. I sent down six or seven men who fired at the natives on the other side of the river and say one was killed. Put the other well men on to building two towers, one at the W. centre and the other at S.E. angle of the Fort.

Water is a very serious difficulty here. The river is 900 yards off and is the only drinkable water obtainable. There are some water holes in the bush 560 yards away but the water is always disturbed by elephants at night and when brought here has the appearance of ordinary "country hotel" soup in England.

Gave a kid to Parke for the sick ones.*

15th January Tuesday
... There are some of the very worst and laziest of scoundrels in the expedition ... There is a great big hulk of a chap [who] sometimes I think this man is just laying himself out to give as much trouble as he can. By George, he will get more than he reckons on if he persists in his little games!

16th January Wednesday
Finished the latrine, the S. East tower and brought up a long pole for a flagstaff. At work on the W.N. West Tower and the N.E. tower ...

17th January Thursday
Finished all the towers. Started building officers' houses. By evening had finished one and about ¼ of another ... Our men are constantly seeing natives

---

*Parke was under no illusions about why the porters needed to be fed: "... Stairs and Nelson and myself fully realize the value of keeping these men alive as we have barely enough Zanzibaris with us to reach Zanzibar, for we can never face the forest again" (*Surgeon-Major Parke's African Journey*, p.126).

in the bananas. They said they saw yesterday some of the *rugga rugga* shoot a native on the other side of the river. I know this is untrue though. It is certain though that the natives have stolen the canoes.

Stanley should be near the edge of the hills over the Lake by now. It will certainly be an anxious time for him if Emin is not at the south end of the Lake. I should think he would hear of Emin's whereabouts either from Kavalli's [words illegible] but the news may not be very reliable.

Sick ones getting on slowly. Our huts should be very comfortable when finished.

18th January Friday
... Parke is very seedy again. He suffers intense pain. Nelson injected morphine. It is some form of fever.

19th January Saturday
Two years ago since we left England. Parke very bad. He has bilious intermittent again, a very bad form. It generally lasts about 14 days or so ... A Soudanese died to-day from ulcers. His foot had simply decayed away ...

20th January Sunday
Poor Parke is really dangerously ill to-day. He has agonizing pains in his stomach and back and groans at time with heart-rending sounds. Both of us are now very anxious about him.

To-day a Madi and a Zanzibari [straggler?] came into camp. It is 16 days since they were left behind by the column. Both were weak and sickly. Three other Zanzibaris ... died on the road. Of the three sick Madis two were caught by the Masongora and killed ...

Just two years ago to-day since we sailed away from Gravesend in the *Navarino* ... I wish I could only get my spirits up a little. I declare at times it is heartbreaking work dealing with some of these men, remonstrating, entreating, threatening, fining, nothing seems to be of any use.

I will never come into this part of Africa again unless I have the command of the thing myself or else it be a military concern.

21st January Monday
Rugga rugga returned. Brought two goats but of course killed a great many more. Some 10 of them reached the plains and brought back sweet potatoes. I feel sure Laki killed a native on the plains, but the stories differ so I cannot get quite at the bottom of the affair. I afterwards learnt that the men got ten goats.

Parke much better.

◆   ◆   ◆

23rd January Wednesday

Two men died to-day ... Finished latrine of whites. Started building the inner *boma*. A slave woman ... also died to-day. The old [?] ulcers and dysentery are the two chief causes.

24th Thursday

... One of my very sick chaps died to-day. It is a mercy for all that he is gone. For 14 days he had been kept alive by pouring liquid food down his throat ... another Zanzibari died this afternoon. Poor chap has been seven months doing no work. Just as he was getting better an attack of dysentery took him off.

♦   ♦   ♦

26th January Saturday

Mending our houses which leaked very badly last night. We have had severe thunderstorms for the last three nights running ... I am terribly afraid of fire, situated as we are on this windy hill top and the men's huts only 60 feet from the ammunition. Every night just before the hurricane comes on I go round among the huts and put out all the fires.

The poor Madis generally get let in for a hammering. They are so slow a stick is the only method of making them move.

The absence of the 32 men from the Fort makes an astonishing difference. At times one spends very anxious moments dreading a rush at night on the part of the natives or an outburst of fire. With these 32 men though I feel very little apprehension. [One man] I had buried on the hillside leading down to the river as the old burying ground was so stony that our hoes were being seriously damaged ...

27th January Sunday

Am making a new hat out of canvas and leather. Put a new buffalo hide sole on one of my boots.

Yesterday I cleaned up the Maxim gun and fired a few rounds. To-day I made a new stand for the water tank [for cooling the gun]. Formerly this tank used to be suspended on the steel shield; this Stanley would not let me bring on and so now I have no protection from arrows in front as before. On the plains, however, I shall rig up some sort of invention for a shield. Expected the *rugga rugga* back to-day but they did not come ...

28th January Monday

Started doing up the loads, made new bags, weighed and did up six loads ... *Rugga rugga* came in about 11 a.m. They brought four goats and some fowls but got about 24 goats all told. The men will get very fat and strong here. As they have played the fool in wasting ammunition and only brought me four goats, I fell them all in and swore I should put any man in chains who endeavoured to go raiding. I would not allow any more forays at all. They all felt awfully ashamed of themselves as in the way of meat with me they get four or five times as much as they would if Stanley were here.

Two [natives] were killed and none of our men hurt. Many of the natives would appear to have fled to the other side of the river.

Stanley has been away 18 days now – no news from him. If we get no news by next Sunday then I shall feel sure Emin is not at the south end of the Lake, that he is not ready to come out, and that perhaps he does not intend doing so. Should I have to send native couriers of Kavalli's north to one of Emin's stations we may be here another month without any news. Most of the Manyuema here are going down hill very fast, whereas our men are picking up and the ulcers healing splendidly. The Manyuema get soup, medicine and the same care as our men, but they are so low in condition (many of them) that food appears to do them no good ...

My brother Jack's birthday: he must be 27 years old to-day if I am not mistaken. I often wonder if he is married yet and my sisters, Anna and Hilda.* The gap of three years will seem very strange to one on getting back ...

29th January Tuesday
Nelson and I all day doing up loads in sacks, these afterwards we weighed and put into old powder boxes. The loads average about 54 lbs.

Cleaning all the spare rifles. The Yambuya men I find cannot take a Remington rifle to pieces yet they say their rifles were taken from them and locked up in a house. "Yes," I told them, "that was because the Major knew you would ... desert if he gave you rifles".

Started building the large central tower in the inner *boma*, it will hold 12 rifles and the floor is 12 off the ground. From it one will be able to see the whole fort and surrounding ground ... Up to the hilt with all sorts of work now. Good for us though as it makes the time pass by and all are healthier and happier for it.

30th January Wednesday
Finished re-doing up the loads and cowries this afternoon. At work on the new tower. The view from this tower is a very fine one. The bush on the S. can be seen stretching away till one loses sight of it some 25 miles off at the

---

*Six months after Stairs's diary entry, Jack, who was born in 1862, married the daughter of the Italian bandmaster of a British regiment in the Halifax garrison. After a few years they separated. Jack, much enamoured of horse racing, pursued a lacklustre business career in Nova Scotia and Ontario. Anna, unmarried, lived in Britain from 1917 to 1940 and died in Halifax in 1953. For Hilda, see the note on p.73.

crest of a range of hills. Mount Pisgah in the mornings when low banks of clouds seem to stick about half way up its side is a very fine sight. The plains at their nearest point to us are about four or five miles off I should say ...

31st January Thursday

... Should Emin Pasha be at the Lake and communication easily and rapidly assured between he [sic] and Stanley, then his couriers should be on their way here. Now if no couriers reach here by the 6th or 8th February then I shall feel sure that Stanley had to procure natives to convey news of his arrival to Mswa or some other station of Emin's and that Emin Pasha has either been inexcusably dilatory in his movements or else he is held a prisoner by his people. I never yet thought for an instant or felt it that Jephson was dead. He may have been very ill but he is not dead.

1st February [1889] Friday

... Saw two native elephant spear falls and set one of them off. A heavy log is suspended in the air about 30 feet from the ground, to the lower end of this is securely fastened a short, stout stick pointed at the lower end and finished off at the extreme point with an iron shoe. A stout vine is attached to the bushes with the ordinary cross pin fastening used by the Wasongora natives and runs up over a stick lashed high up in a tall tree and thence over and down to the big log first mentioned. Upon an elephant or any large animal passing through the bushes the cross pin arrangement is detached and the log falls, the spear piercing and pinning down the elephant. The one we set off stuck deep into hard ground and supported the log at an angle. So I should say quite 5' of a thick, strong spear 3" in diameter goes into the elephant backed up by about 500 lbs. of wood: quite enough to finish him off then and there.

Some men I sent out for corn encountered nine natives and shot one, bringing in the hand,* the others ran dropping some bows of the open country pattern.

2nd February Saturday

... It is 23 days now since Stanley left here. Life here is very much the same as at Fort Bodo only that there are more men and they are a much livelier lot. Not a day passes but the drums are going and always a dance in the evening. Some of the men are very graceful [sic] in their movements in these dances. Then there is no scarcity of food here as at the old Fort [Bodo] and in consequence one does not have the same complaints and whinings about food. The position here also is a better one, being on a hill top we can see about us

---

*As proof that they had actually killed the person, a common practice in the Congo Free State.

on every side for miles. The natives about here appear to have a wholesome dread of the rifle.

I am glad to say that the ulcers are getting better very fast and almost all the men getting better. Still there are some eight or nine Zanzibaris and an equal number of Manyuema who remain pretty much in the same state as when they came here. We have 42 men or perhaps more who could carry loads now.

3rd February Sunday
Mending boots and shirts. Long ago my boots having given out, I am now using those of my own manufacture, a wretched substitute as the skin is untanned or unprepared in any way. Nelson gave me an old pair of his boots. These I have patched and sewn up quite out of shape. Every time I use them though my feet suffer. I don't see what I am to do: ahead are nine months of a march and I have no boots to march in. I only hope that I will not get ulcers. One's feet in this country are the most important part of one and to be unable to use them means perhaps death.

4th February Monday
Took four men early this morning and went on to the plains to try and get a shot at something. Reached plains in one hour's easy walk, fired at a buffalo but missed and saw nothing else ... The African buffalo is one of the most dangerously active animals at charging one knows of. A single beast if wounded and away from its comrades almost invariably charges. Then on the plains there are no friendly trees one can slip up and so avoid a pair of sharp horns. We saw no natives.

It is just 12½ months since I was in open country last, the longest period on end I have ever lived in the bush. Any day now I expect Stanley's *tarishi* (couriers) from the Lake. Gave Baraka Wadi Moussa twelve strokes for sleeping on guard.

5th February Tuesday
Great sport was caused in camp to-day by a Manyuema woman. This woman got herself up in feathers and flowers and with a native rattle went all about the camp singing to the devil. About 10 o'clock though the sun got very fierce and she strolled back to her hut having been unsuccessful in calling up his majesty! I believe she is quite mad at times. At night all of a sudden one hears the most blood curdling yells and imagines about 40,000 Washenzi coming on against the camp. After a few inquiries, it generally turns out to be this woman ...

A girl ...who was sleeping outside one of the gates of the Fort and suffering terribly from gangrene in the foot was taken off last night by a leopard. This morning with some men I followed up the tracks for some distance but lost them in the bananas. The beast is certain to return in a night or two and make another try. The gates are shut at sundown and all kept inside but still men have to go out at night and the position is a dangerous one.

6th February Wednesday
Sent off a party of *rugga rugga* to-day in a S.S.E. direction ...

The road from the plains that I returned to the Fort by a few days ago is a bit longer than that of Stanley's, but in the end the distance is about the same as Stanley turns to the south apparently after reaching the plains and my road cuts his.

On this road there are three large banana plantations all in very poor order. Such quantities of ripe bananas on the trees I really think I never saw before. One plantation is only 40 minutes from here, so that when we have eaten out the bananas here it will be an easy matter to procure more.

When I use the word bananas I really mean plantains, that is the big coarse sort with corners [*sic*]. The real banana such as one eats in England or gets from the West Indies is very scarce in this part of Africa. They are much the nicest to eat raw and ripe, but flour cannot be made from them. From the plantain one can make flour, beer, cakes, fritters, have them roasted either ripe or unripe, boiled ripe or unripe. From the flour one makes porridge or *njarri* which is simply scalded meal, much in the same form as the stuffing inside a fowl at home. From the stalk and leaves one can make baskets, rope, roofs of huts, neat little wrappers for butter or other food and last of all the root is edible, many a feed I have had of it when there was nothing else to be had.

The natives about here have small crops of corn but of an inferior kind. Of tobacco there is a great quantity.

7th February Thursday
Collected a lot of castor oil beans to make oil of for the sick and also for our rifles, in all got three large *chungus* (pots). Wadi Khamis and I started on a trap for "the leopard." It will have two ordinary Remington rifles loaded and a goat as bait. A Monbuttu woman was out getting firewood yesterday and when only a short distance outside the Fort gates was sprung upon by the leopard and had arms and back scratched. She escaped, however, and came screaming into the Fort.

Last night I sat up outside the Fort with a rifle till midnight. At this hour I had to retire though as the moon set and I could not see the goat I had tied up as a lure to his majesty.

A Manyuema died to-day.

This afternoon six of the *rugga rugga* I sent off yesterday turned up. They had got separated from the main body and had gone off on their own account. After an hour or so they struck a native track newly opened up, following this they came to a very large native camp and rushing in, the natives fled. The bag consisted of some five goats, 40 or 50 fowls and beans. The natives had word of their approach, and just as our men sailed in, were making up their goods into loads ready for the flight. To-night our fowls rose from two up to 25, of these there are 12 well-developed hens so we stand a chance for an egg or two now.

... the chief of the main party of raiders is off somewhere on the Ituri River after goats. I expect him in to-morrow with a good bag. Every goat we kill here we give half of to the sick and weakly. We have been killing every three days up to this.

It is a great thing for the men getting all this meat. A few feeds or rather gorges of goat meat is better for the men than all the ulcer medicines the doctor has in his boxes.

If Stanley does not come until the end of this month he will find the men as a rule in splendid condition. Now only 20 to 25 men get soup and meat. When we started at first we had to give 40 rations. A Manyuema ... died to-day of dysentry. Some of the Madis are yet very thin. One fellow is simply a skeleton, absolutely no flesh can be seen on any part of his body, his system will not absorb the slightest particle of nutriment, I should say.

I often wonder what English people would say if they knew of the way in which we "go for" these natives. Friendship we don't want as then we should get very little meat and probably have to pay for the bananas. Every male native capable of using the bow is shot, this of course we must do. All the children and women are taken as slaves by our men to do work in the camps. Of course they are well treated and rarely beaten as we whites soon stop that. After 3 or 4 weeks with the men they get to be as happy as clams and gorge themselves with food almost to bursting. It always seems very funny to me to see a native woman who yesterday was running wild in the bush come up to the doctor with the rest of the men and slaves for medicine for her ulcers. They all of course have heard of the white men from our former trips to the Lake, but still also appear very much astonished on actually seeing [them].

8th February Friday

... It is a great thing on coming to a new place where one is likely to remain for some time to make a sketch of the different roads, valleys and hills and to explore in every direction for five miles or so, the country on every side of your position. Of course all books recommend one to do this but it is only now that I fully see the real use of it. Now I know nearly every road, creek, village and hill for some miles from the camp. The satisfaction and comfort one feels after making this rough survey more than atones for the work. I can never rest now for a day unless I know just what exists on every side of me.

This evening ... I went down to the leopard trap and put in a fowl for bait and put a cartridge in the rifle. It is now all ready and should "that leopard" try to steal "that fowl" he is a deader as sure as nails are nails. I don't believe in the chicken as bait; a goat is much better as he bleats all night long and attracts the leopard or hyena to the trap ...

9th February Saturday

... In the afternoon the *rugga rugga* sailed into the Fort absolutely laden with loot. They brought me six goats and some fowls, beans, corn, skins, spears, shields and arrows and bows, head dresses, and what I have not seen for 700 miles , an idol or rather the head of an idol or god that is solicited when rain, success in war, or anything else is wanted.

It would be very interesting to know really what form of worship these people have if any.

I should like to get some of these curios home but there is absolutely no chance as every man is wanted to carry ammunition. At every camp I get splendid collections of skins, bows and arrows, shields, pipes, pots, knives, bill-hooks, baskets and hats, but have always to leave them behind.

Three natives were shot and the hands brought in.

The numbers of slaves in the camp are increasing to an alarming extent. I hope no epidemic is likely to break out. Smallpox our column was once attacked by and though the slaves died off like rats yet the vaccinated Wangwana escaped scot free; only two cases occurred. These bush people, unvisited by either Arabs or whitemen or any outsider and living their peaceful lives in the forest, nevertheless have periodical visits of the smallpox. They also suffer from venereal poisons as peoples of other countries.

William Hoffman, Stanley's servant, is really about as low a character as one could possibly imagine. From first to last he has done nothing but lie and steal. Stanley never has used him of late. He has simply lived outside, at times depending on the charity of the Zanzibaris ...

I purchased a leopard's skin for 6' of Emin Pasha's cloth. These skins are things I should like very much to get home.

10th February Sunday

... to-day Rashid came into the Fort, bringing 35 Zanzibaris and 100 Wazamboni carriers from Kavalli's village.

I got two long letters from Stanley, one from Jephson and a note from Bonny. Stanley is camped near Kavallis' village being [in] good now with all the natives from here to the Lake. On his way east at Majambonis' village he heard of Emin Pasha and Jephson. The news was conflicting but still he was able to make out that a revolt had occurred in the Equatorial province and that the Pasha, Jephson and Casati, the Italian, were all prisoners. Stanley received definite news of them at Mpinga's village about 2½ days this side of the Lake. Kavalli had sent a packet on to him and on opening it, Stanley found one letter from Jephson dated Dufilé Nov. 7 '88; a p.s. was added Wadelai

Nov. 24th and another Iunguru Dec. 18th 1888. He also got two brief letters from the Pasha.

The general thread of Jephson's letter was about as follows. The letter warned Stanley to be very cautious as a revolt had broken out. A meeting of Emin's officers instigated by his chief clerk and a lieutenant ... was formed. This assembly deposed Emin Pasha from his position and on the 18th August both Emin and Jephson were made prisoners. This was about the time we expected Jephson with relief at Fort Bodo ...

Soon after this, however, the "old crowd," the Mahdists, ... sailed up the Nile in force and landed near Lado. Their head ... sent dervishes to the commander of Rejaf demanding the surrender of the garrison. These [three emissaries] were seized and the garrison prepared for resistance. In a few days Rejaf fell, five officers and many soldiers being killed. Rejaf is the Pasha's northernmost station. A panic then was the result on all sides, and three stations, Bedden, Kirri, and Muggi, were abandoned; the ammunition at Kirri was seized by some natives. At Dufilai Jephson says, "we are like rats in a hole and unless you come very soon you will be too late and our fate will be like that of the rest of the garrison of the Soudan." The last words of Jephson's letter are doleful enough, "If we are not able to get out of the country, please remember me to my friends."

Emin's soldiers ... were so angry after these stations were abandoned that they declined to fight unless the Pasha was set at liberty which was done. The Pasha and Jephson were thereupon sent to Wadelai, but [Emin was] not re-instated.

The Mahdists have sent down to Khartoum for re-inforcements. All were anxiously looking out for the expedition's arrival at the Lake and appeared to be dreadfully afraid of the Mahdis.

Stanley says there is a report about of a second relief expedition being at the north end of the lake. The men of this are said to be armed with rifles like ours, to carry their loads just as our men do and that they are led by white men, not Arabs. Can this be Joseph Thomson? Not at all unlikely ...

The Wazamboni ... are as a rule fine, fat-looking fellows, but they are unused to load carrying and many of them are mere boys. I expect by the time we reach Majambonis' four days off, most of them will have enough of it.

Jephson was well. I fancy now Emin will have to come out. He is now making his way south collecting whom he can. Both steamers were seized by the rebels and our boat, the *Advance*, destroyed. It would seem now though that Emin has possession again of at least one steamer.

11th February Monday
... Tomorrow we shall make a start and by next Tuesday 19th I hope once more to see Mr. Stanley and Jephson. Stanley's orders and directions are very explicit.

White men in this strange African country seem to have a universal suspicion of each other. Each would imagine the other to be a "bit canny," or to put it plainly every white man in this country thinks everyone else either a rogue or a good-for-nothing. No use to say, "Oh, this is absurd, or what nonsense!"

In the evening the Wazamboni gave us an exhibition of their dancing powers. Many of them are very active in the usual wriggling and squirming performances of all natives, but all are especially clever in keeping time and following the beat of the drum ...

Four generations ago a general disturbance took place in the western part of Uganda. A certain body of men becoming discontented with the doings of the king then in power, collected together and moved off to the country west of Albert Nyanza, between Kavalli's and the forest, these the forefathers of the present Majamboni. Since then they have prospered and beyond several local wars and attacks on the part of Kabba Rega have lived a peaceful, pastoral life.

◆   ◆   ◆

13th February Wednesday
... How pleasant it is to once more get out on to the plain and feel the breezes...!

I find these natives just as Baker describes those of Unyoro and other parts. As long as they are with friends who have rifles they are very brave and want to fight their neighbour's all together forgetting that when the white man and his gun leave them that these same neighbours are bound to retaliate.

All night long the Wazamboni made a horrible noise dancing, swaying and beating their drums. Our caravan is about 300 all told.

14th February Thursday
... The track we are marching on now is about 10-15 miles south of that by which I went to the Lake before. The Wazamboni are not bad carriers but every day there are constant squabbles and loud talking between our men and them. They complain bitterly that our men push them on the road.

15th February Friday
Left camp and in one hour came up on parties of Wazamboni who had come out from their villages to meet their friends. Soon these increased and our men got their loads carried by these most obliging people. ... at once, the chief, Majamboni, came to see me and brought a jar of milk. We had long *shauris*. I am going to stay here to-morrow. He promises to have plenty of carriers ready the day after to-morrow, and will give my men food to-morrow.

All day long a regular fair day in camp. Our men selling and buying and the crowds of natives made the camp quite lively. Our men gave two cowries for one fowl, quite twice too much.

A letter from Stanley awaited me. Emin Pasha now will come out, there is no doubt. The first lot of those willing to follow us have already come down by steamer and another lot will shortly follow. The whole of the Equatorial province will be wrecked and many lives lost and work undone.

Stanley wants me to get along as fast as possible. I sent off couriers to him with a letter telling him we are coming along well.

The women here are really very pretty and the men handsome looking fellows. The dress of the women is a little sprig of green bush which is renewed every morning. These ladies therefore are provided with a brand new gown every day, a thing many white ladies I know would be proud of.

In the evening Majamboni's warriors gave a war dance. These are the same lot of howling wretches who 14 months ago howled and yelled at Stanley.

Jephson and I were enclosed in our mimosa *boma* on the hill top just behind this camp. For three days we stayed there trying to make friends but as it was no use. Jephson and I burnt down at that time every house, granary, cattle *kraal*, destroyed their crops and bananas and punished them in every way we could. Now they are our best friends.

It was very amusing watching the young women dancing with the men, and the particular wriggle they give very "fetching." The young girls and women yell at the tops of their voices in the wildest excitement. One woman I noticed with a baby under her arm frantically wriggling about in and out among the crowds of men. She appeared to quite forget her baby which was squalling most horribly.

These people value cowrie shells more than any other article of trade except perhaps cloth. They also value arrowheads, long straight sticks for spear shafts, axes and things of this sort. Bill-hooks too they are very fond of. We whites are absolutely without any means of buying anything so that we are in some cases solely dependent on the native chiefs' charity!

16th February Saturday
Stanley will be expecting us to-morrow or next day. Majamboni says the carriers will be ready to-morrow morning but a native chief's word is never up to much, simply because in many cases his men will not listen to him.

To-day I was presented with two head of cattle, four jars of milk, potatoes, flour, sugar cane, corn and beans. The cattle I had slaughtered at once and issued to our chaps as well as flour, *mtama*, (kaffir corn), potatoes, etc ... The milk which is always drunk when sour in this country was very good. I gave Majamboni a bolt of blue serge (4 yds.), my own property. We under officers are not given one cent to spend on chiefs.

17th February Sunday

Left Majamboni's after some trouble about getting enough carriers; travelled over a very good road north of our old one and reached Mpinga's about 3 p.m. Here a year ago we had a big fight. Mpinga is not nearly such a fine looking man as Majamboni. His people speak the same language as the Wazamboni. The women are very much disfigured by the way they do their lips up. The upper lip is pierced and a large ring inserted. Gradually increasing this ring the lip protrudes quite four inches in many cases ...

18th February Monday

... Met Stanley, Emin Pasha and officers, Jephson and Bonny. I think there is now no doubt that Emin will come out with us and Stanley will give his [Emin's] officers time to return to Wadelai and bring out their men ...

Jephson has had a lucky escape.

19th February Tuesday

... had a yarn with the Pasha. He of course feels very keenly having to leave the country he has been governor of for so any years ... The Pasha is a very spare little man with, I fancy, not a very strong mind.

The difference in discipline between his men and ours is very marked. Ours at once spring to an order like shots, whereas his men have to be coaxed and asked to do any work. Here there are some 10 or 11 clerks and officers who joined the rebels but afterwards asked forgiveness and expressed a desire to go out with us. At least two of these beauties were sent up from Egypt to undergo a period of seven years of confinement for *murder*. One of them also desired very much to have the Pasha shot only a few weeks back. These people will go back to Wadelai and try and persuade their men to come out. Some I fancy will never return.

Jephson told me his story which is very interesting.

20th February Wednesday

Put up the Maxim [gun] and explained the mechanism of it to the Pasha and his officers. They were all very much surprised at the rate of firing possible. Emin had two mountain guns which are now in the hands of the rebels. I believe there is very little ammunition for them. Emin tells me that if he gets out safely with us he will go to England and thank them first. Then he will urge the English Government to take over that part of Masai land east of [Lake] Victoria Nyanza and the Kingdom of Kavirondo. He says he has not yet finished with Africa and one day will return ...

Casati is still down there [at Lake Albert]. He says he only wants 80 carriers. Fancy *only* 80. He'll d_____ well get 10 if he comes with us and be thankfull [*sic*].

21st February Thursday
... A report came in from Bonny that Kabba Rega's people were on the war path and had raided some villages 10 miles from here. The Pasha went down to the Lake with Nelson and 60 escort, who will sail into Kabba Rega's people if they can engage them.

22nd February Friday
At work building huts for the Pasha's people, a job our men do not seem to appreciate very much. The officers often seem to be a shaky lot. Of course as yet one only knows from Jephson what a lot of blackguards they are, but perhaps later on we shall find out more about them. I should like him to bring out, say, 100 guns. These added to ours, say 240, would make a very respectable force and quite enough to get out of the country with and yet too many to overrule the Wanywana. One looks upon our Zanzibari boys now as heroes and friends and not merely as porters. They have brought us so far and I hope will take us out to the coast, they can help themselves and others whereas those belly-jobs from the Soudan would appear unable even to help themselves. How we shall all get on peacefully I can hardly see. The officers appear to be frightened of the men, according to Jephson. Emin's soldiers say the white man is played out in the Soudan. All these yellow bellies are called white!

23rd February Saturday
Same work as yesterday. Bonny came back and brought up Signor Marco, the Greek merchant, who has been caged up in Emin's country for goodness knows how many years.
    Food is scarce in camp. The levy taxes on the friendly natives about here, each chief giving his quota of flour every few days, but this is not really half enough.

24th February Sunday
Building houses for the Pasha's officers, clerks, etc. A piece of work which makes one's back get up. However, I suppose it is work that must be done and may as well be done cheerily as not.

25th February Monday
Went off with some sixty rifles to stir up some natives near Mwites' [?] village who would not bring in food. After threats they brought forth supplies and we returned.

26th February Tuesday
This morning I took sixty Zanzibaris and marched off to ... about 9 miles N.N.E of this place. As the natives beyond would not bring in food I descended

into their country and sailed out with 127 head of cattle. A most acceptable piece of loot. Got back by 4 p.m., tired out.

27th February Wednesday
At work in camp building a brush stockade to hold our swollen herd of cattle. Took pretty well all day at this. The Pasha came up from the Lake again to-day. I hope he will not go down again. These Turks of his are up to any game.

28th February Thursday
... down to the lake to bring up loads and people. Reached the foot of the mountains by 5:35 p.m. and camped. Feet and joints of legs terribly sore from descending the steep slopes.

Chapter Thirteen

By March 1889 Stanley had decided to wait no longer for the garrisons who were still procrastinating – as he saw it – about whether they wanted to leave Equatoria. Stanley was wary of the intentions of Emin's followers. He feared that if they became sufficiently numerous and aggressive, they could overcome his own men and seize ammunition and other supplies in order to stay where they were.

Stanley was determined that Emin would accompany him to the coast. He had not spent more than two years in the African bush only to return without tangible evidence of his success. Stanley regarded his whole reputation as being at stake in the "rescue" of Emin. No one would be allowed to prevent him from realizing his goal, not even a reluctant Pasha. Stanley set 10 April 1889 as the day on which the Expedition would begin its long march to the coast. Any of Emin's followers who had not joined it by then would be left behind.

It had now become obvious that no effective force would be available to Emin to hold the north end of Lake Victoria for the Imperial British East Africa Company as Mackinnon had suggested when the expedition had first been mooted more than two years before. Emin, in Stanley's words, "had no force to do anything for him, for you, or for me ... Nolens volens the pasha had to come."

One historian of the expedition has noted:

... Emin could summon no enthusiasm for the prospect of a withdrawal from the area and the people he had come to know so well, although he readily admitted the truth of all that Stanley and the others had to say about the impossible position he would be in if he remained. At no point did Emin express a firm intention to withdraw with Stanley's expedition, rather, as the choices before him diminished, he simply accommodated himself to circumstances – and these soon came to be dominated by the more forceful personality of Stanley.[1]

Stairs and the other officers strongly supported Stanley in his demands on Emin. They did not believe that the procrastinating garrisons intended to travel to the coast with them.

1st March [1889] Friday

Left camp at the foot of the mountains at 5 a.m. In three hours reached the Lake and Casati's camp. The camp is on the lakeside in a very pleasant spot. How jolly it was to see once more the waves rolling in over the sand! It reminded me very much of home.

Off again back across the plain and reached the foothills by 5 p.m. and made camp. Am bringing up 100 loads and Vita Hassan, the Tunisian apothecary, some Egyptians, etc.*

2nd March Saturday

Reached Kavalli's and Stanley at 1 p.m. Feet very sore. Nelson laid up with fever. Everyone else well.

One of the women gave birth to a child on the road with the utmost unconcern of her surroundings. Then marched on again quite cheerily and as proud as a "Lord Mayor."

Vita Hassan has been ten years in Emin's country and at times has been very useful to the Pasha.

What a caravan we made up to-day to be sure. Women, babies, parrots, beds, chairs, every sort of odds and ends in the Soudan must have been represented. Casati is a captain in the Italian service. He was formerly A.D.C. to General Soldeve. He is quite grey now.

3rd March Sunday

... One has now and then long talks with the Pasha about the state of affairs. Felkin** and Junker are terribly to blame about the ideas Europeans have or had of the Pasha's country and people. For years a smothered rebellion has been only waiting for wind to fan it into flames. The proposition of the Pasha's that he should leave the country afforded them their chance. The Pasha's, Jephson's, Casati's and Vita Hassan's lives for some time were merely

---

*Jephson noted in his diary that Vita Hassan, the Jewish apothecary from Tunisia, was "a very decent little fellow and very useful to Emin Pasha, he was sent out some eight years ago by the Egyptian Government when Emin Pasha applied for a doctor, he is now his apothecary, storekeeper, and general helper." (*The Diary of*, p. 249). Hassan published his memoirs in two books: *Die Wahrheit über Emin Pascha* (Berlin, 1893) and *Emin Pascha, die Aequatorial Provinz und der Mahdismus* (Berlin, 1895).

**Robert Felkin (1853–1926), the noted Scottish physician, missionary, and explorer, had published "The Position of Dr. Emin Bey" in the *Scottish Geographical Magazine*,

suspended on the slightest threads. They were insulted, disobeyed, jeered at and at last told to clear out of the country. The second advent of the ... Mahdists will bring these beauties to reason I have no doubt.

I feel very anxious and I'm sure Stanley does about what is now going on at Wadelai. It is true we have the Pasha, but what if Selim Bey, who has gone up to Wadelai, should return and bring a lot of cut throats with the name of soldiers here? Might they not seize our powder and ammunition? They are quite able to do it. Every one knows our Zanzibaris are no fighters against guns and determined men. The apathy, the indifference with which these people, including the Pasha himself, seemed to look upon our relief expedition, their absolute helplessness in acting promptly are simply appalling and to us quite beyond understanding. That we who have for two years patiently toiled through forest, dangers, fevers and sickness of all sorts should be met at last by people who will not help themselves (let alone others) is so maddening as to almost make one say, Well! Go then and be hanged: the Mahdists will cut your throats and serve you right. These people consider us their slaves I fully believe. No, we will be your servants for some little time but never your slaves.

Emin's soldiers, boys and women all have the same sullen, sulky, doggish, arrogant expression, one sees very few jolly, smiling boys as among our Zanzibaris.

4th March Monday
Yesterday Bonny went off to the Lake. Stanley is a bit seedy to-day. His bowels are out of order.

Finished building the huts for the Egyptians. It is as yet very hard to say how many guns will come out with us. I say perhaps 70. We shall see afterwards how near the mark this is.

... our head Zanzibari has fever. I cannot help thinking this camp is an unhealthy one in spite of its elevated position.

We get more food now from the natives than formerly; perhaps this is owing to my two raids.

The features of Kavalli's men and the natives about here are much more refined that those of the Wasongora bush natives. The huge lip ring disfigures the appearance of the women very much. At Majamboni's I thought the women and girls the prettiest and most really formed of any I had yet seen in Africa. Here the women wear dressed skins for covering, as well as the small spray of grass before and behind, freshly put on every morning.

---

vol. 2, no. 12 (December 1886), which had contributed to the concerns he had already raised about the plight of his friend. Once the expedition was launched, he joined in editing an account of Emin's service in the southern Sudan: G. Schweinfurth, F. Ratzel, R.W. Felkin, and G. Hartland, eds., *Emin Pasha in Central Africa* (London, 1888).

This place is about 5,200 feet above the sea. The Warezza hills to the east close by are probably quite 6,000 feet high. I am awfully sorry that I lost my watch, etc. I can do nothing. However, the Pasha is taking careful observations...

5th March Tuesday
I doubt if the letter the Pasha wrote the other day ever reaches Shookri Aga [Shukri Agha] as the Pasha imagines it has.

Some of these days Stanley will rush out of his tent and make things move a bit quicker ...

♦   ♦   ♦

8th March Friday
Parke went down [to the lake] with some men for more loads.

These clerks and people of the Pasha's are simply maddening. Though they all know we shall have to throw away their rubbishy loads on leaving here, still they will not do this down at the Lake and avoid our having to carry them up the mountains.

The Pasha really has no control over his people. When one sees what goes on here one readily becomes aware of the state of affairs that must have existed in the Equatorial Province. We have finished building houses for these people and many, I have no doubt, consider Jephson and myself as simply their slaves.

9th March Saturday
... The natives have stopped coming in to us as carriers now. We used to give them six cowries per man for the round trip to the Lake and now and then slaughter a bullock for them. Apparently the mountain slope with a heavy load has been too much for them. This is a great pity, especially as the stony track is playing the mischief with our men.

10th March Sunday
Parke arrived up. The steamer has not yet come. What is the matter? Are we to get Shookri Aga and his people from M'swa or shall we have only those intend coming down from Wadelai ... ?

♦   ♦   ♦

13th March Wednesday
Left camp for Lake with 50 carriers. Marched all day up to 8:30 p.m. Made 16 miles and reached the Albert Nyanza at a fishing village of Kavalli's. The natives had plenty of fish and gave us some and some salt.

14th March Thursday
Left the fishing village, reached Pasha's camp 8:30 a.m. at once started off and reached the top of hill by nightfall.

Bad fever, terrible pull up the mountainside.

15th March Friday
At last reached camp. We left long before daylight and reached Stanley about 9:30 a.m.

I thought I would have to give it up and send to camp for men to carry me in, but thank heavens I pulled through and got in. Fell down on my bed and simply rested all day.

♦   ♦   ♦

17th March Sunday
Went up the hills on a picnic with Pasha, Jephson, Parke, Nelson, and Bonny. Spent the day collecting birds, beetles, insects, etc. for the Pasha. The highest hill I was on was 5,500 feet odd. We had a capital lunch and enjoyed ourselves very much. This must be remembered as a great day to us all as it is the very first of its kind we have had since the expedition left England.

Bonny shot a good specimen of a plantain eater which delighted the old Pasha very much. He is a tremendous enthusiast in things botanical, zoological, entomological, etc. He is such a funny looking little man with his crooked nose and spectacles peering over some insect that one always feels inclined to laugh at him. But he is such a good old soul, so kind and generous and so sympathetic. One can see he never could make a governor.

The natives on the shore take hippopotami with a harpoon which is thrown in the ordinary way but attached to a large float of ambatch wood. In this way many are captured.

♦   ♦   ♦

18th March Monday
The Pasha and Stanley have agreed together about the length of time we are to give the officers who went to Wadelai. It is fixed as the 10th of April, on that day we move from here ... .

The Pasha was delighted with the survey I made for him from the Lake up to camp. I am also making a section of the mountains with aneroid for him. He has given me some maps of his country, two pairs of new cotton trousers, a notebook and pencil, and paint brush. He is a most generous person ...

The Pasha is only going to get 11 or 12 loads carried by Stanley, Vita Hassan gets 3, Marco 3, and Casati 3. Just the same number as we officers.

The yellow-bellied Egyptian clerks of the Pasha will just have to flounder along as best they can ... .

Bonny has been given charge of the Soudanese now numbering 17 in all. We have still some 18 or 20 Madis. These I surmise will follow as far as Zanzibar. Poor devils, they will never see their country again or their families. The Manyuema are fast being trained down into something like submission by Stanley. There is said to be a settlement of Arabs (probably Manyuema) somewhere off to the southwest of here about 7 days' march. Should these be Manyuema, then most likely our Manyuema boys will desert over to them. From here Stanley proposes to move to Majamboni's and from there make a final start for "the unknown".

Vita Hassan, the apothecary, is not at all a bad sort of chap. He is endowed with more common sense than any of Emin's under officers and other followers.

As for the generality of these yellow-faced, indolent people, one can see that there will be some stranger sights when once we get on the march. What quantities of women and children there are in this camp alone, I should say 50 helpless ones quite. They have about 15 or 16 donkeys which will be some sort of help to them.

19th March Tuesday
Fell in our companies and gave men notice that we should leave here on the 10th April. They were all very much delighted at learning that a date had been definitely fixed.

◆   ◆   ◆

21st March Thursday
Jephson and I started off at 5 a.m. with our companies on a foraging party. We marched hard and fast till 10 a.m. ... Jephson went to the right with No. One company and I took my company to the left. At 2 p.m. we met, he having got about 200 cattle and I about 90, a good take.

The natives were very bold on the right. Many of Jephson's men fired off 10 rounds. We afterwards learned that four men of theirs were killed outright and two others wounded. One of our men got an arrow in the calf of his leg but it amounts to nothing ...

Jephson and I with the last of the cattle reached camp about 9 p.m. pretty tired out. We must have gone 25 miles quite. Several bulls we had to shoot to prevent disturbance. This must be considered a most successful day's work.

22nd March Friday
This morning we gave over the cattle to Ngudgu (a chief who lives close by); these were some of his cattle which were stolen by a chief about 10 miles

from here and which we raided yesterday morning. We slaughtered 5 cattle also, 2 of these we gave to No. 1 and 2 to my company No. 2. The other was given to the Pasha.

The Pasha and Signor Marco, the Greek merchant, went out collecting birds, beetles, etc. One effect of our raiding yesterday was that plenty of flour was brought into camp to-day. We got about 5 gallons of milk from our herd this evening, giving each of the officers 15 cups, the Pasha and some of his clerks and our sick also got some ...

◆   ◆   ◆

24th March Sunday.
Casati's leg is pretty bad yet; he has two nasty suppurating ulcers on his ankle which will be a long time before they get well.

25th March Monday
Today letters came from Shookri Aga [Shukri Agha] and Selim Bey. The steamer arrived yesterday from M'swa. The letter from Wadelai came in a canoe to M' swa and was forwarded by steamer.

Selim Bey's letter or rather the letter from the officers and clerks at Wadelai to a man almost, asks the Pasha's forgiveness and states that now all [are] desirous of coming out with us to Egypt via Zanzibar and that already large parties have been sent off by land and water. Those going by water will collect at Tunguru first, then move on M'swa and then here.

Shookri Aga stated he would wait until [he received] further orders from the Pasha.

Stanley, shortly after getting the letter from Selim Bey, called Jephson, Parke, Nelson and myself into his tent with the Pasha to talk over matters. Emin Pasha asked Mr. Stanley what he had decided upon. Stanley then asked me if I thought we should be justified in leaving here on the 10th of April or not, taking everything into consideration, the way they had rebelled and taken their governor and one of our officers prisoners, had insulted them, threatened their lives; how already we have waited nearly a year for them, how slow and dilatory in their movements they are and a score of other things. Of course, I answered that the 10th of April was ample time and that those really desirous of leaving and joining us would be readily able to do so. The whole of the other officers answered in the same way. The Pasha, one could see, had hoped that we should extend the time beyond that date, but nevertheless he promised for himself that on that date he would be ready to march. Stanley spoke to the Pasha very strongly and at times I fancied there would be a split. Luckily, however, things blew over.

Now among those coming from Wadelai will be some 600 men ... at least so the Pasha says! We'll say 300 of these will come. Now several times these lambs have expressed a desire to settle down in the country to the south of the Lake and follow us a few days then leave us, but before doing so they openly said, "We will rob them of every round of ammunition possible". I feel certain that this is just the sort of thing they are capable of doing. This Stanley expressed in very strong terms to the Pasha and stated he would never allow these men to come into his camp armed.

What a strange man Emin Pasha is where matters of common sense business are concerned. In conversation generally [?] and in many ways I believe there can be few more pleasant and entertaining men than the Pasha. Leave these scenes and start on any business matter or affairs where it is a question of duty and the Pasha is entirely incapable of seeing things in their true light. Have not some of his people [word illegible] at least three successive times? Have they not even threatened to hang him? To chain him up? And yet he can say, "No, they will never rebel again." How stupid; how [word illegible] it is of him to speak like this! Fancy trusting these blackguards!

I hope it will never be said of Stanley or his officers that they trusted these brutes one jot. They're just as ready now to do mischief as they were before. To tell the truth, I earnestly hope that when we finally leave this place on the 10th of April not one soldier from Wadelai or one of their split-tongued officers will put in an appearance.*

About Shookri Aga and his irregular soldiers [word illegible] M'swa according to all accounts they would be a very able addition to our strength. Their people, however, not having any idea of the value of time, are pretty sure to put off coming by that date and so miss us.

At the end of the *shauri* both Stanley and the Pasha decided to send strong letters to Shoori Aga [*sic*] to move on this matter at once. Stanley's letter will be all right, but that of the Pasha will "not be straight" and as a man should write. The Pasha cannot order anyone to do a thing; he requests them always.

26th March Tuesday
The time is now rapidly coming when we must make a partial move on Majamboni's. Stanley and, in fact, all of us are getting desperately tired of this awful waiting. All of us are burning to move off from here and feel we are on our long road to the coast and home, but the Pasha and his people seem to be affected with a lethargy which they do not appear able to throw off.

---

*Stairs was eager to depart and to be done with Emin's officers of whom he had a low opinion: "Of the late Egyptian officers of Equatoria who accompanied us to the coast, with one or two exceptions, but little can be said in their favour. They were a standing example of the saying, Trust a pure black or a pure white man; but a yellow one, *never*" (*The Nineteenth Century*, vol. XXIX, p. 963).

27th March Wednesday
To-day we heard from Kavalli's natives that a large party ... dressed just as our men are and with rifles, had arrived at Majamboni's village some 18 miles west-south-west of here. Immediately we all began thinking who on earth this could be? Could it be Jameson following us up? This indeed would be good news if true ...

I said at once that it was a hoax and on going down and getting a man to speak with Kavalli's people my impression was only strengthened.

Jephson left at 12 noon with about 30 men to march over and see what the truth might be. He has orders at any rate to bring 200 natives as carriers so his mission will not be fruitless even should the reports of the natives prove untrue. He will reach Majamboni's to-night.

◆   ◆   ◆

29th March Friday
Mlengi and six natives came in at 1 a.m. this morning with a note from Jephson. The report of any strangers arriving at Majamboni's was absolutely untrue. Jephson should reach here to-day with 170 - 200 carriers ... This is only another instance of the general falsity of vague native reports.

I leave on the 31st for Majamboni's, there to await Stanley's arrival. We shall in all probability be there some 15 days, I should say. There will be a regular to-and-fro traffic between the two places, I expect, when we once get established there. I don't mind the job much, but would rather stay here till the end.

When the final move is made from here there will be weeping and wailing and knashing [sic] of teeth in the loudest tones on the part of some of the Pasha's people. Even though we have had so much meat, still a great many of our people are still in very poor order for long and continued marching.

30th March Saturday
Jephson got in about 5:00 this evening, bringing about 56 carriers (they promised 200) of Majamboni's. When natives promise to give you carriers in numbers like grass, you may know that this means about 50 men. When they tell you that the chief himself will "see all about it" and send you plenty of men, you may book it for certain none will come at all.

◆   ◆   ◆

1 April [1889] Monday
Got off about 8 a.m. with a heterogeneous mass of natives, Nubians and Zanzibari. All together it would make but a poor caravan for a long march. The natives about here, as I suppose also in most parts of Africa, are but

faint-hearted porters. At every dirty pool and stream they come to on the road they fill up their bellies with water and in consequence soon slacken and get faint. The best sort of money in this country is livestock, of this there can be not a doubt. The natives here will do anything for meat. Poor devils, they will seldom get it, I expect, when we are out of the country.

Musiri's country appears much more fertile than that of Kavalli and one notices very fine patches of grazing land all well watered with good streams. In most of the gullies leading down to these little streams are planted banana trees (strange to say one only notices *young plantations* of bananas. They never seem to arrive to maturity). There appear to be a great many herds of cattle scattered over the country judging from the number of *kraals* one sees...

2nd April Tuesday
Reached Majamboni's about noon. Here I pitch my tent and wait for Stanley who brings up the rear with the Pasha and his people.

Majamboni is the same old stick as ever. He will sit from daylight 'till dark in front of the tent smoking his pipe and not saying a word all the time. I sometimes fancy he does it to impress one with his greatness. If he does he makes a huge mistake.

It is strange how really poor these people are in spite of the extreme fertility of this valley. Their settlement is beautifully planted in a green, grassy valley with a clear pebbly stream flowing through its centre. *Mtama*, corn and potatoes will grow splendidly; yet a jar of *merissa* containing perhaps a quart is considered a desperate present to make to one. The natives themselves will fight over a few potatoes or cobs of corn while for a piece of meat the brains of the entire settlement will be turned topsy-turvy and one would think when we give them a cow that a civil war was taking place, such a din and uproar there is.

3rd April Wednesday
... Sent a note announcing my arrival to Stanley ...

Poor boys [the Zanzibari], what bricks you are, and how one notices it when you are put side by side with those skulking, scowling negroes of the north. What cheery, happy, open faces our Zanzibaris have! What brutal, doggish, cunning ones the Pasha's men possess!

...who could like these people? Hawash Effendi, immediately on reaching here, plagued me to get carriers for him to send on to the Pasha. To-day it is the same thing, if left to work his own will, he would soon break the existing friendship between us and Majamboni ...

4th April Thursday

... Majamboni, the old coot, wants me to go and fight a chief one day S.E. of here. Fancy gentle stranger, only one day off. Majamboni will supply 600 warriors, he mildly states. What fools! This is just like the African savage. When he has the support of the white man's guns he will fight his best friend just for the sake of robbing him of his cattle and women (even though the two tribes intermarry). Then when the white man goes, he in his turn gets robbed by the man he has just despoiled.

Conversation between Hawash Effendi (a major) and myself to-day. First let me say that the Pasha told me at Kavalli's that Hawash Effendi would build the Pasha's house here. Hawash Effendi was present and said, "Of course." The following then may shew up the ways and wiles of these yellow-bellied Egyptians.

Hawash Effendi: My men have already built two houses and tell me there are no poles to be got in this valley and so I shall have to build a house like those the Zanzibaris build.

Stairs: Yes, that seems to be the best thing you can do.

H. Effendi: Now will you give me some Zanzibaris to go out and cut the necessary poles and rods since they know best just what to cut?

Stairs: No, I can't do that as it will establish a precedent and besides the Pasha distinctly told you in my presence that you were to build his hut.

Hawash Effendi.: Yes, I know, but can't you just lend me then six Zanzibaris to fit and tie on the poles? My men do not know how to do this.

Stairs: No, I cannot even do that.

H. Effendi: Well then, just give me two men for quarter of an hour to fix on say six poles. Now that is all I will ask.

Stairs: No (getting mad), if you can't build the house why then the Pasha must sleep out of doors. I will not let one Zanzibari help any of you with your houses. You look on them as dogs whereas we consider them our friends; not one will stretch out his little finger to help you if I can help it.

H. Effendi: Well then, will you exert yourself with Majamboni to get his men to cut the poles?

Stairs: No.

I then turned round and walked off. Do these beauties imagine us to be their slaves? Men who number murderers, rebels, and thieves in their list? Why only yesterday one Effendi stole salt from another and threw it into the river to avoid detection. I told this lamb I would fire him out of the camp with his wife, babies and all if he tried any more tricks of that sort.

By the Khedive's orders, we are only "to escort by any route that Mr. Stanley may choose such persons as are desirous of making their way out to the coast and Egypt." We are not told that we should be their slaves. We have quite enough work with the natives generally to have much time to spend on these people who almost to a man are rebels against the Pasha ...

5th April Friday

How wild these natives make one sometimes with their jabbering and yelling! At a pow-wow they all talk together like so many parrots, nothing will stop them, it is their meat, this incessant talking. I often wonder half the time what they are talking about. An Irish night in the House of Commons is deathly stillness compared with this.

The men are to come like "grass" to-morrow to carry loads for us. This means perhaps about 40 will come.

The chiefs' wives came to see me this evening, two of them were pleasant looking enough but the third was really a very pretty woman of about 18 or 19 years old. She has just been married and as yet has had no children.

What a lazy, aimless life these savages live! They barely plant enough to keep themselves alive. The rest of the time they smoke, talk or sleep. It is most amazing to see a man going about with his pipe and some tobacco wrapped up in grass and "lashed" on to some part of his body. From time to time he will look to see if his precious tobacco is "all there". Should any other native steal this, it is almost tantamount to a tribal war. The tobacco in question would generally go into an ordinary thimble. This shows their poorness, for all are extremely fond of smoking.

6th April Saturday

... This afternoon the women of all the valley came up to my house and danced before me from 3 to 6 p.m. It was a most lively and interesting sight; a great many are very clever with their feet. The dress they wore was the ordinary one, a bit of bough stuck through a belt and let hang down in front and also another bit behind. They got intensely excited after the first half hour yelling and working their bodies like demons. This would have made a great catch for the manager of the Alhambra. He would have full houses every night.

Some of the head women came up and asked me for a cow which I had to give. Women are the sauce all the world over. Now, if these had been men I certainly should have refused, but being women they can wriggle anything out of an ordinary man.

Fever struck me in the evening just as if I had been hit with a big pole across the back. I had to go in at once and till eleven o'clock I suffered the tortures of this most cursed of African troubles.

7th April Sunday

... I get the milk from some six cows every morning and evening. Though they do not give anything like the quantity ordinary English cows do, still I get a huge bucket 2/3rds full ... of the best I drink or make into butter, which is very good. Every morning one of the men churns for me in a large gourd. It is a great pull having this milk. All my meat I sell for eggs which are ever so much more acceptable than tough, tasteless cow meat.

The women are all collecting and making a terrible noise. What happy, careless animals these females are! No cares about dress have they, the nearest bush affords them a completely new outfit every morning. They were just as ravenous as the men for meat and made just as much noise. Meat I suppose they taste once a year. The milk they are not allowed to drink; this is all kept for the men.

8th April Monday
The time is drawing near for Stanley's appearance. The carriers I sent off the day before yesterday should leave Kavalli's to-day ...

9th April Tuesday
... This is the eve of the Pasha's leaving Kavalli's. Poor old chap, he will be in a terrible state of uneasiness all day, the more so should Shookri Aga not have turned up.

It must be a terrible blow after twelve or fourteen years life in this country, and after having nursed his infant so long, to have that infant grown now up into a man, turn upon him and force him out.

It is a lesson that I hope I shall never forget should circumstances ever place me in any position where Nubians or Soudanese are to be dealt with. I sincerely hope I shall be able to work up to this maxim: "Never trust a Soudanese anywhere, at any time, with any power, in anything." He will deceive you sooner or later, but *some* time he will deceive you, you may be certain of that. Up to now no man knew how to handle the Soudanese as Baker did, all will say that in this country.*

What were Baker's principles? "To keep a sufficient force always at his beck and call, say 100 men or so, and with this force crush at once the slightest attempt at an outbreak or even murmurings." When he did punish a man he did so before as many people as possible and if for insubordination he flogged the men to within death's door!! He knew always what was going on about him. All reports, all the opinions of his underlings, he knew to a nicety, and he was thus always ready for any emergency by being so informed.

To-day even the best things in this country are those brought out by Baker; his steamers, chairs, lamps, everything that is good and lasting was brought here by Sir Samuel Baker ...

---

*Sir Samuel Baker (1821–93), one of the greatest explorers of the upper Nile and of central Africa, was accompanied on his travels by a Hungarian who later became his second wife. A rich man, he was able to explore as his interests took him. Samuel and Florence Baker eventually reached Stanley's goal of Lake Albert Nyanza in 1863-65.

10th April Wednesday

At last the day has arrived when the "Emin Pasha Relief expedition" is to move off from the [Lake Albert] Nyanza camp and start on its long march to the coast (all well) and home.

We of the expedition who have for weeks and weeks past looked forward to the 10th of April as a red letter day and as one which would give us our deliverance from that "huge monster", the Soudan, and all connected with it, now feel in great spirits that at last the day has arrived.

Emin Pasha, on the other hand, who twice got the date of final departure postponed, cannot but feel sorrowful and disappointed. If Shookri Aga has not arrived by this time at Kavalli's it will only add to the Pasha's bitter disappointment, and also be detrimental to us. The chief personages, or those whom we would wish most to get out of the country, we have secured. Heaven alone knows even yet if we shall be able to secure the Pasha. His ways are so strange. Now for our sake let us be off and away from influences this blackest of countries may possess over the Pasha's mind. Let us swing away east and southward to the snow capped mountains of Ruwenzori, and far across the central plains to Msalala and the Central African sea [i.e., the Indian Ocean].

There we shall see our white brothers and learn the news from the busy European world. Then we shall know what we all have been burning to know for the last 2½ years. How are our friends? (for there will be letters for us there). What is the state of affairs in England? Has there been another European war? What is happening in America? in Canada?

Then to me there is the all and ever-important question about my "service for pension and promotion" being counted or not. If these three years I am out here do not count for pension and promotion then there is nothing for it but I must leave the service. At present one does not know what the state of affairs will be when we reach home, but I hope I shall not have to leave the service on account of three years' work in Africa ...

Will Stanley keep to his promise and come to-morrow? Or will he listen to the Pasha's pleadings for more time and give in to another postponement? How I hope we shall move at once, and move steadily forward, and clear away ... to Zanzibar and more genial climes.

Now I should just like to say something about drinking, that is drinking to excess. Drinking is almost as prevalent among these people here ... as it is in England. Their chief drink is almost always a beer made either from bananas, mtama, corn or grain of some sort.

Quantities of this beer are brewed, the drums start going about sundown, and by midnight 2/3rds of the people, between the dancing, singing and drinking, are as drunk as fools. When drunk they make a terrible amount of noise, and often at night I can trace a party of roisterers on their way home, as they move along some path down the valley, simply by their continued shouting. The women are very fond of their beer, just as much as the men.

11th April Thursday

The natives had another big drinking bout last night. All night long we could hear them blowing horns and shouting to each other. They must have got through a great lot of *pombe*.

Will Stanley come to-day or not? If the Pasha is given into this time there is no saying what he might not ask for.

Spring time at home now. In Canada the ice is loosening its iron grasp on the lakes and streams and the dusky trout begins to move about ready for the season ...

Some natives came in this morning from Mpinga's with the news that Stanley had arrived there last evening with the Pasha and all hands. They stated that Kavalli had also moved with them and that the old camp at his place was burnt down on leaving. He and all hands will be here to-morrow. Stanley might have at least sent a note to me ...

12th April Friday

... The first lot of Stanley's people came in at 10 a.m., the others at all hours up 'till 4 p.m. Stanley was carried and does not appear well. Nelson had to wait with Parke at Mpinga's till nearly noon as Mpinga's carriers ran away. They threw away some twenty loads of the Pasha's people amid general swearing and then came over here, bringing Mpinga a prisoner.

A great row had taken place at Kavallis' between Stanley and some of the Pasha's people. It appears from Jephson's account that some of the Pasha's soldiers at night time went in among the Zanzibari quarters and endeavoured to seize some rifles belonging to our men ...

Next morning Stanley went down to the Pasha and endeavoured to reason with him. Either he, the Pasha, must fall in his men and investigate the case, or Stanley must take matters into his own hands. Stanley proposed two things to the Pasha, both of which the Pasha declined to follow. One was that he, the Pasha, and Stanley should move off at once, or that a camp should be formed some two miles off and the Pasha move on there and let Stanley clear out the people on the 10th.

When the Pasha had answered Stanley in his aggravating, dilly-dallying way, Stanley jumped up and swore he would then take everything into his own hands. He rushed out, fell in the Zanzibaris, had all the Turks and Soudanese driven into the square and with his rifle loaded and ready asked for "those who dared to say they would stay behind stand out here and let me see you, you dogs". The Pasha, I believe, chased Stanley all about the yard imploring him not to do anything rash. All Stanley answered in his rage was, "I am resolved, I am resolved." He made the culprits lay down their arms and had them all bound up. He then gave all the clerks, servants and soldiers to understand that everyone present must follow him. Those that disobeyed would be shot.

This was a most wholesome lesson to these people. They will now perhaps see that they cannot play the same game with us as they did with the Pasha. They will know now who are their masters and will see that we shall stand no nonsense from any of them at any rate. What fools these people are, even now most of them would be quite content to settle down in the country here and take their chances as to an untimely fate.

The whole history of this part of the Soudan has been one long series of acts of treachery and rebellion. Not one bright side of the question could be thrown up for view by even the most enthusiastic admirer of the Pasha's doings for the past seven or eight years. Most of the trouble has been caused by the Egyptians in the country, not directly by the soldiers. When the soldiers have acted badly they have invariably been instigated to do so by the Egyptian clerks and other officials.

One thing difficult for any white governor in the country to contend with of course must be religious fanaticism. The Mussulmen look with the greatest contempt upon a white dog of a Christian, no matter however great that Christian's abilities may be and no matter how infinitely superior in every way he may be over themselves. He is a Christian and cannot but have ideas counter to those of Islam. Now the Egyptians sow seeds of discontent among the Mussulmanized natives by installing these ideas in their heads and many, many unpleasant scenes owe their origin to these poisonous doctrines simply *in toto*. The natives themselves (the Soudanese) are not fanatics; they are only made so through the machinations of these miserable, yellow-bellied Egyptians.

At two p.m. I went off eastwards with my company to do some raiding; after I had gone about 7 or 8 miles I was re-called by a letter of Stanley and reached camp about 8 p.m.

13th April Saturday
Last night some 57 people of the Pasha's, chiefly those belonging to Hawash Effendi, took it into their heads to desert, taking some 4 or 5 guns, food, tools, clothes, etc. It is only just what Stanley told the Pasha they would do.

Stanley was taken very ill during the night with vomiting fits and cramps in his stomach. To-day he is really very bad.

Stanley's camp is about 100 yards from mine. Jephson and I occupy my hut, all the other fellows living up above with Stanley.

14th April Sunday
I am very much afraid our stay here will be a prolonged one owing to Stanley's illness. We must all try and wait patiently and get him well as quick as we can, though the stay will be tortuous to all of us.

The Pasha now owns that Stanley must take affairs absolutely into his own hands. There can be no "dual control" here. The Pasha has shown himself incompetent and Stanley to look after and take care of his own people must "perforce" look after those of the Pasha. It is well this state of affairs should have come about as it did. To us it was a foreseen thing, and merely a question of time ...

15th-21st April Sunday

From the 15th to the 21st Stanley has been in various stages of illness, at times being really bad and now to-day, the 21st, he is much better and able to sit up. During the week, Jephson and I went on a raid ... in the dead of night and captured some sixty cattle and a lot of women and children. The Pasha's people were out in force under Shookri Aga.

What a poor patient Stanley is! How inconsiderate for others and how selfish for his own ends!

Poor Parke succumbed to the constant night watching [over Stanley] and now has a severe attack of bilious remittent fever. The Pasha's slaves and people continue to run away nightly in spite of our cautions to him.

Jephson is sickly to-day 21st.

21st to 29th April

During this time we were all waiting for Stanley and Parke's recoveries. Now the 29th, it will be yet some 6 days before we shall be able to start. Yesterday, the 28th, some natives (Wahuma) very nice looking fellows with very fine looking features, came into camp. One has lived near Ruwenzori (the big snow mountain) for many years. He and his people were compelled to leave their country to the southwest and move up near Mpinga's owing to the constant raids of Kabba Rega and his people.

They told us that it was six days' easy marching from here to Ruwenzori ... Cultivation goes on up the mountainsides to almost the snow line: on the top they say are white men, cannibals and the lower natives dare not go up to the summit. From Ruwenzori the track goes westward a little to avoid the mountain spurs and there turns S.S.E. to the lake, a path the natives frequently use when going to the lake to buy salt. What a field of wonders lie before us, this lake, does a river run out of it into the Albert? The natives say so.

How Grant's and Baker's apple carts will be upset should this new lake be a big one and its waters run into Lake Albert.

Then the mountain: there is snow all the year round, it is on the equator and therefore if snow exists the snow line would be quite 15,500 or 16,000 feet above sea level. This mountain must be 18,000 ft. high. We all hope it may top Kilimanjaro and thus be the highest mountain in Africa.*

---

*Stair's first rough estimate was inaccurate; Kilimanjaro is more than 2500 feet higher the Ruwenzori.

The Pasha's people, men, women and children have been deserting for the last ten days at a terrible rate. A report has been spread that we intend to return to the sea by the bush route [i.e., by the Congo route]. All have heard of our suffering in this deadly bush and so getting frightened run away.

We held a court martial the other day and sentenced, among many other sentences, one man to be hanged. He was afterwards let off through the shilly-shallying of the Pasha ...

Stanley is rapidly getting better, while Parke may be said to be well, but weak.

All of us are burning to get on the march and see the "unknown land" ahead.

May 1st Thursday to 4th Saturday

Nothing much goes on in camp from day to day. On the 2nd the party under Shookri Aga returned from their search for deserters, having caught two men and some women. Among these was a deserter of ours, Rehani. Stanley ordered us to hold a court of inquiry into his case. He had induced about forty of the Pasha's people to desert, but we found out the plot and disarmed all those intending ones.

After hours of careful investigation of the case by Nelson, Parke, Jephson and I as president, we found him guilty and Stanley sentenced him to death. All hands were fallen in and in half an hour after this we hanged him on the nearest tree, leaving his body suspended in mid-air all night. This will have a wholesome effect on any others who may have intended to desert.

The Pasha and Stanley hate each other now to an extent almost incredible. We officers all hope another outbreak will not take place as the Pasha feels he is being treated very badly by Stanley and even now has suffered enough to make him leave us at Msalala, a proceeding very much to be regretted, should it occur.

It is impossible to get any straightforward answer from the Pasha even in small matters. He is too long a resident of the Orient for that (24 years or so). There is only one course that can be adopted to prevent the breach widening and that is that the Pasha should hand over to Stanley all his people, and he, the Pasha, have absolutely nothing to do with them. Let him then come and live in our camp with his household and all will go smoothly and cheerfully. This though, I'm afraid, he will never do and it will perforce have to be done by Stanley and the result will be a violent storm on both sides. This state of things existing is a great misfortune for all of us and should it continue, many damaging things about the expedition may be made know to the European public.

♦   ♦   ♦

Chapter Fourteen

On 7 May 1889 Stanley's fever had sufficiently abated that he was able to travel. More than two years had passed since the expedition had landed at the mouth of the Congo. It was finally to embark upon the long march back to Zanzibar, with the humiliated and resentful Emin being escorted as virtually Stanley's captive. During the first fortnight of the march Stairs was too ill with fever to walk – or to make more than brief entries in his increasingly cursory diary.

Stanley later wrote,
The total collapse of the Government of Equatoria thrust upon us the duty of conveying in hammocks so many aged and sick people, and protecting so many helpless and feeble folk, that we became transformed from a small fighting column of tired men into a mere Hospital Corps to whom active adventure was denied. The Governor [Emin] was half blind and possessed much luggage, Casati was weakly and had to be carried, and 90 per cent of their followers were, soon after starting, scarcely able to travel from age, disease, weakness or infancy. Without sacrificing our sacred charge, to assist which was the object of the expedition, we could neither deviate to the right or to the left, from the most direct road to the sea[1].

The progress of the expedition was slow, encumbered as it was by an immense amount of baggage, but also by the halt, the lame and the seriously ill. Nevertheless, discoveries of some geographic importance were recorded as the expedition crossed through regions where no European had preceded it. However, as the expedition finally got under way on 8 May 1889, the discoveries remained secondary to the goal of reaching the coast. After almost one month of cajoling, urging, and pushing forward the straggling column of Emin's followers and the long-suffering survivors of their own expedition, Stanley, Stairs and the other officers arrived at the base of the Ruwenzori mountains.

The Ruwenzori are not a long chain; they are rather a cluster of peaks more than three thousand metres high which rise suddenly from the plains. No European had yet climbed them, although Pliny had supposedly reported their existence two millenia before.* Although the mountains are almost invariably covered in cloud, one year before, Parke and Jephson had first sighted the distant, snow-covered peaks. Stairs caught only brief glimpses of what awaited him as he volunteered to attempt to scale them. (Stanley records Stairs as proclaiming, "I'll go like a shot," but Jephson, with a fever of 106°, was obviously much too ill to go.)

◆   ◆   ◆

7th May Tuesday
Getting everything ready for the start to-morrow.

In the evening two letters were brought on to the Pasha by Kavalli's people from the Lake. The[y] said 20 soldiers and 3 officers had been sent by Selim Bey, the new governor of the Soudan (elected by the officers), to enquire into alleged mistreatment of the Egyptian officers with the expedition. He, Selim Bey, had heard from some deserters from us that the Pasha had been tying up his people, beating them and had given them loads to carry and in consequence "as Governor of the Soudan" he thought it necessary to enquire into these matters and see if they were true. This is pretty good from an officer who is a rebel and just like the sort of thing these people are fond of doing.

I hope no more than twenty rifles will come with the party as our Zanzibaris, though the best of carriers, are not much when it comes to fighting with rifles. Who can say that these people will not try and bring things to a head? Many of the people with us want to go back. Many are frightened of the punishment they will receive on reaching Egypt, so that with a few rifles and determined men they might work a great deal of mischief. With his own people the Pasha has not a vestige of authority nor do they even respect him. It is only their fear of Stanley and the other European officers that keeps them in order.

---

*During their 1875 crossing of Africa, Frank Pocock had told Stanley that he had seen a snow-covered mountain (or mountains) approximately where the Ruwenzori are, but Stanley does not mention the fact in *In Darkest Africa*, presumably because he wanted no other European to be credited with their discovery. Parke and Jephson saw the "Snow Mountain" on 20 April 1888, one year before Stairs's ascent, during their first trek to Lake Albert Nyanza.

8th May Wednesday

At last off on the march and our faces toward the southeast. All the Zanzibaris are wild with joy at getting away on the route again and so, of course, are all the whites...

9th May Thursday

Got away early from camp, The confusion at first was indescribable, all tried to push forward at the same time. Our regular order of march was completely broken up. Instead of it, people and cattle were huddled together four or five abreast, pushing and cursing each other heartily ...

The Pasha's people as yet are but poor marchers. Of course they are soft and unused to the road and no doubt in time will improve, but still they will give us endless trouble before they become drilled into the thing ... We are going in a South and S.W. direction following a deep valley by keeping along the east slope. This, of course, makes the marching bad.

Across the valley about six miles distant is the edge of the "Great Forest" we had to pass through and lost so many lives in. It reminds one of a great big devil with outstretched claws ever on the watch to catch passersby and draw them into its fathomless bosom, never afterwards to be heard of by man.

Stanley will have to be carried many days. His legs are very thin yet, though he is picking up ...

10th May Friday

... I had great trouble with the women and children and at times thought I should go crazy with the broiling sun [and] the endless nagging at the people to go on and the steep hill slopes. Our column now beggars decription.

Ahead is Stanley and his company. Behind him generally come the Pasha, Casati and one of our officers. Then follow all the Pasha's officers and their wives, children and slaves, the most motley crowd to be found anywhere. They are awful people to fight among themselves and the noise of shouting sometimes can be heard quite a mile away I should say. Behind all this crowd come the cattle, say 150. These of course mix up with the people and add to the confusion; behind these come the weary and sick and stragglers, and driving them with curses, shouts and sticks comes the rear guard, moving like a snail across a garden path. Nelson and I take turns day by day at rear guard duty.

11th May Saturday

... Made a short though trying march up and down over hills and camped at ... altitude 4928.7 [feet]. This place is remarkable as being on the summit of the range overlooking the Semliki River running into the [Lake] Albert Nyanza whose waters one can see glittering far away in the sunlight some 18 miles away ...

Some of our people out collecting food were attacked by 12 or 15 of Kabba Regas' people and had to retire. Shookri Aga, one of the Pasha's captains, was with them and when they came to sum up, it was found that three of Kabba Regas' men had bitten the dust and one of ours, ... a boy belonging to Signor Casati, the Italian.

On this news being brought into camp, I took off about 130 rifles and went out to meet the enemy. On our descending quickly on to their position, however, they ran away like the mischief and no shots were fired. These people will certainly attack us when we cross the Semliki River.

◆   ◆   ◆

14th May Tuesday
Marched to Kiriawa, a wretched sort of place in a hot dusty hollow. My fever became very bad. All night long I had violent pains in my kidneys accompanied by vomiting. It is "bilious remittent." Jephson and I are both in the same hut, both laid flat on our backs. My temp is 105°. I am in for a bad dose.

15th May Wednesday
Stayed at Kiriawa. Nelson went out and found the Semliki River.
    Am perfectly helpless. My urine is blood red. Heavens, how I should only like some ice to cool my burning head!

16th May Thursday
Went off to the Semliki River. This River runs into the [Lake] Albert Nyanza about 20 miles N.E. of here and is the most important addition to its waters after the Victoria Nile, of course.
    Both Jephson and I were carried. I remember very little of what happened.
    Started crossing people over at once. Nelson and Parke looking after the work. In evening were fired upon by Kabba Rega's people's guns, sallied out and drove them off. Uladi and Saat Tatu swam the river and under a fire of arrows cut a canoe adrift and brought her over to our side. Saat Tatu unfortunately was badly wounded.
    Temperature going down but am dreadfully weak. Jephson very bad yet.

◆   ◆   ◆

19th May Sunday
Finished crossing people over the river. There were 1168 people ferried over the stream. Of this only about 190 are Zanzibaris, so the strength of the Pasha's people, mostly women and children, may be estimated.

◆   ◆   ◆

22nd May Wednesday
... To-day I partly walked and was partly carried. We made rather a trying march of six miles or so S.S.W. Nelson did not reach camp at night.
  Feel much better.

23rd May Thursday
Acted as rear guard and walked the whole distance, a short march of 3½ miles south toward the mountains. Nelson had a rather bad time of it last night with the rain and mosquitoes. The Pasha's people in this bush (for we have had bush ever since the Semliki River) give us great trouble every day in rear. For instance, Stanley and the advance get to camp say at 10:00 a.m., whereas we in rear will not reach camp till 3:30 or 5:00 p.m., weary and worn out with driving these people along and halting at every old village and creek on the road.
  Our camp is in a largish village, from which we get a grand view of the mighty Ruwenzori now only 16 miles off.

24th May Friday
... The name of this country is Uvamba, the next Toru, a name well known on all maps and placed by Stanley when going across the Dark Continent so that we are gradually coming into countries known to geography ...
  In these woods there is a numerous dwarf population said to be bad people who lie in wait behind trees and shoot passersby. We should be out again in open country in three days or so.
  Read *Through Masai Land*. Not intensely interesting, but shows great energy, and plucky work throughout and a keen idea as to geological history. He will make a great traveller, Thomson.*

25th May Saturday
... Bush rather open and stunted. The Pasha's people are beginning to dislike Nelson and I [*sic*] very much as we push them on every day and yell out at them, offending their dignity very much.

---

*Joseph Thomson (1858–95) had been an explorer in Africa from the early age of twenty-one. The book of which Stairs had somehow obtained a copy was the recently published *Through Masai Land: A Journey of an expedition Among the Tribes of Eastern Equatorial Africa, Being the Narrative of the Royal Geographical Society's expedition to Mount Kenia and Lake Victoria Nyanza, 1883–1884* (London, 1887). As did Stanley, Thomson also wrote a novel, but his principal book is *To the Central African Lakes and Back*, 2 vols. (London, 1881).

26th May Sunday
Reached village at foothills of the big range, Nelson in rear.

27th May Monday
... Never in my life have I seen such quantities of bananas as there are hereabouts. On every hillside and hilltop there are plantations of splendid bananas and plantains. Look wherever you will along the edge of the bush and plain, you will see these fine plantations.

Boiled thermometer and found height of camp to be 2,942 ft. above sea. Also found height of range opposite the camp to be 9,147 feet and distance 3½ miles off. I should say by comparing this height with Ruwenzori that the latter will prove to be about 15,500 feet.*

Since coming here we have not even caught a glimpse of the snow mountain now 10 miles off owing to the dense masses of clouds which hang constantly over the mountains at an altitude of 6,000 or 7,000 feet. We know though that a great part of Ruwenzori is covered with dense bush. In another march or so we should be abreast of the mountain and then perhaps some of us will try and make an ascent.

The Pasha's people are very weary of the bush, even though we have been such a short time in it. The mud, streams and twigs have done up a great many of them about the feet. They are poor stock, these people, with very little life or go in them.

28th May Tuesday
To-day's march was a very trying one to all, but to those in rear it was especially fatiguing. From 6:30 a.m. till 3:30 p.m., we in the rear plunged along through mud, up and down slippery hills, every few minutes receiving a check as someone of the Pasha's people would go down with his or her load and block the road. At times I thought we should not reach the camp, so obstinately stupid the people seemed to be in stopping at every hilltop and village we came to. About 2:00 p.m. we came to open country, but such open country I never saw before, just one mass of ups and down covered with grass ... quite 14 inches high.

---

*Stairs's calculations were reasonably accurate. The highest peak of the Ruwenzori range is in fact 16,795 feet. The range was ascended and thoroughly explored by the Duke of Abruzzi in 1906. See Filippo de Filippi, *Ruwenzori: An Account of the Expedition of H.R.H. Luigi Amadeo of Savoy* (London, 1909) and R.M. Bere, "The Exploration of the Ruwenzori," *Uganda Journal*, vol.10, no.2 (1946) and vol. 19, no. 2 (1955). John Batchelor, *In Stanley's Footsteps*, (London, 1936) states that an orchid found on the slopes of the Ruwenzori Mountains, was later named "Orchid Stairsii".

Some of the women from the north are very plucky load carriers, but their brutal masters load them down cruelly, so much so that on a slippery, hilly road they can hardly get along at all. We have, I should think, some 25 or 30 Egyptian Coptic and halfbreed women, the wives of the different clerks and officers. It is most amusing to see them on the march, walking through mud up to their knees. They do not mind the black men at all and will make a great demonstration of healthy looking limbs, but should a white man appear, down go their clothes and they appear most prim and proper. They are terribly afraid of their husbands, I fancy. With us they will scarcely say a word ...

29th May Wednesday

... camped ... near the mountains. Here an old man was caught, out of whom some information was got. The country we passed through to-day was fairly level and all covered with long, tangled grass. We marched parallel to the mountains at a distance of about 1½ miles from where the big hills spring up ... The old man caught was a frightful looking old cannibal, a regular bush man. Here the mountains must be quite 10,000 feet high.

30th May Thursday

A most disastrous day. After Stanley had reached camp about 11:00 this morning and things had been made busy, 8 or 10 of our men and Manyuema went off as usual prowling about in search of loot. At a short distance from camp they were fired at by some persons hidden in the grass at a distance of only a few yards. Uledi Sadi had his elbow shot away. A boy of Sadi, the Manyuema chief's, was killed. Poor little Faraj Ala, my old boy, was terribly shot in the stomach and chest and died at night. Khani Unyamwezi was badly wounded and two others slightly wounded. Of course, our men replied, thinking the people in ambush must be those of Kabba Rega. After some time, however, it was found that instead of them being Kabba Rega's people, they were Manyuema of a party of Kilonga-Longa's ivory hunters camped only about two hours from us. They had come up here from camp after bananas and hearing us had taken us for Wanyoro raiders and so had ambushed [us] and fired on us. Our men killed three of their party.

It was a most disastrous affair and we felt quite sad at Faraj Ala's death. He was such a bright, cheery little soul, the life of his own camp and alway had a cheery "Mornin', Master" for me everyday as I passed him.

This is the second *saffari* Kilonga-Longa's men have made on to the plain and now they are settled just at the foot of Ruwenzori for the purpose of collecting ivory, though I should think Kabba Rega's men have already taken most of that article out of the country ...

◆   ◆   ◆

1st June [1889] Saturday
... This book, the fifth I have had to use to account for what has happened
since we have been in Africa, was very kindly given to me by the Pasha. I am
always sorry I did not bring out with me three or four good substantial journals.
Perhaps had I known we were to be such a long time in this country I should
have done so.

Our courses of late have been all over the country. We can make no southing
owing to the mountain range lying directly in our track. In two or three days'
march we hope to be able to turn the corner of the range and slant a little
more to the southward. Some streams from the mountain passing near camp
... are very cold, the temperature in some cases being as low as 16° centrigrade.
The height of the mountains opposite here is about 11,000 feet ...*

2nd June Sunday
All along the foot of the mountain range, which now runs S.S.W., is very
broken country, covered with scrubby bush. In many places the ravines are
100 feet deep and create a great deal of trouble for the Pasha's people, who
are only accustomed to open country and make but a poor show of it in the
bush. Many of the plants and trees one used to see in the big Congo forest
one notices here. One also notices many of the same birds throughout the
bush, though there is one great distinction and that is the presence here of the
prickly acacia which is absent in the forest between the Congo and [Lake]
Albert Nyanza.

The effect of the Manyuema's residence in the country is most plainly
marked by the numbers of deserted villages and ruined plantations we passed
to-day. The paths also are all grown up with grass, showing no signs of native
traffic at all.

We have now turned the corner of the range, as it were, and ahead of us on
our left appears a huge broken mass of precipitous mountain cones, all
separated and defined by deep, rocky ravines. The lower spurs and gullies are
covered with dense forests of large trees, making an ascent anywhere about
here impossible.

---

*In 1891 Stairs wrote in an article in *The Nineteenth Century* (vol. XXIX, p. 959), "On
the 30th of May we found ourselves camping directly under one of the loftiest spurs of
Ruwenzori. We had reached at last the mountain we had seen from afar so often, and
were now camping under its shades. I trust, therefore, reader, that you will pardon us
for a little fling of honest pride that it had been left to us to discover what many brave
men had failed in doing for centuries before – the snow-capped peaks of the ' Mountains of the Moon,' and the birthplace of the Western Nile for below us flowed the same
water that runs past Khartoum and Cairo, in a stream so small that a native with ease
could throw an knobkerry over it."

In a few marches more we shall be ... among hostile natives. Perhaps we shall also have Kabba Rega's guns against us. The danger to the column is very great, should this happen, presenting as it does a long, huge, unwieldy flank, formed of women and children and badly provided with guns. At times the length of the column in rough country would be quite three miles. Up to this it has been quite impossible to close the people up on to the front and thus make a compact body of the column and so make ourselves stronger by being able to concentrate our men and fire on a given point quickly. We hope, however, to organize the Pasha's guns into a company and try to get the people licked into better shape when we reach the short-grass country some 8 or 10 marches from here.

◆   ◆   ◆

4th June Tuesday
... From time to time we got glimpses of the snow-capped peaks, but on the whole we could see very little of the upper mountains, owing to masses of vapour which shrouded them ... Every gully appears to have its banana plantation and every coign of vantage its huts. Many of the huts present a very strange appearance, perched far away up on some cone-like hill, with desperately steep tracks leading up to them. Almost all the bush natives, I should say, have fled up to these mountain villages, many on hearing of our approach, and many on account of the Manyuema.

5th June Wednesday
After an up-and-down hill march of only three miles, reached camp. Plenty of food. Stanley and I had a talk about going up the big mountain.

6th June Thursday
Started off with 40 rifles up the mountain.* I knew it could not be a good place for trying an ascent, the bush was too thick by far. Well, I went on and on and camped at night at 8,570 feet among the heather. Next morning I reached 10,677 feet at 9:00 a.m., but there I had to stop. The men had no food. It would take us 1¼ days yet to reach the snow. I had not time to do this and to go on would end disastrously. I therefore ordered the men back.

---

*In an article for *The Nineteenth Century* (vol. XXIX, pp. 959-60) Stairs wrote,"On the 6th of June I started up the mountain with an escort of forty rifles, to find out if it were possible that an ascent to the very summit could be made. It was not our intention this time to go for more than a two days' journey upwards, but merely to sketch out the mountain, and try to find a leading spur which might enable us to ascend to the top from some future camp."

I took two aneroids and a thermometer. The above elevation is with all corrections made. As I have made a long report of this to Stanley and as it will some day most likely be printed, I do not write anything else about this ascent.*

I was able to give Emin Pasha 37 specimens of different plants some two of which are new to science I believe. At 10,000 feet I found blueberries and blackberries and lower down violets. I am sorry I could not have gone on to the snow and brought some down, but this was out of the question, provided as we were with no food.

7th June Friday
Reached Stanley in the afternoon. He was greatly pleased at our getting even as far as we did. The Pasha was also delighted at getting the plants ...

8th June Saturday
Gave our men another day to prepare food. I am exceedingly glad I brought down the blueberries and plants for the Pasha. The pleasure he evidently feels far more than compensates for the trouble.

9th June Sunday
Camped in forest. I in rear guard got in at 5:30 p.m., being just thus 11 hours on foot, driving along the weak and sickly ones of the Pasha. It is terribly trying work this, both to body and mind. On the road we passed a hot spring. The water, though quite clear, had a taste of sulphur. Its temperature was 102°F.

10th June Monday
Marched 6½ miles. Were attacked by natives but after two hours in camp they came in to make friends. This is a great gain to us, as we shall now be shown a short road and will not lose any sick who may have strayed off the path ... Here the forest ends and ahead is nothing but open country.

11th & 12th June Tuesday & Wednesday
... Here the natives report a large river coming out of Lutan Nzige [Lake Albert] and going N.W. Does this go into the Nile or Congo? The long-vexed question in England.

13th & 14th June Thursday and Friday
Took 60 rifles and went to examine river. I returned on the 14th to Stanley and in my report to him I say, "I have now not the slightest doubt in my mind

---

*The text of Stairs's report to Stanley of his ascent of the Ruwenzori mountains is at appendix two on p. 405

but this is the Semliki running into the [Lake] Albert Nyanza and on to the Nile and that therefore the long vexed question to all geographers is now definitely settled and the Lutan Nzige [Lake Albert] helps to swell the Nile."

◆   ◆   ◆

19th June Wednesday

... Jephson and I went down to the salt lake this afternoon and saw some of the most marvellous sights I have ever seen in my life. The water of the lake is of a blood-red colour, something like Condy's Fluid, and intensely salt. That of Salt Lake City [Utah] would only have the 1/20 part of salt in a given volume of water that this has.

The method of making the salt is as follows. Pans of 20' diameter are made in the mud on the flat shores and quite close to the water. This is then allowed to run in and the pan is dammed up. In a short time the sun causes the water to evaporate, leaving a thin coating of ice-like salt on the top. This soon sinks and more is formed on the surface. The salt sinking to the bottom forms the most perfect crystals, on a stratum of pink salt whose crystals are smaller. The natives then come and with their hands take out these cakes of salt.

We got some of these cakes 1¼ inches thick. An enormous amount of salt must be taken out of this lake which Kabba Rega's people have deemed politic to take. The country for many miles about, even as far as Ruanda, is supplied from this source alone.

Stanley took some men and went out on the lake for a look about in the canoe I got the day before yesterday. They went along the eastern shore some seven miles, but had then to come back as the canoe was such a poor one. Some of the Wabuma natives say one can go to the far end of the lake in 1½ days in a canoe; others again say it takes as many as nine days paddling. I am very much afraid that Stanley will never be able to circumnavigate this Lake.

The duties of looking after the Pasha's people, fighting natives, etc., have made this expedition more like a small army fighting its way through the country than a geographical expedition. We have no time to sit down with 1,100 people; food cannot be got for them.

Kabba Rega's people too are ever ready to cut off any detached party of ours that comes in their way.

Of course, he [Stanley] can get a very good idea of the extent of the lake and can make a faithful map of some of it, and then we know its waters flow into the Nile, therefore most people in England will be satisfied.

20th June Thursday

... We are to-day exactly on the equator ... We saw vast quantities of spur winged geese and plover, cranes, herons, vultures and other birds and caught a fish and shot some geese and plover. The spur winged plover is a poor bird to eat, but I believe the geese and crested cranes are very good eating. We had a brace of plover and a dove for dinner.

Our cows give us now two cups of milk all round the officers, or a total of 16 cups to 20 cups per milking. It is a great addition to porridge and tea and makes one enjoy one's meals ever so much more than when we had no milk at all ...

The mosquitos are terrible here. For two nights the men have had no sleep at all. They simply sit up and talk and yawn all night over the fires.

♦   ♦   ♦

24th June Monday
... Our guides left us to-day. The Wahuma are splendid fellows; such tall, lithe figures and fine features. A Wahuma is excesssively proud of his small hands and feet and looks with contempt on the big appendages of the ordinary Bantu negro. A Wahuma will only drink out of his own or comrade's vessel, but will never allow another native to drink out of it. Their passion for following cattle and attending to them is their ruling one.

In some cases where their cattle have been driven off by Kabba Rega's people, they have followed up and given themselves up as prisoners just to be able to hang about and milk their beloved cows. They rarely till the soil. Sometimes one will see a few potatoes and pumpkins about their huts but this is all. Their chief food is milk, but very little meat is killed by them.

25th June Tuesday
... Fever is raging like a plague among the men; it is the ordinary intermittent type that they are affected with. It has been fatal only in one case ... in his case, however, pneumonia came on and killed him in two days. The Manyuema and the Pasha's people are suffering to an extent never before seen since the expedition began. The causes are malaria from the low lake levels and bad water.

26th June Wednesday
Reached camp on plateau of 900 feet above lake level, probably fevers will abate. Both Jephson and Parke have fever and I feel seedy. Encountered Wanyasura who fired off their guns and then ran away.

27th June Thursday
Remained in camp. Pasha and Farida [Emin's daughter] both have fever. Went back to get Parke's tent.

The Wanyasura had killed a woman of the Pasha's who had dawdled behind the rear guard. I and my party were fired upon by some Wanyasura at a distance of about 400 yards. Several bullets whistled over our heads but on our returning a volley they at once made off. One can hardly say that Kabba Rega's people are distinguished for bravery.

28th June Friday
... I had fever last night. This was a very trying march for me. It was just as much as I could get along ... Stanley, Parke, Bonny, Jephson and I have all got fever of a very sharp type.

29th June Saturday
... Stanley is pretty bad.
Here we are right on the edge of the lake and have made friends with the natives. We got some fairly good fish here.
The Pasha is better. On all sides one sees the men down with fever. Zanzibaris when they do get it go under at once and they will not help themselves at all, just lying like so many logs.

◆   ◆   ◆

1st July Monday
My 26th birthday. By the shores of Lutan Nzige [Lake Albert], the Unknown. Who will settle the question about this Lake? How far south does it go? We shall not be able to, owing to want of food and canoes of a suitable size.
What are one's people doing, I wonder? Great changes must have taken place since I left England. How intense is one's curiosity to know what has happened!

◆   ◆   ◆

3rd July Wednesday
... Had a big palaver in the evening as to which road eastward and southward to the Alexandra Nile we should take. It was decided to pass through the warlike Ankori and thence south to Kitanguli on the Nile. This is the quickest road home. In 30 camps we should reach the Nile unless turned by the Wanyankori. Most probably though we shall be able to make friends with them.

4th July Thursday
... many natives came in to see the white men and their caravan and thanked us for opening up ... the salt lake to trade again by our driving away the Wanyasura. This stroke will I fancy make our journey through Ankori a simple one. From here we get our last view of the Nyanza. Stanley's old camp must be north of us some five miles ...

Although Stairs had been able to climb the Ruwenzori, intermittent malaria continued to dog him. Stairs attempted to march with the column but by the first week of July, much to his distress, he had again to be carried from time to time.

Stairs made no diary entries between 11 and 24 July. Thereafter, his entries, frequently no more than short summaries of ten days or a fortnight, are without much substance. It is as if he, along with the Zanzibari, regarded the final march as an ordeal to be endured, not as a journey full of geographic, anthropological or other interest. In any event, the erratic progress of the straggling column left little time for observation of the world around it. Emin's people were generally wholly unsuited to the hardships of the long trek eastward to the Indian Ocean. Children, especially babies, began to be abandoned, the sick left along the way, and disease went untreated. In addition, hostile warriors of Kebba Rega harassed the column as it pressed through the forests and across the uplands. Only when it reached the Church Missionary Society station at Usambiro on 28 August 1889 did the end of the expedition's long ordeal appear to be in sight.

5th July Friday

To-day we reached Kiwiga. The natives are strolling about camp in numbers. We are firm friends. I bought a very neat pipe from them for some meat. Our peaceful passage through Ankori is now fairly assured I fancy.

◆   ◆   ◆

10th July Wednesday

... Many of the people have left Uganda and fled to neighbouring countries ... It is to be hoped that some power such as England will step in soon and take over this splendid country.

◆   ◆   ◆

11th-24th July

I write this on the 24th. From the 11th onwards I had so many attacks of fever that I could not muster up enough energy to write even a few remarks each day. These fevers have made us all look like so many spectres; we are all pale and thin with pinched faces and miserable, bony appendages for legs. It is most exhausting in this state to march even a few miles and one arrives in camp and flings oneself down praying that nothing will come to disturb one's weary rest. "Oh, for a temperate climate!" This cursed fever will ever be a drawback to colonization in Africa.

18th 19th and 20th July

... I with a bad fever and Stanley also knocked over. Goodness only knows how these continual attacks of fever are likely to end. All of us are subject to them. They leave us quite exhausted and feeble as cats. The causes Parke lays down are bad water, cold winds and extremes of temperature between night and day ... [This camp] is very badly off for water. The usual supply is from some filthy stagnant hole where men and animals drink alike. Oh for a temperate climate again and good health! Oh for a Canadian summer and the woods and good food! How one's spirits and strength would go up and how one would again think life worth living ...

♦   ♦   ♦

23rd July Tuesday
... We have heard ... that Bagamoyo had been shelled and burnt by the Germans. This is most likely true enough, and is in revenge for the Germans who have been killed up country. This must have happened over a year ago, I should think. It is hard to say what the Arabs will do. They could make it pretty hot for whites ...

♦   ♦   ♦

25th July Thursday
S.S.W. ten miles. Fever bad, had a hard time of it to get along, luckily Parke sent some men back from camp to meet me and these helped me along greatly...

♦   ♦   ♦

28th July Sunday
... Fever bad. I was carried to-day in a hammock I was so weak. A terrible comedown. I can only walk two hundred yards without a rest.

29th July Monday
Again carried. Reached the hot springs of Mtagata, these are about four in number in a shady bit of bush in a gully surrounded on the south by hills and open to the north. At one place the water rushes out of the earth in a goodly sized stream whose temperature is 120° about. This stream is perfectly tasteless and is excellent water for washing and cooking. When it gets cool it is also good for drinking. The other springs are pools of warmish water. It is in these that the natives delight to loll about in and wash their troublous sores. They say it effects wonderfully quick cures on ulcers and other sores. But most probably it is the exchange from dirt to cleanliness that works the cures. The prospect around the springs is a most dreary one, nothing but bleak, stony, bare hills. Perhaps in the rainy season things look brighter.

30th July Tuesday
... The meaness of these natives surpasses anything one has ever seen. For a little flour they want a doti of cloth, just fancy the sharks ... Perhaps there is no ivory to be got here now.

We rejoice in having plenty of hot water always ready; a great blessing. All of us drink the waters!

◆   ◆   ◆

3rd August
Reached Kafurro, the old Arab trading establishment ... This place was visited by Grant and Speke in 1863 and by Stanley some thirteen years ago, It was then a flourishing station with some four or five Arabs of Zanzibar ... After thirty years of semi-civilization then, Kafurro has resumed its natural state. To mark the sojourn of these Arabs here there are two lemon trees, a lime, three mango trees and some onions, besides these there are old remains of houses, some long-legged coast fowls and tomatoes. Of these latter we eat a great many and with lemon juice squeezed over them. They are a great change to us. Kafurro is not the residence of the kings of the country; this is about three miles northeast of here ...

Jephson went over to see the king yesterday with a company of Zanzibaris. He was shown through several dirty cattle kraals into His Majesty's presence and found him to be a boy of sixteen or seventeen years old, clad in an exceedingly filthy rag of "Amerikani" cloth. He received Jephson sitting at the door of his hut (which Jephson says was a small one) smoking his pipe and surrounded by about two hundred natives squatting in a semi-circle and clad in bark cloth. Not a decent piece of clean cloth was visible among the whole assembly. The King asked for Jephson's gun which Jephson refused.

Guides ... were arranged for and the King promised to send down quantities of food. The "quantities" turned out to be three jars of pombe, a few packets of beans and some bananas, just enough to feed thirty to forty men; whereas we are a 1000 strong. This is a true account of the present "King" of Karagwe...*

---

*In his own diary, Jephson, in describing his visit to the village, was scathing about the way in which Stanley "writes flowery descriptions of King's palaces, court pages, etc., of colonels, generals and regiments, of pomp and show, and gives people at home a most false idea. I have no doubt he would have written of the King's Kraal quite differently to the way I have written, there would have been palaces and courtyards, with the King sitting in his divan surrounded by courtiers and generals, with his wives dressed in their court dresses, while a string of clients and courtiers streamed through the palace

From July 2nd to August 4th the Pasha has lost 141 of his people by desertion, death, stolen by natives and sold to natives for food. This is a great loss in numbers, but in reality a great gain to the strength of the column.

♦   ♦   ♦

7th August
Made a march of seven miles ... on Speke and Grant's old track. Here the men got plenty of food.

Stanley is sick again. It is strange how hard he tries to hide his illnesses from us, I fancy he likes to crow over us officers who cannot hide our fevers. He is terribly jealous of anyone being carried, though he himself has been carried every day since leaving Majamboni's. Jephson fever again ...

8th August
... The morning was bitterly cold with a driving rain and strong wind. Many were knocked over (of the slaves and children) and it was only on the sun coming out that they recovered and came on. The men raided quantities of groundnuts and beans. We are to stay here two days really because Stanley wants a rest.

The Wanyankori and the people of Karagwe have the finest and most useful looking spears I have yet seen. They are used for stabbing, not throwing. Both tribes are very much afraid of our guns. They have never seen many before and marvel at the rate of fire of the Winchester and Remingtons. With four hundred rifles, one could go clean through Karagwe, Ankori, Unyoro or Uganda and take whatever one liked. The fighting prowess of all these peoples have been exaggerated greatly by former travellers ...

---

gates etc., etc., etc. I only saw a dirtily clothed youth seated in the door of a small hut in which were a lot of black sluts, whilst some 250 natives squatted around upon the straw which had [been] spread on the ground for their accommodation, all of them very dirty and had an exceedingly unpleasant smell and thought a great deal of themselves. I think people like Stanley who write in that absurdly exaggerated style do a great deal of harm in Africa ... All this talk of kings and emperors and princes of the royal blood, with their residences, courts and palaces sound all very fine in books of travel, but it is nothing but bosh and conveys a very false idea to the people for whose instruction the book is published" (*The Diary of*, p.390).

9th August

... Held an inquiry into the conduct of Wm. Hoffmann, Stanley's former servant.*

10th August

Reached the Lake of Urigi ... Speke and Grant passed up the west side of this Lake, but we go to the eastward to avoid the land [word illegible] of the King of Usui ...

Speke is fearfully out in his delineating of this Lake. Instead of being a small lake, as he has got it, it is quite 25 miles long and irregular in shape; it is also out of position in latitude and longitude.

There are quantities of game hereabouts; giraffe, zebra, rhinoceroses, hippos, elephant, eland, hartebeest, water buck, springbok and many others. The prettiest sight of all is to see the zebras running about just like ponies in a grass paddock at home ...

◆   ◆   ◆

12th August

A Nubian of ours shot two natives on reaching camp. We found him out and gave him over to the natives who speared him to death at night: blood for blood. We are now in a friendly country and must try to keep up the friendships as we hope to try to send a canoe from some point on the Lake Victoria [across] to Msalala with letters.

These letters would reach quite twenty days before us as we have to march round the southwest bend or bay of the Lake. We all hope that there may be white men and letters for us there and also perhaps some rice and good, healthy food.

Each day we talk more and more among ourselves about the chances of there being missionaries there and look upon Msalala almost as home, though it is four and one half months' journey from there to the coast. There should be one hundred bales of cloth there for us and twelve boxes of European provisions.

Grouse shooting commences [to-day in Britain].

---

*In what escapades Hoffman indulged is never spelled out in the diaries of the officers, although Parke suggested one direction as early as 25 July 1887 when he noted that "our chief's cockney servant [i.e., Hoffman] says that the girls are the ansomest as I has ever seen" (*My Personal Experiences*, p.84). More darkly, Nelson hinted that Hoffman joined in cannibalism (Nelson papers auctioned in Newcastle upon Tyne, 1993). Note that in 1889 Stairs describes Hoffman as Stanley's "former" servant.

13th August

Reached a new country ... the chief of which is Kaduma ... The natives, at first, were threatening and wanted us to pay in cloth for passing through their country. However, we firmly impressed them that that was not our custom ... They are now fast friends. Kaduma is an old friend of Stanley's. He met his people thirteen years ago when circumnavigating Victoria Nyanza which Lake is two days to the east.

♦   ♦   ♦

18th August

... Shortly after leaving camp we came out on some bluffs right over the Victoria Nyanza and got one of the finest sights of anything we have yet seen. Far away to the east to the horizon stretched the Lake, glittering like gold in the morning sun and here and there studded with islands of all sizes. Ahead of us is a big bay which we shall have to march around. It is unlike either the Albert [Nyanza] or Albert Edward Lakes, having bold shores and looking much like one of the Canadian lakes.

Chapter Fifteen

*From 28 August to 18 September 1889 the expedition revelled in the abundant food
and hospitality of Alexander Mackay's mission station at Usambiro. The missionaries Mackay and Deeks were the first Europeans the expedition had encountered
since June 1887. More than one thousand kilometres still separated the expedition
from the coast, but for the Europeans, Mackay's kindness acted as a reminder of
the need to begin to adjust themselves to the values of white communities.*

*At Usambiro the expedition received its first mail and news from the outside
world in over two years. From a few British newspaper clippings Stanley had the
first inklings of the controversy that was already beginning to surround his conduct of the expedition and the death of Barttelot. Stanley had anticipated that some
criticism would arise, if for no other reason than Barttelot's family was well placed
to attack Stanley's leadership, if it chose to do so. Stairs too began to realize that
controversy would await the expedition's return to Britain. He noted that both Ward
and Rose Troup, back in London, were already publishing articles about it.* His*

---

*Rose Troup, seriously ill, had arrived back in Britain during the summer of 1888 and
Ward a year later, during the summer of 1889, following his virtual dismissal by Barttelot.
Rose Troup married upon his return to Britain, but his later life remains obscure. Ward,
on the other hand, became a noted sculptor – as well as an ambulance driver in the First
World War. He assisted Morel and Casement in their campaign against Leopold's Congo
Free State, writing *Five Years with the Congo Cannibals* (London, 1890) and *A Voice
from the Congo* (London, 1910) as well as *Mr. Poilu; Notes and Sketches of the
Fighting French* (London, 1916). Eight years after his death in 1919 his wife, Sarita
Ward, published *A Valiant Gentleman : The Biography of Herbert Ward, Artist and
Man of Action* (London, 1927).

few diary entries after Usambiro become increasingly curt. Whether he felt that discretion had become desirable or whether it was from a feeling that there was no longer anything novel to say – that the adventure was almost over – Stairs reduced his diaries to brief notations and even they soon trailed off.

At a final muster on 14 September 1889, preparatory to its departure for the coast, the expedition totalled only 559, little more than a third of the 1,510 who had set forth from Kavalli's. In five months, almost one thousand men, women, and children had died, deserted, or simply disappeared along the route.

19th-28th August

From this onwards to Mackay whom we reached on the 28th, the country was covered with light bush.* We all felt the hot, trying marches very much. One can hardly express one's feelings of delight on pulling up at the mission station, seeing two Englishmen, Mr. Deeks and Mr. A.M. Mackay. They also were very much pleased at seeing us and thus feeling certain we were not dead.

A mail for us had arrived from the coast. There were two letters for me, one from my [step] mother and another from Jack. Both told me the saddest and heart-breaking news I could have read. Our dear old father had died [of cancer] in Cannes on the 21st March 1887. This is a terrible blow to me. I am burning to know all about it and can find nothing except bare facts. How they all must have felt it at home! One hardly takes everything in now there is so much in the way of news.

Poor Jameson died at Bangala on his way down Congo of fever.

The new German Emperor is also dead and now it is Kaiser Wilhelm again.

My sister was burnt out in Burmah and appears to have had a terrible time of it.**

What will become of our old home now? Will the place be sold? What a blow! Our old home at the [North West] Arm broken up, it is too much. Shall I never again roam about the old place and potter about among the boats down

---

*Alexander M. Mackay (1849–90), the intrepid and long-serving Church Missionary Society representative in Buganda, had in 1885 urged Emin to remain at Wadelai, pending British assistance which Mackay was certain would be sent. See J.W. Harrison, *The Story of the Life of Mackay of Uganda* (London, 1898).

**For Mary Bourke, see note on page 60. Jephson recorded in his diary, "There were no letters or papers for us. Stairs had two, one announcing the death of his father, and another containing the news that his sister, whose husband is stationed in Burmah, was burnt out of house and home by the Decoits [*sic*] and had to take refuge in the jungle until she was rescued. Ah! the bitter, bitter disappointment it was to us to hear that all our letters had been stupidly sent on to Uganda and had been destroyed by the Arabs. In our low and depressed state of spirits we imagined all sorts of things happening to our people and news equally bad as that which poor Stairs had received" (*The Diary of*, p. 397).

at the shore? Shall we never have any more pleasant evenings together near the bathing house? The brightest thing I always had to look back to when far away from home and the place I always delighted to return to was Fairfield. Shall I never go back there again among the brown birches and spruce trees, back by the side of the dear old Arm, back to the old places of our younger days? How many times have I started away from the old place with a well-loaded basket off to the woods trout-fishing ... Shall I ever return to it again? Perhaps so and perhaps in the hands of others. No, never shall I go there if it belongs to other hands.

In what state my father's affairs were when he died I cannot tell. If we are left well or badly off I do not know nor can I guess. That he should have been buried in France is very sad, I think! But what a blow to us all this is! However, I saw it coming, though those at home never did.

Mackay and Deeks made us very comfortable, good food, books, chairs, papers and English tobacco, how we did revel in these things! Such stories have got about in England concerning us: how Stanley was wounded; how the "White Pasha" was marching on Khartoum; etc., and the excitement caused in England over the expedition. Poor Barttelot's death caused a great deal of indignation against the Manyuema, but in reality we know it to have been his own fault. Ward and Troup have been making statements apparently, though perhaps not actually publishing them over their names.

Here at Mackay's how we enjoy ourselves: first, there is the coffee in the morning and chat, then a little work and breakfast. Biscuits, coffee, sugar, pepper, good stews, etc., why one hardly knows how to use all these things after such a long sojourn in the wilds! Mr. Deeks, though staying here, really belongs to Nyanza Station, some four days off on the east side of the Lake, and Mackay's real place is in Uganda ...

Mackay is the very ideal of a good chap for African colonization; he is wasted as a missionary in the position he is in. His treatment of us we shall never forget: a more kind-hearted and generous man I never met. We were able to obtain some European provisions here which will be a perfect godsend to us on the road. Mr. Deeks also has been very kind to us in a hundred different ways. Both of these missionaries are of the opinion that the Uganda mission will be a success.

◆   ◆   ◆

18th September
To-day we left Mackay and started off on our 700 miles of a march to the coast ...

◆   ◆   ◆

21st & 22nd October

... Water is very scarce and our people suffer considerably.
Should meet letters from the coast soon.

23rd October

... In this hot weather, marching along a dusty track 'till one's throat is dried
up and one's lips parched, how grateful one is for a drink of water no matter
how muddy or salty and think then how all these women must suffer when
they "have not got this cup full"; nevertheless this is what actually does happen,
for poor creatures they drain their gourds as a rule early in the day and so
suffer all the rest of the march. But to me how good a cup or two of tea is
when one is "red hot" on the march. Nothing that I know of quenches the
thirst so thoroughly as hot tea: cold tea or coffee are not thirst quenchers,
but quinine if taken in the morning will stave off thirst for some time ...

◆　　　◆　　　◆

26th October

... It is astonishing to us how people had apparently lost their heads in England
about this expedition. Now, most probably, they have received Stanley's
letters from Yambuya fourteen months ago and have stopped all this trash
about cannibalism, slaving, etc. But the cuttings we have read from English
and American papers show an ignorance about Africa and things African that
is appalling. A Mr. Wilmot Brookes (?) writes to his father a letter which is
published in (I think) *The Standard*. This letter is either written in a vindictive
and utterly spiteful tone or else is the result of a writer utterly ignorant of the
true state of affairs at Yambuya. He had heard of arms and legs sticking out of
cooking pots! Has he? Now, my experience of the very worst cannibal natives
is that they know it is wrong to eat human flesh and that they not only hide
away any human meat from white men but also from other natives. They will
never allow themselves to be caught with human flesh. Even Manyuemas who
eat dogs are ashamed of it and hide the flesh away if one comes into their
camp. Natives are always ashamed of themselves and try to put off any
questions as to their cannibalistic propensities ...

On 26 October 1889 Stairs had made his final diary entry, almost three years after his
first (Jephson had concluded his diary even earlier: on 2 August 1889). However, six
weeks still separated the expedition from the Indian Ocean. Stairs later described the
final stage of the expedition's long trek to the coast in an article, "From the Albert Nyanza
to the Indian Ocean," in *The Nineteenth Century*, vol. 29 (June 1891), pp. 953-67 and in
The Nova Scotian (30 May 1891), pp. 45-62. The following summary account is from
the two periodicals.

[From *The Nineteenth Century*]

On the 19th of November, about 10:30 a.m., we caught sight of the German flag waving over Fort Mpwapwa, and soon after halted under the two guns of the fort and made camp. Here we were welcomed by some German officers, who informed us that this was their farthest point west. [The garrison of four whites and one hundred Zulu mercenaries was commanded by Lieutenant Rochus Schmidt of the Imperial German Army.*] Fort Mpwapwa was well able to withstand the attacks of any number of Arabs, provided its water supply would only hold out. It is very striking to see our Zanzibaris beside the Zulu and Soudani soldiers of the Germans. Our men never salute us, and know no drill that could be of use to them; while, on the other hand, the Germans have their men drilled to almost perfection. While it is of the greatest importance to have men well trained in the use of their arms – i.e., to be good shots – I doubt if all this fancy drilling does much good; it is apt to break down in such a country as this.

Six days after leaving Mpwapwa we received as a gift from Major [Hermann] von Wissmann** some hams, champagne, and cigars. Needless to say, we soon made these disappear. Later on we received still further presents, this time Mr. J.G. Bennett, of the *New York Herald*. These certainly showed we were approaching civilisation, for among them were tooth-brushes, Florida water, and soap.

On the evening of the 4th of December we found ourselves encamped ... only eight miles from Bagamoyo and the Indian Ocean. The men were in great spirits, singing the whole day long, as the thought arose that home and friends were near.

---

*Rochus Schmidt (1860–1928) was later to achieve general officer's rank and to play a major role in the military government of Lithuania during the First World War. For a discussion of the German training of the African *Schütztruppen* such as Schmidt commanded and which appeared to Stairs so rigidly disciplined, see L.H. Gann and Peter Duignan, *The Rulers of German Africa, 1884–1914* (Stanford University Press, 1977), especially chapter six.

**Hermann von Wissman (1835–1905), a Prussian army officer, had become bored with life in German garrison towns and sought adventure in Africa. On leave from the army he had led two expeditions (he worked with de Winton in 1884) before Bismarck employed him to secure the littoral of East Africa for Germany. At the head of his mercenaries drawn from the Sudan, Mozambique, and Somaliland, von Wissman did more than anyone to consolidate German rule, but he was nevertheless passed over for the governorship of the resultant German protectorate (he did serve for one year as governor in 1895, but the fact that he was a morphine addict appears to have been a factor in the brevity of his tenure). For his own account of his early work in Africa, see H. von Wissmann, *My Second Journey through Equatorial Africa from the Congo in the Years 1886–1887* (London, 1891).

[From *The Nova Scotian*]

About eight o'clock in the evening, while the men were leaning over the camp fires cooking their evening meal, all of a sudden came the long, low "boom" of the Sultan of Zanzibar's evening gun from the island far across the sea. It was the gun that summons all true Mahommedans to prayer in the evening. Like some long-lost and forgotten chord being again heard it reminded the Zanzibaris that their homes were near. With a roar of cheering that I still can hear, the men bounded through the camp. Again and again the volleys of cheers rang out in the still night air. The men left their fires and surrounded the tents of the officers.

"*Tumefika pwani*; we have reached the coast".

"*Tumefika mwisho*; we have come to the end".

Reader, could you have seen how those men cheered Stanley, you would have felt that with such men as these he could go anywhere.

Next day, December 5th, 1889, we marched into Bagamoyo.

The sea again, boys, our work is done!

With bursting hearts and quickened pulses we met Englishmen and Americans again.* The feelings that came over us, when once again we saw the old flag flying from the peaks of the British men-of-war in the bay, are never likely to be forgotten by any of us.

Good-bye, boys!

Each and every one of you have passed through the fire and proved himself a hero true as steel. Through the forests and across the plains of Africa, you have stuck to us like the men you are. Over five thousand miles have some of you marched step by step with but poor food. Backwards and forwards through that forest which seemed unending, through fevers, starvation, and scenes of death have you marched, like Trojans. We white men who have served with you for three long years, who have fought and starved, have marched and camped with you, now go to our homes far across the sea.

But deep down in our hearts has sunk the remembrance of your deeds and, in the home of the white men who knows you, will your names be kept bright.

In after life we may meet with more brilliant examples of daring, more carefully wrought out schemes of progress than you were capable of achieving.

---

*The Americans were Edward Vizetelly of Stanley's former employer, The *New York Herald*, and Thomas Stevens (1855–1935) of The *New York World*. Stevens, who had travelled much of the world on a bicycle, wrote at length about the Emin Relief expedition. When back in London, he became a friend of Stanley and published *Scouting for Stanley in East Africa* (London, 1890). Vizetelly proved a rather more difficult companion. Highly excitable and seldom sober, he apparently believed that Stanley's porters were threatening him. Stanley had Nelson disarm him and place him under guard. Vizetelly later published his African memoirs, *From Cyprus to Zanzibar by the Egyptian Delta* (London, 1901).

But never are we likely to see again such splendid fortitude during dark and trying days as has been shown by you, the Zanzibaris of the Emin Pasha Relief expedition!

Medwisha tumepata.

It is finished; we have won.

With the expedition's arrival on the shores of the Indian Ocean on 2 December 1889, almost three years after it had embarked in Zanzibar for the Congo, Stairs concluded his account of his adventures. He did not write about the sorry aftermath of the expedition. The expedition's crossing of the African continent had been marred throughout by brutality, disease, starvation, and death. Of the 708 recruits who sailed from Zanzibar in February 1887, only 210 returned in December 1889. But even after its arrival at Bagamoyo, mishap continued to dog the expedition. Wissmann, the *Reichskommissar* of German East Africa, had a banquet prepared to celebrate the completion of the expedition. During the dinner on 4 December at the gubernatorial residence, Emin somehow fell fourteen feet from a balcony and fractured his skull (it was assumed by most that Emin, being myopic and possibly befuddled by alcohol, had missed his step). Parke joined briefly the German surgeons in attending him in the small German hospital at Bagamoyo.

Before their departure for Zanzibar, Stanley, Stairs, and Jephson each visited Emin once, urging him to take the mail steamer to Egypt, but it was clear that he had decided to accept the German offer of employment. They never saw him again. Within two years Emin was dead, his throat cut by Arab slavers as he and a few African followers wandered, seemingly purposelessly, in the eastern Congo, following a German decision to terminate the employment of someone who so evidently marched to his own drum rather than to that of Berlin. Stanley never displayed much remorse at Emin's fate, either at his near fatal accident or his later murder. His final word about Emin is quoted in his authorized biography:

We could only see dimly that he dreaded a return to civilization or coming into contact with civilized society, and therefore, as we were the unconscious agents of his return to the sea, we became as odious to him as the Germans were regarded as friendly when they eagerly equipped him with the means of returning to his aimless, objectless life in inner Africa.[1]

Stanley had got what he wanted by forcing his reluctant trophy to march to the coast. Thereafter, he appeared indifferent to Emin's future.*

---

*Emin's enthusiasm for re-establishing long-neglected ties with Germany may have been blunted by the fact that the Transylvanian widow of the Turkish governor who claimed to be his wife had successfully sued him. "Frau Schnitzer in Germany recognized her husband's picture in a fashionable magazine, sued him for alimony and was awarded ten thousand marks by a German court. Presumably she could not collect the money from her distant husband ."

Except in one respect. Upon learning of Barttelot's murder, Stanley had begun to suspect that his conduct of the Emin Relief Expedition would be closely scrutinized in London and very likely attacked. Being of a decidedly pugnacious character and no believer in half measures, Stanley immediately began to plan a counterattack. Part of his response would be to continue to denigrate the dead Barttelot; another part would be to denigrate Emin. To do so successfully, however, Stanley could not risk being contradicted by the one European survivor of the rear column. During the last months of the expedition and thereafter, he had to tolerate the continuing misdemeanours and imbecilities of Bonny, whom he privately regarded as a "specious rogue." Stanley needed Bonny's corroboration that, in the end, Barttelot was responsible for his own death.

Beginning with letters sent to London from Usambiro, Stanley systematically developed his counterattack on Barttelot's family and other detractors. In Cairo in a remarkable fifty days starting in January 1890, he wrote the two volumes of *In Darkest Africa, or, the Quest, Rescue and Retreat of Emin, Governor of Equatoria*, his heavily biased and even tendentious apologia for his leadership of the expedition, leaving the reader with the decided impression that he himself had behaved in a notably correct and manly fashion, while Tippu Tib had been deceitful and treacherous and both Barttelot and Emin had been patently foolish, inadequate and, worst of all, unreliable.*

Not surprisingly, this did not wash with Barttelot's influential family. They vigorously fuelled the controversy which would, in any case, have attended the conclusion of any expedition that had caused such widespread havoc and suffering. Stanley's belligerent character alone had long since ensured that he would never lack detractors. That distaste, combined with revulsion at the way in which Stanley had conducted the expedition, was more than enough to ensure that following his return to Britain, he was at the centre of a major tempest.

At first, however, all seemed to be well. From Cairo, Stanley and Parke had made their way first across the Mediterranean, then to Brussels to report to King Leopold, and finally in late April 1890 to London where Stanley and his officers were repeatedly feted, honoured, and lauded. Never easy in the company of women and ambiguous in his sexual preferences, he nevertheless married Dorothy Tennant on 12 July 1890 at a resplendent ceremony in Westminster Abbey where Parke, Jephson, and Stairs were all groomsmen. Following Stanley's prolonged honeymoon and upon the eve of extensive lecture tours in North America and Australia, the storm broke over his conduct of the expedition. Both Barttelot's family and Rose Troup had refrained from publishing any comment in light of the six-month limitation accepted by all the officers of the expedition, but when they did publish, the immediate controversy and public revulsion was such that Stanley's reputation

---

*Stanley's rapid writing so impressed his publisher that he wrote a book about Stanley writing his book: E. Marston, *How Stanley Wrote In Darkest Africa* (London, 1890). Stanley's account sold well, although it was not without its critics. Emma, the wife of Charles Darwin, regarded it as "the most tiresome book in the world – he observes nothing."

never fully recovered.* Stanley had his advocates – although they were never many – but two quotations may suffice to convey something of the devastating attacks of his detractors. On 11 April 1889, when the expedition was still eight months from Zanzibar, a writer in Henry Labouchere's periodical *Truth* condemned it roundly:

It is impossible not to admire Mr. Stanley's pluck and endurance. But I venture to question the use of marches like his into the interior of Africa. The plea was that Emin Pasha wished to be relieved. He does not want to be. He is only desirous to be left alone. What benefit, then, is it to the cause of civilisation that a white man should hire a vast number of carriers and undertake an expedition, in which half of them die of fatigue, and some are hanged for wishing to desert, in order to force his way through tribes by burning their villages and shooting them? The net result seems to be that it has been discovered that one lake is not so deep as it was a hundred years ago, that another lake lies to the south of the first, that there is a very dense forest, mainly inhabited by dwarfs, on the road to these lakes, and that somewhere in the vicinity of this forest there is a high mountain (hitherto unknown), the top of which is covered with snow. All this is, no doubt, interesting. But is it worth impressing carriers who die of fatigue or are hanged, shooting dwarfs, and destroying villages? I should like to hear a carrier or a dwarf on the subject.

Even more scathing was Gladstone's chancellor of the exchequer, the anti-imperialist Sir John Harcourt, who thundered that Stanley had led one of those

filibustering expeditions in the mixed guise of commerce, religion, geography and imperialism, under which names any and every atrocity is regarded as permissible ... an armed expedition like Stanley's claims and exercises the power of life and death and outrage upon all with whom they meet, powers which are exercised without remorse. They enlist men whom they call carriers, but who are really slaves, driven in by contract by the established slave drivers of the country. They work these men to death, and if they are recalcitrant flog or shoot them... what is really wanted is to concentrate public opinion on the real nature of these transactions which are the worst form of piratical jingoism.[2]

What Stairs thought of the bitter controversy that surrounded Stanley throughout the late autumn and winter of 1890 – and, indeed, for the remainder of his own short life – is

---

*Something of the contemporary animosity can be gauged from H.R. Fox Bourne, *The Other Side of the Emin Pasha Relief Expedition* (London, 1891). Richard Fox Bourne had long been a severe critic of European colonization of Africa. He later wrote, *inter alia, Civilization in Congoland; A Story of International Wrong-doing* (London, 1903), a book that assisted Casement and Morel in their case against Leopold's Congo Free State.

unclear. What is clear is that somewhat paradoxically Stairs, along with the other officers, began to modify the hard things that they had to say about Stanley.

♦   ♦   ♦

By 13 January 1890 Stairs and the officers of the expedition were back in Cairo, Parke to rejoin the army medical service, the remainder to return to Britain after being feted by the Egyptian government and the British community in Cairo. During his few weeks in Cairo, Stairs wrote to his younger brother, Jack, that he had planned how he would spend the four months' leave that awaited him, but he doubted that it would include a winter visit to Halifax (after three years in Africa the cold might be too much). On 30 January Stairs also wrote from Cairo to the editor of the Halifax *Morning Chronicle,* asking him to convey his thanks "to the many Haligonians who have so generously sent their congratulations on the successful termination of the Emin Pasha Relief expedition. During the many trying periods ... I never forgot them, or the many happy days spent in and about old Halifax ." In an answer to a journalist of *The New York World* whether he would return to Africa, Stairs replied that "the next time he would go as chief or not at all."[3]

Stanley, once in Cairo, praised extravagantly the qualities of Stairs, Jephson, Parke, and Nelson. On 30 January 1890 Stanley wrote to Lord Wolseley, the adjutant general, who had originally approved the applications of Barttelot and Stairs, that

Lt. Stairs is certainly unique for the ready and prompt obedience he pays to orders. He does not argue about orders or his duties but sets about them in a workmanlike manner which is more pleasing to a commander than any other merit in my opinion. I have tried him several times on most arduous enterprises in the Great Congo forest and the open country in matters which required tact and courage, and he has always returned with his missions performed truly, rightly and cleverly. I have sent him to cope against subtle arabs and given him authority to fight, if tact failed. He gained what I wanted by tact ... Had any accident occurred to me he was my successor. Were he a little more studious, I should say he would be a general before he was 45.[4]

At a reception in London held in honour of the officers of the expedition by Mackinnon and the Emin Relief Committee, Stanley was again notably fulsome in his praise of Stairs, despite the fact that, having read Stairs' s letter to Barttelot, he was fully aware of Stairs' low opinion of him. Perhaps recalling Stairs's criticism that Stanley offered no praise for a job well done, Stanley added eloquently that "I never permitted myself in Africa to indulge in laudation of any act, however well done. To faithful performance of imperative duties I considered myself entitled, meed or no meed; it was what they each and all had pledged to do."

Stanley's encomium of Stairs to the committee (paralleling his praise of Stairs to Wolseley) presumably represented another instance in which he could contrast the foresight, ingenuity, diligence, and perseverance of Stairs with what he sought to present as the opposite traits in Barttelot. At the height of the controversy with Barttelot's family and Jameson's widow, Stanley was travelling through North America on one of his lucrative lecture tours. In Toronto in January 1891, Stanley again praised Stairs extravagantly and by implication denigrated Barttelot.

For their part, Stairs, Parke, Jephson, and Nelson were notably more circumspect in what they said about Stanley following their return to London. At first they had not been so restrained. Colonel Euan-Smith, Kirk's successor as British consul general in Zanzibar, wrote in December 1889 that the four officers were "certainly a splendid quartet of Englishmen, but there is no love lost between them and Stanley who, I fancy, though an unequalled leader of natives, does not understand how to treat Englishmen."[5] However, a few weeks later in Cairo, Stairs began to praise Stanley. He said to a journalist of *The New York World,*

Stanley is one of the most remarkable men I ever met and Parke and Jephson and Nelson will tell you the same ... Stanley's is not an ordinary nature ... He is a wonderful man. Ask Jephson, ask Parke, ask Nelson; not one of us believe there is another man in existence who would have made a success of this expedition ... [6]

Jephson, who was also present at the Cairo interview, joined Stairs in his observation that

There have been times when we have thought Stanley a harsh, unfeeling man who had no sympathy for the suffering of others and was bent on working us to death. I have seen days when if I could have had the ear of the public at home I should have felt inclined to vent in the columns of the paper some grievance that seemed very real ... But now that it is all over, I can look back and see that Stanley was right. Without the hard, exacting work, we should never have pulled through, and Stanley's seeming harshness never goes beyond the point necessary for the success of the undertaking he is engaged in.

Even allowing for the passage of a few weeks to ease the dislike and resentment which all his officers felt for Stanley, this is a marked departure from the varying degrees of opprobrium that they had recorded in their diaries.

Why did the officers progressively soften and eventually end altogether their criticism of Stanley? Presumably they believed that if Stanley were widely denigrated and condemned, they would be also. As Stanley's leadership of the Emin Relief Expedition became the subject of formidable criticism in London, the officers must have concluded that they would do well to hang together and to support Stanley. For his part, Stairs did not excise from his diary his searing criticisms of Stanley, but equally he did not seek their early publication. To the contrary, he asked his brother Jack to ensure that his diaries were not published until after Stanley's death. In the meantime, Stairs would remain silent about Stanley's brutality – and perform himself acts of no less brutality.

◆   ◆   ◆

While Stanley remained in Cairo rapidly completing the two volumes of *In Darkest Africa,* Stairs had crossed the Mediterranean to Italy and on 4 February 1890 had arrived in Cannes where he had sketched his father's grave. He was back in London a few days later, more than three years after he had embarked for Zanzibar.

In London, Stairs was gratified to learn that he had retained his army seniority and pay and that he had been offered the appointment of adjutant of the Royal Engineers at Aldershot. He was soon elected a Fellow of both the Royal Geographical and the Royal Scottish Geographical societies. More tangible recognition arrived in the form of a "first donation" of £400 from the Emin Relief Committee, an unexpected honorarium voted to each officer (the hapless Bonny, not being an officer, received only one-half the amount) from the surplus funds of the committee.

When near starvation in Africa, Stairs had frequently craved European cuisine: he could now indulge himself until surfeited since Stanley and his officers were the lions of the London season of 1890. First in Brussels on 19-26 April (where Stairs went with Jephson and Nelson to join Stanley and Parke) and subsequently in London, the dinners and receptions were so many that Stairs declined to attend several. He was, however, at receptions by the Emin Relief Committee, the Corporation of the City of London, a ball at Buckingham Palace, a reception by the Canada Club, and a dinner in the presence of the Prince of Wales. At the last, organized by the American community in London in May, the Prince of Wales presented each officer with the replica of a large silver medallion (the original was sent later).* The menu card included a comment by Stanley on each of the four officers present: Parke, Stairs, Nelson, and Jephson. Of Stairs, Stanley had written, "One of those rare personalities, oftener visible among military men than among civilians, who could obey orders without argument, who could accept a command, and without ado or fuss execute it religiously – courageous, careful, watchful, diligent and faithful."

Eventually the dinners and speeches palled on Stairs – who was, in any event, unwell. Despite the fact that he was suffering from recurring malaria, he did serve as a groomsman at Stanley's wedding on 12 July before embarking in Liverpool three weeks later for a summer visit to his stepmother, several siblings and boyhood and R.M.C. friends in Halifax. His evident ill-health may, however, have been the reason why, a week after Stanley's wedding, Stairs declined an offer from the London agent of Cecil Rhodes's British South Africa Company to participate in an expedition to the region between the Zambesi and the Congo. Such an expedition would have entered Katanga and laid claim to it for Rhodes. Stairs, however, refused the proposal of 18 July and recommended Nelson in his place (who also declined). Whether Stairs did so because of persistent illness or for some reason connected with Leopold's claim on the area is now unknown. Instead Stairs sailed for Canada.

◆   ◆   ◆

---

*By the time the medallions were actually completed, three of the four officers were dead; only Jephson, ill and fragile, had survived to receive one.

Stairs disembarked in Halifax on 12 August 1890. He had been feted in London and praised at a dinner at his old school in Edinburgh. Now it was the turn of Halifax. Only a few days after his arrival, the 66th Princess Louise Fusiliers received enthusiastically his brief after-dinner speech to the effect that his thoughts in Africa had been that the eyes of his native city were upon him and that, in a sense, the reputation of his country had been in his hands. On 29 August a committee appointed by the mayor of Halifax to decide upon a gift for Stairs recommended a sword to be made in London of Nova Scotia steel.* On 4 September the North West Arm was illuminated, boats were festooned with lanterns, and the passage of Stairs's boat was greeted by the music of bands and the cheers of the assembled yachtsmen.

The culmination of Halifax's honours for its "illustrious son" came on 11 September at a civic reception attended by the lieutenant- governor. After a military band had played "Here the Conquering Hero Comes," Stairs was presented with a scroll. In his brief speech of thanks, Stairs offered his somewhat laboured apologia for the expedition.

In some quarters doubts have been thrown upon the sincere work performed by Mr. Stanley's expedition ... though the expedition as well as most other African expeditions was accompanied by great sacrifice, and must have to some extent changed the existing political conditions of affairs [sic] among the tribes of Central Africa, still the benefits that have and will accrue to the British Empire and civilization generally, are such as to have fully warranted the expenditure of life, money and labour necessary to its fulfilment. The openings that will be offered to the expansion of English and other trade in supplying new markets for the goods of the world, the improved condition of the native that will ensue, the suppression of the slave trade through the influence of the railway and telegraph lines are only some of the benefits that will spring directly from such an undertaking as that of the Emin Pasha Relief expedition.[7]

◆   ◆   ◆

In late September Stairs sailed from Halifax for Liverpool to rejoin the Royal Engineers, but it was to Africa that he wanted to return. King Leopold, that *malo orgio* of so much that went wrong in Africa in the late nineteenth century, soon provided him with the opportunity. It seems that Sir William Mackinnon, Verney Cameron, and Sir John Kirk joined in recommending Stairs as leader of one of several expeditions which Leopold was planning to send to Katanga to secure that mineral-rich region for the Congo Free State. The invitation to Stairs to lead an expedition came from the *Compagnie du Katanga*

---

*For some reason a silver plate was substituted for the sword. The plate was ordered by the Canadian High Commissioner in London, Sir Charles Tupper, who knew Stairs's family, at the not inconsiderable sum of £209. He presented it to Stairs in London in the autumn of 1890.

(which, not surprisingly, was under Leopold's thumb), but before Stairs could accept, he had again to secure a long leave of absence from the army. The Royal Engineers were not, apparently, disposed to do so a second time, so Stairs transferred on 25 March 1891 to the Welsh Regiment from which it would be easier to obtain the necessary leave. Upon doing so, Stairs agreed to lead an expedition which would be one part of Leopold's wider plan to thwart Rhodes and to win international recognition of Katanga as part of the Congo Free State. No doubt it had occurred to Leopold that to have a British officer leading one of his expeditions at the express urgings of his British associates might also do something to counter the ambitions of Rhodes.

Why Stairs accepted the invitation of a Belgian company, having already declined a similar invitation from a British company, is puzzling, especially given his obvious distaste both for the men who administered the Congo Free State and for Leopold's boundless ambitions (see, for example, Stairs's diary entry of 31 May 1887). Perhaps the reason was no more than the Belgian offer meant the command of an expedition, whereas the British offer may have not. In any event, within seven weeks of transferring from the Royal Engineers to the Welsh Regiment, he was again en route to Zanzibar.

Stairs was patently ill-advised to return to the fevers of Africa only sixteen months after the Emin Relief Expedition. A companion on the Katanga expedition later noted that Stairs "was fully conscious of the rashness of the experiment, since his constitution had been severely tried by malaria and exertion, nor was its tone entirely restored. Indeed, before leaving England, he told more than one of his friends that they might never see him again."[8] Stairs's companions on the Emin Relief Expedition did not. Almost all died early deaths, debilitated by disease. Barttelot and Jameson predeceased Stairs, and Nelson and Parke followed him within months.*

---

*Nelson was the first. He died of dysentery on Boxing Day 1892 (six months after Stairs) while employed by the Imperial British East Africa Company in the Kikuyu district of Kenya. Parke died in September 1893, nine months after Nelson, while on the staff of the military hospital at Netley in southern England. Bonny died in the Fulham workhouse in 1899. Jephson, like Stairs and Nelson, wanted to return to Africa, but persistent ill health forced him to decline both British and Belgian offers. (Leopold even sounded him on leading an expedition to Katanga to succour Stairs). Jephson died in 1908, having been an invalid for much of his later life. Hoffman lasted longer than them all. Following his year in Mombasa, he accompanied Stanley to South Africa and later was employed in the Congo Free State. He presumably died sometime after the publication of his curious memoirs in 1938.

Chapter Sixteen

From at least the eighth century it seems that the rich copper and gold deposits of Katanga were worked by local tribes. During the subsequent centuries, reports of the deposits had reached Europe via the coast Arabs and the first Portuguese explorers, but the area remained difficult of access from either the Congo or Zambezi rivers. Overland journeys were hazardous, not least because of the hostility of local tribes.

By the second half of the nineteenth century, both Livingstone and a young Royal Navy officer and noted explorer, Verney Cameron, had reported on the mineral wealth of Katanga.[1] Cameron had claimed the region for Queen Victoria in 1874–75, but the Disraeli government, wanting no additional colonial entanglements in Africa, was quick to repudiate his claim. When in 1885 Leopold had gained international recognition of himself as sole proprietor of the Congo, the status of Katanga remained in a sort of penumbra. British missionaries and later Cecil Rhodes spread the impression among those few in Britain who were interested that Katanga was an especially desirable part of Africa. Rhodes, believing in the existence of a continuous reef of gold and copper from the Rand to Katanga, eventually advanced the claims of his British South Africa Company, despite the fact that Katanga had been nominally included within the boundaries of the Congo Free State by the Berlin Conference. No state officials, however, visited the region and limited resources meant that the expense of establishing a station there received no priority from Leopold.

By 1890 Leopold had become decidedly uneasy about the continuing uncertainties regarding the status of Katanga. East Africa was being rapidly carved up. In July 1890 Germany and Britain concluded an agreement that redefined and made more formal their earlier "spheres of influence". Almost a year before Stairs embarked upon his second expedition, the new German colony of East Africa had been recognized by London. Equally, Britain's protectorate over Zanzibar and the territory to the north had been recognized by Berlin. During the eighteen months since Stairs had been in Zanzibar, the German grip on the mainland opposite had tightened.

Unlike his three-year crossing of Africa, Stairs on his second expedition would not only follow a well-established trade route to Lake Tanganyika – pioneered by Burton, Speke, and Grant as well as by the Arabs – but he would pass through a region where local turmoil was being suppressed by increasingly rigid German rule. Beyond the mainland territories being claimed by Britain and Germany – the protests of the Sultan of Zanzibar were simply brushed aside – Leopold was determined that there should be no disputing his rights in Katanga.

Leopold's eagerness to secure Katanga may have been fuelled by growing concerns in Europe that slavery in East Africa was not in fact being eradicated, but rather remained as a continuing scourge costing the lives of thousands of blacks annually and relegating others to a sub-human existence. A great impetus to the anti-slavery movements was provided in 1888 by the campaign mounted by Cardinal Lavigerie, the Archbishop of Algiers and founder in 1868 of the White Fathers of Africa (*La Société de Notre Dame d'Afrique*). Money and volunteers were sought to undertake a latter-day crusade. While ostensibly supportive, Leopold was privately concerned that, sooner or later, the intrusions into his territory of the anti-slave crusaders would expose his Congo regime as being in several respects as brutal as that of the slavers themselves. With luck, however, the impetus and some of the funds of the anti-slavery movement might somehow be harnessed to supplement the notably meagre resources of the Congo Free State.

Accordingly, Leopold made a great show of demonstrating his commitment to the eradication of the slave trade by inviting to an eight-month conference in Brussels the leading advocates across Europe. What eventually emerged was a partial solution to the king's continuing fiscal problems. The Congo was gradually bankrupting him. Through the device of an import duty approved by the Brussels conference, supposedly to finance anti-slavery actions, Leopold extricated himself from his earlier pledges to keep the Congo free for all trade. Neither imports nor exports had hitherto been taxed. The Congo was a "Free State". Now, finally, a way was opened to raise state revenue by imposing a ten per cent duty on all imports.

All this was reason enough for Leopold to act promptly to assert "effective occupation" of Katanga and to define and win recognition for the borders of the Congo Free State, established by the Berlin Conference of 1885. More pressing, however, was the fact that in 1889 Cecil Rhodes (then prime minister of the Cape Colony) had despatched northward the young but experienced explorer and geologist Joseph Thomson to attempt to claim Katanga for his British South Africa Company. By way of back-up, Rhodes sent a second expedition under the command of Alfred Sharpe, a hunter who doubled as British vice-consul in Nyasaland. Rhodes's ambitions were not wholly unwelcome in Britain. British missionary reports had told of work in an otherwise neglected part of Africa and some British entrepreneurs, in addition to Rhodes, were beginning to covet the mineral and ivory riches of Katanga. Harry Johnston, the newly appointed commissioner of the British Central Africa Protectorate, wrote to Lord Salisbury in August 1890:

... Garenganze called by the Swahili Arabs Katanga [is] ... the richest country in minerals (gold & copper) in all Central Africa ... The king of the Belgians has no right to it ... From a Belgian point of view he is an admirable patient who has by many a hook and crook, by many a wile and intrigue, by much expenditure of his own and not a little of that subscribed by the rich English people whom he bamboozled, created a fine African Empire for little Belgium. But why his enterprise should be received by us ... with indulgence ... I cannot conceive.[2]

For his part, Leopold soon realized that since his protests to London about Rhodes's intentions were of no avail, he must act without further delay to assert his effective occupation of Katanga. Expeditions would have to be mounted to establish beyond further question the inclusion of Katanga in the Congo Free State.* Two were organized under the aegis of the recently incorporated *Compagnie du Congo pour le Commerce et l'Industrie*. Two more expeditions were soon mounted by the even more recent *Compagnie du Katanga* which in March 1891 had been granted one-third of the state lands in Katanga and a century-long concession for the exploitation of its mineral riches.** Both companies – and hence all four expeditions – were in fact directly or indirectly controlled by Leopold. Verney Cameron, back in Britain, helped to bring together both continental and British investors in the *Compagnie du Katanga*, one of whom was Sir William MacKinnon.

What awaited Leopold's four expeditions to Katanga was a regime under Msiri, the son of an ambitious Nyamwezi trader who had established his

---

*Two German explorers, Paul Reichard and Wilhelm Böhm, had reached Katanga in 1883, followed shortly by two Portuguese naval officers, Hermenegildo Carlos de Brito-Capello and Roberto Svens, both of whom had been with Serpa Pinto on his travels in southern Africa. Plymouth Brethren missionaries from Britain had established themselves in Katanga by 1885.

**Both the ubiquitous Sir William Mackinnon and the former British consul general in Zanzibar, Sir John Kirk, were directors of *la Compagnie du Katanga*.

control over a region about as large as Britain. Msiri's regime – and that of
his father – was typical of

the loose, military overlordships created by the magnates of the caravan trade to safeguard
the sources of their wealth. Especially where traditional politics were small and weak,
traders defended themselves by travelling with armed escorts and establishing fortified
depots for their goods. From there it was a short step to taking hostages or seizing cattle
in order to ensure the supply of ivory, slaves or rubber at attractive prices, and this in turn
often led on to the trader settling down as ruler, taking tribute from the indigenous population
by military means.[3]

Msiri was, in effect, the paramount ruler over a variety of tribes and chiefs
whom he had cowed into submission by his ruthless and random use of terror.
In his fiefdom, he punished with death anyone suspected of disloyalty and
with mutilation (particularly by cutting off hands) anyone suspected of other
misdemeanours. Throughout Msiri's large territory he was everywhere feared
and hated by those over whom he ruled. Paul Reichard, the German explorer
who arrived in Bunkeya in 1883, was shocked by what he saw: "a man of
subtle cruelty, [Msiri] is most at home playing the role of executioner and he
very much enjoys burying his victims up to the waist and letting them die of
hunger."[4] Frederick Arnot, the first British missionary to penetrate the area,
was soon equally disturbed: "The sensation creeps over one of being in a
monster's den."[5] Msiri's hold on the region and its trade in copper, salt, ivory,
and slaves was certain enough as long as no European allies of dissidents
were at hand. A member of one of Leopold's expeditions later described how
to Msiri's capital of Bunkeya (variously Bunkeia) came "from Zanzibar, from
Uganda, from the Zambezi, from Angola, and from the Congo basin ...
merchants who exchanged ammunition and cloth for ivory, copper, and slaves.
The Arabs also succeeded in foisting upon Msiri a wonderful collection of
music-boxes, concertinas, American clocks, a policeman's uniform, and all
kinds of firearms, some good and some indifferent."[6]

On 18 April 1891 the first of Leopold's four expeditions to reach Bunkeya
was well received by Msiri. It came from the nearest Congo Free State station
and was led by Paul le Marinel, a long-time employee of the state. However,
he failed to induce Msiri to fly the state's flag. No more successful was the
second expedition under Alexandre Delcommune, a highly experienced
explorer who had served on the lower Congo under both Stanley and de Winton.
Delcommune arrived in Bunkeya on 6 October 1891 (two months before
Stairs), only to realize that unrest was increasing amongst several subject
tribes. Msiri, then aged about sixty, no longer had the energy of his youth.
Revolt was spreading and famine mounting. There was equally a growing sense
among the tribes that the arrival of the European expeditions meant that Msiri

would be unable to pursue indefinitely his ruthless punishments and widespread slaughter.

The third of Leopold's expeditions was led by Stairs; the fourth by Captain Lucien Bia of the *Deuxième Guides* of the Belgian army. Although by coincidence Bia's expedition embarked in Antwerp the same day (18 May 1891) that Stairs left London, it was assumed that Stairs's expedition would arrive first by following the direct trade route through German territory and across Lake Tanganyika. Stairs's sense of urgency was strong: "we [could not] allow time to run to waste, otherwise the claim stood in considerable danger of being jumped"[7] Bia's expedition would follow a somewhat more circuitous route, but would be available as back-up for Stairs's expedition. Both Stairs and Bia were instructed by Leopold to urge local tribes encountered along their routes to accept the flag of the Congo Free State. Once in Bunkeya, if they found that the British South Africa Company had already concluded a treaty with Msiri, they were to content themselves with attempting to reach similar agreements with surrounding tribes so that Leopold would have additional bargaining chips in any subsequent negotiations with the British. Stairs was not required to fire upon any British expedition.

By the autumn of 1891 Msiri was becoming uneasy about Leopold's interests in Katanga. He sent a message to Alfred Sharpe, the British vice-consul in Nyasaland (and employee of the British South Africa Company who had earlier visited Msiri in search of gold), hoping that he would provide British support to counter the Congo Free State's claim to his territory. Msiri, upon learning of the approach of Stairs's expedition, assumed that since it was reportedly led by a British army officer, Stairs must be the answer to his letter to Sharpe.

Msiri's mistake was understandable. Why indeed would a British army officer be commanding an expedition for the King of the Belgians to secure Katanga against the claims of the British? The short answer is that the British government was not interested in even the most indirect involvement in Katanga. Its principal interest in the Congo was to exclude the French. Since the British government had no direct ambitions in Katanga, it was not opposed to Leopold's recruitment of Stairs, anymore than it had been to Leopold's earlier employment of Stanley or de Winton. For a second time the War Office granted Stairs a long leave of absence.

No record remains of how Stairs was first contracted by Leopold, but his contract, signed in Brussels on 9 May 1891 with the *Compagnie du Katanga* is extant. "His stay in Africa will not go beyond two years and six months ... in remuneration for [which he will receive] a monthly salary of eighty pounds ... [to] run from the day of his shipping [first class] at London". As a priority, Stairs was required to recognize that mineral discoveries which he might make "remain the exclusive property of the Company." More generally, Stairs would incur a fine of £1000 if he communicated to anyone "intelligences of a commercial or mining kind concerning the territories of the Congo Free State ..." Not only was Stairs explicitly precluded from trading on his own or anyone else's account, but he was most definitely not to publish anything about the progress of his expedition. Following the completion Stairs could publish an account but only if he had first submitted the proofs to the Company, "so that the latter should be in [the] situation of being assured that these publications contain no intelligence that could [be] turn[ed] to good use of competitors." In return, Stairs was to have a minimum of five porters for his personal belongings (as was each officer of the expedition) and "feeding, lodgings and medicines .. [but] no indemnity of any kind shall be due by the Company to the inheritors of the Captain W.G. Stairs, in case he should perish."[8] Nor is any record extant of how Stairs in turn recruited the following members of his expedition, other than the brief account in a book published in 1893 by the expedition's Irish physician.

Stairs's deputy was Captain *Omer Bodson*, an officer in the Belgian Carbineers who was seven years older than Stairs. Bodson had served for more than three years in the Congo (like all Belgian army officers in the service of the Free State, he had retained his military seniority and pay). He may have been known to Stairs at least by name: he provided some assistance to the Emin Relief Expedition as it passed up the Congo and had been one of three Belgian officers who in August 1888 had joined Jameson in a sort of kangaroo court which had promptly condemned to death the murderer of Barttelot.

The third officer of the expedition, the French *Marquis de Bonchamps*, was, like Jameson, Jephson, and Rose Troup, something of a traveller. Christian de Bonchamps was also seven years older than Stairs, had served in a French cavalry regiment, and was an ardent hunter in the Canadian Rockies.

Joseph Moloney, the medical officer, was an Irishman. Having completed his medical studies at St. Thomas' Hospital in London, he practised for some years in south London. His only contact with Africa had been a hunting trip in Morocco. It was, however, Moloney who was to write the only firsthand account of the expedition, *With Captain Stairs to Katanga* (London 1893).

The fifth European, *Thomas Robinson*, was a former Grenadier Guardsman, who was employed by Stairs as "carpenter and general factotum". Little is said about Robinson; he remains shadowy in something of the same way that Hoffman is in the accounts of the Emin Relief Expedition – but unlike Hoffman, he appears to have been honest, disciplined and dependable.

Soon after returning from his hunting trip to Morocco, Moloney successfully applied to Stairs at his London hotel to join the expedition. And presumably it was Stairs who selected Robinson from among the many applicants (both had to be endorsed by Brussels). Possibly Stairs also accepted in the first instance the application of the Marquis de Bonchamps, but it is likely that it was Leopold himself who assigned Bodson to the expedition.

(He had been noticed by Leopold: upon his return from the Congo, he had distinguished himself in the military suppression of civil riots in Liège.) Moloney later wrote:

... we were a mixed staff acting under an international syndicate ... such enterprises are less likely to succeed than those conducted on more homogeneous lines. Political considerations naturally cause a company thus constituted to adopt a somewhat flabby and vacillating policy ... differences of race are accentuated by the worries and fatigue of a long march overland, and ... the small band splits into yet smaller cliques – Britons on the one side and Continentals on the other ... the existence of some unnecessary friction on the Stairs expedition cannot be wholly ignored.[9]

This friction was presumably largely between Bodson and Stairs. Whether it would have been less if Stairs had been able to speak French (he had learned Swahili but he had little French), or if Bodson or Bonchamps had been able to speak English is now impossible to say. More likely, friction may have arisen over what Bodson understood to be Leopold's instructions (via *la Compagnie du Katanga*) and Stairs's more flexible and lenient methods of carrying them out. From Bodson's role on the Congo, in the suppression of the Liège riots, and his eventual killing of Msiri, he seems to have been a ruthless man.

◆   ◆   ◆

In his Katanga diaries Stairs was writing primarily for the corporate reader in Brussels – and in London – rather than for a broader public. In his written instructions as leader of one of the four expeditions Leopold despatched to Katanga, Stairs was to prepare a daily journal for *la Compagnie du Katanga*. His diaries were to relate the principal events of the expedition, and his own observations on the nature of the terrain crossed and the inhabitants along the way, their resources, and their likely future. Accordingly, the Katanga diaries are replete with factual descriptions from the Indian Ocean to Katanga, information that would assist in the later exploitation of the region.

Insofar as the French translation reflects the English original, Stairs's year-long diary is both decidedly shorter than his three-year diary of the Emin Relief Expedition and is markedly different in texture, tone, and tenor. Almost wholly absent are his lively personal asides about his companions which pepper his Emin journals. Nor are there the nostalgic if somewhat contrived recollections of boyhood days in Nova Scotia. Even Stairs's accounts of his clashes with tribes on his way to Katanga and of Msiri's death lack immediacy. In fact, the account by Moloney of the expedition is more vivid, providing a useful corollary to Stairs's spare record.

Some of the differences between Stairs's two diaries is the result of a drainage of vitality from the Katanga diary by the stultifying process of translation from English into French and back into English. The fact remains, however, that Stairs himself excluded from his Katanga diary those personal digressions or reminiscences that would have added to its dimensions. It is as if the past barely existed.

For example, Stairs offers no information about how he was recruited, although Mackinnon, Kirk, de Winton, and Stanley were all probably involved. He does not record the fact that on his way to Katanga he was crossing the return route of the Emin Relief Expedition (or, for that matter, routes of Livingstone, Speke, Grant, and Stanley). He seldom refers to Stanley or Emin or the Relief Expedition, except for the occasional mention of a Zanzibari veteran. Stairs and Bodson – however limited their ability to converse with each other – would presumably have spoken at least briefly of Barttelot's death, an event which had stirred troubling controversy not only in Britain but also in the continental press. Bodson had met Barttelot in the Congo. As noted above, he had later presided over the "court martial" which had condemned to death his murderer. Equally, Captain Bia, who relieved Stairs at Bunkeya, had carried out the execution. In a more personal and less commercially inclined diary it is inconceivable that Stairs would not have recorded whatever Bodson or Bia told him about the Barttelot affair – and surely they told him something.

One other instance may serve to reinforce the point about the austerity and distance of Stairs's Katanga diaries. Stairs does not more than note in passing that an American woman traveller was on the east coast of Africa when he arrived. In fact, May French Sheldon (1848–1936) was not only a close friend of Stanley but someone whom Stairs himself knew and had assisted in her remarkable travel plans.

May Sheldon, her father, and her rich husband were long-time friends of Stanley. All were Americans, although Sheldon had received much of her schooling in France and Italy (whose languages she spoke). According to one account, she had emulated her mother by qualifying as a physician (a still rare event for a woman), but by the time that Stanley knew the Sheldons in London in the 1880s, she had become a novelist and a successful translator and publisher. (It was, incidentally, through the Sheldons that Stanley had employed his unlikely servant, Hoffman.)

In 1891, at the age of forty-three, May Sheldon set out to see something of the continent that her friend Stanley knew so well. Presumably at Stanley's instigation, Parke offered her medical advice* and accompanied her from London to Dover on the first stage of her long journey to East Africa (she

---

*Two years later, Parke published *A Guide to Health in Africa* (London, 1893).

travelled to Zanzibar on the sailing immediately before Stairs of the *Madura*, the same ship that had carried the Emin Relief Expedition from Zanzibar to the mouth of the Congo). Presumably again at Stanley's prompting, Stairs wrote her a long letter of general advice about travel in the African hinterland. In return, she described Stairs in her book about her African travels as that "lovable friend".[10]

Stairs refers to none of this in his Katanga diaries. Nor does he take notice of the presence in Katanga of a fellow Canadian, the Plymouth Brethren missionary William Henry Faulknor. It is likely that he would have written much more about the people whom he encountered and his reactions to them – as he did in his Emin diaries – if his Katanga diary was not primarily a factual account by an expert observer of the exploitability of the region by European capitalists.

"Fierce fight at Avi Sibba: Lieut. Stairs wounded with an arrow" on 13 August 1887. Only fifteen months later was Surgeon Parke finally able to remove the fragments of the arrowhead from Stairs's chest. (*Penny Illustrated Paper*)

An imagined reconstruction of a "brisk encounter in Majamboni's village" on
7 December 1887 from *The Illustrated London News*. One of the men of the
Expedition fires the village as an unidentified officer kills a native.

The nocturnal encounter of Emin Pasha and Stanley at Kavalli on Lake Albert Nyanza on 29 April 1888. Casati is on Emin's right and Jephson on Stanley's left; Stairs was still at Fort Bodo. (*Penny Illustrated Paper*)

THE AFRICAN MARCH OF CIVILISATION.

INTERPRETER.—"Chief Wangbo wants no more beads and brass wire. He says you cannot cross his country unless you agree to pay his price."
AFRICAN EXPLORER.—"What does he want?"
INTERPRETER.—"Two thirds of the royalties on your next book."

An iconoclastic comment on the eagerness of African travellers to profit from their adventures. Stanley, a former journalist, was himself invariably in the vanguard of those rushing into print, so much so that he required the officers of the Emin Expedition to sign an undertaking that they would publish nothing for six months following its conclusion. In Cairo beginning in January 1890, Stanley wrote the two volumes of *In Darkest Africa* in fifty days to be certain that he would capture the market and establish the benchmark for subsequent discussions of his already controversial expedition. (*Punch*)

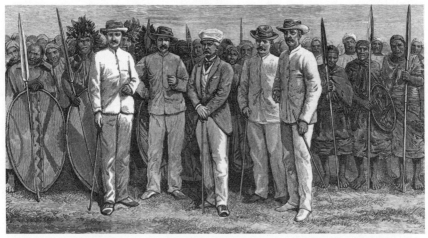

A drawing from *The Illustrated London News* (based upon a photograph, presumably made at or near Bagamoyo upon the completion of the Emin Pasha Relief Expedition): "Mr. Stanley and his Gallant Comrades 'in Darkest Africa': Masai Warriors in the Rear." From left to right: Jephson, Nelson, Stanley, Parke, Stairs. (*Illustrated London News*, 1 March 1890)

The officers of the Emin Pasha Relief Expedition on board the *Katronia* on their way from Mombassa to Cairo en route to Britain, in late December 1889 (Stanley is waving at the taffrail while Parke recuperates in a *transatlantique*). (*Illustrated London News*)

Surgeon Parke. Capt. Nelson. H.M.S. Capt. Stairs. Mr Mounteney Jephson.

Henry M. Stanley and his officers 1890.

The officers of the Advance Column in Cairo in December 1890. From left seated:
Surgeon Capt. Thomas Parke; Henry Stanley; Mounteney Jephson; from left
standing Capt. Robert Nelson; Lt. William Stairs. All have aged as a result of their
hardships and illness. (Stanley, *Autobiography*)

A studio photograph taken of Stairs following the completion of the expedition. It appears from his clothing to have been taken at the same time as his portrait in safari kit. (McCord Museum of Canadian History)

Dr. Joseph Moloney, the Irish physician who accompanied Stairs on his Katanga Expedition and who attended him at his death on 9 June 1892. Moloney's book *With Captain Stairs to Katanga* is the only first-hand account of Stairs's Katanga Expedition (Moloney was such an enthusiastic African traveller that he later also volunteered to lead an expedition for King Leopold of the Belgians). (*With Captain Stairs to Katanga*)

Stairs's tombstone at Chinde at the mouth of
the Zambesi River, erected by his sister, Hilda.
(McCord Museum of Canadian History)

Chapter Seventeen

The Madura *of Mackinnon's British India Steamship Company carried Stairs's expedition to Zanzibar (as it had the Emin Relief Expedition to the Congo). Bodson, Moloney, and Robinson sailed in the* Madura *from London Docks on 11 May 1891. One week later, Stairs left London for Paris where the Marquis de Bonchamps joined him. They embarked together in the* Madura *in Naples on 20 May.*

18 May 1891
Left Charing Cross at 10:00 for Folkstone and Naples, where I shall join the *Madura* for Zanzibar. I have spent fifteen months in England. During that time I learned much and greatly enjoyed myself. Good-bye, old England! I hope to return in two and a half years, safe, sound and successful ...

◆   ◆   ◆

20 May
... This afternoon I arrived in Naples to find letters awaiting me, including a note for Alex. Delcommune who is somewhere in central Africa, near the sources of the Congo.

21 May
Left Naples [in the *Madura*] for Port Said. Aboard is Saleh, Stanley's servant on the Emin Relief Expedition. He made a small fortune during his travels in Europe and America. Now he wants to return to his homeland, but I doubt very much that he will ever attain a high appointment despite his real

intelligence. He will resume the carefree and lazy habits of Zanzibar and, little by little, will forget everything that he has seen.

Among the passengers is the Rev. Mr. Ashe, formerly a missionary with Mackay in Uganda. He seems knowledgeable about everything concerning East Africa and is, to a point, an admirer of Stanley. Ashe has written a learned and useful little book entitled *Two Kings of Uganda.**

I dislike all sea voyages which last more than two hours! I agree with the hindoo: "They're poison." One always seems to leave ashore some part of one's energy. It is only with the greatest effort that one achieves anything at all.

The names of the members of the expedition are: 1. W.G. Stairs (British); 2. Captain Bodson (Belgian); 3. Marquis de Bonchamps (French); 4. Dr. J.A. Moloney (British); and 5. Thomas Robinson (British).

◆   ◆   ◆

25 May

Disembarked in Port Said, bought some cigarettes and dined ashore. It seems strange to see these yellow-bellied Egyptians again. A world of memories returns about the difficult days of the Emin Relief Expedition in bringing those Egyptian clerks to the coast.

During the year that I passed in Britain, I met in London at least 300 people. But how few friends I made! They are indeed rare those whom I can call by the name of friend ... In London, there are hardly ten people from whom I could borrow £10 if I were in serious need, and I know only three families to whom I could call at dinner without being invited – and without a dinner jacket.

Shall I ever again see the young women with whom I dined last year in London or those hundreds with whom I waltzed – in town and whom I have now half-forgotten? I do not in general admire very much the young women in town. They are empty-headed, following each other in both ideas and dress like a flock of sheep. The young woman in the country, who comes to town only infrequently, is both more interesting and better educated.

The ideas of the average Englishman about Africa are both bizarre and irritating. But one must admit for sheer ignorance about Africa, the continental nations beat Britain hands down.

◆   ◆   ◆

---

*Robert Pickering Ashe, *Two Kings of Uganda; or, Life by the Shores of Victoria Nyanza; Being an Account of Six Years in Eastern Equatorial Africa* (London, 1889). Ashe had served with Mackay in Buganda in 1885 and, having survived the dangerous turmoil there, had returned to Britain to recuperate. See also Ashe's *Chronicles of Uganda* (London, 1894).

30 May

I have had several good conversations with Mr. Ashe, the Uganda missionary. He seems to have sensible ideas about Africa. The more I read the reports of the work of missionaries and the more I chat with them, the more I am convinced of the truth that for preaching to produce a lasting effect on the souls of Africans, it is first necessary for laymen to establish, by force if necessary, a stable and just government.

Have we [whites] the right to divide among ourselves this vast continent, to throw out the local chiefs and impose our own ideas? To that there can be only one answer: yes! What value would it have in the hands of the blacks who, in their natural state, are crueller to each other than the worst Arabs or whites? And could one suppose for a single moment that the Arabs would leave the continent to remain unexploited? Certainly not. The Arab will seize control of the central Africans and introduce his own semi-barbaric institutions, unless the white man intervenes....

As I say, before the arrival of the missionary, it is necessary first to establish a stable government. We've followed a false route, beginning the task at the wrong end by first sending missionaries, unsupported by arms. The blacks then perceive our weakness. Further, white traders arrive without regard for either law or religion, providing a bad example for the blacks.

And how could one compare, for example, the practices of the British Government with those of the Arabs? Britain's experience in central Africa should be followed by all true friends of the natives. May success crown the efforts of the British!

What more solid bond is there than that which exists among Parke, Jephson, Nelson and me? I have never read anything comparable to the achievements of four Englishmen who had survived so much together and who remain such close friends. I consider Parke as one of the bravest and one of the best fellows I have ever met.*

I have named one of my boats *Dorothy* in honour of Mrs. Stanley who christened her. The other I have called the *Bluenose,* the nickname I was given by some of my contemporaries.

◆   ◆   ◆

---

*Although Stairs had been highly critical of Nelson during the Emin Pasha Expedition (see, for example, Stairs's diary entries for 22 and 23 June, 1888), once back in London he presented Nelson with a watercolour sketch of "Starvation Camp" with the inscription, "In admiration of his pluck in sticking to the ammunition of the Emin Pasha Relief Expedition during 23 days of starvation".

1 June [1891]
Arrived at Aden. I have spent two agreeable days awaiting the *Arcadia* of the
P. and O. Line. Dined at the mess. As always in Aden, the heat is stifling.

◆   ◆   ◆

3 June
Sailed for Zanzibar this evening. I received letters from Sir John Kirk,
informing me that the Sultan no longer opposes my recruitment of porters
there. I understand that the missionaries of Cardinal Lavigerie [the White
Fathers of Africa] seek to recruit 400 porters at Zanzibar. A famine will
probably confront us along the route, adding to all the other challenges facing
us.

◆   ◆   ◆

11 June
Arrived at Mombassa. I am staying ... with Mr. Pigott, who is acting
Administrator here. Remarkable progress is being made ...

12 June
Visited the grave of my old friend H. B. Mackay, R.E., in the cemetery at Free
Town. Poor fellow! The news of his death was a terrible blow. To be cut off in
one's prime is a dreadful business.*
    I have received a telegram from Nicol [of Smith, McKenzie and Co. in
Zanzibar] informing me that, to date, he has succeeded in recruiting only
sixty men because he was unable to begin until last Monday. This is
disappointing, since at Aden I received a telegram telling me that all was
going well and upon my arrival in Zanzibar, I would find ready both my porters
and my goods. With the assistance of Mr. Pigott, I have been able to recruit at
Mombassa 56 porters. I hope to recruit 50 more next week. I have recruited
a headman, 56 porters, 1 cook, 4 *askaris*, in total 62 men, of which one
missed the embarkation [for Zanzibar].
    Here in Mombassa there arrived recently a large number of people from
Baluchistan [in India] whom, as far as I can judge, are as pretty a group of
absolutely useless human beings as imaginable...**

---

*Stairs's friend from the Royal Military College of Canada, Huntly Mackay (see note on
    page 60), had died of fever in Mombasa on 16 April 1891, two months before Stairs's
    arrival.
**The "Baluchis" (or "Baluchitis" or even "Beloochee" as Stairs variously called them)
    were warlike people from Baluchistau, northwest of Karachi. Having crossed the Ara-
    bian Sea to East Africa, they had initially been employed as mercenaries by the Sultan

13 June

I embarked my men [for Zanzibar] after having them sign contracts for two years at a total cost of £183/7/-. From Zanzibar has come the news that the large number of caravans leaving for the interior is causing a shortage of porters.

We sailed from Mombassa at 1330. I understand that Miss Sheldon, the American traveller, has reached the coast near Pangani, in the German territory.*

14 June

Arrived at Zanzibar. I met with Nicol of Smith, McKenzie and Co.** I succeeded in leasing a dhow which will carry the men whom I recruited in Mombassa to Dar-es-Salaam. I am afraid that they may desert if I let them disembark here.

I have sent a telegram to Baron von Soden, the German Governor, seeking permission to land both men and arms in German territory.***

---

of Zanzibar, but many soon became traders and slavers in the hinterland or merchants in the port.

*May French Sheldon, during her visit to the east coast of Africa in 1891, is reported to have worn "a court gown, artificial jewels and a blonde wig to impress tribal chiefs." She later described her adventure in *Sultan to Sultan* (Boston, 1892). Despite her illness in 1891 (see Stairs's diary entry for 18 June 1891), Sheldon travelled to the Congo Free State in 1894 under the auspices of King Leopold who hoped that she would report favourably about his personal fiefdom. Independent explorers and casual visitors were discouraged; presumably Leopold knew whom he was authorizing to visit the Congo Free State. He was not disappointed. Even when Congolese atrocities were becoming widely know, the ardent advocacy of Sheldon could still impress Lady Stanley; see also Dorothy Middleton, *Victorian Lady Travellers* (London, 1965), pp. 90-103.

**W.J.W. Nichol was the representative in Zanzibar of Smith, Mackenzie and Co., the agents whom Stairs had retained to supply both goods and porters to his expedition. Nichol had joined the company as an assistant in 1887, he became a partner in 1890, and remained with the company until 1936. Nichol had sailed to Zanzibar with Stanley and Stairs in 1887, but Stairs does not mention the fact in either diary. Stairs had met George Mackenzie at the outset of the Emin Relief expedition. For an account of the central role the company played in helping to ready expeditions for the interior, see Smith, *The History of Smith, Mackenzie Co. Ltd.* (London, 1938).

***Freiherr Julius von Soden (1846–1921), a career diplomatist and former governor of the German colony of the Cameroon, had been appointed governor of German East Africa, instead of Major Hermann von Wissmann (see p. 296). Between 1900 and 1914 von Soden served as a minister in the government of Württemburg.

On 8 September 1891 Stairs wrote to Brussels, "The good effects of the German policy in this part of Africa in quieting the people and subduing vicious chiefs have been most

15 June

I sent Bodson with a dhow to Dar-es-Salaam to carry letters to von Soden and a hindoo merchant. I landed most of our goods and placed them in a warehouse pending our departure.

At noon I saw C.S. Smith, the British Consul, with whom I chatted for an hour. He is in no way hostile to what I am trying to do, but insists that all our porters must be free men. Their contracts must be signed in his presence and approved by him. I have obtained a copy of Johnston's contract to serve as a model.*

I have also seen the Belgian and French Consuls, the Belgian to obtain letters to the Governor of Tabora. The French priests appear ready to forward my letters by the way of Mpala. Nicol does everything to advance our interests, but I nevertheless foresee being delayed here until 30 June.

The Belgian Consul, for his part, has asked [the Sultan] that Captain Jacques be allowed to recruit porters here. Jacques, who is going to Karema on behalf of the Belgian anti-slavery society, needs 500 men. My couriers to Karema, who should have been sent on their way by the French consulate, are still here and the French fathers have had no word about them.

Stokes arrives at the coast to-morrow. Famine has reached Tabora, but I am assured that the route remains peaceful.**

---

marked to me, as I saw the country two years ago in a very wild state. And all through, I and my officers and men have been shown nothing but the greatest kindness by the Germans. And I take this opportunity of expressing officially that much of the usual trouble experienced on expeditions leaving the coast was entirely dispensed with in our own case owing to His Excellency Baron von Soden's kindness."

*This is the first mention of (Sir) Harry Johnston in Stairs's Katanga diary. Johnston was to have a notable career in the British colonial service, initially as a protégé of Lord Salisbury. Of his service in Nyasaland when Stairs was en route to Katanga, Gann and Duignan have written that Johnston "was as untypical an empire builder as the imagination might conceive. In 1891 he was appointed to take charge of a forlorn outpost [as first comissioner and consul general of the British Central Africa Protectorate] where British influence was limited to a few mission stations and trading posts. Within a few years, the ex-art student – plump, squeaky-voiced and undersized – had wrought a complete transformation ... Aided by a few gunboats supplied by the Admiralty, Johnston smashed the local supremacy of ... Swahili-speaking [Arab] slave traders" (*The Rulers of British Africa,* pp. 84-85).

**The presence of both Captain Jacques and of the White Fathers reflected in part the anti-slavery movement that had been unleashed by Cardinal Lavigerie in 1888 and given additional impetus by the Brussels anti-slavery conference of 1890.

Charlie Stokes was a boisterous Irish adventurer and ivory trader who was later hanged by an officer of the Congo Free State for supplying arms to natives. See Louis William Roger, "Great Britain and the Stokes Case," *Uganda Journal,* vol. XXVIII (1964) and Nicholas Harman, *Bwana Stokesi* (London, 1986).

16 June

I saw Bonstead and arranged with him that sixty loads of rice and two of biscuit will be sent by him to the missionary station at Mamboia on the route inland from Bagamoyo. I also arranged with him to send three postal couriers each month to Karema – if that is possible.

I recruited about a dozen porters today. I met many former members of the Emin Relief Expedition. Unfortunately, they are already committed to going with Johnston to Nyassaland.

17 June

Forwarded letters of introduction from the Sultan .... He has granted me a personal audience on Saturday. I recruited twelve porters. Abedi, my former boy, will go with me. Dine... with Henderson, the captain of H.M.S. *Conquest;* C.S. Smith, the Consul; [Captain Bertram Lutley] Sclater, R.E.; and Dr. Charlesworth, the local physician ....

18 June

I received a telegram from Bodson in Dar-es-Salaam. Everything is well. He has been received by von Soden. I replied that he should seek the assistance of the Germans in recruiting thirty Zanzibari porters.

I understand that the caravan of Mr. Ashe is being dispersed. I hope to obtain several of his porters ... I am becoming concerned about being able to recruit sufficient numbers. My only hope is that the Sultan will support me, following my audience with him. Someone here seems to have spoken to him against me.

Miss Sheldon arrived here today from the mainland. She has been very sick. She was being carried aboard the steamer, even as I was learning something of her travels. I continue to attempt to enrol some of her porters, with the help of Bonstead, her agent.

Mr. Ashe, having been unable to pay an advance exceeding two months' wages to his porters – they had asked for three months – they tore up their contracts and are again on the market. If I began to hire them, however, there would be a terrible row, missionaries being able to do as they please. [Yet] the men are eager to join me – they would be better paid.

Smith has presented me, along with Bonchamps and Moloney, to His Highness the Sultan ...*

♦   ♦   ♦

---

*Seyyid Ali bin Said succeeded Seyyid Khalifa bin Said as Sultan of Zanzibar on 13 February 1890 and reigned for three years. Seyyid Khalifa bin Said had succeeded Seyyid Bargash on 27 March 1888 and had reigned for less than two years.

20 June

Recruitment goes well, but the men are largely those whom Mr. Ashe refused to accept and who might yet opt to go with him. It wouldn't surprise me if I might still lose them.

Johnston's men are enrolled for two years, with the title of police agent. Their salary is at least fifteen rupees a month, plus food. Johnston has with him eight horses, two 9-bore guns, a mountain cannon, 600 Sniders, a hundredweight of cloth, £100 in silver coin, postal material, a safe, seeds, a Customs officer, and an officer of the Royal Engineers. At the expense of the British government, the S.S. *Juba* will carry them to Quelimane [on the African coast near the mouth of the Zambesi]. There all the goods will be transferred to two sternwheeler gunboats on the Zambesi. In that way they will be in the Shiré itself. With the gunboats making two trips, Johnston's loads should be north of Lake Nyassa by 27 July.

At 1600, I went with Nicol for a [second] audience with the Sultan. I explained to His Highness the purpose of my expedition. I asked him to support me in my recruiting efforts and to give me letters calling upon the people of Karema, Rua, Itawa and Katanga to assist me. I have also invited him to write to the Consul [Smith] to assist me in the recruitment of porters.

The Sultan promised me the letters I sought.

♦   ♦   ♦

22 June

Several of Ashe's former porters simply did not show up this morning. The number recruited to date is about 220, of which perhaps 150 will actually go with me.

23 June

... I recruited today sixteen or eighteen from among those who crossed the continent with me on the Emin Pasha Relief Expedition.

24 June

I hope to send 150 men [to the mainland] Saturday, having obtained the Consul's permission to embark them at the wharf of Smith, Mackenzie and Co. I have 300 men enrolled, of whom I estimate only 200 have any real intention of working. Bonstead, Ridley & Co. are experiencing difficulties in forwarding my rice to Mpwampwa. As always, it is a problem of porters.

♦   ♦   ♦

26 June
I loaded our supplies on two dhows and made the arrangements for the embarkation of our men tomorrow morning.

27 June
At 07:15 a.m. I formally enrolled our men. At 11:00, 175 were assembled before the Sultan's palace and subsequently in the courtyard of Smith, Mackenzie where they received four months' advance pay. They then boarded the dhows. Dr. Moloney commanded one, Bonchamps the second and Bedoe, my former headman, the third. At 7:15 a.m. the dhows [with 205 men aboard] sailed from Zanzibar for Bagamoyo.

While I was paying the wages in advance, I learned to my consternation that the steamer, the *Henry Wright*, had let us down. I had counted on it going direct from Mombassa to Dar-es-Salaam to collect Bodson and his men and to leave them at Bagamoyo. Now Bodson will not arrive in Bagamoyo until 2:30 p.m. Sunday at the earliest.

The intrigues, the filth, the stench and the confusion which were everywhere evident when the men were enrolled was unbelievable. To complete such a dreadful task, one needed many a pipeful of tobacco and much patience.

I wired Bodson and the [German] commandant at Bagamoyo. I expect Customs difficulties there....

♦   ♦   ♦

29 June
I have succeeded in recruiting several more men; I still need fifty more.

Smith [the British vice-consul] has asked that I see him. He showed me a telegram from the Foreign Office, enquiring whether the refusal of the Sultan to allow me to enrol slaves was an obstacle to my departure.* I answered that for the moment it was not an obstacle, but that the prohibition had proven to be tiresome and time-consuming. The prohibition had entailed an additional expense of £300 and had delayed my departure by a fortnight. I now hope to leave here on Wednesday.

I have unpacked the *Bluenose* and prepared it to be embarked tomorrow on a dhow. The German Consul tells me that von Soden has arranged for our goods to be received at Bagamoyo.

---

*Stairs was evidently prepared to recruit slaves while the parallel Belgian expedition of Captain Jacques had been sent to help suppress the slave trade.

How many improvements must still be made in Zanzibar! The Customs, the police and the army must all be reformed, the coastal shipping should be licensed, and order needs to be maintained everywhere. Portal, when he arrives, may perhaps be able to improve things.*

The *Bluenose* carries 13 loads, the *Dorothy*, 12 ...

30 June
I have been able to recruit several more men, but what a tedious business this recruiting is!

1 July 1891
My 28th birthday. I'm beginning to get old. I hope, during the next two years, to be able to do some good work for others and for myself.

I sailed from Zanzibar [for Bagamoyo] about 2:00, after much difficulty and after having spent a total of seventeen days in Zanzibar.

I have received letters from the Foreign Office, enclosing copies of orders to both Smith and Johnston to assist me. It's a little late to-day for that to be of much help.

We arrived at Bagamoyo at 9:00. I stayed with my officers at the house of... the Indian who is my agent on the coast.**

2 July
Dozens of caravans are leaving for the interior. Numerous columns of Wanyamwezi arrive almost every day.

The Germans have passed onto me bad news from Karema. It seems that the Arabs have expelled the French Fathers. If that is true, what a blow! The cloth, which I forwarded to Karema, will no doubt be missing when I call there to collect it.

3 July
... I expect to begin tomorrow.

---

*Sir Gerald Portal (1858-94) was appointed consul general in Zanzibar in 1891, following his service in Egypt and Abyssinia. After successfully urging a British protectorate in Uganda, he died in Zanzibar in 1894, age thirty-six.

**Although Stairs does not mention it, he also saw Emin's daughter Ferida in Bagamoyo.

Chapter Eighteen

By the first days of July 1891, Stairs had concluded that no additional porters could be recruited in either Zanzibar or Bagamoyo. After a final effort at organizing its supplies, the expedition began its long trek inland following the now well-established route to Tabora and then on to Lake Tanganyika.

4 July
The caravan departed at 9:00 and I followed at 12:15.
    Tippoo Tib arrived this morning. I gave him the letters ... from Sir John Kirk. He in turn gave me letters for Tabora and Ujiji.*

---

*Stairs's diary entry about his encounter with Tippu Tib is remarkably laconic. In writing his journal primarily for *La Compagnie du Katanga*, he may have had good reason not to rehearse the circumstances regarding Tippu Tib's journey to Zanzibar. He was there to defend himself in the consular court against Stanley's charge of fraud (which Stanley had brought partly to divert attention away from himself and the rear column débâcle). Eventually Stanley withdrew his charge.
Moloney offers a little more detail about their encounter with Tippu Tib. When asked his opinion of Stanley, Tippu Tib not surprisingly answered that "his shortcomings on the score of veracity were notorious ... In fact, Tippoo Tib considered that Mr. Stanley's unpopularity would endanger his life were he to return to the Congo; and even at Zanzibar he might run some risk of assassination" (*With Captain Stairs*, p. 35). Frederick Jackson (later Sir Frederick Jackson, governor of Uganda), who travelled extensively

I saw Schmidt [von Soden's lieutenant] and received two letters from von Soden for [German] stations in the interior. I also had a conversation yesterday with ... Stokes.

My men total 304 porters, 30 *askari*, 16 servants and 9 headmen. As always when a *saffari* is first on the road, there is confusion. In a few days I hope that Bodson and Bonchamps will have become more knowledgeable about their tasks. For the moment, they are a little green, but they are both full of good intentions, which is the main thing. I wired to Nicol to say that we had left the coast.

A large number of Wanyamwezi come and go each day along the route which seems peaceful. Unfortunately, everyone agrees that food is scarce. The portable German steamer destined for Lake Victoria Nyanza is to be sent along the route in a few days. Some of its components weigh up to 500 lbs. I hear that a [German] officer is to go in advance to get food for the porters.

Mr. Ashe will soon set out from Pangani.

5 July

This morning it took no less than 2¼ hours to get the caravan in marching order. Abundant patience is necessary so as to ensure that one does not lose either one's head or one's judgement. Everyone is still new and not yet up to his task. My greatest worry is desertions. Between here and Mpwapwa, I expect at least fifty men deserters. These men tire easily – and get blisters on their feet. Besides, it's easy for them to return to Bagamoyo. Many porters have no other role in life other than to sign up with a caravan to obtain the advance pay and then desert to the squalid back alleys of Bagamoyo. I attempt to instruct the new men and to feed them all as well as possible.

The real route to Katanga is not this one, but rather via either the Zambesi or the Congo.

We crossed by ferry the River Lufu, a crossing that took a total of 2 hours and 40 minutes. We established our camp about a half mile to the west, having left behind us all traces of coconut palms and other coastal vegetation. If one were to judge by the appearance of the countryside alone, we might well be in the centre of the continent, for the strip of cultivation along the coast extends only a few miles inland. A letter from H.H. Johnston overtook me today with a

---

in East Africa at that time, recorded the impression which Stanley had left in Zanzibar ... "a man of undoubtedly great courage and determination, but self-centered, overbearing, ruthless and a man who would stick at nothing; not quite the hero he was in Europe and America." See *Early Days in East Africa* (London, 1969), p. 142.

long explanation of why he would not recommend the Nyassa route. Famine reigns there. He cannot, in any case, offer us sufficient transport ....

6 July

Marched at 7:10 for two hours and camped near the marsh where the Emin Expedition had spent its last night before entering Bagamoyo.

Caught a deserter *in flagrante delicto*. He has been put in chains. The threat of desertions hangs over my head, night and day. One is almost powerless to prevent it ...

Quarrels among the men break out all the time. They lack discipline. It will be some time yet before they are up to scratch. The Zanzibari are excessively quarrelsome and shout and talk all at the same time. Imagine the cacophony! When they have been restrained for some time by the discipline of the white man, they change fundamentally, but for the first days following departure from the coast, they could hardly be less disciplined. Add to that the fact that our caravan includes not only Zanzibari but also men from Dar-es-Salaam, Bagamoyo and Mombassa – and all these beauties go at each other like cats and dogs.

7 July

Left camp at 4:50 a.m ... after 2hrs. 40 mins. we made camp. At 10:30 Dr. Moloney arrived and told me that eight loads are still in the camp with Bonchamps, who commands the rearguard. It is the same old story of porters who are badly mismatched and Europeans who overload them with their excessive personal baggage.

During the night another man from Dar-es-Salaam deserted. I shall lose all of them, one after another!

It is strange to see how aggressive, in general, the Zanzibari is toward an inoffensive native. He acts like a bully, but in fact is himself frequently a coward.

Pray that the Jacques expedition doesn't catch up to us or overtake us.* There is no one between Bagamoyo and here: the country is deserted. Those who were living here became fearful of maltreatment and abandoned their huts along the route. Consequently it is impossible to obtain provisions here. German policy should encourage the natives to erect villages along the routes and then guarantee them effective protection. There would then be an abundance of food in no time at all.

Bedoe, my headman, served to with Joseph Thomson in two expeditions ... He was also headman of the caravan of Bishop Hannington when he was

---

*Captain Jacques had not surprisingly decided to follow the same route inland as that proposed by Stairs since it was the most established and direct route.

murdered. Bedoe says that the poor bishop was stubborn to the point of madness. Invariably, he had his tent pitched away from the men so as to avoid the noise of the camp.*

Another of my headmen ... accompanied Stanley on his voyage across the dark continent. He's an active fellow – who will serve me well, I think. Masudi ... was a porter in our last expedition. He's loyal and will keep his men well in hand.

Thank God that I have no more than 21 men from Dar-es-Salaam. They're useless!

Well, here I am again in the midst of a caravan, camping amidst the grasses and the trees, far from the great world and all its bustle. How good it feels! Despite all the worries, difficulties, bad food, and the certainty of fevers, I find this life, for a variety of reasons, vastly superior to that which one lives within the four walls of a barracks.

Three months ago I was at Aldershot, in the company of the best fellows in the world, enjoying their agreeable society, an exquisite special friend and the town nearby. I was not, however, happy in the true sense of the word. I felt that my life was passing while I was doing nothing worthwhile. Now, I travel across the coastal plain with more than 300 men under my orders. My least word is law. I am truly the chief.

Two years in this country, always on the alert on interminable marches, is quite enough, for human nature cannot endure more. I don't think that it's possible to avoid the fevers in this region. Anyone who works as we do everyday in the full sun is likely to succumb, sooner or later, to fever.

8 July

After a two-hour march, we established camp ... By 10:50 everyone had arrived at the camp. It's very good progress.

We have about a dozen sick and lame. The average ratio of the sick to the total is about 5 per cent, but, in a few days, will reach 8 or 9 per cent. It's always the same with those freshly arrived from Zanzibar, still ill at ease with the march and the loads. The cases of illness are ordinarily among the porters, caused by a weakening of their constitution following abuses of all sorts, including their addiction to smoking hemp. It is only after a month of hard work and good nourishment that the poison is expelled from them. Moreover, the least abrasion of the skin can re-open old ulcers imperfectly healed.

Considerable quantities of ivory, quite beautiful, are now on their way towards the coast, coming from the Wanyamwezi, two months from here. By this morning,

---

*James Hannington was the first missionary bishop of East Equatorial Africa and an enthusiastic explorer. He was killed in November 1885 while attempting to enter Buganda from Mombasa.

we have seen almost 1500 tusks, which will net the Germans $14,200 in export duties ...

9 July

... the rearguard arrived at the camp about two hours after the vanguard ... The commanders of the companies have some difficulties with their men whose language and habits they do not yet understand. I myself must speak French with my officers – and I don't know the language. I hope to speak it adequately within three months.

10 July

... Bedoe woke me this morning with the cheerful news that during the night seven of my men from Dar-es-Salaam had deserted, bringing the number of deserters to eleven of the total of twenty-one. So far, in all, a grand total of seventeen desertions.

The most dangerous moment for a caravan is now. Not yet fully accustomed to their duties, the men become stiff, their morale deteriorates and they desert. Not less than a fortnight is required for the muscles of the porters to become both firm and supple.... I do everything that I can to move things along. Beatings and harsh language are forbidden. Our daily stages are short and I am generous in the distribution of *posho* [to buy food]. I hope in that way to advance slowly during the next ten stages. We should thereafter be able to complete daily stages of about eight miles, establishing our camp before noon. Unfortunately, there are still delays and complaints every morning ...

◆   ◆   ◆

12 July

... I had a long and instructive conversation with one of the chiefs of Kisemo. I asked him why he did not plant onions, orange trees or coconut palms, instead of limiting himself to *mtama* [sorghum] and maize. He replied, "God forbid that I plant anything other than *mtama* and *corii*. If I tried anything else, we should all die." How ridiculous! For two hundred years, this has been a frequented place of passage, no more than six hours from the coast, but only the coarsest grains are grown which at Zanzibar would be fed only to donkeys. From the Luvu River to Kisemo, there are no coconut palms, no lemon or orange trees. The Germans have so far succeeded only in planting their flags along the route. There is food here, but it is the same food that one would have found here a century ago. No progress has been realized from the point of view of either quantity or quality.

Here is a small insight into the native character. Mungo ... contracted to carry a bale as far as Kisemo for one rupee. The contract was quite clear and he carried the bale here. I offered him the rupee. After a moment's hesitation, he accepted, but then asked also for four ells of cloth. I refused, but went to the trouble of explaining to him what a contract is. He listened – and then asked for some tobacco. The natives cannot understand that things have a certain value – and no more ...

The local chiefs have come to call on me, sitting for hours outside my tent awaiting any small gift. Time does not matter to them. They might as well squat here as in their villages – although that does not benefit the white man!...

13 July

... I hope to give the sick the opportunity to recover. Three or four are gravely ill ... I am thinking of sending them back to the coast, but that would cost me something since each received $20 in advance ...

After we leave here, I hope that we shall make steady progress, the men having by now become accustomed to the regular march of a caravan. Desertions are not yet as frequent as I had feared, the happy result of our endless vigilance ...

14 July

... At mid-point in our route to-day, we saw for the first time the hills which border on the coastal plain. In two days we shall begin our ascent of those hills and reach the plateau which is about 1,200 feet above sea level ... In the vicinity of our camp is a splendid alluvial plain where one could grow almost anything. Mangoes and coconuts would flourish ... I am told that there were once here at least ten or twelve small villages. [Now there are only three], the result of the war two years ago between the Germans and the Arabs ...

15 July

... Mkoa was once of populous village, but its habitants became terrified by the constant pillages of passing caravans. They abandoned their village and built another two miles to the north. They were afraid of the Soudanese soldiers in the service of the Germans. Their faces reflect their terror when they describe the extortions and raids of those beauties. That does not surprise me, for I doubt if one would find anywhere in the world such brutes as the Soudanese...

◆   ◆   ◆

17 July

... How little Europe understands what is involved in the exploration of Africa! We speak of a route when in reality there is no trace of one. What in other countries is called a road proves here to be no more than a path which leads from one place to another in a tortuous way which is by no means the shortest distance. On these paths one must walk in an "Indian file," the result of which is that our 350 men are strung out over no less than two miles. There is no way for the white man in either the vanguard or the rearguard to be certain how those in the centre are behaving themselves, whether they are sitting down, wandering about, or moving on ahead, for the long grass and the trees generally prevent anyone from seeing ahead for more than 200 or 300 yards.

Every morning I get up at 5:10 a.m. I breakfast as well as I can on the leftovers of the day before, to which I add a cup of tea ... It seems to me more important to fill one's stomach at breakfast than at any other time of the day. During the morning hours one is exposed to the full strength of the sun; it is reasonable that one's belly should then be full. Who could work under the full rays of the sun, without being well fed ...

... On the question of how a caravan marches, more sheer nonsense has been written ... than I can possibly cite. One must first take into account the condition of the men. If a stage is long, one should do it in one go, stopping only once for 45 minutes ... In a stage of twenty miles, for example, if one were to heed the "experts," one should do the first twelve miles, then rest during the heat of midday and complete the remaining miles during the remainder of the afternoon and evening. To do that, however, would be a serious mistake ... during two or three hours of rest, the men would become stiff as logs ...

18 July

... French missionaries invariably choose the best place for their missions, which is more than one can say for the sites chosen by British missionaries. The French fathers do better than ours: they teach the blacks to be carpenters, masons, farmers, cooks, whereas often the British missionaries teach the blacks little more than how to sing hymns ...

19 July

... At our present pace, I'm beginning to worry whether we have enough goods to see us through to Mamboia. Our daily stages are no more than two hours ... Captain Jacques, I fear, will overtake us. We must at all costs keep ahead of him, so that his 500 men do not eat what little food there is in the villages along the way ...

... It is scarcely two months since I left Britain, but it already seems like six ... In the army, one would not do as much in a year. But two years of work is more than enough in the tropics ... My tent is quite comfortable, with a bed, a chair, candles and books to read at night. What a difference from Stanley's journey! We had almost nothing of luxury during those three years. I slept on the ground and dined seated on a box with another box serving as my table.

What a strange life has been mine when I compare it with that of other fellows in the army. I left Canada scarcely twelve years old to attend school in another country. I was then four years in Kingston before spending two years and nine months in the virgin forests of New Zealand ... Then suddenly I found myself in Chatham and London, leading an utterly different life, eating my full, sleeping as much as I wanted, not needing to take any special precautions for my safety, not having to think or work very much. Then suddenly another complete change, from a placid, boring life to one filled with challenge. I crossed Africa with Stanley for three years ... working every day an average of eleven hours and finally reaching the east coast with the feeling that I had accomplished something worthwhile. And then London again and Aldershot with plenty of leisure time and money, dining, dancing and visiting country houses until I grew weary of it all. Then yet another profound change and I find myself to-day back on the road to the heart of darkness [literally, the black centre].

In any case, I certainly have not let the grass grow under my feet: at age 28, I find myself in command of a large expedition, charged with an important mission and all sorts of difficulties to overcome.

There are three things I hope to achieve:

1)   above all, to be successful with regard to Msiri and my work in Katanga;
2)   to discover mines in Katanga that can be exploited; and
3)   to make some useful geographic discoveries west of Lake Tanganyika.

In short, I seek success all along the line, a rapid journey and a return home in good health.

Smith, Mackenzie and Co. should have forwarded mail from Britain ... I like to have news of the great world for as long as I can, but when I know that I can no longer, I don't miss it.

I take great care in making observations of longitude and latitude ...

◆   ◆   ◆

22 July
.... I read last night Cameron's *Across Africa*. He had great difficulty in crossing the same plains that we crossed in five hours. In the floods he had water and mud up to his knees and it took him two days.

[This village] is badly situated. I don't know how one could place a village here, when there are so many excellent sites ready at hand. Only rarely do Africans think of approving their lot: they repeat what their fathers did and their sons and grandsons will do the same ...

23 July
... the only work the people here do during the course of the year is to sow and reap. It's hardly demanding ...

... All these villages are as poor as church mice although with a little effort they could live in some affluence. One thing impresses the newly-arrived European: the length of time it takes to get anything worthwhile from the natives, all the result of their laziness and horror of any work whatever. One single good Zanzibari does more work than fifteen of these lazy villagers. I have gradually concluded that a sound thrashing is the best medicine for the natives ... A good beating would be salutary, for it would show them just how wrong they are in believing that they are the greatest people in the world ...

24 July

... The natives could not be more arrogant ... [but] I have inspired in them a healthy fear. They are among the laziest people that I have ever encountered. ...

25 July

... one of the men ... has deserted ... He has stolen a gun. If I catch him, I shall make such an example of him that others will never have such ideas. The men are well fed, our stages are short, and justice is quick and fair ... in such a case as this, the white man has the moral right to execute deserters ... One gains nothing, and loses much, in handing over to the authorities those who have committed crimes. His comrades will not be present at his salutary execution ...

Unlike whites, there is no diversity among blacks. They lead the same kind of life; eat the same food, and concentrate their thoughts on the same few subjects. The result is that, little by little, they now have the same identical brain. We whites, on the other hand, learn to know so many different countries, inhabited by such varied people and we encounter so many different things that our ideas become as diverse as our characters.

The opinion some travellers have about the east coast Africans is laughable. Their thoughts do not go beyond their daily needs. It follows that they are even incapable of so conducting themselves as to promote their slow evolution toward a higher level of existence. Left to themselves, one would find them in the year 3000 in exactly the same state that they are to-day ... the level of wild, fearful animals.

26 July

... met the caravan of the Rev. Mr. Ashe, headed toward Uganda. He has been 21 days on the route... Greaves, one of his missionaries, has fallen ill ... and has been sent back, dying, to the coast. ... Ashe himself travels by bicycle. If the path is too rough, a black, who hurries along behind him, pushes the bicycle until Ashe can remount. In that way Ashe can arrive at the campsite two hours before his caravan.

I write on the 27th; yesterday I had fever which left me prostrate all day ... I know the symptoms so well ... Robinson is reduced to a shadow of his former self. I'm afraid that he simply cannot stand the climate.

◆   ◆   ◆

28 July

... the Zanzibari boy makes a wretched servant ... In intelligence and abilities he is as far below the hindoo and the Singalese as they are below the white. [He] is often faithful and extraordinarily honest and obedient, but he has no notion whatever of the needs of whites ... The chief boy can frequently be of immense help to the commander of a caravan. He can inform his master of the plots and intrigues which arise among the porters. But rare is the boy who can... offer useful ideas to his master ....

29 July

... the inhabitants of the village fled at our approach. Seeing that, our men began to pillage their huts, stealing dozens of goats, chickens, bows and arrows. This morning I have restored to the owners whatever I have been able to recover and for the remainder I have paid a fair price, which I shall deduct from the wages of the Zanzibari. We shall see whether this has a salutary effect and will put an end to this deplorable practice of plundering ...

30 July

... I climbed up to the British mission to visit Mr. and Mrs. Wood ... Their house and garden are delightfully situated ... Mr. Wood is a remarkable gardener. Thanks to his efforts all sorts of European vegetables grow in his garden. A good man, who has been wonderfully kind to me ... Ashe, it seems, has had the same problems that I have had with thieving porters ...

Wrote my last letters which I gave to [Cyril] Gordon, a missionary from Uganda who passed through here this morning on his return to Britain. Having lived in Africa for nine years, he certainly deserves the rest that awaits him. No news or letters from the coast. Ashe leaves here Monday ...

31 July

... as we were arriving at our camp, we were overtaken by a caravan of about 300 whose chiefs sought my protection, which will increase our total to about 900. I agreed, on the condition that they obey my orders and not steal chickens or grain from the villages.

... In Uganda, Smith, Williams and Lugard were in a fight with the Wanyoro, but Gordon [the C.M.S. missionary] says that they soon had to retreat in the face of the floods which covered the whole area ...*

---

*For a full account of this skirmish, which had occurred three months prior to Stairs's diary entry, see Perham, *Lugard*, vol. I, pp. 254-57, and *Diaries of Lord Lugard*, vol. II, pp. 162-71. Stairs's reference to Williams is to Captain H.W. Williams (1857–1938), who although senior to Lugard in army terms, had volunteered to serve under him; Smith, second-in-command of the column, was not in fact in the skirmish; the

1 August [1891]

... The three Wanyamwezi caravans which are following us arrived an hour or so after us ... They travel peacefully and comfortably, the more affluent among them each having a tent, a cook and women in train. The reason why the Wanyamwezi travel so well is that their wives and daughters follow them, carrying their supplies, their tents and their dishes. When they reach their campsite, the exhausted porters stretch themselves out, light their pipes and chat together while the women cook, cut wood and do all the chores ... Each Wanyamwezi caravan carries a German flag and over each headman's tent is the black, white and red standard ...

2 August

... With a telescope I can make out the German flag flying .. 11 miles from here.

... The natives [here] have pierced ears and hang little iron chains from them. They have bracelets of fine copper wire. Their skin is generally darker than that of the coastal tribes ... It is difficult to be certain of their real colour; they smear themselves with yellow clay ...

... In Britain preparations must be well under way for the "glorious twelfth" [the first day of the annual grouse shoot]. The subalterns at Aldershot see their chance to have some sport, far from bugle calls and their commanding officer. I doubt that I shall ever be able to resume the humdrum life of the barracks. That would be a slow death, an inch at a time. The work does not frighten me; on the contrary, it appeals to me, but life in the mess is awful. Always the same people and the same stale jokes. I loathe hearing the anteroom soldiers apply the term "medal hunter" to those who are not content with an idle military life. It seems to me fifty times more honourable to be a "medal hunter" than to warm one's feet on the hearth bench in an anteroom where one can spend five or six years awaiting promotion, with occasional excursions into town, to balls and to the races. Such an existence is a dreadful waste; no man of action would even consider it.

My ideal existence is English life in the country: a large estate, far from the hurly burly of town, with great lawns soft as velvet on which to play lawn tennis under the shade of great trees ... That's the life I should like to lead during my leave upon returning from Africa. Following my leave, I should like to return to the active life of London, doing something worthwhile.

---

other British with Lugard were the physician, Dr. J.S. Macpherson, and William Grant. Lugard, who had with him two Maxim guns (one of which had been with Stairs), was in Uganda under the direction of Sir Francis de Winton, who had become administrator of the Imperial British East Africa Company's territories. In his travels through Uganda, Lugard was only weeks behind the peripatetic Emin and at one point had in his own train both Shukri Agha and Selim Bey, two of Emin's former lieutenants.

Look at my present life. I command 400 men, with more power and more freedom of decision than a general commanding a division. Without doubt, there are challenges... but also opportunities to distinguish myself. I feel my responsibilities, but I can also breathe freely... one learns what is valuable in life...

3 August
... the earth is as dry as a stick ... The hills which seem endless nearly drive us wild ...

4 August
We arrived at Mpwampwa after a march of 4½ hours. I sent my letter of introduction to Lieutenant von Elpon. I also notified Mr. Price, the C.M.S. missionary, that we had arrived ... As I was going to the [German] fort, I met von Elpon and invited him to my tent where we had a long conversation about African affairs ...

A great number of cattle (4,500 head) have died around Mpwampwa of pulmonary epizootic disease. The unfortunate natives are helpless to do anything about it ...

5 August
... I called upon Mr. Price at his mission ... He forecasts that in three weeks famine will overtake the region. Crops have failed from the prolonged drought ... I called upon von Elpon at the German fort. He kindly gave me a fat sheep which is very welcome.

6 August
... Tomorrow we start across the desert which will take at least twelve hours to cross. It is one of the worst obstacles on our route ... At this time of the year there exists in this region a stretch of about thirty miles where it is simply impossible to obtain even a drop of water. Kisokwe is a station of the Church Missionary Society, but as the mission is situated two miles from our route, I am afraid to risk the burning sun in order to visit Mr. Beverley, the missionary, who, I am told, has been ill recently ...

7 August
Left Kisokwe at 6:00 a.m. ... Everyone has been ordered to fill his gourd and to prepare his food since from noon we shall begin to cross the desert ...

8 August
Left at 5:30 a.m. and following the most difficult march I have ever made in Africa we camped ... at 10:00 a.m.. The heat is stifling and when we finally reached water it was brackish. Many of the men drank endless amounts – and

became ill. At the camp itself, there was fresh water. My men were prostrate from the two days of [desert] march ... I have every sympathy for my men, but among them are thirty who must count as among the laziest and most useless of human beings.

◆   ◆   ◆

10 August

... I buried one man who died of exhaustion and thirst during the crossing, but I consider myself fortunate, for certainly other whole caravans have been destroyed in attempting to cross the desert. ...

... The Arabs have a healthy fear of the Germans. They dare not sell a slave at Bagamoyo ... a great number of the slaves are better fed and better cared for than they are in their own land, where they practise their fetishism and fight endlessly with each other. That the slaves are better fed and treated is true of 90 per cent of the 2,000 slaves whom I have encountered since I left the coast. They were plump and sleek ... It is the slave-hunting which is so diabolical. However, once they have been taken, their fate is better than that of the thousands of "slaves" who live in Christian Britain. I have never seen anyone in Africa in a worse state or in more frightful circumstances than is to be seen in Whitechapel or Liverpool. On the other hand, one encounters here crueller acts and crueller punishments by whipping than one does at home ...

◆   ◆   ◆

12 August

... We are in the heart of Ugogoland ... The Wagogo [tribe] has a bad reputation as caravan thieves. Unlike the Wahehe who set an ambush, knife the laggards and take off with their loads, they enter the camp at night in twos or threes ... stealing whatever they can lay their hands on, particularily rifles ...

◆   ◆   ◆

14 August

... Upon arriving at our campsite, the Wanyamwezi began to loot the village. They stopped only when ... [we] chased them with our sticks. I have threatened their chiefs with banishing them from my safeguard ... they came to me in a body to seek my pardon ... There are more than 900 Wanyamwezi who travel with us. I have a total of 1,350 men under my orders, a small army and more men than I have ever commanded ...

◆   ◆   ◆

16 August

... Most of my men are exhausted by the eleven stages since Mpwampwa, across the parched desert with only bad water and thin rations. It is 85 miles from Mpwampwa here, so we have marched well, considering that we are badly fed, badly supplied with water and encumbered with the sick ...

17 August

... still fifteen stages to Tabora [on Lake Tanganyika]. The boys [servants] on the expedition are a constant disappointment to me. I enrolled two as stewards (or "stewedi" as one says in Zanzibar). They were to be the chief boys, each paid seven dollars monthly. However, one of them is quite incapable of understanding the first thing of how to serve a white ... when they serve at my table they hold the plate in such a way that everything slides off. I have reduced them to $5 per month, the same as the other boys. Fortunately, I have a good cook.

◆   ◆   ◆

18 August

... black and white alike suffer in this intense heat. During the day, the body is overheated; the cold at night makes one shiver and fever follows ...

◆   ◆   ◆

20 August*

... I have no one with whom I can chat. I greatly miss this. I cannot, given my inability to speak French, engage in a sustained conversation with Bodson or Bonchamps. In any case, we differ completely in our ideas. Moloney is a good fellow, but unfortunately has no small talk. It's always a business, when we do talk, to fill an evening. The result is that, outside the hours of work, I live entirely alone. There are moments when I think that my brain will shrink from the absence of any companion with whom I can discuss anything ... I am able to take pleasure in reading at night, but I cannot during the day.... I pass my days in isolation. This manner of life, I know, makes me self-centred and narrow, but it is imposed by the need to take constant care and to behave sensibly. For

---

*On 20 August 1891 Stairs again crossed the route of the Emin Relief Expedition, but he did not record the occasion, although in a letter of 8 September 1891 to Brussels, he sensed the precarious position in which Emin had placed himself. "I hear that Emin Pasha is still working northward and is now in English territory. I fancy he is on his way to claim for Germany all that territory which lies to the northwest of the Congo Independent State. He is poorly armed and has but little ammunition left."

example, if I took my meals with the other Europeans, we would soon quarrel over trifles ... *

21 August
... Towards the end of the afternoon, Chief Mgogo [of the Wagogo] arrived, after I had twice sent for him. I spoke harshly first to him and then to his followers. I told him that he was a thief and a coward who attacks the weak caravans of the Arabs or Wanyamwezi, extorting from them 200 or 300 dotis in the name of *hongo* ... I added that soon the Germans would send a hundred soldiers who would take over the Makengi territory and at the same time kill "all thieves of any sort." I told him that when one of my men steals a *single* chicken your woman wail and your men shout for a half hour. Then the following day when the chicken is returned along with some cloth, you promptly attack a poor Wanyamwezi caravan. You are not men, you Wagogo ... Try stealing my goods and I shall shoot you like rats.

This warning seemed to make a great impression ... With people of this sort, there is no remedy but a complete thrashing and confiscation of all their goats and chickens. That may seem hard, but it is necessary ... Africa is an immense continent, peopled by an enormous number of tribes who differ greatly from one another in their practices, appearance, what they wear, their ideas and languages. Some among them have a rough idea of justice, of what is yours and what is mine. Others are simply fierce savages, without any culture whatever, living like animals, incapable of understanding anything but the most elementary ideas and acting invariably on the principle that might is right ...

The former, given time and with a strong government of whites, can be made into competent farmers ... on the other hand, the lazy tribes, the vicious and savage ... will remain into the next century in a state similar to that in which they have lived for the past five centuries ... They will never rise above that level and will remain ignorant savages. They will finally disappear to make room for tribes better disciplined, more active and stronger who will eventually resolve the question of the future of the black continent ...

... We speak too quickly about the African native, too superficially and with too many generalizations. One should study a tribe or a race before judging them and one should analyse them in detail so as to base oneself on a sure foundation before one pontificates on the subject of the African.

22 August
... my caravan now totals 2,250. Our campsite covers more than eleven acres. Perhaps I shall never again have so many men under my command ... There is

---

*Stairs may have adopted from Stanley this practice of dining alone although he had earlier deprecated his example (see his diary entry for 7 September 1887).

no satisfaction on earth that can compare with commanding so many of my fellow men in a good cause.

... The uneducated and uncivilized black understands nothing of a nature of a contract. It is the same with the Arabs. A contract negotiated in good faith and form, duly witnessed and understood clause-by-clause by both blacks and whites, is signed. If, as is possible, the contract no longer appears convenient to the black, he will without hesitation violate it and let things go. If, on the contrary, he finds that all is well and that he is benefitting from the contract, he refuses to understand why, in his turn, the white may want to cancel it. In reality, many blacks think that everything is there to take and nothing to give.

Too much has been written about the good nature of the black. He certainly has many admirable qualities: cheerful, seldom vindictive and with many amusing sides to his character. In general, however, one can hardly see him as that paragon of virtues described by some travellers ...

Europeans when they return home judge the continent with pessimism ... But the optimists who describe with a golden pen more things than they have seen, who multiply a hundred head of cattle until they become thousands, who depict the country as somewhere everyone can live and flourish, those should be condemned by all who love truth ... Africa is like any other country: there are good places and bad, fertile areas and arid. In such a country, the white, if wise and prudent, will prosper; otherwise he will be overcome by fever and will not in several centuries be able to create a viable community.

With a good administration and a true sense of purpose, with railways and roads to the coast, enormous regions could be exploited and produce great wealth while enriching themselves ... It is important that we all be prudent in our descriptions, for if we overdo it, people may base themselves on our descriptions and risk losing all their capital and even their lives.

◆   ◆   ◆

25 August

... Yesterday, upon arriving at our campsite, I sat myself beside the water holes and watched, out of curiosity, while a thousand people came to draw water. What any interesting study of African manners! About dusk 300 Wanyamwezi arrived and threw themselves into the puddles of water that were supposed to slake our thirst. The result was that the water was disturbed, the mud came to the surface and changed the waterholes into mud baths. No more than 30 or 40 of our people were able to get enough water to satisfy their thirst ...

I have often noticed that if the blacks strive hard to meet their individual needs, it is only rarely that they work one for another, unless they see some personal profit in doing so. There does not exist with them any central power which obliges them to work for the common good. All will work together to build a *boma* for the common defence or to plant a crop, but if a water hole needs to be cleaned, who can be bothered? They simply dig a new one.

A tree is across the path at the entrance to a village, but who will remove it? No one. Everyone passes around it until the tree finally rots away. The women will take some of the wood to burn and the white ants ... will dispose of the remainder. Or take the example of a large branch of a tree which hangs over a path which forces the porters to stoop and to carry their loads in that position at great exertion – and even at some danger. A caravan of 3,000 Wanyamwezi will pass under the branch, each porter lowering his head and his load, when it would have been a simple matter for the man at the head of the column to clear away the obstacle with three or four blows of his hatchet. But for that to be done, a white man or an Arab must be there – it would never occur to a native.

♦   ♦   ♦

26 August
Arrived at the village of Chief Kwawamba following a march of 1¾ hours. In the distant on a small hill I noticed amidst some palm trees ... giraffes stretching their long necks to see us pass ...

27 August
... I have tried, during my leisure hours, to write some verse. I certainly have not achieved anything notable, but if I have been able to analyse faithfully the changing lights and shadows of the daily life of an African expedition, I shall have realized a long-held goal ...

28 August
... Tomorrow we must *tirika*: sleep in the bush without water ... an eleven hour march almost twenty miles from here to the next water. A camp without water worries me, for on the following day, the men are good for nothing ...

29 August
We have marched twenty kilometres in five hours and fifty minutes. We passed the place where poor Carter was killed several years ago* ... Our camp is near the Lake Cheia which at the moment is simply a parched expanse without a

---

*On a trek from Zanzibar to Karema, Thomas Carter, a British army officer in the employ of Leopold's *Association International Africaine*, had vainly attempted to introduce Indian elephants and their mahouts to Africa. Carter was killed in 1881 with another Englishman, Tom Cadenhead, when they blundered into a tribal war.

drop of water. I sent natives on ahead to search for water ... they report only empty wells, surrounded by decomposing buffaloes, giraffes, and antelopes, all dead from thirst. Extraordinary as it is for this region, there is also the corpse of an elephant upon whose putrid flesh the Africans feed ...

30 August
Marched from 5:15 a.m. until 10:15 a.m., when we arrived at Itura with my caravan dying of thirst and exhaustion. In the wells there was no more than a small ribbon of water. An Arab whose caravan preceded ours assured the natives along the route that we rob the natives. The result is that only with the greatest difficulty have I been able to buy any food. And to think how kind and courteous I have been to the Arabs ...

31 August
... 6½ hours of march to cover fifteen miles. We camp amidst the brush, tired beyond description and without water. Tomorrow we shall reach water after a 2½ hour march, but the following day there is a wasteland of fifteen miles to Rubuga.

This morning I sent letters to the German commandant at Tabora, to the local chief and to eight or nine of the principal Arabs ... I asked the German to provide a campsite for my caravan. As we approach Tabora I fear increasingly the desertions of more of my men. These long marches without water terrify them and I sense that they would prefer to desert than to continue in such conditions ... The hardships and the weariness cause me such endless cares ... that I have become as thin as a rail and my cheekbones stand out in my face ...

Chapter Nineteen

By 1 September 1891 the expedition had finally left behind the drought stricken land to the east of Lake Tanganyika. It crossed the watershed dividing the rivers that flow eastward to the Indian Ocean and those that flow westward to Lake Tanganyika or the Congo. Eight days later the expedition reached Tabora, the Arab slavers' town which marked the northernmost point of its route before it descended toward Lake Tanganyika. Moloney describes the "habits" of Tabora as "those of pillage and general lawlessness," but the arrival of a small German force six months before Stairs had imposed rudimentary order.

The day before entering Tabora, the Belgian Anti-Slavery Expedition, led by Captain Jacques and two other Belgian officers, overtook Stairs's expedition. The two expeditions marched together into Tabora where they remained together until Stairs departed for Lake Tanganyika on 21 September.

Moloney, with wry humour, describes how Arabs who travelled alongside the expedition were carrying powder and arms for the Manyuema who collaborated with them in their slaving, while the Jacques' expedition had been organized to suppress slaving:

... one of the caravans travelling with us, carried two hundred rifles and ten barrels of gunpowder, destined for the Manyuema country. Yet, immediately behind them marched Captain Jacques, on a mission for the suppression of slavery, which might necessitate close acquaintance with those very weapons of war. If the nigger entertains a latent sense of humour, he must be vastly tickled by these strangely contradictory products of our much-vaunted civilization. And if officials, for the sake of revenue, persist in winking at these wholly illegal importations [of arms], how can the [European] Powers escape, not only the charges of cant and avarice, but – what is far more calculated to produce amendment – some crushing military disaster?[1]

Stairs was not amused. He reported to Brussels on 8 September 1891 that

powder is passing fully into the *Etat Independant*. Captain Jacques marches with his anti-slavery expedition while one camp ahead of him marches Shadolia the Beloochee [sic] with over 1,800 pounds of powder ... chiefly of course to promote and further the slave trade. It is simply ridiculous that this sort of thing should go on. Anti-slavery societies and powder importers are things that will not work together in this country.

Stairs fails to record that from 19 September to mid-October he was constantly ill, suffering so badly from haematuric fever that he had to be carried in hammock or on a donkey. Moloney was increasingly concerned about the long-term prospects for Stairs's health.

1 September [1891]
... the river here has become no more than a trickle, as a result of the drought ... [but] thank heaven we found enough water to match our thirst, cook our food and even wash ourselves and our clothes. It is the first time since leaving Bagamoyo that we have drunk water from a river which flows into the Congo and thence into the Atlantic Ocean ...

There has been no rain for 65 days and apparently water is scarce even at Tabora. We left Bagamoyo 59 days ago, of which we marched 52 days, an average of about ten miles a day. An excellent pace. The Arabs who accompany us have been on the march for 85 days.

2 September
A seven hour march, camped near fresh water.* ... I caught a porter who had deserted with a tool box ... which contained the wrenches for my boat's bolts, some of the bolts themselves and all my tools. I have not slept from worry about whether my boat would become useless. Learning from this experience, I have now distributed my eggs among several baskets. I remain concerned that as we approach Tabora, porters will desert, taking with them bales to sell

---

* Moloney's account is different. "... just as we were pitching tents after a long day's march, Captain Stairs decided that the *saffari* must proceed again, as the water was undrinkable. Whereupon Gallic indignation [presumably Bodson's] waxed uncontrollable – if this was Stanley's training the less said of it the better; never had an expedition been arranged in such a careless manner; men ought to have been sent ahead and so forth. However, Stanley or no Stanley, we had to tramp until 2:30 p.m., and then halted in a plain without an atom of shade" (*With Captain Stairs*, p.105). Perhaps it was this type of incident which Moloney had in mind when he spoke of "unnecessary friction on the Stairs expedition" (p.16).

in Tabora. That being so, I watch them like a hawk and have organized a network of informers who are continually on watch ...

3 September
... I have received a letter from Captain Jacques who tells me that he has had much trouble along his route, including several skirmishes.

There is a crowd of porters available in Tabora ... Many are deserters by profession. They seek to be employed, then once employed they disappear into the *pori* [jungle] with their load ... and become rich without doing any work. Their thievery enables them to live for a month like game cocks and then they start their little tricks again.

I plan to remain in Tabora for ten days to rest my men and make up for the desertions that I foresee. I've chained two deserters who were caught red-handed. ... The Germans should make a clean sweep through here.

4 September
... Emin Pasha is now in Rwanda, south of Lake Albert Nyanza ... His geographical discoveries should be most interesting ... *

5 September
The "Arabs" of Africa are not those tall, well-built, open, athletic fellows one reads about in books ... No more than 5 per cent have ever mounted a camel and all are very poor shots. They cannot sustain a long march and are decidedly inferior to whites in this regard.**

6 September
... camped five miles from Tabora.*** Couriers brought me a letter from the German commandant of the station ... everything is ready for our arrival...

---

*Stairs does not note that one year before, in the autumn of 1890, Emin on his ill-fated journey inland had passed through Tabora, raising the German flag over the town, although he had not been asked to do so. Presumably the Germans or Arabs would have told Stairs, if he did not already know it, of Emin's passage, but throughout his Katanga diaries he seldom mentions him, and then only fleetingly.

**Moloney, but not Stairs, records that on the evening of 5 September the expedition had a brisk skirmish with natives who had attempted an ambush.

***Tabora had been visited by Livingstone, Speke, Burton, and Grant. It was there that Verney Cameron, leading an expedition sent by the Royal Geographic Society to succour Livingstone, had in September 1873 learned of the great missionary's death.

7 September

Arrived at Tabora at 9:50 a.m. ... I went to see Baron von Sigl [Sigel], the German commandant. Alone here, he has a hard time with the Arabs ...

Yesterday Captain Jacques [and his expedition] caught up with us. He's a splendid fellow, healthy and strong.

◆   ◆   ◆

11 September

I am ready to leave. My men are becoming demoralized by drinking so much *pombe*. Several of my boat porters haven't eaten any solid food since we arrived here. Sigl and [the local Arab chief] get along well. Both are tactful and patient men doing their best to keep the lid on things. Sigl has a difficult task here, but he's equal to it. He's a congenial fellow, knowledgeable about African life.

... All the Arabs want to know the purpose of my expedition. I believe that they organize a large caravan to follow in our tracks with the purpose of plundering the region west of Lake Tanganyika. They see us as clearing the way for them and, by our own high standards, leading the natives along the way to believe that the Arabs' caravan is as peaceful as ours.

12 September

Sigl has somehow managed to maintain order here. Before his arrival, there was an average of forty murders a month; now there are only two or three. If he were to leave, everything would fall apart.

Tomorrow we are on our way again.

13 September

At 6:45 a.m. I saw the expedition depart Tabora. I remained behind until 10 in an effort to recover four deserters...

As a result of the recent pulmonary epizootic disease, all the hyenas have died from eating the infected carcasses ... This terrible epidemic has at least delivered the villages from the hyenas which stole the goats and sheep and terrified the villagers. The hyenas in any case are not needed here to eat the human cadavers that are thrown into the bush. Ants and insects take care of that.

14 September

... in general, the Arabs, especially those of the interior, regard us as fools. In twenty-five years they will have changed their opinion. The most respected people in all of East Africa are the Germans. They have shown both Arabs and blacks their superiority in arms and inspired in them that fear which is the beginning of wisdom...

15 September
... The natives hereabouts are hostile ... without the presence of the Germans in Tabora, we would have been attacked ... They are cowards, yet for the sake of one or two bales of cloth, they will attempt an attack. We must pass through a bad *pori*. I expect to be attacked by the more aggressive natives hoping to get cloth ...

◆   ◆   ◆

17 September
... in our tents there is two inches of sand and the temperature is 93°F ...

18 September
... In Africa the only cause of war is simply fear. If I hadn't sent ahead messages to the local natives that I did not intend to attack them, they would have all fled into the bush upon my approach. Later they would have prowled around our camp and, upon seeing my men return laden with food, would have attacked them and perhaps killed two or three. Naturally, our men would have responded in kind and the fighting would have begun in earnest. If the natives leave us alone, they have nothing to fear. My men will not steal from them. They have been well trained and fear punishment if they steal. I have no patience with deserters or thieves ... certain of our Zanzibari are frightful cowards and only steal from the natives when they are certain the natives are intimidated ...

19 September
... Some of my headmen are the worst old women that I have ever seen. I shall demote several and replace them with more dynamic fellows.

Robinson, my servant, has fever, as do seventeen of my men ... I shall have it soon too.

Our men now know that we are going to Msiri's. I expect that there will be desertions at Mpala.

◆   ◆   ◆

21 September
... Many men down with fever caused by the terrible heat ...

22 September
... 37 cases of fever. From 7:30 a.m. to 3:50 p.m., the sun is blinding and even at night the heat is stifling ... Unless there is some shade, the porters lie on the ground and gasp like fish out of water. They consume enormous amounts of water which, since it is frequently contaminated, gives them violent fevers ...

During the last week of September it was evident that Stairs was seriously ill with fever. Moloney became increasingly concerned.

On the 24th we all implored him to suspend the march for a day or two, so as to give himself a chance of recovery; but the only answer to be obtained was, "I have undertaken to reach Karema on the 9th of October, and on that day I intend to be there." Next day his debility was extreme, and he had to be carried in a hammock by four men. This condition of comparative inactivity became unendurable to him on the 26th; and he informed me that he intended to leave the hammock after the morrow at all risks, and march with the caravan, as people "played about" in his absence. Certain it was that, directly his watchful eye was removed, everybody began to take matters easily; and the start, which should have been at six o'clock, was frequently delayed until 6:30. According to his determination, he mounted his donkey on the 28th, and gradually began to mend. At the same time, I could see that his constitution was far less robust than he imagined, and that prolonged exertion would probably result in a breakdown. Unfortunately he was generally at high pressure, keenly ambitious of the expedition's success, and unable, therefore, to rest satisfied, unless acquainted with the smallest detail. If the hackneyed expression, "a martyr to duty," can be applied to any man, it can be used without fear of contradiction of Captain Stairs.[2]

27 September
At 4:30 p.m. messengers arrived from Karema [on Lake Tanganyika]... They gave me a letter from Father Camille Randabel of 22 September (five days ago), telling me that he had received my letter of 19 September and that he will do all that he can to assist me. Father Randabel promises me three boats to go to Captain Joubert's south of Mpala. He says that Rumaliza has laid waste the whole area to the north-west of Lake Tanganyika and is preparing to do the same to the south. Rumaliza was about to attack Joubert when he learned of our approach and that of Captain Jacques. That was enough to keep him in the north ... I have sent a messenger to Captain Jacques.

◆   ◆   ◆

29 September
... I have six headmen who give good service; the rest are not worth much. As soon as they are out from under the eye of a white man, they dawdle about or hide themselves among their men. Here it is certainly not as in India. There they have native NCOs who do the really hard work while the European sleeps in his tent or bungalow. Here the white man must himself supervise the work and oversee its completion if he wants things to go forward well and rapidly.

◆   ◆   ◆

2 October [1891]

We reached Gongwe ... The village, where we pitched our tents, was once a
lively, populous place but is now poor and almost deserted, thanks to the war
launched by Kasogera who lives a day away ... He ... breached the stockade,
killed more than 100 men, carried off 100 women and 70 cattle ... [and] sold most
of the women into slavery at Umkaila from where they were sent on to Tabora
to be sold to the Arabs. That was the real reason for the war. Kasogera needed
to have slaves to sell so that he could buy cloth. Gongwe is in a pitiful state.
The thatched huts have been burned. The chief, in effect, camps in his own
village.*

♦   ♦   ♦

5 October

... I wanted to camp near a pond about two miles back, but when we arrived
there, we found only stinking mud and dead fish.

♦   ♦   ♦

8 October

... This march has been the most difficult since we left the coast. We sank into
the sand and crossed over sharp stones taken from a river bed ... From my tent,
I am able to see the blue mountains which border Lake Tanganyika ...

As we near the lake, the landscape changes. Instead of *pori* with its short
grass and large trees, we are crossing hills, dotted with shrub, and through
valleys with tall mimosas, and acacias and long, dry grass. The terrain is
intersected by streams and rocky ravines which, in the rainy season, are
transformed into torrents that empty into the Kifume and from it into the lake.
The natives are few and poor ...

*On 9 October the expedition reached the eastern shore of Lake Tanganyika. A long,
narrow lake, it was only about twenty miles across. A steamboat owned by missionaries
was on the lake, but it was at the south end to meet the commissioner of the British
Central African Protectorate, H.H. Johnston. All that Stairs had available to take his
expedition across the lake were his two portable steel boats and a few crude dhows or
sailing canoes.*

---

*The chief had executed sixteen captives and placed their heads on poles throughout the
remnants of his village. Moloney proclaimed himself shocked by this practice; presumably he did not know that Stairs had done the same on the Emin Relief Expedition.
See Stairs's diary entry for 21 August 1888.

9 October

We broke camp at 5:45 a.m.. We first saw Lake Tanganyika about 9:00. About ten minutes later, I entered [Father Randabel's] mission station at Karema where I was warmly welcomed ... I drank happily of the lake water, which seemed like nectar after the muddy filth upon which we have existed for so long. We rejoiced at the sight of this vast stretch of blue water ... I immediately began to make arrangements to cross the lake.

At 10:50 p.m., I embarked 110 men and 60 loads in three canoes for the camp of Captain Joubert at Mount Rumbi on the opposite side of the lake, a little to the north, 25 or 30 miles distant. One boat returned with a bad leak ... One of the boats took 33 men and 14 sailors plus 69 loads, which gives a good idea of their capacity. I have been able to use the priests' boats as a result of sending a courier ahead when we were in Tabora – which means that the caravan has not been delayed.

Captain Joubert has two boats on the opposite shore. One of the missionaries has gone over to Mount Rumbi to bring them over. Then I shall have a total of five boats to transport both my men and those of Captain Jacques. He should be here in three days. At this time of the year, the return journey takes five days. The best moment to embark is midnight. One rows until dawn. With the dawn comes a S.S.W. wind which pushes one along to Mount Rumbi or Mpala where one arrives at dusk ... The width of the Lake at Karema is about 23 miles.

The missionaries have given us a standing invitation to dine with them. How good it was to taste again fresh vegetables and European bread ...

10 October

At 8:00 this morning I sent away the boat that had sprung a leak. The wind being good, it was out of sight within three hours. ... The boats are made from tree trunks from the shore opposite. The sides of the hollowed out trunk are raised by nailing rough planks together ... The oars are poor; they consist simply of a stout stick, with a spade-like paddle nailed to the end. I've sent my own oars with the Marquis de Bonchamps to see whether they wouldn't be more useful to the men than their own wretched contrivances. The mast is no better; the rigging is for a dhow.

Captain Joubert is the only white man [across the lake] at Mount Rumbi, but there are four [White] Fathers at Mpala and as many again at Kibanga, seven days north of Mpala on the western shore.

... My letter to Swan [Alfred Swann], who is at the south end of the lake, should have reached him three days ago. I sought the use of his steamer which could carry all my men across in a total of six days, whereas I shall now spend twelve days to do so. I won't launch my two [portable] boats on the Lake since the waves are strong and their steel is thin ... The waters of Lake Tanganyika are fresh and clear, better than those of Lake Victoria and far superior to the brackish water of Lakes Albert and Edward.

I employed a guide to-day to take us to Msiri's ... I estimate the distance to be about 35 days.

11 October

... Nothing could surpass the generosity of the [White] Fathers. They go out of their way to help us. They have given us a standing invitation to all meals. Every day at noon I go to their station which is about a half-mile from our camp. I lunch with them and remain there generally until about 3 in the afternoon, when the temperature begins to decline a little. Nevertheless, I am eager to be on my way across the lake, for my men become remarkably demoralized by remaining in camp with nothing to do ...

Father Randabel gave me to-day a fibre that looks like flax but is found only at the northwest side of the lake. It would make excellent cloth. Randabel has sown some seeds and given me some which I shall take to Europe ...

The men have had a great dance ... I like them to dance for it distracts them from other subjects. Idle hands make for mischief, especially in camp ...

12 October

I had one of the [two steel] boats assembled this morning and ventured out on the lake to test it...

13 October

At 9:00 a.m. I received a letter from Swan [sic] in reply to the one that I wrote him from Tabora. It is dated 4 October 1891 from Kimyamkdo, ... the southernmost point of Lake Tanganyika. My messengers returned after three weeks: nine days to get there, two days there and nine days to return. Swan, in answering my request for his steamer to carry my men across the lake, regrets that he is unable to bring it to me as there is no one to take charge of his station in his absence ...

At 2:00 p.m. I was pleased to see one of the boats arrive back from Mount Rumbi. Bonchamps sent me a letter reporting that all is well, although the boats were too heavily laden and had taken in much water ...

14 October

... To date, we have sent across the Lake a total of 140 men and 120 loads ...

... Our guide and I have estimated that there are 25 stages, or one month, between Joubert's camp and Msiri's ...

At 7:30 this evening, after much difficulty, I was able to dispatch the boat that had arrived this morning ... After midnight the third boat arrived and, within forty minutes, I was able to send it off ...

15 October
... We have now been here for a full five days. I expect that we'll be here for another five or six before all our people are across the lake ...

Chapter Twenty

The expedition took the second fortnight of October 1891 to cross to the west (or Congo Free State) side of Lake Tanganyika. Stairs's immediate goal was the station of one Captain Joubert, a former French soldier of fortune who had become a sort of lay missionary, living for the past twelve years among the peoples on the western shore (Joubert had a camera, but no trace remains of the photographs which he took of Stairs's arrival.)

Captain Jacques's expedition overtook Stairs near Lake Tanganyika and again travelled with it. On 31 October Stairs led his expedition out of Joubert's station to begin the third and final stage of its long march to Msiri's capital of Bunkeya.

17 October
Jacques's caravan arrived this morning. He is taking only a few *askari* with him across the lake. His porters are being paid off here.

Days are passing rapidly, but I have been unable to accelerate the lake crossing of my expedition. One feels absolutely powerless. For 48 hours the wind has blown from the south which prevents any of my boats returning from the west side of the lake ...

18 October
Captain Jacques and his officers, Father Randabel and another missionary visited me to-day. Randabel, who is the Superior of the mission station, is a delightful fellow and I understand his French perfectly. He loves the natives, but hates the Arabs and would like nothing better than to drive them from the country. They are, by their immoral examples, the very contrary of the teachings of the missionaries.

... It will still take four boatloads to complete the crossing. A total of eight trips have already been made. I hope to complete the crossing by Wednesday [21 October].

19 October
I caught three big fish this morning. Two ... weighed about 40 lbs. each. The third was smaller, weighing nine or ten pounds ... A most curious fish, spotted yellow and green, and with a bullet-shaped head and jutting teeth. It is fun to fish, for it runs like a salmon ... In places the lakeshore is covered with shells thrown up by the waves ...

20 October
... Captain Jacques is an intelligent and far-seeing man. Unfortunately he, like the French missionaries, is convinced that the Arabs should be exterminated and that would lead to the pacification of the country. What nonsense! The country would not be pacified by the massacre of the Arabs. The natives must first be subdued. More than one tribe would greet the white man as its saviour against the Arabs, but later the tribe would come to hate him and try to be rid of him. The white man would have to be strong enough to defeat such a scheme and remain the ruler over the blacks instead of being their slave. Nothing abases a European more than to be in an inferior role to a black savage.

21 October
... I prepared a package of mail for the coast, thirty-one letters sown into an envelope of thick, waterproof material...

22 October
... I left camp last night at midnight in a boat belonging to the White Fathers ... With eight paddlers and bright moonlight, we did the journey [along the coast] in an hour, sleeping the rest of the night on the sandbank. From dawn to 8:00 a.m., I roamed along the beach, shooting in total eight fat ducks. They are numerous, but very wild ... There were four or five different types of duck (one the common Egyptian duck with ringed eyes), two kinds of goose, three of plover, large curlews, red-footed waders, storks, cranes, herons, dotterels ...

23 October
... Wherever there is a French mission, one finds cooking oil, bread and vegetables, whereas few British missions can offer such useful additions to the African diet. Among other things, the fathers make tapioca from manioc and vinegar from bananas. They have thirty head of cattle ...

In front of the principal building is a cemetery where there are the simple but well maintained graves of three fathers who gave their lives in cause of salvation of the African from barbarism. There is one inscription in the cemetery which is particularily touching in its simplicity: that of Father Josset, the former Superior, who died the same day we set out from Bagamoyo ... A simple wooden cross is inscribed:

Ici repose
le R.P. Josset, décédé le 4 juillet 1891.
R.I.P.

By boat the missionaries visit regularily Mount Rumbi, Mpala and Kibanga ... They don't teach the natives to read or write nor do they require them to do things useless to them in the future, but rather make them into artisans, carpenters, blacksmiths, etc. I am greatly impressed with the quiet commitment of the Fathers. It is something new and rare in Africa, especially in contrast to the noise and haste of caravans.

I do not, however, agree with the political games to which the Fathers lend themselves in the lake region. Their aim seems to be ... the complete eradication of all Arab or Mohammedan influence in the regions where they hope to spread Christianity. That is perfectly understandable from their point of view: the Mohammedan has great power over the natives and is hostile to the spread of Christianity. But there is another factor that must also be taken into account: the Arabs are powerful, they know the country better than we do; they close ranks when danger faces them and they have arms and the men to use them. They hate the European intruders, the dogs of the Nazarene ...

If, in such circumstances, the Arabs were forced to fight, who knows what the result would be? Distant in the heart of the country some isolated missions would certainly be surprised and everyone massacred. Life and property would face all sorts of risks. Have priests, whoever they might be, out of their mistaken sincerity and ill-considered zeal for their branch of religion, the right to run such risks? I think not. It is up to governments who have the force and who, by force, can win respect for their administration. It is up to governments, I say, to take on the Arabs and bring them, if necessary by force, to behave in an orderly way, not because they are Mohammedans, but because they are slavers. And that brings me to insist again on what I have said before, that is, in order to obtain real success, missionaries must follow the establishment of stable government, not precede it. The missionaries will thus gain security and the native will respect them, the first step to get him to believe in their teachings.

24 October

It is futile to say that missionaries should not interfere in politics in the country where they find themselves. They almost invariably do. They are almost forced into it by the local chief under whose protection they are. The chief begins by first asking for advice, then comes to tell the missionary about his troubles, and finally he asks how he should behave towards another chief with whom he has been fighting. In order to protect their interests and their property, the missionaries are obliged to side with one chief against another ...

25 October

... My boys are wretched fellows, not half as good as those on the Emin Relief Expedition ... If only hindoo servants could travel with one in this country, what a blessing it would be for the white man. A Zanzibari servant doesn't know the use of a strap or a buckle and hammers in a screw as if it were a nail. Generally he cannot follow the instructions he has been given and one must repeat two or three times the least explanation ...

26 October

Two boats returned from across the lake and I finally leave at dusk. Only the great kindness of the White Fathers made bearable the weariness of waiting.

27 October

... We arrived at Mount Rumbi at 1:00 in the morning. The whole population, black and white [i.e., Captain Joubert] were on hand to welcome us ...

◆   ◆   ◆

30 October

[Having crossed Lake Tanganyika] we are now in the Congo Free State.

... On his slaving raids, Rumaliza has been destroying villages only three leagues from Mount Rumbi. He claims the western side of the lake and regards whites as intruders in his domain who must be expelled by force.

Captain Joubert, a thin, wiry little man of dark complexion, appears to be in poor health. He has lived near Lake Tanganyika for almost twelve years and has apparently given over any idea of ever returning to Europe ... An energetic man, he lives rough, rather like the bush farmers of New Zealand. He eats what the natives eat. A former Papal Zouave, Joubert was sent here to help put down the slave trade. He has built a chapel and, although a layman, is as devoted to the salvation of the blacks as much as any missionary. Joubert ... is a first-class gardener. He is adored and not feared by the natives, calm, patient, faithful to his vocation, always working, wholly absorbed by his daily tasks ...

Tanganyika is a splendid lake, with beautifully clear blue water set amidst high mountains. What a wonderful place for holiday resorts when a direct [rail?] line is built from Lake Nyassa and along the Shiré.

31 October

We are once again on our way, following a total of 22 days at the lake ... Smallpox is raging throughout the region. If we were infected, it would be a disaster for the expedition, for news of it would spread and we would be denied access to Msiri's kingdom...

1 November [1891]

.... Of our six superb donkeys, there remain only two. Our nights are no longer punctuated by their braying, for the four strongest have bitten the dust ... The donkeys were placed aboard the boats [to cross Lake Tanganyika] under the care of the donkey-boys. Of the ten [sic] donkeys embarked, four died at Mount Rumbi as a result of the voyage and the barbarous cruelty of the donkey-boys who, to quiet them on the boats, tied their legs so tightly that their skin and muscles were destroyed. My poor donkey was so tightly bound that three of his hooves were destroyed. Bonchamps' donkey was given nothing to drink for three days, although the boat was sailing on the fresh water of Lake Tanganyika. Another donkey had its intestines spilling out!

The Zanzibari boy is brutal and cruel toward animals and is so by sheer stupidity. He doesn't beat a donkey to excess, he does not overload it, he doesn't make it run too fast, but he is wholly negligent. The white man must personally ensure, day after day, that his donkey is fed. If one leaves that task to the boy, the donkey will simply fade away and die. Is it possible to imagine a more refined cruelty than that of leaving a donkey, his four feet tied, exposed to a burning sun for three days and nothing to drink? As soon as I arrived, I gave the donkey-boy a tongue-lashing and fined him 48 dollars [deducted from his pay...] Despite that, he is convinced that he did nothing wrong. If only I could drive it into their heads that they must do their work!

... I forgot to note that my two steel boats, the *Dorothy* and the *Bluenose*, crossed Lake Tanganyika in good condition ...

◆   ◆   ◆

3 November

... Along our route, one sees many deserted villages and destroyed plantations which shows that Makatubu [a former slave] has been wholly successful in his sack of the region. The natives fled at our approach, but I sent messages assuring them that I meant no harm and urging them to return which, in the evening, large numbers did.

Our altitude is 5,777 feet, our greatest height so far ... The mountain air is fresh and at night the temperature is about 65°F ...

4 November

... The perpetrators of the destruction are Kafindo and Uturutu, two Balutchis who live on the [Luapula] River, and Makatubu who is originally from the coast and is in Zanzibar at this moment. They have together reduced the region to ruin. The unfortunate natives were forced to flee into the hills where they are dying of starvation.

There is much work here for Joubert. If he gave flags to the strongest chiefs and formed them into a confederation against these villains he could [be certain] that his region was rid of Mohammedan half-castes, the torturers of the hapless natives, too weak and cowardly to resist the brigands with guns. If I am so fortunate with Msiri as to pacify at least a small part of his kingdom, I shall be only too happy to descend on the villains!

The natives are not without blame. Even when they have arms, they flee, abandoning their women [to the slavers]. They never set sentinels at night or in the early hours of the morning – invariably the time when raiders attack!

These marauders, in the service of Arabs and half-castes from the coast, give themselves grand airs, calling themselves *wangwana*, free men, yet it would be difficult to find any among them who is not a slave or even the slave of a slave ... You have thieves of all races and tribes... who delight in pillaging and destroying, and are hopeful of becoming rich through their slaving ...

5 November

... The countryside through which we are passing is fresh and green. If I could have 50,000 such acres in a temperate climate, in New Zealand for example, I would be wholly independent. One could raise three sheep to the acre, all year round. The sale of timber would cover the costs of building a house and a shed for the wool ...

Makatubu must be a cunning fellow, as capable of using his head as his gun. At first, he presented himself in the Lufuko valley as a simple ivory trader, asking the short-sighted chiefs of the region for permission to build his station. This permission was granted and, little by little, he attracted more and more soldiers around him and fortified his *boma*. One day, he threw off his mask and defied all the chiefs of the region. It was too late for them to protest against such deception. As quick as lightning, Makatubu's slaves fell upon the villages, shooting, stabbing and capturing every man, woman and child. The stupid natives were reduced to camping in the mountains and sleeping outdoors. It took Makatubu two years of pillage to depopulate this valley. Then he crossed Lake Tanganyika at Kirando, to sell his human booty and ill-gotten ivory. Today Makatubu is in Zanzibar, rich and yet still the humble slave of Abdallah Shaash, the Arab you meet in its streets ...

... Would it not be a thousand times less expensive for the anti-slavery societies to lock up for life men like Makatubu while they are at the coast, instead of sending expeditions charged with ending the slave trade and which do absolutely no good and cost a great deal of money? If Makabutu and Abdallah Shaash were imprisoned in Zanzibar, other populous and fertile regions would be spared the fate of the unhappy land we are now crossing. It certainly wouldn't cost the anti-slavery societies much. As things stand, Abdallah Shaash is a man who, in Zanzibar, considers himself as good as any European, and who assumes that whites are complete fools. I understand that Makatubu is openly organizing in Zanzibar a large caravan of gunpowder, cloth, etc. It is known that he is preparing to conduct new raids in the [Congo] Free State, using Kirando as his base!

Look too at the other side of the question. Everyone who has visited Africa knows that the black is selfish, boastful and a great lover of talk and *pombe*. He considers himself the elect, the chosen, beyond whom there is nothing else. He retains this good opinion of himself until he has received a sound thrashing from someone whom he then recognizes as his superior.

Boastful and full of talk, the chiefs, without the slightest mistrust, authorize an Arab to enter their territory with a fixed number of guns in order to "trade," that is, to exchange ivory for gunpowder, cloth, hoes, etc. The Arab arrives with his soldiers, selects a place that he first examines from the point of view of its suitability for his future attacks and is soon comfortably installed. The Arab is a past master at intrigue, has great presence of mind, a good deal of composure and is gifted with remarkable lucidity compared with the poor, *pombe*-filled brains of the native chiefs.

Here is how he [the Arab] proceeds: he begins by stirring up Chief A against Chief B. Then he allies himself with A to fight B and, when the latter is defeated, he turns against his ally A and routs him in turn. Then the pillage of the countryside begins. Right, left, everywhere, the Arab attacks the natives, too limited in their thinking and too attached to their village to think of allying themselves with their neighbours to organize their common defence. Finally, when the whole region is soaked in blood, when the population has completely disappeared, the Arab withdraws ... Although one pities the natives, one cannot prevent oneself from despising them because of their narrow selfishness, which blinds them to every danger.

I constantly tell the chiefs that their own drunkenness and their craze for chattering are the surest allies of the Arabs and the half-castes from the coast. Even during a war, the villagers neglect to set sentries, when they should know very well that it is always at nightfall that the hunters of human flesh make their raids upon them. The palisades enclosing the villages are built according to half-a-dozen different plans, and the enemy is at the centre before the occupants have had time to realize what is going on and seize their guns. The chiefs have such a good opinion of themselves that they consider themselves superior to their colleagues on the other side of the mountain. None will stoop to unite with another in order to join forces and to fight the enemy.

And yet, generally, these petty chiefs govern (badly) territory the size of a good Canadian farm ... The pride of these small tribes make them easy prey to the Arabs who come here to ruin and depopulate the country, and not to establish flourishing stations like an honest, right-thinking white man ... Should authority over the negroes be exercised by Arabs, half-castes or whites? That is the question. I have no doubt about the answer. Authority should be exercised by whites to the exclusion of all others, and the sooner the better ...

[This region] could flourish by the cultivation of sugar cane and rice and cattle farming. Unfortunately, however, the country is so depopulated and ravaged that we have been marching for four days without being able to buy even a pound of any food.

Once cotton cloth used to be made in these regions ... It is solid, long-lasting material to judge by the samples I have seen ... The principal element in the [local] clothing is, however, a sort of waistcoat made from the bark of a tree ... which grows nearly everywhere. Rope, too, is made from it; certain other fibrous trees are also used, and in villages one sees the tree, a sort of ficus, from which cloth is made ...

6 November

... The country we have travelled through can be considered as some of the best in Africa for crops and the raising of cattle and goats ...

Yesterday evening ... Dr. Moloney came to inform me that he had found another case of smallpox. What a catastrophe if it were to spread through my caravan! ... Smallpox has ... spread, south and west, to Msiri's territory. Yet it seems that few natives die of it.

The rain is having its usual effect on my people: There are a great number of stomach-aches. I make everyone erect dry huts, but the men's clothing is so light that they are subject to feverish chills.

7 November

... Kassongomona's men left yesterday to announce our arrival to their master. Last night they camped near huts of the Wamarungu which they raided. During the night the Wamarungu returned and killed three of Kassongomona's men with their poisoned arrows. That's commonplace in Africa and nothing to worry about ...

In Europe, there are false ideas about the physique of the central African. There are several different types in this region, but none resembles the flat-nosed, thick-lipped negro of the west coast of Africa. The east coast, with its swamps and fevers and its unhealthy climate is not the place to look for a perfect type of black. Rather it is here in the mountains where the air is fresh and the water pure that one finds the finest specimens of Africans ...

...We have seen bamboo, cardamon and other vegetation which flourishes in a humid climate. The cardamon brought back memories of the terrible days in the Aruwimi forests with the Emin Relief Expedition when those plants were almost the only food our men had.

8 November

...I've heard of a caravan from Lake Nyassa which has arrived at Mpueto's north of Lake Moero. The Wasumba say that it is a British caravan. If so, it must be Crawshay's which will establish a station on Lake Moero.* I've also heard of a second caravan, this one travelling south ... Could it be Thomson or perhaps Delcommune? There is no reliable information, and I am reluctant to send any men to search for it; my caravan is already so overladen that it is all that we can do to move forward, stage by stage.

... It would be a quite simple [to suppress the Arabs in the region] if I did not need the good will of these same Arabs and Balutchis, who are powerful hereabouts. If I don't get on with them, there will be great difficulties across my path. And yet, I would like to do the Wanyamwezi a favour and take some of them with me to see Msiri, for he is of their race. That could be an immense step forward in negotiations with this powerful chief. I have letters for Kafindo and Uturutu, and shall write some myself that I shall send from the Luapula. The former is at war with Msiri, which further increases my difficulties in Katanga, for if I were to be seen as Kafindo's friend, that would not please Msiri.

The Arabs ... have forbidden Mpueto, the chief of the northern part of Lake Moero, to build a *boma* around his village. The chief replied that he was not the slave of any Arab and that he had gone to Joubert on Lake Tanganyika to ask him for his help and a [Congo Free State] flag.

Kassongomona arrived in Katanga before Msiri, but he soon had to withdraw in the face of the latter's greater power. In this part of Africa there is an extraordinary mixture of Arabs, Balutchis, whites, Wasumbwa, and natives, all crossing each others' paths, some to obtain ivory, others to seize possession of various regions. It's a sad spectacle to see these splendid valleys formed of alluvial soil and rich in humus, which still lie fallow, except here where they cultivate a little maize. Tobacco, rice, vegetables of every kind, and sugar cane could be grown in abundance, but the most that one sees is maize and millet! The blacks of the interior are fond of mangoes, guavas and pawpaws, but the simple idea of planting these fruits has never occurred to them. I noted this in Tabora and Karema, where not a single fruit-tree has been planted by the natives. That is a pity and denotes an inferior race, neglecting to surround itself with the most elementary comforts, which would cost neither trouble nor care.

When one asks a native why he does not cultivate vegetables when it is so easy for him to obtain seed, he invariably replies, "Mungu makatara" (God forbid). What is the origin of this fatalistic expression? What a mystery! The natives have never even tried planting rice or special grains! In any event, the native is always prone to cultivate the produce requiring the least attention for the largest yield. It is rare to note, from one period to another, any improvement whatsoever in their way of life. There are explorers who, on their return to

---

*William Crawshay, a former subaltern in the 5th Inniskilling Dragoon Guards, was employed by the British South Africa Company.

Europe, have so praised the African that they've come to consider their opinion the truth. Why do that? I prefer to depict the African as he is, with his good and bad points, and leave it to those who have not seen him in his homeland to form their own judgement. The optimists who find everything perfect really do more harm to Africa and Africans than the most passionate pessimists. I have a foreboding of calamity, but I can't tell where it will happen.

9 November

... To-morrow we are having a great *shauri* with all the Wasumbwa chiefs of the region about the doings of the Arabs and the Balutchis. The Wasumbwa claim that they have the right to the ivory they get from hunting, the Balutchis say the opposite, so war has become imminent. It is absolutely necessary for me to remain on good terms with both for I want to take the Wanyamwezi chiefs to Msiri's territory. So I must take their side and that will be considered an offence by the Arabs and the Wangwana ...

Kassongomona has five villages under his domination. He has just come to see me. He is a young man of about twenty-two or twenty-three, quite small but well-built. He looks rather stupid and his eyes are dull, probably the result of dissolute living and too much *pombe*. He has succeeded old Kassongomona, who died some time ago, so ridding Msiri of a powerful rival for the possession of Katanga. He talked for an hour and a half about the affairs of the country with which he is well acquainted. But he draws no advantage from this knowledge as far as his authority is concerned, for he is completely dependent on two or three advisers who tell him what to do.

He would like to attack Msiri, his father's old enemy, and would be ready to follow me to fight him. I made him understand that, as he is an enemy of Kafindo, if he went off with his men to fight against Msiri, leaving his village to the care of the women, this would mean abandoning them and their children as prey to this Balutchi Arab. He had never thought of that. My observations made him change his mind completely *for the moment*.

War, as it is conducted here, involves not only a conflict between two parties, but also tribes beyond the dispute itself. Each tribe hastens to seize any opportunity to avenge personal injuries. If Kassongomona made war on Msiri, he would thus aid his mortal enemy, Kafindo, who is also in conflict with Msiri. There are few African chiefs who have any originality, except perhaps for an unique method of brewing *pombe*. Each one obeys the traditions of the elders and only rarely makes a decision on his own accord. In addition, the chiefs are distinguished by their eternal chatter, praising their own strength and mocking that of others. To prepare a long time for war and to weigh the chances of success are things no one thinks of. Even when their hostilities have begun, they take no defensive measures. The enemy has already invaded the village while the chief is still drinking *pombe* with his wives.

The story of Uleki, the chief who is following me with twenty men, is strange. He had a quarrel in Katanga involving one of Msiri's favourite wives. This woman became pregnant. In time Msiri noticed this and discovered that Uleki had "meddled in his affairs." Msiri sent warriors to seize him, but Uleki managed to reach the Lualaba. Chased from there, he took refuge on the shores of Lake Tanganyika. The poor woman and her child died. Every child of a wife of Msiri's bears the name of Mwanangwa, that is, son of the chief. There are several hundreds, it seems, of these children.

♦   ♦   ♦

13 November
... Food is scarce and hence expensive. Ahead of us lies five days of bush without any food ... If only I knew where Delcommune was!

Chapter Twenty-one

What awaited Stairs in Katanga was decidedly unpromising. Msiri's rule was being challenged from several directions. Other tribes had sensed that his grip was slipping, especially with the rumoured approach of the two expeditions of Cecil Rhodes and the four of King Leopold. Elsewhere in Msiri's territory the hated Arab slavers remained active, causing turmoil and devastation. Both water and food became increasingly scarce. Stairs wrote, "The famine is such that if offered a treasure one could not provide provisions; there are none. No more firewood either and the water is execrable. The English missionaries are terrorized by Msiri."[1]

Plymouth Brethren missionaries were assiduous in their prozletyzing, but were equally persistent in their refusal to involve themselves in questions of how Msiri ruled. Msiri in turn treated the missionaries in a patronizing way which they themselves passively accepted, but reports that Msiri regarded the missionaries almost as captives fuelled concerns in London and Brussels.

The first of Rhodes's two expeditions had reached the marches of Katanga, but not Bunkeya itself, before it turned back in the face of a smallpox epidemic and starvation. The second of Rhodes's representatives, Alfred Sharpe, did reach Bunkeya – in November 1890 – a few days before the arrival there of three Plymouth Brethren missionaries, F.L. Lane, Hugh B. Thompson, and Dan Crawford who joined the two already there, Charles Albert Swan (not be confused with Alfred Swann) and the Canadian, William Henry Faulknor.*

---

*Twenty years later, Dan Crawford published an account of his mission in Africa: *Thinking Black: Twenty-two Years Without a Break in the Long Grass of Central Africa* (London, 1912). Swan, who had known Stanley on the Congo, recorded his adventures in *Fighting the Slave Hunters in Central Africa* (London, 1910).

In his interviews with Msiri, Sharpe employed Swan as his interpreter. Sharpe hoped that the missionary would simply convey to Msiri the statement that the British were his friends. On that bald statement Msiri would be induced to put his mark on a treaty ceding his lands to the British South Africa Company and to raise the Union Jack over Bunkeya. Swan, however, would not participate in this gross deception. He insisted on translating for Msiri the full text of Sharpe's proposed treaty. Not surprisingly, an angry Msiri promptly refused to sign and the discomfited Sharpe had to return hurriedly to Nyasaland. Sharpe was highly displeased with his missionary compatriots:

Msidi [Msiri] would have no interview with me without Mr. Swan being present: this was a nuisance. On speaking to Msidi about treaties and concessions, he refused utterly – said Mr. Arnot had told him to have nothing to do with anyone who wanted him to sign papers, and that it meant giving away his country... These missionaries do a great deal of harm when they take upon themselves to advise native chiefs, as their advice is according to their own narrow views.[2]

Both expeditions of the British South Africa Company having failed in their purpose, Leopold's four expeditions had followed with the same broad goal of laying claim to Katanga. His first two expeditions had been no more successful than those of the British South Africa Company.

This was the volatile situation which awaited Stairs in Katanga. And it was Stairs's expedition, the fifth to arrive in Bunkeya in a little more than a year, which finally decided the fate of Msiri's fragile kingdom.

From 13 to 19 November the expedition camped on the banks of the Lualaba, the tributary of the Congo. From there Stairs sent to Bunkeya an emissary with a letter and a large gift of cloth to ascertain Msiri's welcome. Of one thing Stairs could be certain before the return of his envoy: the possibility of a British protectorate (to counter the Congo Free State's claim) was again in Msiri's mind. Although Stairs does not mention it, he had been given several days before – inadvertently or otherwise – a letter from Msiri intended for Alfred Sharpe, inviting a representative of Rhodes to return to Bunkeya for, presumably, a warmer welcome. Stairs did not hesitate to open the letter to Sharpe nor did he in light of it hesitate to continue to press Leopold's claim, if anything even more determinedly. Yet Stairs signed his letter to Msiri, "Stairs, the Englishman." Whether Stairs was intentionally attempting to mislead Msiri or had some other motive in mind, it remains an odd signature for the leader of an expedition mounted by Leopold to secure Katanga for his Congo Free State. The most likely explanation is that Stairs hoped to secure an undisputed entry into Bunkeya through deceiving Msiri that he was in fact the Englishman coming in response to his invitation.

The week's idleness on the banks of the Lualaba presumably allowed "Stairs, the Englishman" some time to attempt to think through what he could do to induce Msiri to accept the blue flag of the Congo Free State and what he would do if Msiri continued to decline it. From his diary entry of 14 December, it seems clear that

Stairs had decided to depose Msiri, having convinced himself that otherwise "pacification" (i.e., Free State governance) would be impossible.

The week was also time enough for a few of the sick to recover, and it provided Stairs with the opportunity to induce several neighbouring chiefs to fly the flag of the Congo Free State over their villages. Moloney recorded that

Everywhere we experienced a most cordial reception, and in no case did Captain Stairs encounter the smallest reluctance to accept the Congo flag. Indeed, the expedition was universally hailed as an unexpected deliverance from Msiri; and the native bands, composed almost entirely of drums, used to sound in our honour until one's head ached with the noise.[3]

Upon resuming its march southward toward Bunkeya, the expedition passed through scattered forests interspersed by rivers. At first antelope and buffalo were abundant, but food for the expedition became decidedly less the nearer it approached Bunkeya. Crops had been destroyed and no food was for sale.

14 November
... It is now six months since I left Britain. We are nearing Msiri's kingdom ... I await the return of my messengers whom I sent to chiefs Kafindo and Mpueto. This morning I sent messengers to Msiri [with gifts] ... worth £140.

I eagerly await Msiri's reply. If there are whites already in Katanga [i.e., agents of Cecil Rhodes], it's impossible to say what will be the result ...

15 November
... At 5:00 p.m ... one of the messengers whom I had sent to Kafindo ... returned ... Kafindo says that he will come to see me the day after tomorrow. At 7:00 p.m. the messenger whom I sent to Mpueto returned. Mpueto and his chiefs will come to see me tomorrow.

◆   ◆   ◆

17 November
... About 3:00 in the afternoon Mpueto came to our camp ... I said to him, "I asked you to come here so that the long-standing quarrel between you and Chief Ngwena can finally be settled, the country pacified, the land cultivated and all may feel more secure. I know that you have real complaints against Ngwena, but he has many grievances against you and your people. But if you don't be careful, the Arabs will seize your land and ravage it. The best thing for both of you to do is to cultivate your lands in peace."...

18 November

Mpueto signed an act of submission to the Congo Free State. I gave him the flag which some askari will hoist over his village. I have also had the flag raised over Ngwena's village...

19 November

We set off so early that by 8:30 all the men with the loads had crossed to the other side of the Lualaba. The boats performed perfectly. The *Bluenose* took twenty-two loads and the *Dorothy* about sixteen ... The men all crossed quickly in ten boats provided by Ngwena ... Here we set up our first camp in Msiri's territory – which he claims stretches to the Lualaba.

At 2:00 p.m. I learned of the arrival of Kafindo with fifty followers. I had a tent assigned him ... [and] sent him a fat goat, four pigs, six butcher's knives, four pair of scissors ... two tins of snuff, 300 pins and a 30 shilling watch ...

Kafindo says that some months ago three white men left ... to go to Msiri's. They came from Nyangwe and must by now have reached their destination. No doubt that is Delcommune and his expedition. I would like to arrive at Msiri's before Captain Bia, who is in command of another [Congo Free State] expedition coming from the north ...

Kafindo, who is a Balutchi... travelled with me to Tabora. He talks in an open manner, but one can't trust what such people say. He would like to accompany me to Msiri's, but I insist that he must wait another six or eight months. I am anxious that the route should remain open behind me, at least as far back as Mpueto's.

Kafindo's rice crop failed last year. He has nothing left for a new sowing. I gave him some onion seeds ...

◆   ◆   ◆

22 November

After a short 2¼ hour march, we stopped near the Luwule at a place where the river turns south. At 3:00 p.m. four or five of Uturutu's men, laden with merchandise, arrived in my camp with one of my men. Uturutu would not feel easy until he had seen me, so he was marching hard to catch up with me before I arrived at Msiri's. The fool! Does he really think that I believe it is his desire to visit me that brings him and Kafindo here? What he seeks is authorization to follow me to Msiri's. I shall take good care he won't do *that*. Indeed, Msiri would immediately think that we were coming to fight him ... Uturutu is a goose if he imagines that I don't see his little game. No Arab would do a nine days' march just for the pleasure of saying to a white stranger, "How do you do?" If an Arab makes such an effort, it is to make money. In the present instance, the

Arabs hope that, thanks to the white man, they will be able to enter Msiri's territory to seize his ivory and his slaves.

◆   ◆   ◆

24 November

... Game abounds: we shot not less than 22 antelopes and a buffalo this morning. The plains here are large and fertile but, unfortunately, they are not cultivated. Red antelope swarm here. The Luwule flows across the middle of the plain but its bottom is muddy, which would make a crossing difficult in the rainy season. Between the Lufira and the Luapula [rivers] there is, according to the Arabs, a mountain whose lower levels are covered with thick forests, but the summit is bare and rocky. It is isolated and, according to the same source, must be about 10,000 feet high. It is called Kilimani, a word which simply means "place of the mountain" (*kilima* means mountain).

At a late hour, Madjid, the Arab from Kassenga, came to the camp and until midnight, he and Uturutu remained chatting with me in front of my tent. I did my best to impress upon them how important it is for them to keep my route open behind me. I added that if the Arabs want to remain friends with the whites, they must leave the natives alone so they can sow their crops in peace; that we Europeans were tired of their raids and destruction of villages. Sooner or later, we would put an end to it. I told them that if they wanted ivory, they should pay for it like honest people and not steal it from weak, harmless natives, and in turn oblige them to transport it to Tabora. They replied that they were ready to obey me in everything and to help whites. Uturutu asked me to give him the [Congo Free] State flag. I could not, but as I wanted to remain on good terms with him, I told him that Captain Jacques would no doubt let him have one. I gave Uturutu a letter for Jacques...

25 November

We have reached Kassenga, the station of the [Arab] Madjid who accompanied my caravan. By prolonging his stay in this country, Madjid is turning into a real savage. He's been living in the bush now for five years. He belongs to an Arab caste that doesn't cut their hair or shave their beards. His savage appearance puts me in mind of the illustrations from Captain Cook's voyages in the South Seas. Uturutu, Kafindo and Madjid are all much in debt to the Tabora Arabs. These Arab merchants of Africa have nothing of the nobility attributed to the Arabs of *arabia deserta*. They are quite simply Jews, and poor, indebted, needy Jews. They are far from having the shrewdness and ability of the hindoo. But having a stronger physical constitution than the hindoo, they can live in the interior and pursue their baleful trade, while the hindoo would die like a rat. They want everything they see; their fingers itch, even if the object is of no use whatever to them. Thus, seeing me write, Uturutu began to insist that

I give him pens, objects which, for him, have not a shadow of use, for Arabs don't use such pens for writing. If he asks me for them, it is only because he sees that I have some!

Arabs are, besides, accomplished beggars and don't hesitate to ask for all sorts of things. They seem to think that whites were created to heap presents upon them, while they, in return, owe the whites only poor, worthless gifts. I told Uturutu that we whites are tired of these Arab "salaoums" given with a "corrupt heart" in exchange for valuable presents, eagerly sought. I showed him that I saw into his game, and that I knew the worth of the word of the Arab who says, "The country is yours, master, and no longer mine" and who, on the sly, plays monstrous tricks on you.

He answered me, "There is Arab and Arab. There are good ones and bad ones. I am amongst the former." I know what to think about that ...

♦   ♦   ♦

27 November

... The chief came to see me accompanied by his wives, decked out in all their finery. They have bead necklaces cleverly arranged and some of the wives are really pretty. At first, black women are shy and don't dare approach a white man. But, little by little, they get bolder and finally grow familiar. The husbands love their wives, but not love in any real sense of the term, for often the women are treated as beasts of burden, like a "thing" that every man must have, on a par with a spear or a gun ... Married women respect the conjugal bond. It is rare for a girl to be seduced.

We have had good hunting. The best African game is, in my opinion, guinea-fowl, then quail. Giraffe or antelope meat is excellent, but antelopes have a dry flesh, rarely fatty like that of zebra or giraffe.

♦   ♦   ♦

1 December 1891

Arrived at Gera after a splendid march of 21 miles. In two days we have marched 42 miles. Excellent!

♦   ♦   ♦

Chapter Twenty-two

Stairs's emissary to Msiri returned from Bunkeya on 8 December. He reported that Msiri had greeted him in a courteous and friendly manner and sent with him a message to Stairs (dictated to Dan Crawford, missionary at Bunkeya) that the expedition would be welcomed as brothers. Decidedly less promising was an accompanying letter from Crawford himself. Moloney says that "Mr. Crawford's communication to Captain Stairs ... contained a full account of the king's oppression, and the ruin caused thereby; indeed the general condition of the country was painted in the most sombre colours imaginable. 'Well,' remarked our leader, with his wonted decision, 'I'll put a stop to Mr. Msiri's little games.'"

On the 13 December 1891 the expedition unexpectedly encountered Lieutenant André Legat, a Belgian in the employ of the Congo Free State who had visited Bunkeya with the experienced Congo hand, Paul le Marinel. Legat described vividly the excesses of Msiri's reign, based on observations from a Free State fort established with Msiri's agreement some twenty-five miles from Bunkeya. Legat had, however, no news about the progress of King Leopold's fourth expedition led by Captain Bia nor of the fate of Leopold's second expedition under Delcommune who had pressed on southward in search of gold after a brief sojourn at Bunkeya.

The following day, 14 December, five months and ten days after leaving Bagamoyo, Stairs's expedition arrived at Bunkeya. Desolation and famine were evident everywhere. Insurrection was widely reported. The security of the expedition was threatened not only by the anticipated hostility of Msiri, but also by starvation. Further, the rumoured approach of an expedition sent by the British South Africa Company made it, in Stairs' view, imperative to induce Msiri to accept the suzerainty of the Congo Free State by the symbolic act of raising its flag.

8 December [1891]

We crossed the Lufira River at 5:50 a.m.. By 7:10 everyone had crossed the bridge which I had got the men to construct yesterday. Following a two hour march, we camped in the plains near the river which is at an altitude of about 3,000 feet.

At 3:00 p.m., my couriers returned from Msiri's. They had crossed the Lufira River by the eastern route and gone on to Kifuntwe where they were told that I had taken the western route. They brought me a letter from Msiri, written in English by Mr. Crawford, a missionary and a colleague of Mr. Arnot; another, in Swahili, from Msiri himself, and a personal message from Mr. Crawford.

Here roughly is the news contained in these three letters: until my messengers arrived, no one had any inkling of my presence in the region; Msiri professes goodwill and begs me to arrive in Bunkeya as soon as possible; he hopes that we shall be friends and asks me for two head of cattle.

Mr. Crawford tells me that famine is rife in the country. For nine months now there has been continuing guerrilla warfare between Msiri and the Wasanga. A great number of people are leaving Bunkeya at night so as to join the enemy ... The missionaries have no provisions and are living frugally. M. Le Marinel arrived in the country six months ago. He had much difficulty in obtaining authorization to build a station. He left two whites in the region, who put up a post east of the Lufira River, a place where the missionaries also have their settlement. Another expedition arrived from the north about three weeks ago and, after a short stay, went on southward, five days from Msiri's capital. One of the members of this expedition, Karl Hakansson, was killed on Lake Likonia by natives, while he was in command of the rearguard marching south.

Msiri is apparently thinking of abandoning his country and going to ... Lake Moero. What is prompting him toward this decision is the famine which is rife, the drought and the continual warfare against the Wasanga. Msiri eagerly looks forward to my arrival for fear, I think, of his enemies.

Here is the official text of the letter which Mr. Crawford sent me in the name of the great chief of Katanga:

*From Msidi, Chief of Garenganze and Katanga,** *
To the Englishman, Captain Stairs.
Bunkeya, 24th November 1891.

Your five men arrived yesterday, bringing your letters and presents ...
I am happy to receive you in my land and you should not delay coming straight to
my capital. I note that you are an Englishman. That is good, for I know that the

---

*Msiri was variously written Msidi, Muxide, Moshide, and Muside. Garenganze, Katanga and Katangaland were used interchangably.

English are sincere people. You say that the Wasumbwa and other Wanyamwezi are your friends. That is also good; they my relatives. I too am a Wanyamwezi. I would like to move my capital to Kazembe on the Luapula River. Please bring me from Kavunda an ox and a cow. I desire to be on good terms with you. I am happy to learn that that is also your intention.

Your friend,
(S.) Msidi

9 December

... We are 40 miles from Msiri ... The countryside is peopled with Wasanga, always ready to fight Msiri and his friends.

10 December

Two of our men who went off at night to loot were seized by crocodiles while swimming across the river ... Without the antelope which we shoot by the dozen, we would die of hunger.

11 December

Yesterday I sent more messengers to Msiri and to the Belgian officers residing in the country. I wonder who they are?

◆   ◆   ◆

13 December

... A Belgian [Lieutenant] Legat, who had received my letter last night, came to see me. Mr. Legat has been ten years in the Congo. He served under Stanley and has forty soldiers. The news Legat brought is hardly reassuring. The Wasanga have risen everywhere in rebellion against Msiri, and the old potentate is fearful that whites may join them and chase him out.

Msiri is touchy, demanding and selfish in his relations with whites. He tries to get as much out of them as he can without giving anything in return. Mr. Arnot has remained at Bihé and Mr. Thompson, another missionary, has just arrived. After a stay of seven days, Delcommune left Bunkeya, going southward towards Tenke. Since then, there has been no definite news of him. Of the Bia expedition there is no news whatever.

The two Belgians who have a post on the Lufira River belong to Paul Le Marinel's expedition. They have been here for six months and have built a station on the Lufoi, a little tributary of the Lufira which flows from the east. Their post is about three days from the Bunkeya. Le Marinel, his assistants and Mr. Swan, a Scottish missionary who accompanies them, have set out again for Luzambo on the Sankuru River.

There are, at the moment, three missionaries with Msiri. It appears me that Delcommune intends going westwards to the Lualaba, then to follow that river. He does not know that he is no longer in the service of the *Compagnie du Congo pour le commerce et l'industrie* and that he is now in the service of the *Compagnie du Katanga.*

The Wasanga say that they do not want war; their only aim is to see Msiri deposed. He is behaving towards them like a savage beast.

The missionaries are, it seems to me, in a difficult position. Msiri treats them badly and famine is rife as a result of the wars against the Wasanga, who really own the land.

14 December

Purely out of greed and a desire to destroy, the remarkably cruel Msiri has ruined a splendid country. We arrived at Bunkeya at 9:40 this morning and camped near the capital. Mr. Crawford, one of the English missionaries, came to meet me.*

My first impression of the village is bad, but at the moment I refrain from judging too hastily. I shall limit myself to a single observation: we first recognized Msiri's headquarters by the skeletons fixed to stakes round one section of the village and by a terrible pyramid of human heads and amputated hands placed on a sort of pedestal table at the door of his dwelling.

I had a long talk just now with Legat and Crawford. Msiri was furious when he learnt that Legat had come to see me without his authorization. He got it into his head that Legat is attempting to turn me against him.

The famine is so severe that, even if one were to offer a fortune, one could not buy food: there is simply none left. Firewood is scarce and the water is filthy.

The missionaries are treated by the chief on a level with black slaves. They are terribly afraid of him. If the king were deposed, the country would immediately return to order, the Wasanga would be our friends and one could do great things. With the help of 150 Boer mercenaries, the Portugese defeated and captured the black chief of Bihé who had sworn to kill all whites who fell into his hands and who levied heavy *hongo* on travellers. Learning

---

*As early as 1885, a British missionary, Frederick Arnot, had pursued his vocation amidst the uncertainties of Bunkeya. His appeals in Britain for others to join in surmounting the challenges to evangelism in Africa had brought in 1890 a nineteen-year-old Scot, Dan Crawford, to Bunkeya. When Stairs arrived in Msiri's capital, Arnot was at another mission station at Bihé and the irrepressible Crawford was on hand to greet the expedition. See F. Arnot, *Bihé and Garenganze* (London, 1893); Dan Crawford, *Thinking Black (London, 1912)*; and E. Tilsley, *Dan Crawford, Missionary and Pioneer in Africa* (London, 1929).

of this from the Portugese merchant Coïmbra,* Msiri exclaimed that a white would never dare make him captive!

Our first care must be to look out for a secure position, build a station there and live on wildlife until the next harvest.

Having arrived on 15 May, [Paul] Le Marinel set off again at the beginning of July. Delcommune arrived on 6 September, spoke firmly to Msiri, then departed on 5 October for the south after a long stay at the Lufoi station, Legat's post. Our couriers arrived here on the 23 November.

... The three English missionaries now in the country are Crawford, H.B. Thompson, J.F. Lane. The first has been here for a year; the second several months; the third two years. Mr. [Frederick] Arnot is at Bihé with Mr. Faulknor and others.** Mr. Swan has returned to Europe. The missionaries have built a post on the Lufoi River near the Free State station.

15 December

Yesterday evening I succeeded in getting Crawford to induce Senhor Coïmbra, the Portugese, to send two "Bihénos" to follow Delcommune to tell him what is happening and to get him to come back ...

I have got ready the presents to give Msiri during our interview tomorrow. They are: two bales of cloth, one of fine assorted qualities and one of *kanikis* and mixed *joras*; five rolls of copper wire; copper buttons, large quantities of needles and thread; six pairs of scissors; six razors; an assortment of jewels each worth between 200 and 250 francs; six sabre type bayonets of the kind used by the Navy; my own sword; a box of beads; snuff; various trinkets; worth in total 6,000 francs. But I doubt that the chief will be satisfied: what he wants is gunpowder.

The three missionaries came to see me this morning. While we were talking, a messenger arrived from Msiri to tell Mr. Thompson that the missionaries may not return tomorrow to their Lufoi post, as they had intended, unless they give him a piece of cloth. I immediately advised the missionaries to take shelter behind the Lufoi before any serious dangers arise. They propose to set out tomorrow morning. The missionaries are themselves responsible for the contempt that Msiri shows whites. They have been too weak and patient. Msiri has taken advantage of this and is now convinced that all whites are the same.

---

*The "Portuguese merchant Coïmbra" was Lourenco Souza Coïmbra, the son of a Portuguese trader and an African mother. Coïmbra had worked with a notorious slaver and was himself a major trader in slaves. His niece, Maria de Fonseca, one of Msiri's many wives, lived a short distance from Bunkeya.

**William Faulknor was seriously ill during much of his service in Katanga. He and Arnot returned to Britain in 1892 before travelling together to Canada.

The missionaries are going to create difficulties. That will not, however, prevent me from doing all that it is humanly possible to help them. Another consideration is the presence in Bunkeya of two or three of Msiri's advisers, Mohammedans and people from the coast. The only thing that will restore peace and prosperity... is to depose Msiri ... Oh, would to heaven that I could get in touch with Delcommune and plan some joint action with him!

Mr. Thompson told me that [Alfred] Sharpe arrived here in November 1890 with 30 or 40 soldiers. On entering the town, Sharpe fired a salvo which enraged Msiri. A week later Sharpe left. He had made every effort to get Msiri to sign a document declaring the country English [i.e., the British South Africa Company], but he failed. It was Mr. Swan, the missionary, who acted as interpreter during the interviews.*

The missionaries promised to leave tomorrow morning for their station. They must, for their lives are in danger here. One of them said to me just now: "Oh, how I would like to give my life for Africa!" I remonstrated with him, trying to get him to understand that his death would be the signal for that of many others, and that it was selfish of him to be so eager to go to heaven by escaping the danger that lies in preaching the gospel on earth.

16 December

I heard that the missionaries hadn't left so I sought them out. The reason for their hesitation? It had rained during the night. Senhor Coïmbra came to see me. He's an intelligent man who, although black, likes to be called white. He has already travelled six times the Bihé-Katanga route. One could have no better testimony than his as to the extraordinary changes which have occurred in this country. He told me that, three years ago, one could count ten villages where only one is seen now; that the hills to the south-west were covered, just a few years ago, with flourishing villages. To-day, not a single one is left. Msiri's cruelty has caused the exodus of the greater part of the population.

My interview with Msiri is fixed for early to-morrow morning. We shall exchange blood, such is the desire of the chief, who has sent me a message not to listen to the gossip of the other whites, "all bad people."

Senhor Domingo came to see me this morning, imploring me to put an end to the butchering of people that is going on every day.

---

*Sharpe's effort to persuade Msiri to accept the British flag and the suzerainty of the British South Africa Company was a failure. Like Bishop Hannington, Sharpe was the object of Msiri's suspicion since he had come from the east. Worse, he left most of his expedition at some distance from Bunkeya and arrived with only a small entourage and a few gifts. Msiri was not impressed. Worst of all, he relied upon Swan to interpret for him. Given Msiri's enraged reaction, Sharpe was fortunate to be able to return to Nyasaland, empty-handed but at least still in one piece.

17 December

The missionaries have at last departed for the Lufoi, in spite of all the threats of our miniature Nero.

At 9 o'clock my interview with Msiri took place. First I gave him presents, but then I didn't mince matters with him. I told him how Uganda, Unyoro, Unyamwezi and the country of the Masai had fallen to the whites, and asked him if he knew that the King of Bihé was in chains. I reproached him for his cruelty and asked him to explain the half-dry heads on the stakes around the village. I added that the whole region was in a state of desolation as a result of his barbarous proceedings, that he is responsible for the famine and death across this unfortunate land, that it is he who drives the terrified people from their houses and fields. "Who then would dare plant any more crops? That is what has become of this prosperous region which has been so much talked of. A powerful chief isn't even able to give me a handful of flour! I've met on my way chiefs much more powerful than you! You are only a minor chief, evil and hated by your subjects. You must change your ways if you want to be my friend."

Msiri answered me: "I want you, rather than any other white, to be my friend. The other whites are bad. They are trying to set you against me, lying about me, whereas I am good, while the Basanga are bad."

I walked towards him then, and looking him straight in the face, I said, "I don't need the testimony of any other white to know what to think of you. How many heads are on the poles around your quarters, some no more than five days old? What have you done to the Wanyamwezi, always so mild and peaceful? Where is the food with which this village should abound? Answer my questions, and then it will be evident that you are yourself the author of all the calamities."

Then turning round, I addressed the assembled people: Do you want your heads cut off? Do you or don't you want to be able to live in peace, raise your children and live peacefully? If yes, I am ready to help you!"

While I was speaking so frankly, Msiri was trembling with rage and threatening me with violence. I continued regardless and showed him that his fits of anger did not frighten me.

The interview ended with statements made by Msiri in a milder tone: "This country is yours; you are my *Munungu* (god); do what you think is best and be my friend!"

I answered that I was quite willing to be his friend, but on condition that all human sacrifice end immediately. There were about 150 people present, and six or seven of Msiri's wives. One of these was really quite beautiful, with regular pretty features, and certainly the most beautiful woman I have yet seen west of Lake Tanganyika.

There is a palisade surrounding the whole village, and a second within the first ... The interior palisade protects Msiri's residence and is in good condition.

The exterior palisade is not strong. The King's residence is made of *pisé* (clay) and was built by Wangwana from the *mrima* (coast), who came by the Kilwa route. The main square is clean but covered with weeds, and the adult men one meets are few. The huts are round with thatched roofs of the usual sort.

Msiri was wearing a woman's robe, made of red and white pieces of *kaniki*, flannel and cotton. He had a shell necklace, the mark of supreme sovereignty. He had powdered his face with flour and stuck feathers in his hair. As far as one can judge, under the layer of flour with which Msiri had masked his face, his features are full of sly craftiness. His laugh conjures up the memory of those fresh human heads grimacing which are on the stakes in the village. I counted one hundred of these frightful trophies. Some still have the expression that they had at the moment of death, offering a weird testimony to the chief's barbarity. When each man came up to salute him, one could feel the state of abject terror that gripped the unfortunate admitted to such a perilous honour.

18 December

Legat tells me that Msiri spent the night in the village of Maria, making a great row and in a terrible temper, declaring that Legat had set me against him, and that the fire which had followed the explosion on Le Marinel's arrival, a fire which destroyed the present which the King of the Belgians had sent for him, was intentional.

The old fox is busy plotting something. I, for my part, don't miss an opportunity to repeat to his people that if they remain too close to the King, it won't be long before their heads are on the stakes of the *boma*. I liberally hand out *bakshish* to make friends.

If, after a second interview with Msiri, I can arrange matters, I shall go towards the Lufira, where there is meat [urgently needed for the carriers]. Bunkeya is halfway between two hills which overlook the *kwikuru* (capital) and does not have any defences. The hills completely overlook the town. The Unkeia, a small river, flows near the town, but in the dry season, the inhabitants have to go far to get drinking water. The result is that they seldom wash, so they are very dirty.

Around the chief's *boma*, made of *pisé* and furnished with two doors, are the huts of his wives and servants. These huts are separate one from the other but could be set on fire if the wind were blowing. Two badly kept palisades surround the whole.

Maria, the mulatto woman, lives a quarter of a league from Bunkeya. Yesterday Msiri threatened to cut off her head if she went on showing friendship to the whites.

I have received the visit of Tharaia (or Chikako), one of Msiri's partisans. I told him to take care of his head, for if it remained too long within Msiri's reach, it would soon fall. He left frightened. He is, I think, a brother of Msiri and Likuku.

Masite, Msiri's sister, came to see me with her husband, M'Koma Ngombe ...
The chief's horrible dwarf also came. He is a native of Lunda, west of Lualaba
River.

19 December

It rained last night. Msiri says that he will receive me at 2:00 o'clock.

I received a visit of Mukanda Vantu and got him to sense what a brute Msiri
is. He has unbounded ambition.

At 2:00 I visited Msiri. He told me a long, incoherent tale of the way in which
he had become king; he chased away the Wasanga and curses them as the
cause of the war and ruin. "You are," he added, "the only white man still my
friend." Delcommune, he said, had fled from fear.

I replied that he, Msiri, is the only person responsible for the continuing
warfare, and that he certainly didn't become king to massacre the people. "You
are evil and your people hate you. As for Delcommune, you lie about him. He
left because it suited him. "

Msiri started speaking again and continued for a whole hour. Once or twice
he went into a rage, but each time he raised his voice, I lifted mine higher still.

After three hours' debate, I told him that since he is my friend and since I am
shortly going to the Lufoi to shoot the game which my men need for food, he
should accept the [Congo Free State] flag and fly it in order to show the
Wasanga that I am his friend. He refused, "No, I won't, for first I want to see if
you really are my friend."

After more argument which lasted half an hour, he promised me to raise the
flag to-morrow, when I had exchanged blood with his brother Kikako. I rejected
that. Finally, with dusk approaching, he rose to retire to his dwelling. Then I
said to him; "Good! If that's the way things are, I'll act without you and raise
the flag myself."

Taking with me a picket of twenty men, I had the flag raised on a hill near the
village. This act of authority has not provoked any disorder, but all night we
are going to remain armed, ready for anything.

Msiri has left his residence and gone to a village an hour from here.

20 December

Msiri fled during the night. The [Congo Free State] flag continues to fly on the
hill where we placed it.

After vainly trying to get in touch with Msiri ... I sent a troop of 100 men
under the command of Bodson and Bonchamps to persuade him to come to see
me and, should he refuse, to lay hands on him.

Bodson and Bonchamps left at 11:50 for Maiembe where the chief was with
115 guns. They divided their forces. Bodson went with twenty men to the
centre of the village to have an interview with Msiri and Bonchamps waited
outside with the rest of the troop, ready to rush in at the first signal. Msiri, it is

evident, had prepared everything to seize hold of the white man and was surrounded by 60 armed men, of whom several had their fingers on their triggers. Msiri was carrying the sword I had given him.

After talking with Msiri for some time, Captain Bodson told him that he was to accompany him to me. If Msiri would not do so of his own accord, he would force him to do so.

The chief replied, "No, I don't want to come." At the same time he drew his sword, which was a signal that had been agreed upon by the conspirators. At that moment, a man sitting near Msiri raised his gun, aiming at Bodson. It was a son of Msiri, killed shortly afterwards. Bodson, nothing daunted, drew his revolver and fired two bullets into the king's chest, on which Hamadi, head of a squad from No. 2 Company, also fired at Msiri who fell dead. But at the same moment Bodson was shot in the stomach. Poor fellow! The bullet lodged in his pelvis, perforated his bladder and worked awful havoc. He was carried by hammock to the camp, in terrible agony. In the evening he died.

Msiri is no longer, his body is in our camp, but at the cost of poor Bodson!

A number of shots were fired and, back at the camp, I was afraid lest the fighting might spread and our men be divided in two if the camp were attacked. Fortunately, Msiri was so loathed by his subjects that almost no one ran to his assistance, all crouching in their huts waiting to see what would happen. Everyone understood that our intention was not to fight until the moment we seized Msiri.

Bodson is dead, but he has delivered Africa of her cruellest tyrant... His final word, as he breathed his last breath, was the cry "Vive le Roi!"*

---

*On 29 December 1891, nine days after the killing of Msiri, Stairs wrote to Frederick Arnot, who was then on leave in Britain. "I am sent here by King of Belgium to arrange matters in this country. I arrived on the 14th and asked Msiri to take the flag of the State, which he refused. On the 19th I put it up in spite of him. The next day he was to make blood-brotherhood with me, but refused to come, so I sent two officers and 100 men *to tell* him to come. He refused, ordered his men to cock their guns, and drew his sword, one which I had given him as a present only a few days before. On this Capt. Bodson, one of my officers, drew his revolver and shot Msiri dead. There was great commotion, but the country is now quiet and breathes freely, since relieved from the brutal tyranny of Msiri. No more heads will be stuck on poles, ears cut off, or people buried alive, if I can help it. Thompson, Crawford and Lane will have free scope, and no longer be 'Msiri's white slaves,' as he told me they were." [2]

The articles in *Le Mouvement Géographique* (Brussels, 1892), which give a translated and edited account of Stairs's Katanga diaries, also contain a brief description by the Marquis de Bonchamps of the deaths of Msiri and Bodson. They agree materially with Stairs's account. Crawford's account adds that Bodson asked Msiri "what he intended to do, and had only said a few words when Msidi with the drawn sword ...

He was a soldier from head to foot, full of initiative, devoted to the expedition. He never, even for a second, argued about the least order I gave him; as soon as the order was given, it was executed. He was a practical fellow, knowing how to turn everything to advantage and always succeeding. Both this expedition and the Belgian army have lost a valuable officer at a most critical time.

Everything is now in complete disarray. I can do only one thing at the moment: restrain my men and keep them in the camp.

21 December

Everyone has fled except Chamundu, who came to see me. I told him that since Msiri was dead, I did not want to fight. My sole desire was to see peace and prosperity return. I gave him Msiri's body to bury and invited Mulumanyama to come to see me.

Bodson was buried with all possible solemnity this morning at 11:00. His body was wrapped in blankets and sheets. Moloney had the grave dug at the foot of the hills which are about 200 yards behind the village of Maria. The body was borne by our headmen ... When we arrived at the burial place, I had the *askaris* present arms, while earth was piled on the grave where our poor Bodson now lies. We erected a temporary cross at the place ... When we have more time, we shall raise here a cairn with a large cross.

Legat departed this evening at 10 o'clock. He is going to the Lufoi River. For additional security he is taking ten men with him. He hopes to reach his station to-night. I have written to the missionaries telling them to proceed to the [Congo Free] State station until the country is more secure. I've moved my column back to a native village over half a mile from Maria's village. I plan to build a temporary station while waiting for the harvest to ripen in three months. From there I shall fan out, making short forays in order to understand better the lie of the land.

There are no hostile blacks at the moment. What is important is to build solid defences, so I can travel about without fearing for the safety of those I leave behind. I estimate that it will take me a month to construct my fort. We have quite an assortment of seeds. Legat, I hope, will be able to give me some I don't have.

22 December

We have begun the construction of Fort Bunkeya. Trenches have been dug and two-thirds of the *boma* has been built from pieces of Msiri's residence.

---

made a thrust at Captain Bodson, which the latter evaded, and at the same time drawing his revolver he shot Msidi dead through the heart. Msidi had just fallen when the contents of several guns were fired into Captain Bodson's back by some men, wounding him mortally" (Arnot, *Bihé and Garenganze*, p. 126).

When the tyrant's dwelling is destroyed, the debris will serve to build a house for the whites. There are good poles, straight and solid. The fort will take the shape of an irregular hexagon with three towers, a trench and a bullet-proof earthwork parapet.

23 December
Mukanda Vantu, Chamundu, Coïmbra, Maria and others have come to see me. Before naming the new king, I wish to know first the people of the country. I have invited Ntenke and Katanga, chiefs from the south, to come as well.

24 December
The construction of the fort continues steadily. A great amount of the material from Msiri's residence has already gone into the palisades and towers. I've had an excellent table made for myself from the door of the tyrant's house. When we have taken all that there is worthwhile for our fort, we'll set fire to what remains.*

25 December
Christmas Day. My men have a holiday. I invited Bonchamps and Moloney to a banquet. Menu: soup, sardines, pigeons, mutton, custard, an English plum pudding, sweets, a bottle of wine each, coffee and cognac. Everyone had a cigar to end the evening.

26 December
I have sent Legat a complete report of recent events.

After thorough consideration, I believe that Mukanda Vantu, Msiri's son, is the best candidate for chief.

27 December
Mulumanyama, who arrived yesterday, had a long meeting with me. He swears that he will prevent all trafficking in gunpowder from the west coast. He signed an act of submission and I gave him a [Congo Free State] flag.

I have learned from a reliable source that Likuku and Chikako have joined forces. But to what end? The latter has promised, once the harvest is ripe, to come and fight.

---

*Stairs wrote to Dan Crawford on 25 December 1891: "Already the people have returned in great numbers to their hoeing and planting ... We are building our fort out of Msiri's own *boma* and the door of his big hut is now my table, off which this evening we eat our Christmas dinner ... I will work hard to keep the [gun] powder out, and let the country get full breathing ... There are no skulls visible at Bunkeya now."

28 December
Bonchamps is seriously ill. Robinson too. The men feed only on *mbogas* or herbs. Even the whites can find no food to buy. This famine is frightful.

29 December
An important day. I nominated Mukanda Vantu chief of the Wagaranze. I had him sign an act of submission and got him to raise [the Congo Free State] flag above his village. I impressed upon the people present how dangerous it would be to pick a quarrel with the new chief. Chikako declares that he is coming to see me now that a new chief has been elected. I gave Mukanda Vantu my sword as a sign of the authority with which he is now invested.

We have done good work on the fort which is now starting to take shape. The moat will be finished tomorrow, I hope. Two of the towers are more or less complete. The storehouse, in the shape of a *tembe*, is finished, as is my house. A barrack ... is being completed. A second dwelling, for the Europeans, is nearly so ... The men need to be constantly urged on. They are beginning to grow weak as a result of living only on leaves ... under a pitiless sun.

I am still without news of the Bia expedition. I've been told of the approach of an expedition led by whites ... It must be an expedition from South Africa [Rhodes's British South Africa Company]. I have informed Legat.

30 December
I have sent a letter to Legat and given another to two of my men to take to Delcommune. They have orders to go as far as ten days south in search of him.

31 December
Mutwila asks me for a flag in making his submission. The whole country is in disorder. The people are fleeing and are shooting at each other with the sole purpose of provoking pillage. My men, crazed with hunger, have become completely unmanageable and are robbing the natives. They are real devils. Nothing can bring them to reason ...

1 January [1892]
The new year opens amidst gloom. The famine is so terrible that it is impossible to restrain the men. Moloney and I are the only two fit [European] men. Everything falls on our shoulders, so we are exhausted.

The year 1892 seems to be a bad omen for me! May God grant that this year will pass happily and that our efforts will be crowned with success.

What a country for famine! "I'm hungry" is the eternal cry. I have nothing with which to appease the torments of the empty stomachs of all these men who trust in me. Curses be on Msiri, author of all this misery!

A starving man is no longer a human being ... There are no means to control him. He cheats and robs the locals. The name of the white man, who thus acquires, through no fault of his own, a terrible reputation. Everywhere there is suffering and famine!

2 January

Morale is very low for want of food. There will be no harvest, alas, until six or seven weeks from now. Poor devils! I pity them, and yet I have to show them a face of stone and force them to work on. The fort must be finished. Evening comes on quickly and once the darkness falls, body and mind are equally exhausted ...

Chapter Twenty-three

With the deaths of Bodson and Msiri and the decisions made about the departure of the expedition and its return route, Stairs's diary suddenly deteriorates, both in quality and quantity. From 2 January 1892 Stairs made no further diary entries for three months. A parallel reading of Moloney's published account, based on his own diaries, becomes indispensable to an understanding of what happened to Stairs and the expedition during the first six months of 1892.

Part of the reason for the brevity and infrequency of Stairs's journal entries from January to his death in June 1892 may be a result of the fact that once he had crossed from the Congo Free State into British territory his impressions of the people and the terrain and the potential for their exploitation was no longer of interest to Leopold or la Compagnie du Katanga. *A far more important reason, however, was Stairs's ill health. He became seriously ill at Christmas 1891, a few days after the killing of Msiri. Moloney diagnosed a near fatal combination of haematuric fever, pneumonia, and, worst of all, tubercular symptoms. Despite Moloney's constant care, Stairs suffered for more than a month from severe fevers, delirium hallucinations, and persistent debilitation, incapable for the first time of shaking off his illness. So ill was Stairs that by 18 January Moloney did not believe that he would survive the night. In such circumstances, it is hardly surprising that the diary entries are erratic and sketchy. The surprise is that he was able to make any entries at all.*

Stairs's problems following the killing of Msiri were fourfold. While awaiting the arrival of Captain Bia to help establish the presence of the Congo Free State in accordance with his contract, Stairs had first to ensure the security of his small force through the construction of a wooden fort. Second, he sought to plant the flag of the Congo Free State not only in Bunkeya but in the surrounding regions. Third, he had somehow to feed his men, now near starvation in a territory devastated by Msiri (and where, in any case, no crops surplus to immediate needs were traditionally cultivated). Fourth, the threat of mutiny was seldom absent; desertions were frequent. Any one of these tasks would have been challenge enough, even with a healthy and well-fed force. Stairs's men were, to the contrary, much debilitated by both disease and hunger. That Stairs was able to extract from them even a limited effort was a major accomplishment.

To complicate matters further for Stairs, the approach of an European expedition was rumoured at the end of December. Stairs understandably assumed that it might be the expedition of the British South Africa Company, led by Joseph Thomson. (Stairs could not know that Thomson had long since turned back in the face of smallpox epidemic and widespread starvation.) Moloney's account reflects the unease which the news caused. Stairs had apparently determined to fight Thomson if the latter attempted to occupy Katanga. Moloney was deeply disturbed by the prospect:

... the notion of fighting against my own fellow-countrymen while receiving the pay of a foreign monarch, appeared both unnatural and repugnant ... Finally, after a week's anxiety, we ascertained definitely that the caravan in our neighbourhood, was not commanded by Europeans at all, but merely by some Arabs ... But before [our] apprehensions ... ceased to occupy our thoughts, worry and bad food had done their work with Captain Stairs, and he became dangerously ill ... He was soon completely incapacitated from command, and I entertained the most serious doubts if he would ever reach the coast alive.[1]

Writing twenty years later, the missionary Crawford also drew a connection between Stairs's apprehension that duty required him to fight a British expedition and his early death. Crawford, writing of Stairs with light irony, recalled,

... a poor man he, daily embarrassed with the stabbing idea that he, an officer holding the Queen's commission, was called upon to repel the advance of his own Union Jack. He it was who intercepted Mushidi's written command by my hand to recall Sir Alfred Sharpe. Fancy an officer with a delicate and scrupulous sense of honour waking up to the piercing realisation that he had become the tool of a foreigner, drawing Belgian money to combat English pretentions! The truth is, this poor fellow was trapped into a very delicate position, not of his own seeking; and as the days advanced, the monstrous enigma of his anti-English duties became a nightmare to him. Dying as he did before leaving Africa, I have sad reason for believing that this brooding over the dilemma hastened his untimely end.[2]

In the partly finished fort at Bunkeya, Stairs's men died at an average rate of two per day. Bonchamps and Robinson were so ill that they could not leave their tents. Moloney was the sole European still on his feet. The command of the fort and the feeding of the expedition, now near starvation, fell to him alone throughout January 1892. At the end of the month Captain Bia's expedition of 400 men finally *arrived. Stairs, from his sick bed, agreed with Bia that his expedition should now set out for the Indian Ocean.* He so wrote to Bia.*

Fort Bunkeya, February 3, 1892.

Dear Sir,

I have, on deliberate consideration with my officers, decided to return to Europe with my expedition. The deposition of Msiri, the election of his successor, the restoration of tranquility and the provisions for the future peace and happiness throughout the land, encourage me sufficiently to believe that I have done all that can be done at present, both for the Company and the country, by remaining here under the difficulties encountered during the last six months.

We arrived here, found the position a difficult one, with Msiri's word law, with famine and sickness everywhere, and we decided to act in a speedy manner, which we did, but which left us stranded from want of provisions. We remained here until your arrival, getting what best we could to eat, while planting crops which are not yet ripe. Many of our men died of hunger and sickness, and the expedition has had such a hard knock that now the only thing to be done is to march it slowly to the coast.

Three of the white men are ill.

Yours, etc.,

W.G. Stairs

The same day, Stairs wrote to Crawford, "I have been in bed now twenty-nine days, and feel that I am not justified in remaining here any longer." The following day, 4 February 1892, the expedition marched out of Fort Bunkeya, bound first for Lakes Moreo, Tanganyika, and Nyasa and then down the Shiré River to the mouth of the Zambesi and the Indian Ocean. In an old kerosene tin, according to Dan Crawford, was Msiri's head.**

---

*The text of Stairs's letter is in Moloney, *With Captain Stairs*, p. 231. Bia assumed command of the Congo Free State fort at Bunkeya, but as the result of an arduous journey northward to place a British plaque at the place of Livingstone's death he died of malaria on 30 August 1892, two months after Stairs.

**If so, Stairs was not alone in collecting the head of his enemy. In Khartoum six years later in 1898, following the battle of Omdurman, Lord Kitchener ordered the body of the Mahdi to be exhumed, his tomb destroyed and his bones thrown into the Nile. The Mahdi's skull, however, was preserved. Some on Kitchener's staff suggested that he should have it mounted as an inkstand or drinking cup. Queen Victoria was not amused by any of this, including Kitchener's proposal to send the skull to the museum of the College of Surgeons in London. The Mahdi's head was eventually reburied at Khartoum.

A total of 360 men had arrived at Bunkeya with Stairs; 200 departed, the balance either having died or deserted. Several score more died or deserted, en route, including two or three survivors of the Emin Relief Expedition. Swamps, steep hills and valleys, rocky terrain and constant hunger confronted the column, but additional difficulties arose from the hostility of several tribes. In one case Moloney, still in effective command, executed two captives as an example to other would-be assailants). Through March and the first half of April 1892 the remnants of the expedition plodded through swamps and over mountains before finally reaching Lake Tanganyika on 15 April. On its way to Katanga the expedition has crossed the lake in better spirits; "somehow, the enthusiasm displayed on the former occasion hardly prevailed among the wayworn company". However, the expedition had passed into British territory and they were warmly received at the stations of the London Missionary Society and of the African Lakes Company (another venture of Sir William Mackinnon). By mid-May the expedition reached Lake Nyasa, the 350-mile length of which it completed on the Domira, *a steamer of the company. At the southern end of the lake, the commissioner for the British Central African Protectorate, Harry Johnston, boarded the* Domira *and discussed at length with Stairs the situation in the region (Stairs does not mention this important interview, perhaps because he believed that, having taken place in British territory, it was not King Leopold's business).*

1 April [1892]
We have reached Makapula. Food is scarce, *rugga-rugga* have destroyed the crops, all the villages have been wiped out and the wretched natives are wandering about in the mountains.

2 April
We are in Kaputa, 8°12' latitude north. All the natives are in terror of the Wanyamwezi. The chief offered a guide so that I can go to Mwanangwa in the south-east where there'll be difficulties, for I mean to say a few words to the Wanyamwezi and show them they must leave the people alone. We are still in Marungu, hence in the Congo Free State, but the natives are Wawembwa. The highest mountain that we can see is 7,300 feet. The altitude we reached going through the passes was 6,000 feet.

◆   ◆   ◆

8 April
We had to cross the Choma River by boat, which was difficult as it has a current of five or six miles an hour. Sharpe's salt lake is only one day S.W. of here ...

◆   ◆   ◆

28 April

... Tsetse disease is rampant, but even if cattle were immune to it, they still wouldn't survive, for the water is swarming with parasites which... kill them.

I've seen Mr. Swan, who arrived from Ujiji on his steamer the *Good News*. He has given me a leopard, a gift from Rumaliza for the Queen. I shall try to get it to Britain.*

◆   ◆   ◆

2 May 1892

We are in Cherezia, five stages (or fifty miles) from Kituta. Yesterday we had to cross the Saizi River. This part of Stephenson's Road** has never, it seems, been rebuilt. Despite that, the march is quite easy, except in a few places. What is really missing are bridges. Along this route the natives are well supplied at least as far as missionaries are concerned. There are missions at Iwando, Mambwe and Kinymkalo.

3 May

We are at Mambwe, the station of the French Fathers. We were received with touching cordiality by Father Van Oost, a Belgian, and two other fathers.

We had a delicious salad of lettuce, onions, radishes, tomatoes, sorrel, potatoes, cabbages, beetroot, etc. and our baggage is literally stuffed with fresh vegetables.

I've noticed that wherever French Fathers establish a mission one finds clear and fresh water, and admirable vegetable gardens. What a difference from British missionaries whose diet, all year long, is based on flour and preserved food! The French Fathers have been here only five months and have, during that short space of time, made astonishing progress ... I've never seen anything like it in Africa. They have an excellent fold for their sheep and goats, a barn with twenty-five head of cattle, and are busy building a large stone house for themselves. Persevering and energetic, they have dedicated their lives to the success of their mission.

4 May

... Today is the Queen's birthday. God grant her many more! I am sure that foreigners must admire her, an honest, upright woman who always acts prudently and rationally.

------

*The leopard died on the journey to Britain.

**Named after Sir James Stephenson, a former soldier and geologist who, inspired by Livingstone, paid in 1881-82 the costs of opening of a track between Lakes Nyasa and Tanganyika so that a steamer might be carried in sections between them.

The march is delightful with shade trees along the route. If a light breeze were blowing through these, one would think oneself in England. We are making forced marches so as to arrive on the 14th at Lake Nyassa. We still 225 miles to go. If we miss the steamer, that will hold us up for a month.

I wonder how, once back in England in a few months' time, I shall settle into the ways of my new regiment, the Welsh.

5 May
... Our men are exhausted. The guide has no idea of the route to follow. Fortunately, it is well-marked, so it is comparatively easy to find the way.

6 May
We have arrived at the station of Mwengo where we were received by Mr. MacCullock of the African Lakes Company. MacCullock lives alone here and has been ill for some time. He's been a year and a half here at Mwengo, a solidly built station, with well-built and ventilated houses. This is half-way between [Lakes] Tanganyika and Nyassa, and for that reason the place is of strategic importance. I hope to reach Lake Nyassa in eight camps.

7 May
Dr. Moloney has gone ahead to prepare for our embarkation on Lake Nyassa.

8 May
After an easy march, we arrived at Mpanza, a well-built village in a valley with a clear stream. The huts are sheltered in the trees, which protect them against the sun and wind. Caravans have raided the natives' crops so often that they now have placed their plantations far from here, behind the mountains. As soon as a caravan is spotted, they send away their wives and children and hide all their provisions. In Africa it is the practice to steal food from one another, and the natives we have just passed would quite shamelessly steal from their nearest relatives if it were a question of obtaining food.

9 May
We are camping in the bush, having descended about 1,000 feet. This valley ... is wonderfully fertile, with an abundance of timber for building. Sugar cane, coffee, wheat, rice, tobacco and vegetables would all thrive here.

10 May
... A large number of my men want to desert. There is a form of madness for deserting even when the men are approaching a place where they will get a thorough rest.

As from to-day, we shall follow the beaten track or Stevenson [sic] Road, as it is called. Until now, our route had consisted of a path running from village to village, going up and down the mountains. The name "Stevenson Road" is quite inappropriate. It is not a road in any proper sense of the word, but merely a track.

11 May
Camping in the bush. Most of my men are in a state of complete demoralization. When we arrive in camp, they lie on their backs, motionless for hours. Neither my exhortations nor anger can rouse them. They are half dead ...

Stevenson's Road, which we have followed all day, is here and there overrun with weeds, but it is nevertheless very good. Even the stupidest black realizes, on seeing it, that the *Wazungu*, in making roads, are not as crazy as they think. In spite of that, the native always considers himself superior to the white...

12 May
We went down the Lufira Valley, through passes strewn with sharp stones that cut the men's feet. To-morrow we have a rough stage as far as Mpata; the next day we shall reach Lake Nyassa where all our miseries, I hope, will end. I pity my poor porters; they are literally dead-beat. African marches are exhausting, morally rather than physically. What torture it is, this march in slow step, day-by-day for months, in order to attain a goal that we yearnto reach rapidly! One reaches it mentally, yet day after day realizes that it is still so far, far away ...

◆　　　◆　　　◆

14 May
We arrived yesterday at 1:00 p.m. on the banks of the Mpato River and set off again at night, marching by moonlight. I received letters from Karongo, notifying me of the arrival of the steamer on 12 May. We arrived here this morning at 10:45 and were received by Messrs. Whyte and Lagher of the African Lakes Company.

Dr. Moloney rejoined us two hours ago, having done 110 miles in five days. My men are almost wild with joy ... from our camp we can see the *Domira* which will take us to Matope, 400 miles from here. It has taken us one hundred days from Bunkeya here.

15 May
The whole day was taken up with embarking men.

Here are notes that I am copying into my diary:

Seven paramount Katanga chiefs have signed the act of submission:

1.   10 November 1891, Kassongomwana, living in his *kurkuru* in Kassansa. Latitude 7°56'55" south; longitude 29°16' east. He is a stupid young

man who is drunk night and day and is dominated by his sub-chiefs. He is very frightened of the Arabs.

2.   17 November, Mpueto, of Mpueto, chief of Kabuire and Bukongolo. An intelligent fellow, but afraid of the Arabs.

3.   18 November, Gueno, of Guena, on the Lualaba. Latitude 8° 4'44" south; longitude 29° 06'45" east. He is a Msumbwa chief, an old enemy of Mpueto's. Fears the Arabs. A peaceable, sensible man.

4.   19 November, Kimwambula, of Chaowela. Msumbwa chief. Lacks intelligence. Great enemy of the Arabs and Msiri.

5.   3 December, Uturutu, residing on the Lualaba River. He's in fact a Balutchi: his real name is Mohammed ben Selim ben Rashid.

6.   28 December, Mulumanyama. Residence: Myinga. Is a Msanga. Enemy of Msiri. Lives two days west of Bunkeya.

7.   29 December, Mkanda Vantu, of Bunkeya, on the Unkeia. Latitude 10°21' south. Nominated by me as Msiri's successor, 29 December 1891. Son of Msiri.

16 May
We left at daybreak. We camp at Ruaria, 100 miles from Karonga, sleeping in the woods. The scenery is splendid in places.

17 May
We arrived at Bandawa where we took on board Mr. and Mrs. MacCallum.

18 May
Left Bandawa, travelling both day and night.

◆   ◆   ◆

20 May
Arrived at Cape MacClear, mission station of the Livingstone Mission.

21 May
We have reached Fort Johnston, ... on the Shiré, and which overlooks this river as well as the entrance to Lake [Nyassa]. The fort is solidly constructed.

22 May
We rest to-day at Fort Johnston. One of my men was taken by a crocodile last night. I had long interviews with Mr. H. Johnston, the Commissioner of the British Central Africa Protectorate.

◆   ◆   ◆

24 May*
Arrived at Matope where everyone left the steamer. Navigation ends here.

25 May
Left early and after a stage of twenty-two and a half miles, we camp on the banks of the Lungu River.

26 May
Arrived at Mandala [Blantyre]** where we have enjoyed great hospitality in a real English house.

27 May
A twenty-two mile march to Katongo. There we shall board the *Lady Nyassa*.

28 May
We sailed on the *Lady Nyassa*, towing five lighters.

◆   ◆   ◆

30 May
Arrived at Chiromo, a station with a great future, at the junction of the Ruo and the Shiré rivers. The Admiralty has established a small dock here. On the other side of the Ruo, the Portugese have a well established post.

I was able to wire Quelimane, thanks to the Portuguese telegraph which runs from here to the coast.

---

* Moloney gives the date as 26 May, two days later.
**Blantyre is the name of Livingstone's birthplace in Scotland. When Stairs stayed overnight at what was still called Mandala, it was a flourishing village with a small stone Gothic church and a garrison of Sikhs. There Stairs encountered both Captain Bertram Sclater whom he had last seen in Zanzibar, and Alfred Sharpe, the British consul.

31 May
We are continuing our descent. We passed two small British gunboats going up river.

1 June [1892]
Yesterday we camped at Port Harold and have now crossed the Anglo-Portugese frontier. We camped at Morambala at the foot of the mountain of the same name, a Portuguese post.

2 June
Arrived at Vicente at the head of the Zambezi delta, once an important place. Passengers and merchandise were then brought along the Kwakwa River and trans-shipped here. Vicente is the base for ascents of the Zambezi River.

3 June
Stopped at Vicente to allow the up-river steamers to pass.

This was Stairs's final diary entry. The Domira *being unable to carry the expedition any farther down the Shiré toward the Zambesi River and the Indian Ocean, the expedition disembarked to march seventy miles around Murchison Rapids.* * Soon after embarking upon the Lady Nyassa *below Murchison Rapids, the expedition passed two graves which were, in retrospect, a portent for Stairs. He paused at the riverine graves of Bishop Mackenzie and Mary Livingstone. It was near their graves that Stairs became fatally ill. Moloney recorded his commander's last days:*

During the last three or four days Captain Stairs was slightly out of sorts, but the symptoms called for no special precautions. He appeared in excellent spirits, and constantly spoke of Zanzibar as the starting-point of future adventures. But before the night had waned, the hand of death was upon him...
At half-past twelve I was summoned to his bedside, and found him suffering from haematuria in its gravest form. Next day he was carried on board, and in the afternoon we reached Chinde, at the river's mouth ... As he lay dying, the ocean's surf could be heard rolling on the bar, and the s.s. *Rovuma* appeared, ready to take us to Zanzibar in the following week. Mr. Robinson was unceasing in his attentions to the sick man, and on the 6th there appeared some hope of recovery. But restless nights undid the work of quiet

---

*Named by Livingstone after his mentor, Sir Roderick Murchison, a geologist who was president of the Royal Geographic Society. For an account of Murchison's notable contributions to the exploitation of central Africa, see Robert Stafford, *Scientist of Empire* (Cambridge University Press, 1989).

mornings and constant restoratives; and he expired on the 9th at six o'clock in the evening...[5]
Stairs was a few days short of twenty-nine years old when he died on 9 June 1892.

♦   ♦   ♦

News of Stairs's death first reached Halifax via New York, although the Canadian High Commissioner in London, Sir Charles Tupper, soon confirmed the death to William Fielding, the premier of Nova Scotia.
Friends in Britain and Canada contributed for a memorial plaque to Stairs to be placed in the garrison church at Halifax, but the cantankerous commander-in-chief, the Duke of Connaught, would not approve the proposal, possibly because Stairs had died in the service of the King of the Belgians.
At the Royal Military College of Canada, a brass plaque was erected to Stairs, Mackay, and their fellow RMC cadet, Henry Robinson (1863–1892), another Royal Engineer who died in Sierra Leone. A separate brass tablet commemorating Stairs alone was placed on the west wall of the RMC administration building. A memorial to the three was also erected in St. George's Cathedral in Kingston and in Rochester Cathedral in Britain (near the Royal Engineers' depot at Chatham).
One of Stairs's sisters had a stone cross erected over his grave in the small European cemetary at Chinde at the mouth of the Zambesi, recording that he had "died June 9th, 1892 ... on his return from successfully leading an expedition to Katangaland."
His family later donated a small collection of his African artifacts to the McCord Museum in Montreal and, sixty years after his death, deposited his Emin Relief Expedition diaries in the Public Archives of Nova Scotia.

Chapter Twenty-four

Stairs's expedition to Katanga, when combined with that of Bia, established beyond any further doubt – according to the European conventions of the day – the claim of King Leopold to the territory. Cecil Rhodes soon directed elsewhere his abundant energies. However, for a decade, Katanga itself relapsed into obscurity, Leopold having insufficient funds to do more than to maintain a small station there. Msiri's son remained a passive puppet of the Congo Free State. Only in 1903 did Leopold finally sanction additional efforts to expand the presence of the Congo Free State in Katanga. Its administration was, however, short-lived. In 1908, in the face of a massive international controversy over the King's misrule of his personal fiefdom, the government of Belgium reluctantly assumed responsibility from Leopold for the Congo Free State, twenty-three years after its formation. Thereafter, the copper mines of Katanga began to be worked in earnest. The Arabs were gradually banished, but harsh forms of exploitation persisted for several decades.

◆　◆　◆

Stairs's diaries of the Emin Relief Expedition and of his own Katanga expedition recount a progression from an open innocence to a spiritual corruption that Lord Acton would have immediately recognized. In securing Katanga for Leopold, Stairs had changed the direction of the lives of tens of thousands of Africans. In so doing, he himself had incurred the further spiritual corruption and brutalization which had begun in the Emin Relief Expedition.

References to Joseph Conrad's novel *Heart of Darkness* are included in most recent accounts of the Emin Relief Expedition or of Stanley's travels since

Conrad was the first novelist to attempt an analysis of the transformation black Africa wrought in Europeans.* For example, Marlow, the narrator in *Heart of Darkness*, is examined before his departure for the Congo Free State by a Brussels physician who is convinced that all such volunteers must be driven by powerful irrational impulses to take such risks and that their personalities must be altered drastically by the colonial environment. In the event, Marlow barely escapes the transformation. Stairs does not.

There is a great difference between the Lieutenant Stairs of the *Navarino* reading *The Bridal Eve* and sending crates of oranges from Malta to friends in Britain or recalling the piscatorial delights of Nova Scotia and the Captain Stairs of Katanga who had on two expeditions killed many men whose sole offence was that they resisted the entry of the European expeditions and Arab slavers into their homeland. Eventually, Stairs could even write complacently:

It was most interesting, lying in the bush and watching the natives quietly at their day's work; some women were pounding the bark of trees preparatory to making the coarse native cloth ... others were making banana flour ... men we could see building huts and engaged at other such work, boys and girls running about singing ... others playing on a small instrument.... All as it was every day until our discharge of bullets when the usual uproar and screaming of women took place....

On other occasions Stairs ordered his men to kill the wounded. He had the heads cut off the dead and impaled on poles as warnings to others. But it was the severing of hands which he pursued more commonly. As Stairs soon learned, the practice of such mutilation was to be found among several Congo tribes. Certainly Msiri was doing it in Katanga when Stairs was doing it on the Emin Relief Expedition. Perhaps two quotations will give some idea of the prevalence of the practice in the Congo Free State (and for that matter in German East Africa). Describing the actions of black African soldiers in the pay of the Congo Free State at the turn of the century, the Belgian historian, Jean Stengers, has written, [they]" brought back hands cut from the dead or the dying, with the aim of proving to their officers that they had made good use of the cartridges issued to them."[1] By 1908, as Stenger notes, "the cut-off hand [had become] the symbol of the Leopoldian regime", so much so in fact that it played a major part in the successful campaign of Roger Casement and Edmond Morel to end Leopold's atrocities in the Congo.

---

*Some critics have seen Barttelot as Conrad's model for Kurtz but this seems doubtful if for no other reason than Kurtz became enamoured of the life of a local potentate and Barttelot did not. For a discussion of some of the factors involved, see appendix II of Jones, *Rescue of Emin Pasha*, pp. 442-447.

The spread of the practice of mutilation was associated with the growth in demand for rubber. Coercion was increasingly used to force native peoples to collect the latex in the forests. By 1890 reports had begun to seep back to Europe of the brutal methods employed. British missionaries were among the first to tell Europe what was really happening when the cannibal and other tribes of the upper Congo were used in the *Force publique* to exact the rubber quotas. Under the direction of European officers, heads and hands were cut off (how it was thought that a handless survivor could collect rubber is not explained). Stairs had died before these atrocities became common on the upper Congo, but men under his command practiced them.

Before the Emin Relief Expedition, Stairs had not lived among aboriginal peoples. His experience had been that of boarding schools and a small military college (itself similar to a boarding school) and wilderness surveys in New Zealand. Following his departure from home at the age of 12 for boarding school in Edinburgh, Stairs had necessarily learned self-reliance, but he had no experience of the brutality which had so disfigured Stanley's childhood. Nothing in Stairs's life had prepared him for such ruthless and ultimately corrupting encounters with aboriginal people as he experienced on the Congo. Although in both Canada and New Zealand the native peoples had frequently been treated harshly, it was never with such systematic brutality as in Leopold's Congo Free State.

The corruption of absolute power began early in the Emin Relief Expedition: only three weeks up the Congo, Stairs sensed what was beginning to happen. "Certainly nothing that I have ever seen so completely demoralizes a man as driving negro carriers. One's temper is up all the time, kind feelings are knocked on the head and I should think in time a man would become a perfect brute if he did nothing else but this." Given his superior arms, Stairs' power was total over those whom he commanded (save in the case of the Emin Relief Expedition itself where the ultimate authority was of course Stanley's). No African porter could escape the most condign punishment – men died from the lash as well as mutilations and hangings – if Stairs or any of the other officers judged them guilty of some misdemeanour. Valued as mere pack animals, they were severely maltreated if they did not observe in detail the European idea of work and servile obedience.

It was, however, the daily proximity of death which appears to have been central to Stairs' hostility toward all who stood in the way of the two expeditions. Delay meant starvation or disease, either of which was likely to kill off the expedition if the native peoples themselves did not. The only chance for survival was to push on against all opposition or, if in camps, kill any who attempted to steal food or other supplies.

In neither expedition did any of the officers escape the effect on themselves of Stanley's ruthless example of smashing his way across Africa. Moreover, everyone was transformed by the terrible monotony and frustration of each day which was indistinguishable from the preceding or succeeding; by the persistent physical discomforts, including near starvation; and perhaps above all by the poisonous relationship between omnipotent master and near-slave whose only incentive to obey was fear and yet who nevertheless suffered from random acts of violence. One result was that most Europeans, if not all, on Congo expeditions behaved irritably, irrationally and even hysterically. Barttelot was a notable example (he had already killed a recalcitrant native on the Sudan expedition of 1884–85).

In the Rear Column, Barttelot appears to have gradually become unbalanced by the absolute power he wielded over others. Jephson and Jameson, both young men who, like Stairs, had not before been on an African expedition, were also transformed; Jephson eventually outdid even Stanley in calling for the execution of deserters and Jameson appears to have been a willing spectator at a cannibal killing and feast. Only Parke on the first expedition and Moloney on the second – perhaps because of their training in healing – seem to have partly escaped the pervasive spiritual corruption that marked the other officers, especially those of the Emin Relief Expedition, although neither refrained from executing anyone who attempted to leave the expedition.

And yet Stairs, at least to the end of the Emin Relief Expedition, showed occasional signs of uneasiness and remorse at Stanley's actions and even at his own. Stanley considered him too soft on the blacks (but then Sir Richard Burton regarded Stanley as a bully who "shot negroes like monkeys"). Stairs's diary entries, however much they may have been later edited, occasionally manifest either doubt or transparent efforts at self-reassurance. A direct young man, Stairs leaves the impression of occasional misgivings about what was happening around him, but equally an inability to analyze what was happening to himself. Understanding one's own motives is never easy. Stairs's reaction to the appalling circumstances in which he crossed Africa was frequently to retreat into jingo jargon and broad imperialist rationalizations. Occasionally he attempted an apologia for his participation in the two expeditions, but he never rises above banal, conventional superficiality. In the end, his explanations remain sterile. For example, in responding to the acclaim of his native Halifax, Stairs justified the Expedition not in terms of rescuing Emin. He concentrated almost exclusively on material considerations: the Expedition had opened the way for commerce and civilization. The resultant changes to "the existing political conditions of affairs [sic] among the tribes of Central Africa [will benefit] the British Empire...." It is difficult to know whether Stairs really believed such imperial rhetoric. Certainly at his death he left no clear evidence of his personal convictions, despite having participated in the opening of the upper Congo to European as well as to further Arab exploitation and having delivered Katanga from the cruel excesses of Msiri to the brutalities of the Congo Free State.

There is no reflection in Stairs's diaries of a deep commitment to anyone of the three Cs that some have regarded as the driving motives of African explorers: Christianity, commerce and civilization. Stairs is decidedly unenthusiastic about the employees of the Congo Free State, rejecting them as purveyors of civilization. And yet when he himself enters the service of Leopold, he does not offer the explanation that he does so to spread civilization among benighted Africans. Although Stairs on his second expedition was helping to open the way to the commercial exploitation of Katanga, he seldom considers the fact. As for Christianity, some missionaries he respected, but only on a selective basis. There is no sign in his writings of any deep conviction that conversion to Christianity would be a boon for Africa.

At the time of his death, Stairs did not seem much disturbed by the continuing slavery in east Africa. There is no record of regret at the fact that the Emin Relief Expedition opened large new tracts to the Arab slavers. And his very occasional disparagement of slavery did not prevent him from contemplating the employment of slaves in his Katanga expedition. Three weeks before his death, Stairs wrote to Parke, "How things will go with me when I get back [to England] I cannot imagine. I suppose the Anti-Slavery Society will try and jump upon me for employing slaves as they seem to think I am doing and then there will be further outcries about my having being employed by the King [Leopold]. However, I don't fancy these will disturb me to a great extent." It is evident that Stairs was thinking about how his decidedly questionable actions and motives would be judged in Britain, but he died neither repentant nor contrite.

◆   ◆   ◆

Why did Stairs volunteer for the Emin Relief Expedition? Why did he accept Stanley's methods? Why did he later seek the command of an expedition on behalf of Leopold when he had repeatedly recorded his contempt for the Congo Free State and the base character of its officers and their callous methods? Stairs knew that many adventurers in the Congo had sought escape there from their own sense of inferiority by the feeling of superiority that they acquired as Europeans among subject people.

What remains of Stairs's writings (unfortunately few personal letters are extant) would suggest that his initial motive in volunteering for the expeditions was probably nothing more than a desire for adventure as an antidote to the tedium of peacetime soldiering in Britain. As a young bachelor of an apparently uncomplicated character, Stairs, in sending his applications to Stanley and Leopold, was seeking adventure in the same way that other young officers were doing across the Empire. Certainly there is no reflection of a desire to enlarge his own mind by contact with other peoples and other places. From the

Domira on 19 May 1892, Stairs wrote to Parke, then a surgeon major at a military hospital in southern England, "What are you doing now? Are you still at Netley? Take my advice, old man, and do your best to get away on some special business – You will only rot out your life doing the ordinary cut and dried business of the Service – there are too many doing the same."

There is, in fact, little or nothing in Stairs' diaries to suggest that he puzzled overly about what he was doing in Africa. In seeking the command of the Katanga expedition, it is possible that Stairs had convinced himself that there could be no ready reclamation of the early and easy life in the mess or, more broadly, that no one would ever understand what he had endured or witnessed in Africa. Perhaps one should do no more than accept Stairs's own statements that he found irresistible the appeal of commanding his own expedition in a land distant from regimental and traditional constraints. Moloney – who appears to have been an acute observer of human nature – arrived at that conclusion. In describing Stairs's apparent recovery before his sudden and fatal illness, Moloney implies such a final if ultimately ambiguous judgment. "All the suffering and sickness ...he had completely forgotten, and his ardent spirit made light of fresh hardships, provided they were accompanied by fresh discoveries and achievements. Upon him the Dark Continent had laid her spell with an absolutely imperious influence."*

That Stairs and the other European officers were brave men cannot be gainsaid, but they were transformed spiritually as they were caught up in the need to suppress, control and exploit as the scramble for Africa proceeded. Their self-destruction was not that of Kurtz in *Heart of Darkness*. They did not "go native", becoming enamoured of local life and practices. The Africans were not the only victims; they were themselves victims of the corrupting system which they represented. Dostoyevsky knew what the result would be: "Tyranny is a habit; it has a capacity for development; it develops finally into a disease."

Such an evaluation of Stairs reflects in part today's values. During the decades before the First World War, justifications for the suffering and havoc that expeditions brought to central and east Africa were more readily accepted as unavoidable misfortunes on the way to "civilization". All history is reinterpreted by every generation. It is difficult, however, to believe that, without engaging in retrospective moralizing, this or any future generation will conclude that Stairs's undoubted courage, stamina and perseverance in the face of manifold adversities and his undoubted sense of duty and responsibility were not fundamentally misguided and might not have been better employed in a more productive commitment, uncorrupted by absolute power.

---

*With Captain Stairs, p. 273. Moloney might also have been describing himself; he later successfully applied to lead an expedition of the Congo Free State.

Both expeditions in which Stairs served may have upon occasion brought out the best in him, but it was Stairs's particular misfortune to serve successively under the malign command of Stanley and Leopold. Two more unattractive characters it would be difficult to imagine. Their injection into the Congo and the subsequent disequilibrium they caused was a disaster for almost everyone involved. Livingstone and Thomson had each travelled through Africa without arousing enmity, rancour or antagonism. There were no rawhide whips in their limited baggage. Their accomplishments were by peaceful means: as Thomson once observed, "a gentle word was more potent than gunpowder." Stanley and Stairs, however, penetrated Africa in a quite different fashion. They sought no conciliation but rather submission. If it was not forthcoming, they killed to enforce it. Gradually Stairs succumbed. Nowhere in his diaries is there any sign of regret. As was even more the case with Stanley, the penetration of Africa corrupted Stairs. For all its floggings, shootings and hangings, Stanley's last expedition was pointless. Equally pointless was Stairs's expedition to Katanga, leaving a legacy of decades of maltreatment and to this day confusion compounded.

Appendix I

Stairs's report to Stanley on his tenure of command at Fort Bodo:

Dated: Fort Bodo, December 21, 1888.

SIR,

I have the honour to report that, in accordance with your letter of instructions dated Fort Bodo, June 13th, 1888, I took over the charge of Fort Bodo and its garrison.

The strength of the garrison was then as follows: Officers, 3; Zanzibaris, 51; Soudanese, 5; Madis, 5; total, 64.

Soon after your departure from [? for] Yambuya, the natives in the immediate vicinity became excessively bold and aggressive; gangs of them would come into the plantations nearly every day searching for plantains, and at last a party of them came into the gardens east of the Fort at night-time and made off with a quantity of tobacco and beans. On the night of the 21 August they again attempted to steal more tobacco; this time, however, the sentries were on the alert. The lesson they received had the effect of making the natives less bold, but still our bananas were being taken at a great rate. I now found it necessary to send out three parties or patrols per week; these had as much as they could do to keep out the natives and elephants. If fires were not made every few days the elephants came into the bananas, and would destroy in a single night some acres of plantation.

By November 1st we had got the natives well in hand, and at this time I do not believe a single native camp exists within eight miles of the Fort. Those natives to the S.S.E. of the Fort gave us the most trouble, and were the last to move away from our plantations.

At the end of July we all expected the arrival of Mr. Mounteney Jephson from the Albert Nyanza to relieve the garrison, and convey our goods on to the Lake shore. Day after day, however, passed away, and no sign of him or news from him reaching us made many of the men more and more restless as each day passed. Though most of the men wished to remain at the Fort till relief turned up, either in the shape of Mr. Jephson or yourself, still some eight or ten discontented ones, desirous of reaching the Lake and partaking of the plenty there, were quite ready at any time to desert the loads, the white men, and sick.

Seeing how things stood I treated the men at all times with the greatest leniency, and did whatever I could to make their life at the Fort as easy for them as was possible.

Shortly after the time of Mr. Jephson's expected arrival, some of the men came to me and asked for a "shauri"; this I granted. At this shauri the following propositions were made by one of the men (Ali Juma), and assented to by almost every one of the Zanzibaris present: (1) To leave the Fort, march on to the Lake by way of Mazamboni's country, making double trips, and so get on all the loads to the Lake and have plenty of food. (2) Or, to send say fifteen couriers with a letter to the edge of the plain, there to learn if the Bandusuma were still our friends or no; if unfriendly, then to return to the Fort; if friendly, then the couriers would take on the letter to Mr. Jephson, and relief would come.

To the first proposal I replied: (1) Mr. Stanley told me not to move across the plain, whatever else I did, without outside aid. (2) Did not Mr. Stanley tell Emin Pasha it was not safe to cross the plains, even should the natives be friendly, without sixty guns? (3) We had only thirty strong men, the rest were sick; we should lose our loads and sick men.

We all lived on the best of terms after I had told them we could not desert the Fort. We went on hoeing up the ground and planting corn and other crops, as if we expected a prolonged occupation. On the 1st September a severe hurricane accompanied by hail passed over the Fort, destroying fully 60 per cent of the standing corn, and wrecking the banana plantations to such an extent that at least a month passed before trees commenced to send up young shoots. Had it not been for this we should have had great quantities of corn; but as it was I was only able to give each man ten corns [cobs] per week. The weakly ones, recommended by Dr. Parke, got one cup of shelled corn each per day. At one time we had over thirty men suffering from ulcers, but, through the exertion of Dr. Parke, all their ulcers on your arrival had healed up with the exception of some four.

Eight deaths occurred from the time of your departure up to the 20th December, two were killed by arrows, and two were captured by natives.

In all matters where deliberation was necessary the other officers and myself took part. We were unanimous in our determination to await your arrival, knowing that you were using every endeavour to bring relief to us as speedily as possible.

On the 20th December I handed over the charge of the Fort to you, and on the 21st the goods entrusted to my care.

I have the honour to be, Sir,
Your obedient servant,
W.G. STAIRS
Lieut. R.E.

Appendix II

Stairs's report on his attempted ascent of the Ruwenzori mountains:

H.M. Stanley, Esq., Commanding Emin Pasha Relief Expedition. Expedition Camp, June 8th, 1889.

Sir,

I have the honour to present you with the following account of an attempt made by me to reach the snow-capped peaks of Ruwenzori.

Early on the morning of the 6th June, accompanied by some forty Zanzibaris, we made a start from the Expedition's camp at the foot-hills of the range, crossed the stream close to camp, and commenced the ascent of the mountain. With me I had two aneroids, which together we had previously noted and compared with a standard aneroid remaining in camp under your immediate observation; also a Fahrenheit thermometer.

For the first 900 feet above camp the climbing was fairly good, and our progress was greatly aided by a native track which led up to some huts in the hills. These huts we found to be of the ordinary circular type so common on the plains, but with the difference that bamboo was largely used in their interior construction. Here we found the food of the natives to be maize, bananas, and colocasia roots. On moving away from these huts we soon left behind us the long rank grass, and entered a patch of low, scrubby bush, intermixed with bracken and thorns, making the journey more difficult.

At 8:30 a.m. we came upon some more huts of the same type, and found that the natives had decamped from them some days previously. Here the barometer read 23.58 and 22.85; the thermometer 75° F. On all sides of us we could see dracaenas, and here and there an occasional tree-fern and mwab palm; and, tangled in all shapes on either side of the track, were masses of long bracken. The natives now appeared at different hill-tops and points nearby, and did their best to frighten us back down the mountain, by shouting and blowing horns. We, however, kept on our way up the slope, and in a short time they disappeared and gave us very little further trouble.

Of the forest plains, stretching far away below us, we could see nothing, owing to the thick haze that then obscured everything. We were thus prevented from seeing the hills to the west and north-west.

At 10:30 a.m., after some sharp climbing. we reached the last settlement of the natives, the cultivation consisting of beans and colocasias, but no bananas. Here the barometer read 22.36; thermometer 84° F. Beyond this settlement was a rough track leading up the spur to the forest; this we followed, but in many places to get along at all we had to crawl on our hands and knees, so steep were the slopes.

At 11 a.m. we reached this forest and found it to be one of bamboos, at first open, and then getting denser as we ascended. We now noticed a complete and sudden change in the air from that we had just passed through. It became much cooler and more pure and refreshing, and all went along at a faster rate and with lighter hearts. Now that the Zanzibaris had come so far, they all appeared anxious to ascend as high as possible, and began to chaff each other as to who should bring down the biggest load of the "white stuff" on the top of the mountain.

At 12:40 p.m. we emerged from the bamboos and sat down on a grassy spot to eat our lunch. Barometer is 21.10 and 27.95/120. Thermometer 70° F. Ahead of us, and rising in one even slope, stood a peak, in altitude 1200 feet higher than we were. This we now started to climb, and after going up it a short distance came upon the tree-heaths. Some of these bushes must have been 20 feet high, and as we had to cut our way foot by foot through them, our progress was necessarily slow and very fatiguing to those ahead.

At 3:15 we halted among the heaths for a few moments to regain our breath. Here and there were batches of inferior bamboos, almost every stem having holes in it, made by some boring insect, and quite destroying its usefulness. Under foot was a thick spongy carpet of wet moss, and the heaths on all sides of us, we noticed, were covered with "Old Man's Beard." We found great numbers of blue violets and lichens, and from this spot I brought away some specimens of plants for the Pasha to classify. A general feeling of cold dampness prevailed; in spite of our exertions in climbing, we all felt the cold mist very much. It is this continual mist clinging to the hill-tops that no doubt causes all the vegetation to be so heavily charged with moisture and makes the ground under foot so wet and slippy.

Shortly after 4 p.m. we halted among some high heaths for camp. Breaking down the largest bushes, we made rough shelters for ourselves, collected what firewood we could find, and in other ways made ready for the night. Firewood, however, was scarce, owing to the wood being so wet that it would not burn. In consequence of this, the lightly-clad Zanzibaris felt the cold very much, though the altitude was only about 8500 feet. On turning in, the thermometer registered 60° F. From camp I got a view of the peaks ahead, and it was now that I began to fear we should not be able to reach the snow. Ahead of us, lying directly in our path, were three enormous ravines; at the bottoms at least two of these there was dense bush. Over these we should have to travel and cut our way through the bush. It then would resolve itself into a question of time as to whether we could reach the summit or not. I determined to go on in the morning, and see exactly what difficulties lay before us, and if these could be surmounted in a reasonable time to go on as far as we possibly could.

On the morning of the 7th, selecting some of the best men, and sending the others down the mountain, we started off again upwards, the climbing being similar to that we experienced yesterday afternoon. The night had been bitterly cold, and some of the men complained of fever, but all were in good spirits, and quite ready to go on. About 10 a.m. we were stopped by the first of the ravines mentioned above. On looking at this I saw that it would take a long time to cross, and there were ahead of it still two others. We now got our first glimpse of a snow peak, distant about two and a half miles, and I judged it would take us still a day and a half to reach this, the nearest snow. To attempt it, therefore, would only end disastrously, unprovided as we were with food, and some better clothing for at least two of the men. I therefore decided to return, trusting all the time that at some future camp a better opportunity for making an ascent would present itself, and the summit be reached. Across this ravine was a bare, rocky peak, very clearly defined, and known to us as the south-west of the "Twin Cones". The upper part of this was devoid of vegetation, the steep beds of rock only allowing a few grasses and heaths in one or two spots to exist.

The greatest altitude reached by us, after being worked out and all corrections applied, was about 10,677 feet above the sea. The altitude of the snow peak above this would probably be about 6000 feet, making the mountain say, 16,600 feet high. This, though, is not the highest peak in the Ruwenzori cluster. With the aid of a field glass I could make out the form of the mountain tip perfectly. The extreme top of the peak is crowned with an irregular mass of jagged and precipitous rock, and has a distinct crater-like form. I could see, through a gap in the near side, a corresponding rim or edge on the farther, of the same formation and altitude. From this crown of rock, the big peak slopes to the eastward at a slope of about 25°, until shut out from view by an intervening peak; but to the west the slope is much steeper. Of the snow, the greater mass lay on that slope directly nearest us, covering the slope wherever its inclination was not too great. The largest bed of snow would cover a space measuring about 600 by 300 feet, and of such depth that in only two spots did the black rock crop out above its surface.

Smaller patches of snow extended well down into the ravine; the height from the lowest snow to the summit of the peak would be about 1200 feet or 1000 feet. To the E.N.E. our horizon was bounded by the spur which, starting directly behind our main camp, and mounting abruptly, takes a curve in a horizontal plane and centres on to the snow peak. Again, that spur which lay south of us also radiated from the two highest peaks. This would seem to be the general form of the mountain, namely, that the large spurs radiate from the snow peaks as a centre, and spread out to the plains below. This formation on the west side of the mountain would cause the streams to start from a centre, and flow on, gradually separating from each other until they reach the plains below. There they turn to the W.N.W. or trace their courses along the bottom spurs of the range and run into the Semliki River, and on to the Albert Nyanza. Of the second snow peak which we have seen on former occasions I could see nothing, owing to the "Twin Cones" intervening. This peak is merely the termination, I should think, of the snowy range we saw when at Kavalli's, and has a greater elevation, if so, than the peak we endeavoured to ascend. Many things go to show that the existence of these peaks is due to volcanic causes. The greatest proof that this is so lies in the numbers of conical peaks clustering round the central mass and on the western side. These minor cones have been formed by the central volcano getting blocked in its crater, owing to the pressure of its gases not being sufficient to throw out the rock and lava from its interior; and consequently the gases, seeking for weak spots, having burst through the earth's crust and this been the means of forming these minor cones that now exist. Of animal life on the mountain we saw almost nothing. That game of some sort exists is plain from the numbers of pitfalls we saw in the road-sides, and from the fact of our finding small nooses in the natives' huts such as those used for taking ground game. We heard the cries of an ape in a ravine, and saw several dull greyish-brown birds like stone-chats, but beyond these nothing.

We found blueberries and blackberries at an altitude of 10,000 feet and over, and I have been able to hand over to the Pasha some specimens for his collections, the generic names of which he has kindly given me, and which are attached below. That I could not manage to reach the snow and bring back some as evidence of our work, I regret very much, but to have proceeded onwards to the mountain under the conditions which we were situated I felt would be worse than useless; and though all of us were keen and ready to go on, I gave the order to return. I then read off the large aneroid, and found the hand stood at 19.90. I set the index pin directly opposite to the hand, and we started downhill. At 3 p.m. on the 7th I reached you, it having taken 4½ hours of marching from the "Twin Cones."

I have the honour to be, Sir,
Your obedient servant,

Notes

INTRODUCTION

1 *The River War* (London, 1899), p. 68.
2 *Emin Pasha: His Life and Work*, 2 vols. (London, 1898); introduction by R.W. Felkin. *Emin Pasha in Central Africa*, translated by Mrs. R.W. Felkin (London, 1888). Much more is known about Emin's later life than his earlier, partly from his own diaries: Franz Stuhlmann, ed., *Die Tagebücher von Dr. Emin Pascha*, 6 vols. (Hamburg, 1916–27) (a projected seventh volume was never published).
3 Parke, *My Personal Experiences*, p. 382.
4 Smith, *Emin Pasha*, p. 9.
5 Jones, *The Rescue of Emin*, p. 74.
6 McLynn, *Stanley: Sorcerer's Apprentice*, p. 17.
7 See in particular Galbraith, *Mackinnon and East Africa*.
8 J.S. Cotton and E.J. Payne, *Colonies and Dependencies* (London, 1883), p. 114.
9 Letter of 28 December 1884 from Derby to Granville, quoted in Galbraith, *Mackinnon*, p. 10.
10 Quoted in Lady Gwendolyn Cecil, *Life of Robert, Marquis of Salisbury* (London, 1921–32), IV: 310.
11 Anstey, *Britain and the Congo*, p. 201.
12 Quoted in ibid., p. 207.
13 Quoted in ibid.
14 Salisbury to Iddesleigh, 23 September 1886, quoted in Robinson and Gallagher, *Africa and the Victorians*, p. 199.
15 Quoted in Anstey, *Britain and the Congo*, p. 217.
16 Quoted in Smith, *Emin Pasha*, p. 34.

17   Quoted in ibid., p. 36.
18   Quoted in ibid., p. 55.
19   McLynn, *Stanley: Sorcerer's Apprentice*, pp. 158-59.
20   Smith, *Emin Pasha*, p. 87.
21   Ward, *My Life*, p. 33.
22   Troup, *With Stanley's Rear Column*, p. 138.
23   Jameson, *Story of the Rear Column*, p. 264.
24   Ward, *My Life*, p. 122.
25   *Life of Edmund Musgrove Barttelot*, p. 297.
26   Stanley, *In Darkest Africa*, vol. 1: 43.
27   Letter of 30 January 1890 from Stanley to Lord Wolseley; Public Archives of Nova Scotia, MG 29, vol. 63.
28   Ward, *My Life*, p. 11.
29   Letter of 30 January 1890 from Stanley to Lord Wolseley; Public Archives of Nova Scotia, MG 29, vol. 63.
30   Letter of Henry Stairs to his sister, Hilda Johnston, 7 May 1908; ibid.

CHAPTER ONE

1   Published in London, 1872.
2   Henry M. Stanley, *The Congo and the Founding of its Free State* (London, 1885).
3   Published in London, 1878.
4   Quoted in Elizabeth Longford, *Wilfrid Scawen Blunt* (London, 1979), p. 240.

CHAPTER TWO

1   *Lugard*, vol. I: 196.

CHAPTER THREE

1   Jameson, *Story of the Rear Column*, p. 14.
2   Jones, *The Rescue of Emin Pasha*, p. 101.
3   Jameson, *Story of the Rear Column*, p. 48.
4   *Life of Edmund Musgrove Barttelot*, p. 97.
5   Jones, *The Rescue of Emin Pasha*, pp. 101-2.

CHAPTER FOUR

1   D. Stanley, ed., *Autobiography*, pp. 355-56.
2   Parke, *My Personal Experiences*, p. 68.
3   Copy of letter from Stanley to Stairs; Public Archives of Nova Scotia, MG 29, vol. 63.

4   McLynn, *Stanley: Sorcerer's Apprentice*, p. 186.
5   Jameson, *Story of the Rear Column*, p. 75.
6   Jephson, *The Diary of*, p. 111.
7   Parke, *My Personal Experiences*, p. 70.
8   D. Stanley, ed., *Autobiography*, p. 356.

CHAPTER FIVE

1   Jameson, *Story of the Rear Column*, p. 107.
2   D. Stanley, ed., *Autobiography*, p. 358.
3   Hoffman, *With Stanley in Africa*, p. 41.

CHAPTER SIX

1   Jameson, *Story of the Rear Column*, pp. 141-42.

CHAPTER SEVEN

1   D. Stanley, ed., *Autobiography*, p. 360.

CHAPTER EIGHT

1   Note by Stanley in Public Archives of Nova Scotia, MG 92, vol. 63.

CHAPTER NINE

1   Jameson, *Story of the Rear Column*, p. 226.

CHAPTER TEN

1   Quoted in McLynn, *Stanley: Sorcerer's Apprentice*, pp. 249-50.
2   Samuel Austin Allibone, *A Critical Dictionary of English Literature and British and American Authors* (Philadelphia, 1858).

CHAPTER ELEVEN

1   Stanley, *In Darkest Africa*, vol. I: 494.
2   Jephson, *The Diary of*, p. 329.

CHAPTER THIRTEEN

1   Quoted in Smith, *Emin Pasha*, pp. 254-55.

CHAPTER FOURTEEN

1 Stanley, *In Darkest Africa*, vol. II: 212.

CHAPTER FIFTEEN

1 D. Stanley, ed., *Autobiography*, p. 269.
2 Quoted in A.G. Gardiner, *The Life of Sir William Harcourt* (London, 1913),vol. II: 94. Harcourt was using "filibuster" in the original English sense of a pirate on the Spanish Main.
3 Ibid.
4 Quoted in McLynn, *Stanley: Sorcerer's Apprentice*, p. 459.
5 Jones, *The Rescue of Emin*, p. 249.
6 Public Archives of Nova Scotia, MG 29, vol. 63.
7 Ibid.
8 Moloney, *With Captain Stairs*, p. 14.

CHAPTER SIXTEEN

1 Verney Lovett Cameron, *Across Africa*, 2 vols. (London, 1877) (a one-volume edition was published in 1885).
2 Quoted in Rotberg, *Joseph Thomson*, p. 63.
3 Cornet, *Katanga*, pp. 38-39.
4 Quoted in Arnot, *Bihé and Garenganze*, p. 112.
5 Ibid., p. 211.
6 Quoted in Slade, *King Leopold's Congo*, p. 216.
7 Moloney, *With Captain Stairs,* p. 9.
8 Katanga file, *Histoire de la présence belge outre-mer*, 95.U.43, Musée Royal de l'Afrique centrale, Brussels.
9 Ibid., pp. 15-16.
10 Sheldon, *From Sultan to Sultan*, p. 29.

CHAPTER NINETEEN

1 Moloney, *With Captain Stairs*, p. 72.
2 Ibid., p. 92.

CHAPTER TWENTY-ONE

1 Quoted in Martelli, *From Leopold to Lumumba*, p. 133.
2 Sharpe to H.H. Johnston, 8 September 1890, Johnston to the Foreign Office, 3 May 1891; Slade, *English-Speaking Missions*, pp. 118-19.
3 Moloney, *With Captain Stairs*, p. 162.

CHAPTER TWENTY-TWO

1 Moloney, *With Captain Stairs*, p. 166.
2 Arnot, *Missionary Travels,* p. 119.

CHAPTER TWENTY-THREE

1 Moloney, *With Captain Stairs*, pp. 208-10.
2 Crawford, *Thinking Black*, pp. 303-4.
3 Moloney, *With Captain Stairs*, p. 231.
4 Quoted in Arnot, *Bihé and Garenganze*, p. 130.
5 Moloney, *With Captain Stairs*, pp. 275-76.

CHAPTER TWENTY-FOUR

1 Jean Stengers, *Colonialism in Africa 1870–1960*, vol. I: *The History and Politics of Colonialism, 1870–1914*, ed. L.H. Gann and Peter Duignan (Cambridge: Cambridge University Press, 1969) p. 269.
2 Perham, *Lugard*, p. 199. The quotation from Lugard is vol. I, p. 243.

Bibliography

In addition to inspiring a short play (Simon Gray, *The Rear Column*, first presented at the Globe Theatre, London [February 1978]) and a long novel (Peter Forbath, *The Last Hero* [London, 1989]), the Emin Relief Expedition has during the past century spawned a small library of books and articles. So many, in fact, are accounts of the expedition (largely in English and German, although some are in French) that as early as 1960 D.H. Simpson attempted to compile a comprehensive "Bibliography of Emin Pasha", *Uganda Journal*, XXIV, no. 2 (1960).

Since then the number of books and articles about the Emin Relief Expedition has burgeoned. Far less has been written about Stairs's Katanga expedition. The following list records the articles and books which have been especially useful in editing Stairs's diaries of the two expeditions, but makes no claim to be exhaustive (for example, London newspapers and periodicals of 1886 to 1890 contain many news reports and articles about the Emin Pasha Expedition and the several Halifax newspapers of the day record its progress and, in particular, Stairs's participation). Generally brief, these articles are too numerous to merit a detailed listing here, but the interested reader may wish to consult them to gain a first-hand impression of how contemporaries (as well as Stairs himself) wrote about the two expeditions.

Stairs's diaries of the Emin Relief Expedition and related files of press clippings and a scrapbook are in the Public Archives of Nova Scotia, MG 9, vol. 63.

Alpers, Edward A. *The East Africa Slave Trade*. Nairobi, 1967.
Anstey, Roger. *Britain and the Congo in the Nineteenth Century*. London, 1962.
Arnot, Fred S. *Bihé and Garenganze*. London, 1893. *Missionary Travels in Central Africa*. London, 1914.

Ascherson, Neal. *The King Incorporated: Leopold the Second in the Age of Trusts.* London, 1963.

Barttelot, Walter G. ed. *The Life of Edmund Musgrave Barttelot, from his Letters and Diary.* London, 1891.

Beachey, R.W. *The Slave Trade of Eastern Africa.* London, 1976.

Bere, R.M. "The Exploration of the Ruwenzori," *Uganda Journal*, XIX, no. 2 (1955).

Bierman, John. *Dark Safari.* London, 1990.

Boulding, Jack. "Captain Stairs in Katanga," *Atlantic Advocate*, October 1960.

Caillon, Allan. *South from Khartoum.* New York , 1974.

Casati, Gaetano. *Ten Years in Equatoria and the Return with Emin Pasha.* 2 vols., London, 1891.

Collins, R.O. *King Leopold, England, and the Upper Nile, 1899–1909.* Yale University Press, 1968.

Cookey, S.J.S. *Britain and the Congo Question, 1885–1913,* London, 1968.

Coosemans, M. "William Grant Stairs, 1863–1892," *Biographic coloniale belge*, vol. II, 1951.

Cornet, René J. *Katanga: Le Katanga avant les Belges.* Brussels, 1946. *Maniema: La lutte contre les Arabes esclavatiques au Congo.* Brussels, 1952.

Coupland, Reginald. *The Exploitation of East Africa, 1856–1890: The Slave Trade and the Scramble.* London, 1938.

Crawford, D. *Thinking Black: Twenty-Two Years Without a Break in the Long Grass of Central Africa.* London, 1912.

Cuelemans, P. *La Question Arabe et le Congo, 1883–1892.*, Brussels, 1959.

Delcommune, Alexandre. *Vingt années de la vie africaine.* 2 vols., Brussels, 1922.

Emerson, Barbara. *Leopold II of the Belgians; King of Colonialism.* London, 1979.

Farrant, Leda. *Tippu Tib and the East African Slave Trade.* London, 1975.

Farwell, Byron. *The Man Who Presumed.* New York, 1957.

Fitzpatrick, Nigel. "A Victorian Canadian in Africa," *Historic Kingston*, Kingston. Ontario, vol. 35 (January 1987).

Galbraith, John S. *Mackinnon and East Africa, 1878–1895, A Study in the New Imperialism.* Cambridge University Press, 1972.

Gann, L.H. and Peter Duignan. *The Rulers of German Africa 1884–1914.* Stanford University Press, 1977. *The Rulers of British Africa, 1870–1914.* Stanford University Press, 1978. *The Rulers of Belgian Africa, 1884–1914.* Princeton University Press, 1979.

Gould, Tony. *In Limbo: The Story of Stanley's Rear Column.* London, 1979.

Gray, Richard. *A History of the Southern Sudan, 1839-1889.* London, 1961.

Hall, Richard. *Stanley: An Adventurer Explored.* London, 1974.

Hird, Frank. *H.M. Stanley: The Authorized Life.* London, 1935.

Hoffman, William. *With Stanley in Africa.* London, 1938.

Jackson, Sir Frederick. *Early Days in East Africa.* London, 1930.

Jameson, James S. *The Story of the Rear Column of the Emin Pasha Relief Expedition.* London, 1890.

Jephson, A.J. Mountenay. *Emin Pasha and the Rebellion at the Equator*. London, 1890. *The Diary of A.J. Mountenay Jephson*, ed. Dorothy Middleton, Cambridge University Press, 1969.

Johnston, Alex. *The Life and Letters of Sir Harry Johnston*. London, 1929.

Johnston, H. H. *History of the Colonization of Africa by Alien Races*. Cambridge, 1913. *The Story of My Life*. London, 1923.

Jones, Roger. *The Rescue of Emin Pasha*. London, 1972.

Keltie, J. Scott, ed. *The Story of Emin's Rescue as Told in Stanley's Letters*. New York, 1890.

Konczacki, Janina M., "William G. Stairs and the Occupation of Katanga : A Forgotten Episode in the Scramble for Africa," *Dalhousie Review*. vol. 66, no. 3 (1986). ed. *Victorian Explorer: The African Diaries of William G. Stairs 1887–1892*. Halifax, 1994.

Lewis, David. *The Race to Fashoda*. New York, 1987.

Lyons, J.B. *Surgeon Major Parkes' African Journey, 1887–89*. Dublin, 1994.

Macpherson, Fergus. *Anatomy of a Conquest*. London, 1981.

Manning, Olivia. *The Remarkable Expedition, The Story of Stanley's Rescue of Emin Pasha from Equatorial Africa*. London, 1947.

Marston. *How Stanley Wrote "In Darkest Africa"*. London, 1890.

Martelli, G. *From Leopold to Lumumba*. London, 1962.

McLynn, Frank. *Stanley*, 2 vols.: vol. 1, *The Making of an Explorer*, vol. 2, *Sorcerer's Apprentice,* London. 1989 and 1990. *Hearts of Darkness*. London, 1992.

Moloney, Joseph A. *With Captain Stairs to Katanga*, London, 1893.

Oliver, Roland, *The Missionary Factor in East Africa*. London, 1952. *Sir Harry Johnston and the Scramble for Africa.*, London, 1957.

Pakenham, Thomas. *The Scramble for Africa.*, London, 1991.

Parke, T.H. *My Personal Experiences in Equatorial Africa as Medical Officer of the Emin Relief Expedition*. London, 1891.

Peters, Karl. *New Light on Darkest Africa: Being a Narrative of the German Emin Pasha Expedition*. London, 1891.

Robinson, Ronald and John Gallagher with Alice Denny. *Africa and the Victorians : The Official Mind of Imperialism*. London, 1961.

Rotberg, Robert I. *Joseph Thomson and the Exploration of Africa*. London, 1987.

Samarin, William J. *The Black's Man Burden*. Boulder, Co., 1989.

Sanderson, G.N. *England, Europe and the Upper Nile*. Edinburgh, 1965.

Schweitzer, G. *Emin Pasha : His Life and Work*. London, 1898.

Schynse, Père. *A Travers l'Afrique avec Stanley et Emin Pascha*, Paris, 1890.

Sheldon, May. *Sultan to Sultan.*, Boston, 1891.

Simpson, Donald H. *Dark Companions: The African Contribution to the European Exploitation of East Africa.*, London, 1975. "A Bibliography of Emin Pasha", *Uganda Journal,* vol. XXIV, no. 2, 1960.

Slade, Ruth M. *King Leopold's Congo*. Oxford University Press, 1962. *English Speaking Missions in the Congo Independent State, 1878–1908*. Brussels, 1959.

Smith, Iain R. *The Emin Pasha Relief Expedition, 1886–1890*. Oxford University Press, 1972.

Stairs, W.G. "Shut Up in the African Forest" and "From the Albert Nyanza to the Indian Ocean," *The Nineteenth Century*, London, vol. 29 (1891), pp. 45-62 and 953-68. "Practical Hints on Forming Expeditions Proceeding to Central Africa", *The Royal Engineers Journal*, 2 February 1891.

Stanley, Henry M. *In Darkest Africa or the Quest, Rescue and Retreat of Emin Governor of Equatoria*. 2 vols., London, 1890. "The Emin Relief Expedition", *Scribner's Magazine* (June 1890). "The Emin Pasha Relief Expedition", *Scottish Geographical Magazine*, vol. VI (1890).

Stanley, Dorothy, ed. *The Autobiography of Sir Henry Morton Stanley, G.C.B.* London, 1909.

Swan, C.A. *Difficulties and Dangers in Early Days*. London, 1931.

Tilsley, J. *Dan Crawford of Central Africa*. London, 1929.

Troup, J.R. *With Stanley's Rear Column*. London, 1890.

Ward, Herbert. *My Life with Stanley's Rear Guard*. London, 1891.

Wauters, A.J. *Stanley's Emin Pasha Expedition*. Philadelphia, 1890.

Werner, J.R. *A Visit to Stanley's Rearguard*. London, 1890.

White, Stanhope. *Lost Empire on the Nile*. London, 1969.

Index